DIGITAL BUSINESS: CONCEPTS AND STRATEGY

SECOND EDITION

DIGITAL BUSINESS: CONCEPTS AND STRATEGY

Eloise Coupey

Virginia Polytechnic Institute and State University

PEARSON

Prentice
Hall

Upper Saddle River, New Jersey 07458

Library of Congress Cataloging-in-Publication Data

Coupey, Eloise.
  Digital business: concepts and strategy/Eloise Coupey.— 2nd ed.
    p. cm.
  ISBN 0-13-140097-5
  1. Electronic commerce. 2. Internet. I. Title.

HF5548.32.C68 2005
658.8′72—dc22

2004014011

VP/Editorial Director: Jeff Shelstad
Acquisitions Editor: Katie Stevens
Editorial Assistant: Rebecca Lembo
Marketing Manager: Michelle O'Brien
Marketing Assistant: Nicole Macchiarelli
Managing Editor: John Roberts
Production Editor: Suzanne Grappi
Manufacturing Buyer: Michelle Klein

Design Manager: Maria Lange
Cover Design Manager: Jayne Conte
Cover Image: Pierre Coupey
Manager, Print Production: Christy Mahon
Composition/Full-Service Project Management: Ann Imhof/Carlisle Communications
Printer/Binder: Phoenix Color Corp.

Cover image "Late Fragment" is reproduced with permission of the artist, Pierre Coupey. All rights reserved.

Credits and acknowledgments borrowed from other sources and reproduced, with permission, in this textbook appear on appropriate page within text.

Microsoft® and Windows® are registered trademarks of the Microsoft Corporation in the U.S.A. and other countries. Screen shots and icons reprinted with permission from the Microsoft Corporation. This book is not sponsored or endorsed by or affiliated with the Microsoft Corporation.

PEARSON
Prentice
Hall

10 9 8 7 6 5 4 3 2 1
ISBN 0-13-140097-5

To Mark, and to William, Katy, Cameron, and Chloê.
And for Michael, whose accomplishment dwarfs mine.

Brief Contents

Contents

SECTION IV: APPLYING THE FRAMEWORK   223

**CHAPTER 9   Developing Business Intelligence
              with Online Research   224**

Preface

How do you succeed in the digital business environment? How do you make the transition from off-line to online? What aspects of your business will be affected, and how should you manage them? These questions are asked frequently—by businesses large and small—as they begin to navigate the post-dot-com-collapse digital world.

Many digital businesses that were heralded as innovative, important, and potentially lucrative disappeared from the digital landscape in the first years of the century. Business plans that seemed like sure bets foundered in their implementation, often failing to secure the customer bases and sales levels needed to keep the companies afloat. Sky-high valuations and dramatic IPOs dropped like rocks as the digital world adapted to the realization that the traditional concepts of supply and demand also applied to digital business.

As businesses adapt to the realities of the digital world, and build on the hard-won insights of the digital business pioneers, increasing importance is placed on the need to understand how traditional concepts of business strategy and implementation are influenced by the Internet, and to identify the novel aspects of business that are made possible by the Internet. That is why this book was written.

Successful strategies for digital business integrate the capabilities of the Internet with aspects of a company's resources, constraints, and objectives, and with the customer's needs and expectations. Because the Internet is a dynamic, rapidly changing environment for business, it is often difficult to know what types of strategies are likely to be effective, and when, and why. Simply looking at what companies have done in the past may not be sufficient in the rapidly changing digital environment—after all, many of them are gone. The ability to understand and predict what practices will work, and why, can be enhanced by understanding key concepts that define and drive digital business, and by applying them to anticipated situations.

This book is designed to provide you with the conceptual and practical knowledge you need to understand the implications of the Internet for business. By having a general picture of the digital environment and its influences on business activity, it is easier to envision possible outcomes of strategic activity for digital business. This book guides you through the concepts, trends, and characteristics of doing business online, to provide you with the ability to develop and implement effective strategies for digital business.

Sections of the Book

To enable you to develop the skills necessary to understand and integrate Internet technology and characteristics into business activity, this book incorporates business theory with Internet reality to identify business opportunities and target markets, and to develop and implement business activities for attaining strategic objectives. The book contains five main sections. Section I presents the conceptual framework used to organize the text, and it provides an overview of the digital business environment. For instance, while many business texts emphasize the perspectives and influences of companies, customers, and policy makers, this text also includes a discussion of the influence of technology on the nature of the interactions between the other three perspectives. In Section II, we look at the exchange relationships that exist for digital business, from each of the key perspectives. Contrasts are noted between the nature of the relationships in traditional marketplaces and for digital business, and the implications of these contrasts are discussed.

With Section III, we integrate the four perspectives and the framework components of the earlier sections to examine the influence of the Internet on business strategy. In the Section IV, we apply the framework to consider the implications of the Internet for business activity. Topics covered include developing business intelligence with online research, building online business models, and implementing business strategy. Section V extends the framework to examine ways in which businesses can foster relationships, building brand equity and customer loyalty with the Internet. For example, we address the role of the Internet on business-to-business exchanges.

Learning Tools

Building an effective strategy for digital business means that you need to learn two different but related bodies of knowledge. First, you need to have available to you the body of information that presently exists about characteristics of digital business. Second, you need to have available to you the skills you will need to keep abreast of changes in the digital environment.

To make the acquisition of these skills more manageable, this text includes several types of learning tools. For example, to build on skills you have previously acquired for business in venues other than the Internet, the issues discussed in this text are described, where possible, in terms of their similarities to or differences from business in other environments. In addition, real-world examples of companies and organizations using the Internet for business activity are provided to illustrate the key issues throughout the text, in the **InSite** features. The **'Net Knowledge** component of each chapter provides in-depth information about a particular issue or application for digital business, while the **Bits & Bytes** boxes present statistics and pertinent information for digital business. At the end of each chapter, the **Content Management** section is provided to help you determine whether you have mastered sufficiently the skills and topics provided in the text. **Useful Terms** are included, as is a topical review in the **Contents in Brief**. The **Web Applications** feature is a hands-on exercise designed to walk you through the mechanics of applying different concepts for digital business, such as developing an online survey, or enhancing search engine ranking through link strategy and Web page content coding. If you have an interest in a particular topic that you would like to explore in more depth, the list of **Suggested Readings** at the end of each chapter is intended to serve as a research resource. Finally, **Learning Links** are URLs, organized by topic, that illustrate real-world applications of concepts in each chapter.

Acknowledgments

The process of writing a book about digital business bears remarkable similarities to the topic. Dramatic and rapid changes, vast opportunities and pitfalls, and the need for coherent structure and approach to guide thinking and action are all part of the process. One of the most pleasant activities associated with writing the book—next to being finished—is the opportunity to reflect on the thinking and writing process, and to recognize the people who have provided motivation, guidance, and encouragement.

My students provided the motivation for this text, and their patience, feedback, and encouragement are especially noteworthy. They unfailingly provided comments and examples, and challenged my assumptions and logic, and in doing so, they enhanced the quality of the book, and my experience in writing it.

Many of the examples in the text are real-world companies, trying to understand and capitalize on the nature of the Internet as they develop their digital businesses. I am very grateful to the representatives of these companies who were generous with their time and their insights, and the screenshots and figures that liven up the pages of the book.

The people at Pearson Prentice Hall deserve many thanks, too. For the opportunity to write the book, and for supportive guidance throughout the process, I'd like to thank Wendy Craven, Bill Beville, and Jeff Shelstad.

Thank you all, very much!

A Conceptual Framework for Digital Business

The Internet has the potential to influence all aspects of buying and selling. It not only provides businesses with a new environment for commercial activity, but also facilitates exchange activities in traditional marketplaces. This section provides an overview to the study of how businesses use the Internet. In Chapter 1, the impact of the Internet on business activity is described by considering the relationship that has existed throughout history between commerce and technology. For instance, developments in technology provide businesses with new ways to transmit information about products and their benefits. The Internet is a technological development that increases the options for commercial communications. Placing digital business within a historical context of technology, rather than thinking about the Internet as an isolated phenomenon, builds the base for understanding the opportunities and difficulties associated with digital business by contrast with capabilities for business activity prior to the Internet.

Because the Internet environment is growing and changing very rapidly, strategies for integrating the Internet into business activity must be flexible: capable of being adapted as the medium evolves. In Chapter 2, a framework is presented to organize elements of digital business. The Internet environment for commerce is described as exchanges between buyers, sellers, and policy makers. Building on the business and technology basis of Chapter 1, we also include exchanges that involve a technology perspective. The framework provides a "big picture" for understanding the goals and activities of different sets of people in the Internet environment, and the effect of the Internet on business processes to create exchange.

Business and the Internet

Focus and Objectives

This chapter characterizes the importance of the Internet as an influence on business activity. Key topics include the relationship between technology and commercial activity throughout history, and the implications of this relationship for digital business. The origins and growth of the Internet and of the World Wide Web are reviewed.

Your objectives in studying this chapter include the following:

- Understand the need for the study of digital business.
- Recognize the relationship between commerce and the Internet as an outgrowth of the relationship between business and technology.
- Develop familiarity with the history of the Internet and the World Wide Web.
- Recognize the need to integrate traditional business concepts into the study of digital business.
- Be able to differentiate between online business and electronic commerce.

Dot-Combat: The Web Grocer Wars

A gallon of milk, two boxes of linguini, some frozen peas, paper towels, dog food, and a 5-pound bag of sugar—ordered online and delivered to your door. The cost? About the same as if you went to the grocery store and brought it home yourself. The savings, however, can be counted not only in money, but in time. In an age of two-career families, busy parents, and busier kids, the promise of an easier way to knock off a tedious weekly chore held vast potential.

The founders of Peapod and Webvan, two of the earliest entrants in the online grocery market, believed in the potential, as did their investors. Peapod, begun in 1989 using dial-up technology, went public in 1997 and raised $64 million. Webvan began its online grocery effort in June 1999, and went public in November of the same year, and raised $375 million.

Both companies provided well-designed and appealing Web sites, which offered similar arrays of products and services. For instance, a customer's order was "remembered" by the site, so that the next order could be streamlined by editing the previous visit's shopping list. In addition, both companies used recommender technology, software that assessed the contents of a shopping cart and made suggestions about other items. A collection of lettuce, tomatoes, cucumbers, and carrots might trigger a suggestion of boxed croutons and salad dressings. In addition, both companies delivered the groceries to the customer's home, provided the shopper lived in one of the metropolitan areas served by the company.

Given all the similarities, competition between the companies was inevitable, and fierce. Peapod differentiated its service by accepting coupons, and by reducing the time between order and delivery to one day, compared with a 2- or 3-day wait for Webvan. To even the score, Webvan broadened its offerings to include CDs, electronics, and a wider range of household goods. The battle for shoppers intensified as analysts forecast revenues of $1.3 billion for online grocery shopping in 2002.

But did grocery shoppers share the enthusiasm of investors and analysts? Imagine calling your local grocery store and placing an order. What items come to mind? While it's easy to hand off the responsibility for paper towels, flour, and your favorite brand of laundry detergent, how do you feel about having someone else choose your cantaloupe, avocados, and tuna steaks? Even if you have precise product information, would you be comfortable with letting an employee fill your order for personal hygiene products?

If not, you're not alone. Despite high hopes and competitive offerings for the online grocery market, consumer demand did not materialize as predicted. For many consumers, limits on delivery times were too restrictive. For others, giving up the ability to squeeze the Charmin, sample the grapes, and check the sell-by dates was unacceptable. The benefits offered through online grocers simply didn't carry the weight with consumers that marketers had anticipated.

Slow consumer acceptance took its toll. At its peak, Webvan had 46% of the small market for online groceries, while Peapod shared the remainder with several other regional companies. Investors pumped nearly $1 billion into Webvan's vision, enabling Webvan to extend its reach to 13 cities in 2000. Peapod struggled to maintain its presence in 7 cities, eventually selling 51% of its stock to raise $73 million for operations, and pulling out of several markets.

In July 2001, Webvan filed for bankruptcy, reporting an accumulated deficit of $830 million. In contrast, Peapod was at last able to report profitable operations in its Chicago and Massachusetts markets.

Was Webvan's failure inevitable? Can any online grocer succeed?

As is true for many companies that use the Internet as a part of their business, the reasons for success and failure are as many and varied as the business models behind the enterprises. In Webvan's case, several factors may have influenced its demise. Buying groceries online was a novel concept, amounting to only 2% of all grocery sales. Some analysts concluded that Webvan was simply ahead of its time; consumers needed to catch up.

In addition, Webvan invested heavily in building highly automated distribution centers at a time when consumer confidence—and spending—on the Internet was declining. Costs to attract customers to online grocery shopping were high; advertising in excess of 25% of revenues far exceeded the ability of slim margins, typically a 2% to 3% return on sales, to compensate.

The issues that thwarted Webvan are not limited to online grocers. Despite the large numbers of people who have access to the Internet, online commerce is still a young and evolving arena for marketing. The rapid pace of technological developments provides new ways to conduct old and new forms of business activity. What may seem like a good idea can be quickly rendered obsolete by the introduction of an even better idea—or the realization that perhaps old ways were the best ways.

So how do you determine the "best way?" In this book we will examine the role of the Internet on business activity, and we will consider factors that enhance or hinder the influence of the Internet on the success of online efforts. A new framework that enables us to consider new and unique forms of interactions between businesses and consumers, as well as the role of technology and policy developments, will be introduced in Chapter 2 to help you identify and understand ways to use the Internet for effective business activity.

Bits & Bytes 1.1

In a 1999 survey of more than 500 Internet users, only 18% had any interest in buying groceries online.

(*Source:* PricewaterhouseCoopers Retail Intelligence System: Annual Consumer Survey 1999.)

What Is the Internet?

On one level, the **Internet** is simply a means of communication—between consumers, companies, and between millions of other organizations. The Internet enables people to tailor the way they communicate, whether with just one person or with an entire target market, quickly and easily. The ready accessibility of one-to-many communication, once only available through television, radio, or print media, creates opportunities that did not exist with traditional media for all types and sizes of businesses (Figure 1-1). For marketers, communications can be created quickly, and often at lower costs than in

FIGURE 1-1   One-to-Many Communications Can Reach Broad Audiences.

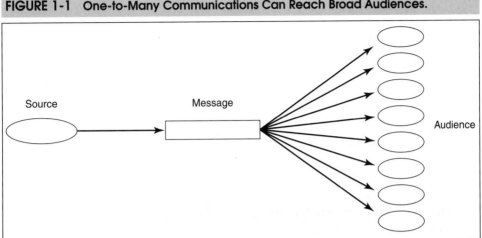

other media. For consumers, exposure to commercial communications is not limited by geography.

Technological Characteristics of the Internet

On a more complex level, the Internet is a product of advances in science, and it can be described largely in terms of its technological components. It is not necessary to understand how the Internet works in order to make use of it as a business tool: Similar to the notion that you don't need to know what makes a car run in order to be a car salesman! A brief description of the technical evolution of the Internet may, however, help you better understand its capabilities and limitations, as well as some of the more prevalent jargon.

The Internet is a network of computer networks (Figure 1-2). *Internet* is a contraction of the words, *international* and *network*; **networks** of computers around the world are connected to each other, enabling rapid transmission of data from point to point. The computers in a single network are each linked to a **server,** which is a large computer that manages the communications for a network. The Internet is primarily a network of these servers, in which communication is accomplished by fiber optic cables, satellite transmissions, phone lines, microwave, and Ethernet lines. A brief history of the development of the Internet is useful for explaining some of the network's characteristics.

The Internet's History

Developed under the sponsorship of the Defense Department's Advanced Research Projects Agency (ARPA), the Internet was envisioned as a decentralized network of computers, with some duplication, or redundancy, between computers. The logic was straightforward. In the aftermath of World War II, including the development of the atomic bomb and the increasing tensions of the Cold War, the government became concerned about the vulnerability of a single, centralized computer system.

FIGURE 1-2 The Internet Is a Network of Networks.

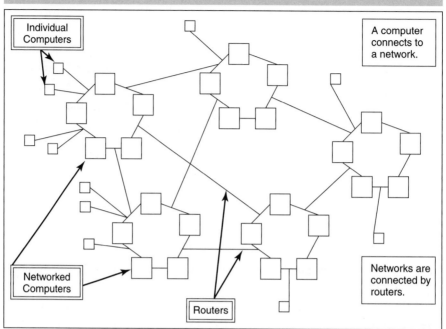

In 1969, the network, then called ARPAnet, became a reality when two nodes were linked. A node is a computer connected to a network. The nodes can communicate by exchanging packets of information, in which chunks of information are forwarded across computers to the network address on the packet. These packets, which may take different network paths to reach the address, are reassembled at the destination computer.

By 1989, the National Science Foundation had replaced the Defense Department as the chief source of support for the network of networks, renamed NSFnet. This new network, designed to link together five supercomputers, served as the backbone of what is now known as the Internet. Originally intended to facilitate research and communication among the scientific community, the Internet has grown to include networks and users across a wide variety of backgrounds and interests. This growth can be attributed in large part to the rapid increase in popularity of personal computers during the 1990s, and in mobile (wireless) access to the Internet, as through personal digital assistants (**PDAs**) and cell phones, in the past few years (Figure 1-3).

Integrating People and Technology: The Rise of the World Wide Web

From its origins as a high-tech tool for facilitating communications between scientists, the Internet has evolved into a communications medium of far greater accessibility to people around the world. This evolution, which reflects the large-scale adoption of the

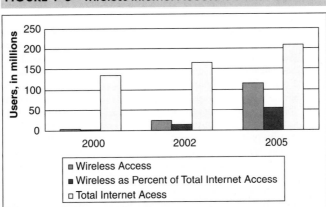

FIGURE 1-3   Wireless Internet Access Is on the Rise.

- ▣ Wireless Access
- ■ Wireless as Percent of Total Internet Access
- ▫ Total Internet Acess

(*Data source:* allNetDevices, as cited by ePaynews.)

technology, can be attributed to the development of the **World Wide Web,** often called simply "the Web," or "WWW."

The Web is a network of electronic documents, called **Web pages.** These pages may be in text, graphic, and even audio or video formats. The documents are integrated through **hyperlinks.** Hyperlinks enable the user to acquire desired information by moving from one page to another through links in a flexible sequence. Information organized and connected by hyperlinks is called **hypertext.** The hypertext approach makes it possible to present information in ways that are more intuitive and user-friendly than the original form of the Internet.

The growth of the Web is reflected in the variety of types of Internet users. The Internet uses the **Domain Name System (DNS)** as a form of address for users. Domain names provide users with a way to describe a particular Internet site without having to know the Internet Protocol (IP) address, which may be a number of up to 12 digits.

The **Internet Corporation for Assigned Names and Numbers (ICANN)** is the organization responsible for managing the DNS. The DNS domains indicate different types of Internet sites, providing structure and organization to the growing medium. The domains are classifications that sort Internet sites by some common aspect, such as site function or geographical location. Site function domains are classified as **generic top-level domains (gTLDs)** as shown in Figure 1-4, and location-oriented domains are known as **country code top-level domains (ccTLDs).** At present, there are 14 generic gTLDs. The original 7 domains were **.com, .net, .org, .edu, .gov, .int,** and **.mil.** In November 2000, ICANN approved the use of 7 new gTLDs. These are **.biz, .info, .name, .pro, .aero, .coop,** and **.museum.**

Simply knowing the domain can tell you something about the affiliation of the person behind an electronic communication. For example, users who are affiliated with an academic institution are designated by ".edu" in the address. Commercial affiliations are denoted by ".com."

Some of the most commonly encountered ccTLDs are shown in Figure 1-5. The ccTLDs are used primarily outside the United States, while gTLDs were historically

FIGURE 1-4 Generic Top-Level Domains In the DNS Reflect Many Interests.

Domain Label	Characteristic Domain User	Example
.com	Commercial, for-profit organizations	Barnes & Noble Bookstore www.barnesandnoble.com
.net	Network resource organizations and gateways	Internet Alaska www.alaska.net
.edu	Educational organizations	Virginia Tech www.vt.edu
.gov	Government organizations	Argonne National Lab www.anl.gov
.mil	Military organizations/branches	Air Force www.af.mil
.int	International not-for-profit groups	www.nato.int
.org	Not-for-profit organizations	Girl Scout Council www.gsusa.org
.biz	Businesses	www.rateme.biz
.pro	Professionals (e.g., accountants, lawyers, physicians)	www.drsmith.pro
.info	Anyone (unrestricted use)	www.internet.info
.name	Individuals	www.eloisecoupey.name
.coop	Cooperatives	www.organicmoo.coop
.aero	Air transport industry	www.pilots.aero
.museum	Museums	www.florida.salvadordali.museum

prevalent in the United States. In recent years, this pattern has changed. Individuals and organizations in countries around the world now use gTLDs .

The rapid increase in the number of Internet users and domains has been mirrored by the growth in the commercial domain, shown in Figure 1-6. These statistics indicate the increasing importance of the Internet for business, and they underscore the need to

FIGURE 1-5 Commonly Used ccTLDs Span the Globe.

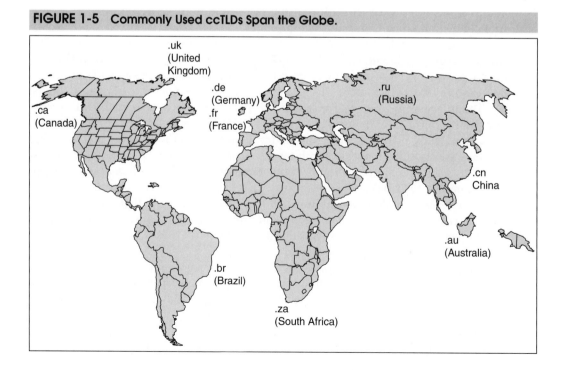

FIGURE 1-6   The Number of Dot-com Sites Grows Quickly.

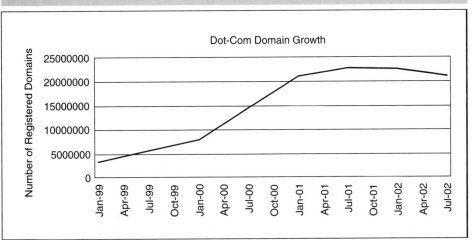

understand how to use the Internet to best advantage. In this book, we will cover a wide range of topics designed to provide you with the background knowledge and abilities needed to integrate business activities with Internet capabilities to develop effective business models and strategies.

The Internet and Business Opportunity

Understanding how the Internet affects business practices is important for several reasons. Despite the ever-changing nature of the Internet, a constant characteristic is its increasing growth and importance in everyday life. An average of user surveys compiled by Nua Internet Surveys estimated a worldwide user population of 580.78 million people as of May 2002, with 182.67 million of those users in North America. These people are using the Internet for many different purposes—including buying and selling. In the United States, the amount of revenue generated by the Internet increased from $377 billion in 2000, to $717 billion in 2001, and $1,234 dollars in 2002.

Where is all this money coming from? Companies who use the Internet to market their products come in all types and sizes, ranging from multinational corporations to home-based, entrepreneurial businesses. Marketing applications of the Internet are equally varied. For example, a company might use the Internet simply as a tool for implementing standard business practices, such as using e-mail to handle catalog requests. Another company might make its entire product line available through an Internet site, as well as through traditional means. This approach is used by retailers such as Barnes and Noble, a book retailer, and by WalMart. Yet another company might market its products solely through a virtual storefront on the Internet, as do Dell.com and Amazon.com. The companies in Figure 1-7 each use the Internet for

FIGURE 1-7   Consumers Access Many Types of Goods and Services Online.

Business Online, From A to Z

——Amazon	a. travel services
——BizRate	b. name-your-own-price shopping
——CNET	c. web browser software
——Dell	d. dating service
——EarthLink	e. home mortgages
——FedEx	f. travel reviews by ordinary people
——Guntella	g. IT news
——Homestead	h. web hosting
——iWon	i. travel services
——Jupiter	j. auction site
——Kashrut	k. web portal
——Lending Tree	l. order tracking, shipping information
——Match	m. media players and programming
——Netscape	n. office supplies
——Orbitz	o. referral-based business opportunities
——Priceline	p. wall display systems for computers
——Quixtar	q. office supplies
——RealNetworks	r. website development
——Staples	s. electronic products comparison and content
——Travelocity	t. high-tech personal electronics
——Ubid	u. kosher food and information
——Verio	v. customised computers
——WalMart	w. online shopping and affiliates
——X10	x. online shopping with offline presence
——yahoo!	y. file-sharing software
——ZDnet	z. comparison shopping guide

some aspect of their business. Can you identify the commercial focus of each company, and the role of the Internet in marketing that product?

The types of online activities are influenced by the goals of the company, and by its experience with Internet technologies. The Internet can be used in many different ways by businesses. As we saw at the beginning of the chapter, some products may be better suited to the online marketplace than others. In addition, some business models may work better for Internet activity than others.

The benefits of the Internet extend far beyond the ability to serve as a resource for acquiring information. The activities in Figure 1-8 represent a subset of the possible ways in which the Internet may influence how we approach and conduct the activities associated with business strategy. In some cases, the influence of the Internet may even affect whether or not the traditional activities are relevant. For instance, promotion efforts associated with the production of product information brochures may become less important for a company who can effectively use the Internet to reach and inform its target market about the benefits of its products.

FIGURE 1-8   The Internet Fills Many Roles in Business Activity.

	Early Applications		Advanced Applications
Sample Applications	Information requests (e-mail) Web publishing	Database development Online transactions	Product production Content development
Characteristics of Internet Use as an Information Resource	Dissemination	Interaction	Customization
Facilitating Dimensions of Internet Use	Physical emphasis		Virtual emphasis
	Lower technological sophistication		Higher technological sophistication

Why Is Digital Business Important?

Despite its youth, the Internet has grown rapidly as a commercial medium. In spite of concerns about the privacy and security of information, such as credit card numbers, and fears about the reputability of online vendors, consumers spend more online, and shop online more frequently, than ever before. Companies have introduced new business models designed to take advantage of the opportunities provided by the Internet medium—both for creating and offering new products, and for finding new ways to sell existing products. An important issue for businesses in the online environment is to understand what types of models and strategies work for reaching company goals.

The Dot-Bomb Phenomenon

Napster.com, Garden.com, Pets.com, eToys.com, Webvan.com—sound familiar? Each of these companies rode the crest of the Internet wave. Now they are gone. In each case, the company achieved widespread awareness among consumers and investors. The disappearance of these companies was not the result of a lack of consumer interest, or a lack of demand for their products and services. Music, plants, pet food, toys and groceries are all widely desired and purchased products.

In each company's case, the reasons for the failure of the business to survive and thrive in the digital business environment may be quite different. For instance, Napster was a casualty of regulatory and legal causes, eToys lost market share to its main competitor, ToysRUs, and Webvan failed to change consumers' perceptions about the benefits of online grocery shopping. The chart in Figure 1-9 shows the distribution of dot-com collapses across industry sectors. Note that the e-commerce sector was hit the hardest.

The graph in Figure 1-10 reports the approximate numbers of dot-coms with significant funding from venture capitalists and others that have disappeared from the Internet landscape between 1999 and 2002. These numbers led people to question the business models that guided the creation and direction of many online companies.

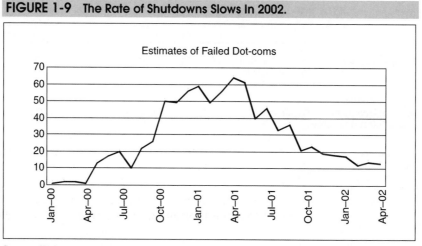

FIGURE 1-9 The Rate of Shutdowns Slows In 2002.

Source: Webmergers.com

As a result, the demise of so many online ventures has had the positive outcome of fostering interest in understanding how the Internet differs from traditional venues for business activity, and what types of business models are more effective than others.

The Impact of Technology on Business

One way to understand the impact of the Internet on the development of successful business models is by understanding the impact of technology on business activity, and of business activity on technology. It is difficult to characterize the development of commerce as we know it today without acknowledging the impact of technological

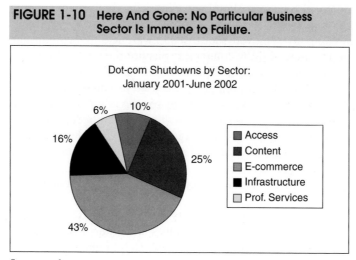

FIGURE 1-10 Here And Gone: No Particular Business Sector Is Immune to Failure.

Source: webmergers.com

development on business practices. In addition, although commerce has often adapted to developments in technology, it has also influenced the course of the Internet's development. The current emphasis of the Internet as a technology for commerce reflects the symbiotic nature of the relationship between technology and business.

An Abbreviated History of the Business-Technology Relationship

Business activities have existed for thousands of years. Early societies relied on barter and exchange methods in local marketplaces, reflecting the need to trade off perishable goods and the absence of a money economy (it is hard to bank cabbages and chickens, and refrigeration had not been invented. . .). With the development of money economies, business activities became increasingly sophisticated; the ability to save money for a purchase lengthened consumption planning horizons and created the opportunity for financial arrangements of credit and interest.

The Industrial Revolution in the later part of the 19th century had a profound impact on commercial activity. The mechanization of many previously hand-done processes enabled the mass production of products; items that were once in scarce supply now existed in abundance—and at lower prices. Technological developments such as the automatic loom and the electric light facilitated mass production in factories, while the invention of the air brake and steel rails combined to provide train systems that were critical to attaining widespread distribution for products.

With the supply in place, the next requirement for a vital business environment was demand. The introduction of technologies that enabled new ways to reach and communicate with consumers fueled the development of a consumer economy with knowledge and interest in available, mass-produced products. Prior to the beginning of the 20th century, the primary avenues for making consumers aware of products were through face-to-face communications, or through print, typically in the form of newspapers. Both methods had limitations. Face-to-face interactions were costly and time consuming. Printed communications ran the risk of missing their target, or of becoming too rapidly outdated.

Mass Communication and Demand

In the 1920s, radio became a common vehicle with which businesses could tout their wares to large audiences of consumers. The RCA Corporation formed the NBC Radio Network in 1926. This network enabled one source to broadcast content to several stations at the same time. The popularity of many of the broadcast radio shows, such as "Amos 'n' Andy" and the "Lone Ranger," made them desirable outlets for commercial messages. By the mid-1930s—the "Golden Age of Radio"—approximately one-third of all radio shows were sponsored by companies. These companies used the shows as forums for advertising their products. The technology behind radio offered advantages over previous ways of delivering commercial communications. Salespeople and newspapers are geographically limited; radio broadcasts are less limited. By advertising on radio networks, businesses could reach audiences that stretched across the country, creating widespread awareness of brands and stimulating demand for these national brands.

Bits & Bytes 1.2

Elapsed time for technologies to reach 50 million users: telephone–40 years; radio–38 years; cable television–10 years; the Internet–5 years.

(*Source:* Netscape CEO Jim Barksdale, as reported in *PC Magazine*, November 4, 1997.)

The advent of television in the 1930s complemented businesses' ability to reach national audiences by enabling them to include visual information about products in their advertising. The technology for television transmissions was largely developed during the 1920s, but it wasn't until 1939 that RCA introduced its fully electronic television to the American public. The first television ad was aired in 1941, by WNBT-New York. The commercial was a 10-second live pitch for the Bulova Watch Company.

Adoption of the television was slowed by World War II. Development and production, not just of television sets, but of many consumer goods, was halted to increase production of war material. The war effort spurred research that led to new products and technologies for their production. These inventions were greeted by an American public flush with money saved during wartime, and pent-up demand due to the scarcity of many products.

The market economy moved quickly forward. To illustrate the speed with which the adoption of the television technology was adopted, consider that in 1946, there were just 6,000 televisions in America. This number increased to 3,000,000 by 1948, and to 12,000,000 by 1951. The only major change to the technology that enabled television was the introduction of color in 1952–an innovation that was not fully supported by the major broadcast networks until the mid-1960s!

From an Industrial Economy to a Digital Economy

Since the 1960s, techniques to create digitized, rapidly transmittable information have led to a shift from an industrial economy to a **digital economy.** The adoption of the personal computer reflects the shift to a digital economy. Similar to the growth of the mass media of radio and television, personal computers have been adopted rapidly. By 1995, 36% of Americans owned computers. That number had increased to 43% in 1998, and to 65% by the end of 1999. Even more dramatic has been the acceptance of the technologies that enable the Internet. In 1995, only 6.7% of the U. S. population used the Internet. By 2002, the online population had grown to over 59%.[1]

In the early and middle years of the 20th century, the widespread electrification of America and the construction of the interstate highway system provided the necessary infrastructure for an industrial economy. In recent years, however, a shift in emphasis from "industry" to "information" has resulted as information networks provide a new infrastructure for a digital economy, one characterized by the importance of networked intelligence in the form of digitized information.

The key to this shift is that there must be a means for transmitting the digitized information. Satellites, wireless technologies, and networked computers are all capable

---

[1] These numbers were reported by Nua Online Surveys (www.nua.com), based on data collected by Nielson Media Research (www.nielson-netratings.com).

vehicles for transmission, and all are components of what has been termed "the Information Highway." Best known to most people, however, is the Internet, which is a network of networks that enables high-speed digital communications.

The Internet has been the focus of many companies interested in taking advantage of interactive media to inform consumers about their products and services and, in many cases, to sell products and services online. **Interactive media,** such as the medium represented by the Internet, enable flexible communications in real time between businesses and their consumers, by technological means, such as computers. This interactivity differentiates the Internet from the traditional communications technologies of television, radio, and print. In addition, interactivity enables businesses to tailor information to meet the needs of different customer targets. This **personalization** is based on the two-way communication between consumer and business that is made possible by the Internet.

Bits & Bytes 1.3

Seventy-three percent of Web sites contain content in English.
(*Source:* Web Characterization Project: www.wcp.oclc.org, 2001.)

The Internet as Just Another Technology

Technology and commerce have coexisted—generally to the benefit of each—for hundreds of years. In this sense, the Internet is merely the most recent technology for the conduct of business activity. The importance of understanding the role of the Internet for businesses, however, lies in recognizing how the technologies that underlie the Internet enable businesses to change the way they carry out commercial activities.

One way to begin to understand the implications of the Internet for business is to consider how past technologies have changed the nature of the interactions between businesses and consumers. We can summarize the history of the relationship between commerce and technology as a timeline, depicted in Figure 1-11.

Consider the types of interactions that the technology enabled. For instance, early commercial activities emphasized one-to-one, face-to-face interactions between the seller and the buyer. With advances in technology, starting with the development of the printing press by Gutenburg in the 15th century, and progressing through radio and television, businesses were able to target larger, more dispersed audiences. With the introduction of the Internet as a tool for business, the shift in capabilities comes full circle as shown in Figure 1-12, but with advantages not previously available through technology. The Internet enables businesses to communicate not only one-to-one, but also in a mass format. In addition, the technologies that define the Internet can improve the efficiency with which commercial activities can be developed and implemented, and the richness of the content of the activities.

How Is Digital Business Different?

The nature of the marketing environment enabled by the Internet means that the scope and nature of marketing business activities are more flexible. For example, with

FIGURE 1-11 Commerce and Technology Have a Long History.

Business			Technology
Dot-com slowdown slows down		2002	.name, .coop, .aero begin registrations
Napster suspends service	2001		.biz, .info, .museum begin registrations
Fist live online musical			
business.com sells for $7.5 million	1999	2000	Number of unique Web pages exceeds one billion
Mr. Clean speaks online			
First full-service Internet bank			Hackers cripple eBay, Yahoo!, eTrade, Datek, CNN with denial-of-service attacks
US Postal Service sells stamps online			
business.com name sells for $150,000	1997		
.com hosts outnumber others		1995	Online dial-up services provide Internet access
Fist online shopping mall	1994		
First commercial interest in Internet		1992	Number of hosts exceeds 1,000,000
		1991	CERN releases WWW
		1989	Number of hosts exceeds 100,000
		1987	Number of hosts exceeds 10,000
		1984	Number of Internet hosts exceeds 1000 Domain Name System introduced
		1975	First Internet mailing list
		1960	Early digital computing technologies Widespread color TV capability
First television ad: Bulova Watch	1941	1939	First all-electronic TV: RCA
One-third of radio shows have commercial sponsors	1935		
		1926	First radio network: RCA
		1921	First radio station
		1890	Majority of production moves to factories
		1880	Industrial Revolution under way (mechanization and mass production)
		c.1450	Printing press invented

the Internet as the tool for communication, physical boundaries become less important in the execution of a transaction than they are for other, more traditional forms of commercial exchange. The impact of the Internet on business processes that reach across wide geographical distances, including communications and transactions, facilitates globalization. **Globalization** refers to company activities across countries that enable it to obtain advantages in reputation and cost.

Suppose that you are interested in selling the furniture produced in your factory in North Carolina. By advertising your product on the Internet, you gain the attention of a potential client—in Bangkok, Thailand. Although you must still face the difficulties associated with transferring the furniture, post-transaction, halfway

FIGURE 1-12 The Full-Circle Effect of Technology on Communications Capability.

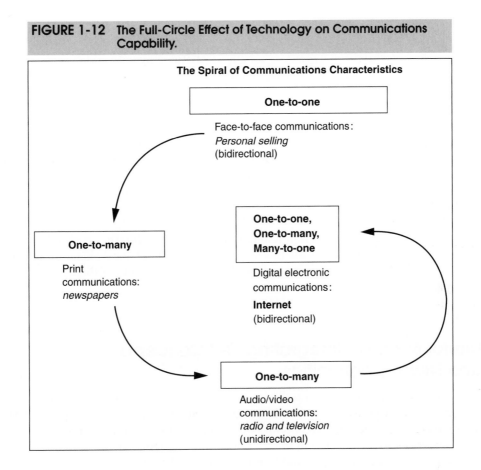

around the world, the physical distance exerts a minimal effect in the negotiation of the deal.

Why? From your perspective as the seller, you can provide information about your product more efficiently to your customer than you could if you had to create a hardcopy brochure or catalog. This means that you can react to competitive forces, adapting flexible elements of your business strategy to stay ahead of the competition.

In addition, the Internet is a more interactive medium than many traditional commercial venues. This interactivity means that you can communicate in real time with your customer though your Web site to provide specific, desired information. Such reciprocal, tailored communication may result in more efficient and satisfying transactions—characteristics that are important for developing long-term relationships with customers.

In summary, the Internet offers businesses several benefits that are not available with traditional vehicles for commerce. The Internet enables companies to create flexible information displays, to provide a greater range and depth of information with interactive technology, and to combine the characteristics of television, print, and radio into a single presentation of video, text, and sound.

Bits & Bytes 1.4

The first registered domain, Symbolics.com, was assigned on March 15, 1985.
(*Source:* Hobbes Internet Timeline at www.isoc.org)

In this book, we focus on the Internet as the primary force behind digital business. At present, more people are familiar with the Internet than with other methods of digital transmission. It is this familiarity and adoption of the technology that has led to the high levels of **interconnectivity,** reflected in the amount of communication between people via the Internet, which makes the Internet an important component of business strategy.

It is necessary to keep in mind, however, that the Internet is merely one way to move information. Given the rate and extent of technological change, it is likely that other means for communicating digitally will quickly become valuable components of effective business strategies.

Digital Business: Integrating Old Concepts and New Opportunities

For companies, it is important to understand the implications of the Internet environment for business activity. The Internet plays a vital role in many aspects of business strategy planning and execution. For instance, target markets can be identified and analyzed with help from the Internet as an information resource, aiding the marketing function of a company. In addition to serving as a rich source of market intelligence about current activities of competitors and consumers, the Internet can be used to gain insights about unmet preferences that may lead to the development of new products and services. By using the Internet as a tool for conducting surveys, a business can conduct market research quickly, and potentially more cheaply, than with the more traditional methods of mail or phone surveys.

The importance of the Internet is not limited to its implications for marketing. Just as the marketing function is only one part of developing and maintaining a successful commercial venture, the Internet often plays a vital role in the types of activities carried out both within and between other functions of commercial organizations. In the following section, we will consider the role of Internet technologies and marketing within the broader context of electronic commerce.

Bits & Bytes 1.5

In June 2002, 3,411,099 Web sites were estimated to be e-commerce capable.
(*Source:* www.netfactual.com)

Functions of Electronic Commerce

Business strategies that include the Internet are often characterized as "electronic commerce." Electronic commerce is a label that encompasses a wide variety of business activities (Figure 1-13). In this text, **electronic commerce** is defined as the sets of activities undertaken by organizations to enable and facilitate the buying and selling of goods and services through electronic, paperless, information systems technologies.

Origins of Electronic Commerce

Electronic commerce had its start in corporations and banks, largely as a means of facilitating aspects of business by computerizing business practices to facilitate information exchange. Two early applications of electronic commerce were **electronic data interchange (EDI)** and **electronic funds transfer (EFT).** These activities within and between companies were desirable because they decreased the impact of constraints such as time and place. Information could be communicated rapidly and in flexible formats to improve communications within a company.

Electronic commerce is quickly becoming a goal for many companies, as they seek to complete purchase transactions and fund transfers over computer networks, and to conduct exchange activities related to new commodities, directly related to the digital medium, such as electronic information. Electronic commerce is more than just a shift from traditional commerce to a digital environment; it enables new products and new types and forms of transactions and businesses.

The Changing Face of Electronic Commerce

Early applications of electronic commerce were focused on within-business and business-to-business uses. This focus is changing to include and emphasize the growing importance of a consumer orientation. The changing emphasis is made possible through the concurrent growth and compatibility of Internet technology and structure, growth of computerized business practices, and spread and adoption of digital information.

This synergy enables electronic commerce to perform as a system comprised not only of revenue-generating transactions, such as buying and selling goods and services, but also of revenue-supporting transactions, such as sales support and customer service. As a result, electronic commerce not only facilitates communications

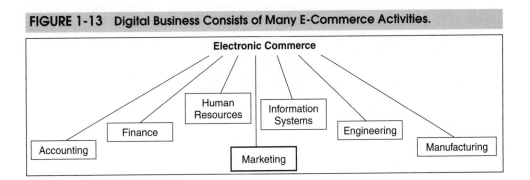

FIGURE 1-13 Digital Business Consists of Many E-Commerce Activities.

'Net Knowledge

I WANT MY DOTTV!

The Internet works its magic in strange ways. For the approximately 11,000 residents of some tiny islands in the South Pacific, the Internet has opened up a world of opportunities and changed the lives of each person. No, it's not the ability to connect digitally to the rest of the world that's made the difference—although that probably has some effect.[1]

What really made the difference was a name, "Tuvalu."

Tuvalu is a Polynesian word that means eight, as in the eight inhabited islands that until 1978 were a British colony known as the Ellice Islands. These islands, which have a combined size of about one-tenth of the District of Columbia, support a chief crop of coconuts, contributing to an average per-capita revenue of $400.

Fortunately for Tuvalu, the Internet country code is .tv. In 2000, Tuvalu traded the use of their domain name to The .tv Corporation International in exchange for $50 million over 12 years. Now owned by VeriSign, the .tv Corporation markets the .tv domain to companies and individuals who want to emphasize the "dynamic online content" of their sites.

As for Tuvalu, the exchange has boosted the country from being one of the poorest in the world to one of the richest. Not bad for a country with fewer than 1,000 TVs!

---

[1]Technology is not a major focus of Tuvaluan life. At the turn of the century, Tuvalu had an estimated 1,000 telephones, 4,000 radios, one AM station, and a sum total of 19.5 miles of highway (none paved).

within a company, but between a company and its consumers, as through customer service, any time, any day. It is this set of capabilities—more and more frequently directed toward consumers—that makes the Internet a desirable component of business strategy.

About this Book

Successful strategies for digital business integrate the capabilities of the Internet with aspects of the company's resources, constraints, and objectives; and with the consumer's needs and expectations. This book is intended to serve as an illustrative introduction to the array of issues related to using the Internet as an integral component of a successful business strategy. The primary objective of the text is to provide you with the knowledge and ability to develop the skills needed to develop effective business practices for the Internet, and to remain on the cutting edge of developments in technology and their role in establishing effective business strategy.

Sections of the Book

To enable you to develop the skills necessary to understand and integrate Internet technology and characteristics into business strategy, this book incorporates theory with Internet reality to address issues in selecting and implementing appropriate business models and activities. The book contains five sections. Section I provides an overview of the unique business environment created by the Internet. For instance, while most business texts emphasize the perspectives and influences of consumers, businesses, and policy makers, this text also includes a discussion of the influence of technology on the nature of the interactions between the other three perspectives. In subsequent sections, we will build on a framework that emphasizes the four key perspectives—consumer, business, technology developer, and policy maker—and their interactions to explore the impact of the Internet on commercial activity.

In Section II, the perspectives are examined in depth to provide you with a clear understanding of the role of each perspective for digital business. Given the rate at which the Internet environment can change, a solid understanding of the concepts that guide online commercial activity will enable you to understand and forecast future activity in each of these areas, and to understand the implications of this activity for business strategy that incorporates the Internet.

With Section III, we put the perspectives together, by building on the basic framework from Section I, to consider the impact of the Internet environment on business strategy. We begin with a general description of businesses within the Internet environment, and then we consider the implications of the Internet for strategic planning. This section serves as the basis for Section IV, in which we look at the role of the Internet in implementing business strategy. We examine the impact of the Internet on aspects of strategy implementation.

In Section V, we extend our basic framework to examine the impact of the Internet on the interactions between companies that conduct business-to-business activities. In the final chapter of the text, we examine ways in which businesses can leverage the Internet to maintain and extend interaction with people in each of the perspectives identified by the basic framework.

Learning Tools

Learning how to use the Internet effectively as a business tool means that you need to learn two different but related bodies of knowledge. First, you need to have available to you the body of information that presently exists about characteristics of the Internet that are useful for business practice. Second, you need to have available to you the skills you will need to keep abreast of changes in the Internet environment.

To make the acquisition of these skills more manageable, this text includes several types of learning tools. For example, to build on skills you have previously acquired for doing business in venues other than the Internet, the issues discussed in this text are described, where possible, in terms of their similarities to or differences from business activity in other environments. In addition, real-world examples of companies and organizations using the Internet to market goods or services are provided to illustrate the key issues throughout the text.

Within each chapter, the *Bits & Bytes* boxes provide you with interesting, historical, and sometimes just-plain-odd background on the development of the Internet as a medium for business. In addition, the *InSites* feature describes Web sites that provide relevant information and a unique perspective on a particular focus or aspect of the chapter. The *'Net Knowledge* sections provide information about the people, places, and things that make the Internet a diverse environment for commerce.

At the end of each chapter, key terms and review questions are provided to help you determine whether you have mastered the skills and topics provided in the text. The Internet exercises provide you with hands-on practice to hone your skills. The *Thinking Points* section is intended to stimulate thinking and discussion of issues related to the chapter material. If you have an interest in a particular topic that you would like to explore in more depth, the list of suggested readings at the end of each section serves as a research resource, as do the lists of recommended links to Web sites.

CHAPTER SUMMARY

The Internet offers companies the opportunity to develop business strategies and to reach consumers in ways that traditional approaches cannot. It is an environment in which consumers and businesses can communicate more rapidly. Speed of communication is enhanced because traditional barriers of time and distance are minimized by the company's ability to create databases of product information, and by the consumer's ability to selectively obtain information.

The interactive medium may serve many functions including advertising and communications, and merchandising and distribution. The chief objective of this textbook is to provide you with a comprehensive introduction to the concept of using the Internet as one component in the development and implementation of effective strategies for digital business.

CONTENT MANAGEMENT
USEFUL TERMS

- .aero
- globalization
- .biz
- ccTLDs
- .com
- .coop
- digital economy
- .info
- Domain Name System
- EDI
- .edu

- EFT
- electronic commerce
- .museum
- .name
- .gov
- gTLDs
- hyperlinks
- hypertext
- ICANN
- personalization
- .int
- interactive media

- interconnectivity
- Internet
- .mil
- .net
- network
- .org
- PDAs
- .pro
- server
- .tv
- Web page
- World Wide Web

REVIEW QUESTIONS

1. What are the key differences between the medium for business created by the Internet and traditional media, such as television, radio, and print?
2. Describe the actual rate of growth of the Internet, compared with its predicted growth.
3. For what purpose was the Internet originally developed?
4. Describe the key differences between an industrial economy and a digital economy.
5. Name several advantages of electronic commerce for businesses and other organizations.
6. How is the World Wide Web different from the Internet?

7. What are the benefits of the Domain Name System?
8. What organization oversees the Domain Name System?
9. What are the 14 gTLDs?
10. Describe two ways that the Internet can be used to facilitate the development of business strategy.
11. Explain the origins and scope of electronic commerce.

WEB APPLICATION

Using Useful Technology: Choose Your News

Because it's a vast collection of constantly changing information and technology, the Internet is a challenging environment for business. It's important to keep up with the trends and capabilities that can affect business activity. Given the amount of information that's out there, however, keeping on top of everything is impossible.

Web portals provide a method for distilling and organizing information into a format that gives you the content you need, in amounts you can handle. This ability to customize the information you see each time you access the Internet can go a long way toward keeping you up-to-date with developments that affect business success.

Setting up your personal portal is not difficult. First, determine your information goals. A sports marketer might require frequent updates on sports scores, while a commodities trader might need news about wheat production. In both cases, frequent travel can make weather information very useful.

Once you know what you need, the next step is to identify your options for getting that information. The major portal sites, such as AOL Anywhere, Yahoo! and MSN (Microsoft Network), allow you to choose content, color, and layout from menus of options. These facilities let you put the information you want into a presentation that matches your priorities.

There are many portals on the Web that do not allow you to customize content. These portals can, however, be an important source of news and information if their content is focused on your particular interests. For example, iVillage.com provides content that is focused on issues of interest to women, and sadgeezer.com specializes in science fiction.

Regardless of the portal you select, there is one step left; you still have to actually read it to get the information. Many portal sites facilitate this step for you by allowing you to set the portal as your default homepage. If the portal does not provide this option, you can reset your default page through your browser.

CONCEPTS IN BRIEF

1. The growth of commercial activity on the Internet has increased steadily since 1992.
2. Companies use the Internet to carry out a wide range of business activities.
3. Business activities on the Internet are influenced by company goals and online experiences.
4. The failure of many dot-coms from 2000 to 2001 led marketers and e-commerce analysts to evaluate the benefits of business models used by companies with some level of online activity.
5. Business has a long history of influencing—and being influenced by—technological developments.
6. Technological characteristics of the Internet create and influence the nature of the Internet as an environment for business activity.
7. An important characteristic of the Internet is its ability to foster interconnectivity between consumers and companies, and others in the digital business environment.
8. Ongoing developments to the Internet enhance the benefits of the Internet as a medium for digital business (e.g., e-mail, World Wide Web).

9. Business theory and its application are influenced by the Internet, but many fundamental principles and practices are still relevant and necessary for developing sound strategy.
10. Electronic commerce is an evolving area, and one of several functions that enables a company to achieve its strategic objectives.

THINKING POINTS

1. What opportunities and advantages do interactive media offer
   a. businesses?
   b. consumers?
2. What challenges and difficulties might interactive media create for
   a. businesses?
   b. consumers?
3. How might the original purpose for the development of the Internet affect its
   a. form?
   b. use for contemporary applications?
4. How might advances in electronic commerce influence the activities typically associated with business?
5. What does the rapid adoption of the Internet—following development of the World Wide Web — suggest is important for businesses that use the medium to sell to consumers?
6. How might the marketing program of an organization that uses the Internet for planning differ from the program of an organization that does not use the Internet for planning?

ENDNOTES

1. These numbers were reported by Nua Online Surveys (www.nua.com), based on data collected by Nielson Media Research (www.nielson-netratings.com).

SUGGESTED READINGS

1. *Where Wizards Stay Up Late: The Origins of the Internet,* by Katie Hafner and Matthew Lyon (Simon and Schuster Inc.: New York, 1996).
2. *Marketing in the Cyber Age: The Why, The What, and The How* (Chapters 1, 2, 3, and 6), by Kurt Rohner (John Wiley & Sons, Inc.: New York, 1998).
3. *The Digital Economy* (Chapters 1, 2, 4, and 7), by Don Tapscott (The McGraw-Hill Companies, Inc.: New York, 1996).
4. "History of the Web," by Shahrooz Feizabadi. In *World Wide Web: Beyond the Basics.* Edited by Marc Abrams (Prentice-Hall, Inc.: Upper Saddle River, NJ, 1998).
5. "The Electronic Marketplace Metaphor: Selling Goods and Services on the I-Way," Part 3 in *Internet Dreams,* edited by Mark Stefik(The MIT Press: Cambridge, MA, 1997).

LEARNING LINKS

Using the Internet to Find Information
owl.english.purdue.edu/internet/search/

www.fool.com
www.redherring.com

Internet-Related News
news.com.com

Internet-Related Statistics
www.glreach.com/globstats

cyberatlas.internet.com
www.nua.ie/surveys
www.internetstats.com
www.statmarket.com

Digital Business Information

www.ecommercetimes.com
www.zdnet.com
live.emarketer.com

www.census.gov/econ/www/
ebusiness614.htm
www.webmergers.com

The Dot-Bomb Phenomenon

www.itworks.be/dotcomfailures
www.hoovers.com/news/detail/0,2417,11_35
83,00.html
www.startupfailures.com
www.thecompost.com

2

A Framework for Digital Business

Focus and Objectives

This chapter presents a framework for thinking about digital business. The framework emphasizes the relationships that exist between people who wish to conduct exchanges of resources, such as goods, information, and money, in the Internet environment. The framework integrates the perspectives of buyers, sellers, technologists, and policy makers and serves as a basis for examining the impact of the Internet on exchanges between the perspectives.

Your objectives in studying this chapter include the following:

- Understand the benefits of using a framework to organize thinking.
- Be able to describe the difference between exchanges and transactions, and their role in business.
- Learn the basic types of resources that can be exchanged on the Internet and what factors guide their exchange.
- Understand the role of relationships as vehicles for resource exchanges.
- Be familiar with a general framework that integrates resource exchanges and relationships to describe a digital business environment.

Moving the Mall

What do you get when you put books, clothes, sporting goods, movies, an arcade, and a food court under one roof? You're right; it's a mall. Americans have flocked to malls since the first strip mall opened, in Kansas City, Missouri, in 1922. Malls provide shopping convenience and entertainment, without the hassles of driving from store to store.

Malls appeal to a wide variety of people. They can provide a sense of community: as meeting place for teens, and as a climate-controlled environment for older customers to get exercise while walking. In addition, typical mall layouts make it easier for parents with young children to move from store to store—pushing strollers without having to maneuver through doors, up stairways, and across thresholds.

Despite the many benefits of malls, they are not for everyone. Sure, they provide shopping convenience, but for many people, the frustration of dealing with crowds, as during sales and holidays, or the limits to the variety of stores in typical malls, outweighs the benefits. For these consumers, shopping from the comfort of home is preferable.

In 1994, the first shopping malls opened for business on the Internet. Like their physical counterparts, these malls were collections of companies and products, clustered under a single address. Similar to off-line malls, the online malls attracted merchants with the promise of foot-traffic, measured in site visits. They lured customers to their sites with the opportunity to sift through the wares of hundreds of merchants, available at the click of a mouse.

Creating a successful online mall isn't easy. Many of the earliest malls didn't last, despite plentiful amounts of investment capital and the availability of business know-how in off-line markets. IBM and MCI each tried and failed. IBM's WorldAvenue mall lasted less than a year, closing in July 1997. MCI's Marketplace MCI, one of the first into the online mall market in 1995, was also one of the first out, in 1996.

What makes some online malls succeed, while others fail? Some of the more successful online malls, such as Yahoo! Shopping and Fashionmall, share several characteristics. Among these are a loyal following of merchants and consumers. The malls have to develop strong relationships with their merchants in order to keep them in the mall. In addition, the mall must work hard as an intermediary between merchants and consumers, to bring new visitors to the mall, and to encourage repeat visits by established customers.

How do online malls develop consumer and merchant loyalty? One answer lies in the role of the Internet as a technological tool that creates new and desirable benefits that businesses can offer to consumers. For instance, when you go to an off-line mall, you may have to visit several stores to find the item you want. If you make several purchases, there is the added inconvenience of hauling your purchases with you. Online malls encourage customer satisfaction with search engines that can hunt for items across stores, and with electronic shopping carts. **Shopping carts** are programs that keep track of your purchases as you move from store to store in the online mall. The malls may also offer **order tracking** from their merchants; a technology that allows the customer to see where purchases are from the time they are shipped, and to estimate delivery.

To encourage merchant loyalty, online malls often help merchants set up their virtual storefronts, and they may provide assistance with sales tax calculation software and online payment abilities. This help can streamline aspects of business management for mall merchants, and it can reduce the effort of complying with tax laws across a wide geographic range. The mall developer may also provide its merchants with Web-based data about store performance, to help the merchant develop a competitive and profitable presence on the Internet.

These benefits reflect the importance of relationships between customers and companies, and between other participants in the digital business environment, such as technology developers. By understanding the customer's experience in an online mall, companies can work in conjunction with technology developers to enhance the quality of the experience, both within a particular setting and across the digital business environment.

The characteristics that describe a successful online mall highlight the unique capabilities of the Internet as an environment for commercial activity, as well as the different sets of people whose interactions influence online exchange. In Chapter 1, we saw how the technologies that make up the Internet can influence the nature of the business environment, as well as the ways in which commercial activities can be completed. In this chapter, we will develop a framework that will serve as the basis for our discussion of business activity in the Internet environment. We will use this framework to examine the ways that exchanges are carried out, with an emphasis on the different partners in the exchanges. The relationships between these partners define the business environment of the Internet and suggest opportunities for commercial activities that are not available in traditional marketplaces.

This chapter is divided into two sections that reflect these different, though related, objectives. We begin with a general framework to reflect the exchanges between customers and companies. Then we discuss the types of things that people exchange. The framework will serve as the basis for organizing the subsequent chapters of this book. The main objectives of this chapter are (1) to describe the framework and its benefits for understanding how to use the Internet as a business tool and (2) to use the framework to illustrate the unique applications and influences of the Internet as a digital business environment.

Bits & Bytes 2.1
In November 1999, the St. Louis Galleria banned all of its 170 stores from promoting any aspect of e-commerce in the off-line mall.*
(*Source:* Associated Press: 25 November 1999).

———
*The policy was retracted within a month.

Why Do We Need a Framework?

A **framework** provides a way to organize lots of different topics that are related to a central purpose. In addition, the framework can be used to specify the relations that exist between different elements it contains. As a result, with a framework we can

FIGURE 2-1   Commerce as a Process: From Exchange to Transaction.

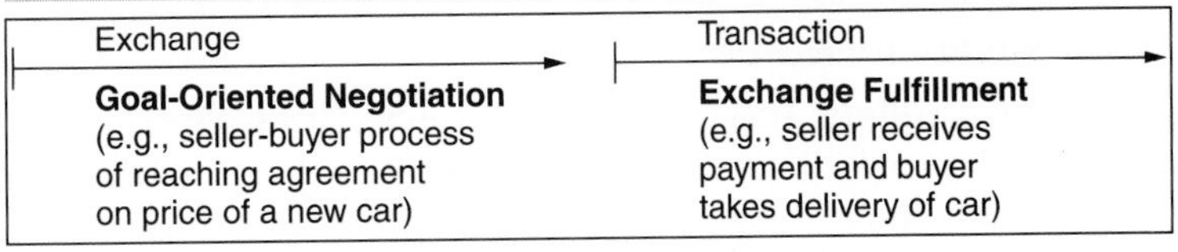

Exchange	Transaction
Goal-Oriented Negotiation (e.g., seller-buyer process of reaching agreement on price of a new car)	**Exchange Fulfillment** (e.g., seller receives payment and buyer takes delivery of car)

systematically and thoroughly examine a wide array of relevant topics in a manner that might otherwise seem disconnected or incoherent.

Think about a blueprint for building a house. The blueprint illustrates what goes where, relating one room or space to the rest of the house. By displaying all of the components in relation to each other, the blueprint may suggest opportunities for improvement (e.g., no window in the shower) or innovation (e.g., a laundry chute that empties into the washer). Our framework functions similarly, by highlighting the key sets of participants in the online marketing environment and indicating the relationships that may exist between them.

Framework Objectives

Our framework is designed to meet several objectives. In addition to describing the focus and direction of the rest of this book, it is also intended to spur your thinking about the ways that the introduction of the Internet may influence business activities. It would be impossible to imagine all of the ways that Internet influences might occur; the topic is a broad one, and the environment is changing so rapidly that new possibilities arise daily. Thus, the framework can be used to suggest avenues for possible effects of Internet influences on business practices, and the implications of these influences, without being limited to the present state of technology. Taking a dynamic perspective to integrating the Internet and business will help you to adapt business activities effectively as the digital business environment continues to evolve.

The Framework's Basic Premise

The framework developed for this book is based on the idea that commercial activity involves processes of exchange between two parties (Figure 2-1). **Exchange processes** occur when parties negotiate with a goal of reaching an agreement. While the process of reaching an agreement reflects exchange, however, the fulfillment of the exchange process is called a **transaction.** The goal of a transaction is that each party receives something he or she values from the other party in the exchange.

Business as Exchange

The concept of business as exchange is fundamental to our characterization of business activity for two reasons. First, an exchange implies the involvement of two parties. Second, the willingness to participate in the exchange process suggests that each participant has something he or she wants to gain from the exchange, and that each participant believes that the other participant has something to exchange that would provide the desired benefit. Simply put, exchange is a two-way street with value for both parties.

Building the General Framework

Buyers and Sellers: The Central Exchange Context

Buyers and sellers are the centerpiece of exchange. Their actions may directly affect each other, and without the participation of both parties, there would be no commercial environment. As you can see in Figure 2-2, the **central exchange environment** consists of the exchange processes that flow between a buyer and a seller. The upper path that links the two parties is a buyer-seller relationship in which the buyer's actions influence the seller. For example, a product complaint initiated by a customer may lead a company to recall all recently manufactured products that are affected. The lower path is also a buyer-seller relationship, but in this instance, the seller's actions influence the customer. This direction is illustrated by the situation in which a company creates, promotes, and sells a product to a particular target segment.

Who Is in the Relationship?   The nature of a bidirectional exchange is described by two factors. One factor is the type of partner in the relationship. We can use the example of an online mall to illustrate types of a relationship. In online malls, for example, merchants sell to customers. Doing so reflects a business→consumer (or business-to-consumer, or **B2C**) relationship. The B2C relationship is familiar to us as the typical interaction that occurs in the exchange processes that result in a transaction of a consumer's money for a company's product. Of course, we could flip the relationship around. A consumer→business relationship exists when consumers serve as the information resource for marketing research, as when a business seeks consumer input to develop a new product or to define target market segments.

In addition to B2C interactions, the online mall must sell its concept and services to potential mall merchants. This activity represents a business→ business (or business-to-business, or **B2B**) relationship. The B2B relationship reflects the exchange processes of many business-to-business activities, a topic we will examine in detail in Chapter 14.

If the mall, or one of its merchants, were to set up chat rooms or bulletin boards to encourage interaction between visitors, the result would be a set of consumer→consumer relationships (**C2C**). C2C relationships exist when information about a company's offering is communicated through word-of-mouth or referral networks.

Who Started the Relationship?   The second factor that describes the nature of an exchange relationship is who initiates the interaction (e.g., the buyer or the seller). This is understandable if you think about the difference in communication between a business

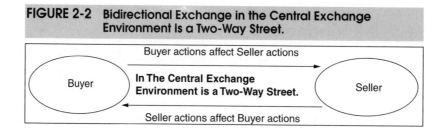

FIGURE 2-2   Bidirectional Exchange in the Central Exchange Environment Is a Two-Way Street.

trying to sell a product to a valuable potential client, and an angry customer who initiates contact with a business after the sale.

The types of activities that may result from the particular types of these relationships are depicted in Figure 2-3.

The Internet can affect the nature of the central exchange environment by altering the ease with which agents, either buyers or sellers, can interact. For instance, finding the right vacation package might take the following steps:

1. Surf the Web → Get online brochures from several travel agents.
2. E-mail brochures to friends → Discuss options via online chat.
3. Contact companies with questions → Use e-mail or live, online help.
4. Check companies' reputations → Read online newsgroups and lists.
5. Purchase package through Web site → Use online payment (e.g., PayPal).
6. Travel → E-mail friends and family who didn't get to go.
7. Upon return, contact company about concerns with accommodations → E-mail digital photos of lumpy mattress.
8. Accept partial refund and participate in service questionnaire, online.

In this scenario, the customer has become aware of different vacation packages (Step 1) and initiated contact with the company (Steps 2 and 7), illustrating consumer→business (C2B) contact. Conversations about the packages with friends and new contacts (Steps 3 and 4) are instances of consumer→consumer (C2C) interactions. The online questionnaire provided by the business to obtain consumer perceptions of the package is an example of a business→consumer (B2C) contact. This example illustrates the central role of the Internet in many aspects of a transaction. In addition, the nature of the bidirectional exchange changes, depending on which partners are involved (e.g., consumers to consumers vs. consumers and businesses), and who initiates the contact (e.g., customer complaining to business vs. business requesting customer feedback).

With the central exchange environment laid out, we are ready to complicate the picture by adding in policy makers and technology developers.

FIGURE 2-3 Relationships in the Central Exchange Environment Take Several Forms.

Receiving Agent		Originating Agent	
		Seller	Buyer
	Seller	Business-to-business transactions	Product complaint Request for product information
	Buyer	Product transactions Marketing research	Word-of-mouth Referral networks Online bulletin boards

Policy and the Digital Business Environment

The central exchange environment is influenced by policy makers, who have the responsibility of balancing the interests of businesses and consumers. Think about sales of alcohol and tobacco. Policy makers routinely place constraints, in the form of restrictive regulations, on the ways that vendors of these products can make them available to consumers. Another example of policy that regulates the exchange environment is the role of taxes. For sales on the Internet, determining which taxes are owed and how to collect them has been an important and hotly debated topic among policy makers. We will take a closer look at tax policy for the Internet in Chapter 6.

Policy can influence the Internet as a digital business environment in different ways. Consider the triad in Figure 2-4. Consumers and businesses interact with each other in the central exchange environment. What they can do (and how they do it), however, may be influenced by policy makers. The arrows between the different groups of people involved in the digital business environment represent different types of relationships, and different effects of these relationships on business activity.

To illustrate the application of this framework, let's look at the path from a buyer to a policy maker to a seller. For instance, a customer, or a consumer group, can complain about a particular business, thus motivating sanctions against the company. An example of this situation is the Federal Trade Commission's 2002 decision to fine the Ohio Art Company, makers of Etch-a-Sketch®, $35,000 for obtaining personal information from children under 13 years of age without parental consent—a violation of the Child Online Privacy Protection Act (COPPA).

Now, let's contrast this path with one that travels from the buyer node to the policy node, and then down to the central exchange environment. Suppose that a group of consumers protests the activities of an entire industry. In response, policy makers might impose regulations that affect all companies within the industry. In this scenario, the impact of policy is shared by all businesses and customers within the central exchange environment for that industry. This situation occurred when the Federal Trade Commission worked with the Food and Drug Administration to clean up the Web promotions practices of companies in the health care industry. Complaints from consumers about fraudulent and misleading claims for product benefits touted on many Web sites led the agencies to initiate Operation Cure.All. The operation was intended to enforce regulatory policies regarding advertising and promotion.

We can also look at the impact of paths that originate with the seller and travel to the policy node. In this case, businesses may initiate the relationship or policy makers can begin one, based on a company's activities.

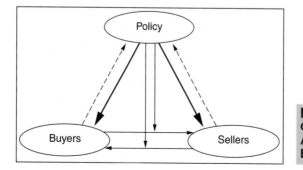

FIGURE 2-4 Policy Operates to Influence Activity in the Digital Business Environment.

In the first situation, businesses can interact with the policy entity to influence the central exchange environment. The path from the business to the policy arm may reflect a lobbying effort by the business, or by a consortium of businesses in an industry, to influence the regulatory climate. The lobbying effort may lead to a decrease in restrictions on the activities that businesses can undertake, or in the way that they can carry out the activities. For instance, effective lobbying pressure may open up new options for promotion (e.g., doctors on television).

In the second situation, commercial activity spurs policy activity. For instance, in August 2002, the FTC proposed to resolve its investigation of Microsoft's privacy practices by requiring substantial changes to the process by which Microsoft collects and stores personal identity information for its .NET Passport service, used for making online purchases. Because these requirements may become the standard for privacy and security of online information, this FTC action, called a *consent order*, has the potential to affect the central exchange environment, and not just Microsoft. In this case, a company's practices initiate policy-based investigation, and result in a benchmark for judging the behaviors of companies with similar processes.

Exchanges between buyers and sellers can be influenced by the relationship between consumers and the policy entity in a variety of ways that are less direct and obvious than those we have just seen. For example, voting behaviors result in the election of politicians and political administrations that appoint policy makers and formulate the agendas for regulatory agencies, thus influencing the nature of the exchange environment.

How and if the Internet should be regulated is a complicated topic that usually sparks heated debate. Issues of whether the Internet should be regulated similarly to other media for commercial activity are often complicated by the geographical scope of the Internet. Policy is additionally complicated by the ease with which Internet content can be created and removed, and by the potential for anonymity. As with Internet taxation, we will examine these issues in greater detail in Chapter 6.

Technology and the Digital Business Environment

The relationships that exist between buyers, sellers, and policy makers in traditional business contexts also exist in the digital business environment of the Internet. In addition to the relationships that exist between the three traditional perspectives, however, the Internet introduces a new set of relationships between buyers and sellers, and the developers of the technologies that make the Internet environment possible. These relationships are represented as another triad (Figure 2-5) in our general framework.

As we saw in Chapter 1, the introduction of the Internet into business planning can be compared to the effects of other technologies when they were new. For instance, the rapid adoption of the television after its introduction to the American public in the 1950s provided companies with a new medium for business activity. The important point is that the role of technology for business is not new. It is the changes to the context in which business activities occur that are new, and that deserve attention.

The nature of the changes to the central exchange environment introduced by the Internet is different, however. Radio and television enabled people to hear and see broadcast information in a mass communication format. Once the basic technology was in place for each innovation, other enhancements to the basic technology made the

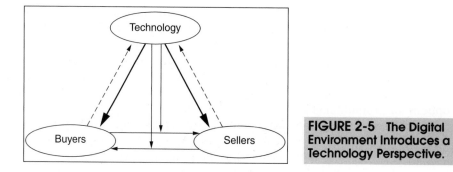

FIGURE 2-5 **The Digital Environment Introduces a Technology Perspective.**

products more effective and economical, but they didn't drastically affect the core benefits of the originally introduced technologies.

The Internet is different. It is characterized by rapid and ongoing technological change. These changes not only improve existing capabilities, but they often add new capabilities. The push for these changes is frequently guided by the relationships between agents in the Internet environment.

With the commercial interest as a dominant focus for Internet development, we need to understand how the relationships between businesses, customers, and technology developers guide changes to the Internet environment, and to business strategy. For instance, a company might work with a technology developer to create a capability for assessing competing product offerings. This exchange might result in a software tool for the Internet that searches online resources for comparable, available products. The information provided by the created technology enables the company to alter elements in its business activity to differentiate the offering. The change to business activity due to a business-technologist exchange may result in a product alteration to meet segment needs, a price reduction, a description of the product that emphasizes benefits desired by customers, or even reconfiguration of the channels through which the product reaches customers.

The business-technology relationship is evident in the development of technology and applications for technology specifically designed to enable companies' goals in the central exchange environment. Amazon's patented 1-Click® ordering speeds the checkout process by eliminating the need to enter credit card information with each shopping visit to the site. 1-Click® can increase loyalty by simplifying online purchasing, and by serving as a barrier against switching between Amazon and non-Amazon sellers by emphasizing the 1-Click® benefits at each Amazon visit.

As we saw in the description of online malls, shopping cart technologies, as well as order tracking software, also enable businesses to enhance the shopping experience for customers. Shopping carts allow visitors to keep track of current quantities and amounts. Once an order is placed, progress of the shipment can be done online with order tracking software. Demand for these capabilities originates with the business, is addressed by the technology developer, and provides benefits for customers who shop at the site and the seller who earns the transaction.

Businesses can also use technology to enhance consumers' online experience with products. Nueweb, a content development company, creates a custom Display-Template for each of its business customers (Figure 2-6). The template enables a business to provide

FIGURE 2-6   Nueweb Technologies Are Used to Implement Business Strategy.

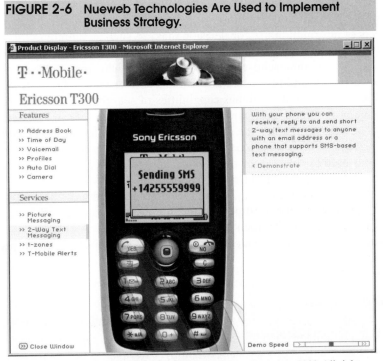

Source: Reproduced with permission of Nueweb, Inc. Copyright 2003. All rights reserved.

its customers with online experiences that capture the product's off-line functionality. The customized nature of the template lets businesses integrate their branding strategies with product display and navigation technologies to optimize company and customer benefits. For example, customers can "try out" the complete range of T-Mobile's wireless handsets online, by interacting with a template that demonstrates the different features of each product in the line. Visual reality is enhanced by the ethereal finger that completes the sequence of operations for each function.

Nueweb has developed its display technology for companies including Sharp, Olympus, and Hoover. The companies who employ this technology receive the direct benefit of improved communications about their products with customers by leveraging the business-technology relationship to further strategic business goals. Retailers like BestBuy and Circuit City also use Nueweb technology to communicate with customers about a broad range of products, while simultaneously integrating their own retail brand strategies into each communication.

The consumer-technology relationship is seen in the development and adoption of technical standards and software tools that facilitate consumers' use of technology for business-related purposes. For instance, user-friendly interfaces to the computer medium provide consumers with easier access to companies' information on the Internet. The development of Netscape, the browser software formerly known as Mosaic, jump-started commercial use of the Web by providing an appealing, easy-to-use, graphical appearance to Web sites.

In addition, intelligent agents can help consumers manage search and use of the available information. **Intelligent agents** are software tools designed to facilitate aspects of information use for decision making, such as searching for specific types of information, storing the results of searches, and constructing displays of stored information. In a commercial context, these agents can make shoppers' comparisons between brands and products more manageable. A **shopping bot** is an example of an intelligent agent that combines capabilities of search engines with other capabilities (e.g., memory of past queries) to refine the results of a search. PricingCentral.com is a portal site that illustrates the consumer-technology relationship (Figure 2-7). The site organizes price search engines and shopping bots by product categories. The different methods used by the search engines and shopping bots provide shoppers with the ability to survey a range of price comparison results.

Uses of technologies like browser software and shopping bots illustrate the link in our framework from consumers to technology developers, with a return link to the central exchange environment. Making product comparisons easier alters the environment as a whole, rather than changing the behavior of just buyers, or just sellers.

Bits & Bytes 2.2

Seventy-five percent of Web customers in the United States have abandoned their shopping carts before completing a purchase.

(*Source:* eMarketer 2001, citing a report by Vividence.)

FIGURE 2-7 Technology Makes Searching Across Sites Easier for Shoppers.

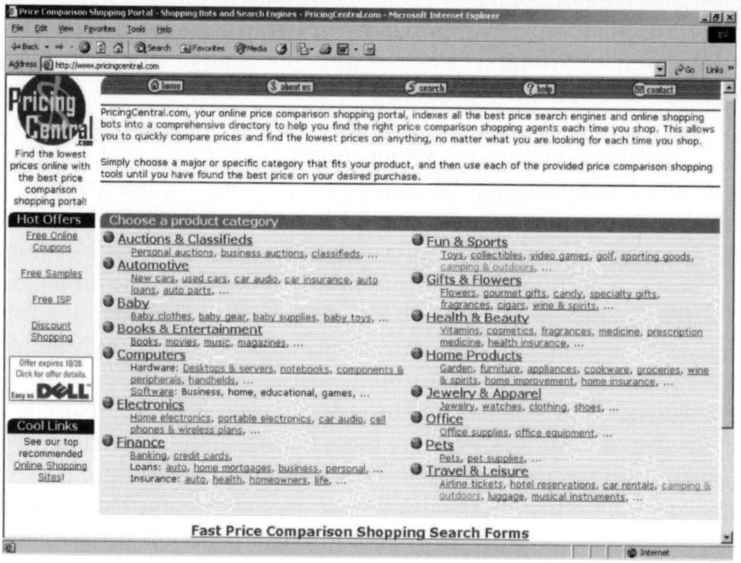

Source: Reproduced with permission of PricingCentral.com. Copyright 2003. All rights reserved.

The General Framework

By combining the policy and technology triads, we arrive at our general framework. This framework describes the marketing environment that is created and influenced by the advent of the Internet into commercial activities. The different elements of the framework are presented in Figure 2-8.

As Figure 2-8 indicates, the roles of policy makers and technology developers in the Internet environment differ from that of buyers and sellers in the central exchange environment. Although they are important influences, policy makers and technologists are not central to the existence of business activity. The primary importance of policy makers and technology developers is their ability to affect the nature of the environment in which exchange processes occur between buyers and sellers, as by regulating the environment or by enabling new capabilities in the environment.

The technology-policy relationship shown in the framework can influence the nature of the Internet as a business environment. As with any of the other relationships, its impact may depend on which party initiates the interaction. To better understand the influence of technology and policy on each other, and on the exchange environment, we can look at the role of encryption technology. **Encryption** refers to processes for encoding information so that it can be read only by someone who has the proper key. These technologies enable users to protect sensitive information sent over digital networks. Many e-commerce activities, such as online banking, require strong encryption to function securely. As a result, there is demand in the central exchange environment for the ability to sell and buy encryption technologies.

Prior to January 2000, trade regulations prohibited the computer industry from exporting strong encryption technologies outside the United States. The Clinton administration believed that making the technology globally available would create a threat to national security. Pressure from the technology sector, and from privacy advocates, eventually led the administration to remove the export ban. In this situation, the technology-policy relationship operated to create greater freedom to market a technology-based product.

FIGURE 2-8   An Exchange-based Framework for the Digital Business Environment.

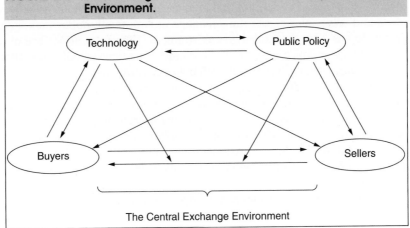

The Central Exchange Environment

Bits & Bytes 2.3

Americans are concerned about giving out personal information online. Only 21.2% of consumers surveyed trust that their information will be protected.
(*Source:* Survey results from NFO Group and Forrester Research, December 2001)

Web-based implementations of the Americans with Disabilities Act (**ADA**) also illustrate the importance of the technology-policy relationship and its influence on the exchange environment. The ADA was instituted in 1990 to insure that Americans with disabilities would have access to the same desirable aspects of American society as Americans without disabilities. Complying with the ADA means that companies with an online presence will implement **Web accessibility.** For example, sites can include text formats that can be accessed by people with visual impairment through screen readers. The ADA regulation reflects the influence of policy makers on technology developers, an influence that can affect buying and selling behaviors in the central exchange environment.

Summarizing the Framework Benefits

The framework allows us to consider the ways in which the effects of integrating business and the Internet may be different for different types of exchange relationships. For example, the ability to post information on the Internet about a product might take a very different form when posted by a company for customers than when posted by a disgruntled customer for other customers, or for the company.

This latter idea illustrates the importance of considering the implications of both directions of the exchange process. While we could simply talk about two partners in a relationship, we would lose much of the ability to understand how the exchange process provides unique opportunities for marketing when combined with Internet capabilities. As a result, an important aspect of this framework is its emphasis on exchange as a process that reflects the influence of both parties on each other. In addition, the framework enables us to describe how the results of business activities and influence attempts may differ, depending on who started the process.

The framework also reflects the ways in which policy makers and technologists influence the types of exchanges that may occur between buyers and sellers. While customers and companies create the exchange environment, policy makers and technology developers alter the exchange environment. These alterations are observed when the technology or policy activities help or hinder the types of behaviors that buyers and sellers can carry out in the central exchange environment.

An important characteristic of our framework is the emphasis placed on relationships—both between and within the four main groups of participants. Relationships for conducting marketing activity take many different forms. For example, a company may form a relationship with a favored supplier to procure parts. That same company may also work to develop a relationship with particular distributor, or even with the end customer. As part of its public relations agenda, the company might maintain a partnership with a nonprofit organization to meet mutually beneficial objectives. Companies work with technology developers to produce new products and marketing

BOX 2-1

INSITE
APPLYING THE FRAMEWORK: WWW.EBAY.COM

Anyone who has ever cleared out an attic, basement, or garage has experienced the challenge of finding the right buyer for that unusual ashtray, or that hula skirt from a long-ago Hawaiian vacation. In contrast, anyone who has searched high and low for the just-right birthday present for a beloved, but quirky, relative knows the difficulty of finding just what you need, just when you need it.

eBay.com, the well-known online auction company, was begun in 1995 by Meg Whitman and Pierre Omidyar to facilitate exchanges of Pez candy dispensers between collectors. Today, the company has a base of nearly 50 million registered users who trade goods worth $30 million every day. In 2001, more than 423 million items were listed for sale.[1] In 2002, the value of goods sold on eBay reached almost $15 *billion*. eBay's mission statement is simple: " . . . to help practically anyone trade practically anything on earth." eBay's founders recognized the opportunity afforded by the Internet to facilitate exchanges between buyers and sellers, creating, in effect, the world's largest yard sale.

eBay's origin and growth illustrate several principles of our framework, and how the framework can be used to describe what works for online businesses, and why. Starting with the basics: Who makes up the central exchange environment for eBay? In one sense, eBay is the seller, selling the opportunity to join the electronic marketplace. People who list items for sale on eBay pay a fee for each listing. The feedback

they provide to management is used to refine and develop the characteristics of the auction-based marketplace. Over the course of its brief history, eBay has continuously adjusted its set of services to meet the needs of a growing and changing user base. It started as an auction site for collectibles—think Beanie Babies and baseball cards—but has since spread to encompass a wide range of products, including cars, real estate, and vacations. As the number of sellers has grown, eBay management has added capabilities to encourage participation by new sellers, and loyalty among all sellers. For instance, the company has added a fixed price purchase component through Half.com, a marketplace for used, mass-market goods, such as computers.

On another level, the exchange environment is also inhabited by people who bid on the listed products. Buyers can interact with sellers to get information about a product, and to clarify transaction-related details. Recognizing that buyers may be uneasy about making purchases from people they don't know, and who don't have a reassuring, physical storefront presence, eBay developed its open feedback system to provide buyers and sellers with a way to check out the reliability of users and the quality of auction items.

eBay's strategic goals have also spurred technological developments that streamline and augment online auction capabilities. An eBay→technology link is reflected in the refinement of online payment methods, such as PayPal. In addition, an eBay seller→technology link has resulted in software developed to automate auction listings for many types of auctions, and not just eBay.

The fourth framework component, policy, is also evident in eBay's history. The vast array of products that can be placed for auction, as well as the anonymity of the online environment has resulted in interactions with policy makers. For instance, attempts by eBay members to auction a human kidney,[2] stocks, and fraudulent Beanie Babies have invited the attention of government agencies. Although these types of issues attract attention and sometimes require changes to the way that eBay conducts business, eBay's members are loyal users, often spending more than 2 hours a week in the Web site.

What makes eBay work? A simple answer is, "the technologies of the Internet." A more complete and complex response, however, includes, ". . . and a large base of people who inspire, accept, and use the technologies."

The history of eBay.com illustrates the nature of the Internet as an environment for commercial activity. The networked communications and graphics capabilities of the Internet make it possible for ordinary consumers to exchange goods with each other through person-to-person auctions, rather than buying from traditional retailers. The company enables interaction between eBay users, and these interactions are the basis for the auction-based, dynamic pricing model that contrasts with the fixed price approaches typically found in traditional, off-line markets.

---

[1] These statistics are available on the company Web site, www.ebay.com, and from eBay's annual report.
[2] The kidney received a high bid of $5,750,100 before the auction was shut down by eBay.

---

capabilities. Policy makers interact with businesses and consumers to determine the appropriate regulatory structure of the central exchange environment. Customers develop exchange relationships with each other, in order to convey information or products. Common across the different partnerships, however, is the process of relational exchange. **Relational exchange** refers to the activities by which partners establish, develop, and maintain patterns of cooperative interaction that enable each partner to meet its objectives. As summarized in Figure 2-9, the primary sets of partners in our exchange framework have representative exchange activities that define and differentiate them from the other perspectives.

Relationships as Vehicles for Exchange

The types of relationships described in Figures 2.4, 2.5 and 2.6 influence the nature of exchange between partners in the relationships. To understand how relationships affect exchange processes, we begin this section with a brief discussion of the characteristics of relationships, and then we consider the nature of the exchanges between partners in the different relationships.

FIGURE 2-9 Many Different Activities Can Foster Relational Exchange.

	Businesses	Customers	Policy Makers	Technologists
	Characteristic Activities of Relational Exchange			
Stage I	Develop commercial opportunites, based on observed and stated consumer needs	Assess needs and survey product offerings	Maintain market balance between buyers and sellers	Determine need for technology development
Stage II	Determine and implement product strategy	Compare and evaluate alternative offerings	Introduce regulation that promotes fair trade and competition between businesses	Develop infrastructure via hardware and software
Stage III	Communicate opportunity to target segment/s	Participate in transaction	Monitor effect of introduced regulation	Develop applications for infrastructure via hardware and software
State IV	Participate in transaction	Consume product	Adjust policy	Refine, improve product

Relationships 101

A relationship can be described in terms of the goals it serves, the general characteristics of the relationship, and the partners in the relationship. We have already looked at the different types of relationships that can exist, such as business-consumer, consumer-consumer, technology-consumer, and policy-business. Now we need to understand how the Internet affects *why* the relationships are formed, and *how* they function.

Goals of Relationships

Relationships make it possible to achieve several different goals. One goal is to manage uncertainty and dependence. For example, developing loyalty to a particular brand or company can reduce uncertainty about product experiences on the part of a shopper. From the company's point-of-view, customer loyalty also reduces uncertainty about the likelihood of a repeat purchase.

In the business environment of the Internet, reducing uncertainty is an important goal for companies. Research results indicate that customers prefer to make online purchases from companies with a familiar off-line, or **bricks-and-mortar,** presence. Retailers with only an online presence (i.e., **pure-players**) were perceived to be less dependable and trustworthy.[1] This perception is due in part to the ease with which **Web site posting,** the process of putting a site online, can be done. Strategic alliances and partnerships are tactics for addressing customer uncertainty. A newly formed company, such as a dot-com, can create a link with an established off-line company, an instance of a business-business relationship. This type of partnership results in a **clicks-and-mortar** company, or a company with a combined online and off-line presence. The "mortar" component provides a reassuring physical presence of the company, while the "clicks" component indicates technological competency to customers. The newly formed company benefits from the relationships that have been developed and fostered by the established company and its customers. When Petco Animal Supplies, Inc. decided to expand from a brick-and-mortar presence to the online environment, the company purchased petopia.com, a pet commerce destination site. The alliance leveraged the solid reputation of the off-line company to penetrate the market for ordering pet supplies online.

A second goal of a relationship is to decrease the costs associated with the exchange activities. For example, extended interaction between a business and its customers provides the business with increased knowledge of the customers' preferences and needs. This knowledge can be used to reduce customers' search costs when a business can tailor product information to provide only the information of value to its customers. Companies can use the Internet to automate the collection and storage of customer preferences, thus reducing exchange costs for both partners. For instance, Amazon.com can track users' search and transaction habits to provide information about product offerings that appear to match customer needs. Knowledge of consumers' needs is also used to guide product development and positioning. As the preceding examples indicate, a single relationship can address more than one goal.

Bits & Bytes 2.4
The White House Web site came online in 1993.
(*Source:* Hobbes Internet Timeline at www.isoc.org)

Features of Relationships

Relationships are described by the extent to which they exhibit four characteristics. One characteristic is the reciprocal exchange between partners; a relationship is a two-way street. A second characteristic of a relationship is that the activities undertaken by the partners are purposive; that is, the partnership has meaning for each partner. Relationships are also described by the amount of activity that occurs in the relational exchange. Multiple activities may occur over the course of the relationship. A fourth characteristic reflects the idea that the set of activities is a process; developing and maintaining a relationship that meets the needs of both parties is an interaction over time, rather than a set of separate transactions.

These characteristics provide us with a way to gauge relationships in order to guide business activity. For instance, a company who recognizes that a relationship is in the later stages of development can tailor interactions with the relationship partner to maximize mutual benefit. The phrase, "the honeymoon is over," illustrates the link that exists between the age of a relationship and behavior—perhaps only too well!

The Internet enables exchange partners to alter these characteristics that describe the relationship. For instance, communications can be facilitated by the ease and speed with which correspondence can be carried out online. In addition, the activities conducted as routine business in a relationship may be affected in number and in efficiency by the ability of the Internet to serve as a resource for information and communication. The Internet can also change the value, or meaning, of a relationship to one or both partners. This situation is observable in situations where the ability to

FIGURE 2-10   The Internet Can Change Aspects of Relationships.

Four Characteristics of Relationships

Reciprocity   (Internet aids communication and exchange)
+   **Activities**   (Internet enables task efficiencies)
+   **Meaning**   (Internet affects dependence and uncertainty)
=   **Process**   (Internet influences relationship)

use the Internet to find alternative sources of products or services reduces the dependence of one partner on the other partner. Changes to one or more of these relationship elements may also change the nature of the process by which pre-Internet exchange patterns were conducted.

To this point, we have considered the groups of people in the Internet exchange environment, and the role of the Internet on the types of relationships they can form. Now we are ready to take a closer look at the types of exchanges that can occur between different combinations of people.

What Is Exchanged?

The idea of business as a set of exchange-based transactions may seem simple and quite obvious. To make things more complicated, consider the variety of types of exchanges that can occur. While we can quickly bring to mind examples in which money is exchanged for goods or for services, people often carry out other types of exchanges. For instance, producing and promoting a new product based on input from consumers is a form of exchange. The consumers and the company have transacted an exchange of information about needs and wants. Word-of-mouth between consumers and negotiations between customers and salespeople are also forms of informational exchange. The existence of different types of exchanges means that we need to develop a framework that includes not only the relationships that exist to enable exchanges, but also the variety of things that can be exchanged.

Resources as the Bases for Exchange

Exchange involves the transfer of something between two parties. In order to make the exchange happen, that "something" has to be valued by the other party in the exchange process. The next step in understanding the exchange process is to determine what we mean by "something." That is, what *is* it that gets exchanged?

One approach is to think of the objects of the exchange process as resources. **Resources** are defined as anything that can be transacted between two parties. From a business point of view, this definition is intuitively appealing; we are used to the idea of a transaction as the exchange of money for a good or a service. The concept of exchanging monetary assets for commodities has been examined in detail by economists, and it has served as a useful way for examining many issues related to economics, such as saving behavior, and the determination of fairness in exchange.

If we look back at the history of commercial activity, however, it quickly becomes evident that commercial exchanges have not always involved money. In the days (or years, or centuries!) before money economies existed, people acquired necessary goods and services through barter and exchange activities. People traded goods for other goods, services for services, and even goods for services. Money, while a familiar resource for commercial exchange, is just one of several types of resources.

Resource Theory and Exchange Processes

Suppose you were asked to make a list of all the things that you could exchange with someone else. The list might get very long. It is also likely that your list would contain a large variety of different items. As a result, it is useful to have a way to classify all possible resources.

The idea that there are different types of resources, and that these resources can serve as the bases for exchange has been formalized as **Resource Theory.** Resource Theory was developed by social psychologists to provide a general framework for describing the sets of resources, and the relationships between the types of resources, that capture the variety of exchanges between people. We can apply this theory to describe relational exchange and the Internet.

Resource theorists classify resources into six categories: money, goods, services, information, status, and love. Each of these six types of resources has been studied in great detail by researchers. As noted earlier, economists have focused on money and commodities as the bases of exchange. In contrast, some psychologists have examined human needs, such as status and affiliation. For instance, researchers have focused on the effect of the Internet as a surrogate for emotional and social interactions.[2] The results suggest that the experience of using the Internet is a resource that replaces the need for some amount of social interaction.

Now we have six sets of resources. The next step is to clarify how they are related to each other. One characteristic of resource theory is that the types of resources can be organized in a perceptual space defined by two dimensions. One dimension is the extent to which the resource is concrete or abstract. For instance, a good is more concrete than love. The second dimension reflects the amount of specificity, or focus on a particular person, in the resource. This dimension, called particularism, is illustrated by the difference between money and love. Money is a universal type of resource; you can exchange it with anyone. In contrast, love—for the majority of people—is specific in nature. We don't walk around expressing generic love for everyone around us. While **concreteness** is focused on the nature of the resource (e.g., its tangibility), **particularism** emphasizes the importance of people as agents in the exchange process. A spatial illustration of the relationships between resources is shown in Figure 2-11.

In the figure, the distance between resources reflects the likelihood that the resources will be seen as reasonable exchanges. This perceptual closeness reflects the idea that resources that are more similar to each other are more likely to be exchanged than resources that are less similar. For example, we can easily think of situations in which money is traded for a good, or a good for a service, or money for information. It is more difficult, however, to find situations in which money is traded for love. The table in Figure 2-12 provides illustrative examples of exchanges between resources. Can you think of any other examples of the resource exchanges in the table?

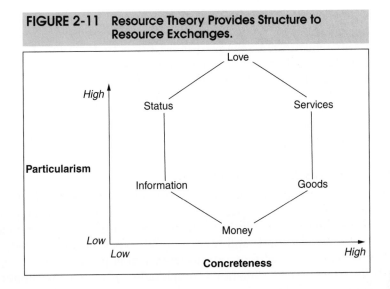

FIGURE 2-11   Resource Theory Provides Structure to Resource Exchanges.

Another insight from resource theory is that exchanges are influenced by context. For example, breakfast served to you on a tray with a flower in a bud vase might engender exchange expectations of a hug or a kiss from a spouse, but probably not from a waiter! The ability to influence the likelihood of exchange has implications for how marketers can induce purchase by positioning products to match situations. For instance, a cell phone can be marketed to professionals as a way to obtain status through improved job performance. For parents, a cell phone can be marketed as a way to stay in touch with children.

FIGURE 2-12   Resource Exchanges Take Many Forms.

Resource	Money	Goods	Services	Information	Status	Love
Money	Financial trades	Buying a hamburger	Getting a haircut	Buying a newspaper	Joining a country club	
Goods		Trading beads for Manhattan	Au-pair for room and board			Engagement ring
Services			Building a website in exchange for landscape maintenance		Providing professional services (e.g., doctors andlawyers)	Running errands for a parent
Information					Espionage. Annual performance review at work	
Status					Socializing at an elite club	Trophy spouses
Love					Celebrities and fans	Support groups

In summary, Resource Theory makes several predictions about the nature of resource exchange. First, it suggests that resources that are perceived to be similar will tend to be exchanged more often than resources perceived to be dissimilar. Second, Resource Theory emphasizes the importance of the context for an exchange, and it predicts that exchanges of identical resources will not always be viewed as equally acceptable (e.g., a kiss for a waiter, instead of a tip). These predictions can be used to understand how people carry out exchanges within the Internet environment, and the implications of these exchanges for digital business activity.

Resource Theory and Digital Business

When we consider the Internet as an aspect of the business environment, many of the concepts associated with Resource Theory are relevant. Each type of resource is reflected in Internet use. For instance, information is readily available from many online sources, and goods and services of all types are increasingly available. In addition, companies can derive status from a .com presence, and people can fulfill needs for affection and affiliation through online personal ads, support groups, and chat rooms.

The dimensions of concreteness and particularism can also be extended to the Internet environment. The concreteness dimension continues to reflect the extent to which the benefits that can be experienced through the different items that comprise resources can be described and experienced in the virtual environment. Particularism also has its Internet analog. The extent to which a resource is targeted toward a specific individual can be described as **personalization.** A reinterpretation of Resource Theory for the Internet is given in Figure 2-13.

FIGURE 2-13   Resource Theory Applied to the Internet Environment.

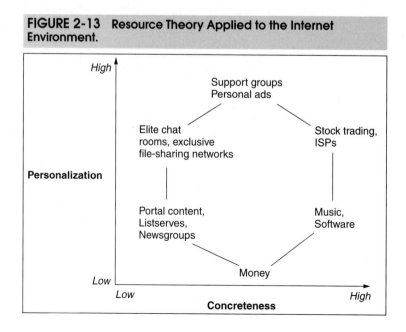

Applying Resource Theory to Business Opportunity on the Internet

Now we consider the implications of Resource Theory for digital business. We can use Resource Theory to look for opportunities for types of exchanges that either may not exist in traditional marketplaces, or that may have other ways in which they can be enacted. For example, we can trace the history of resource exchanges on the Internet to determine whether untapped possibilities exist. By following the path of exchange development over time, we can anticipate where other possible exchange opportunities may be created.

In the commercial domain, one of the first applications of the Internet was to transfer funds from one institution to another. This process of electronic funds transfer (**EFT**) is a form of exchange. As interest in the Internet as a commercial medium increased, companies began to use the Internet as a way to exchange information about products with other businesses and with consumers. Online catalogs were developed, as was **brochureware,** the simple posting of a brochure in its traditional form on a Web site. Sales of goods and services followed rapidly on the heels of informational exchange.

Note that the pattern with which resource exchanges were undertaken on the Internet follows the basic predictions of Resource Theory. Information and goods, both closer to money than services are to money, tended to be the earliest adopted forms of exchange on the Internet. In addition, exchanges between similar resources have tended to occur earlier in the business environment of the Internet than exchanges between more distant resources. For instance, nonmonetary exchanges between information and status are reflected in the provision of content to Web sites with high traffic, in return for name recognition and status. This status, in turn, can be exchanged for money, as when an advertiser secures advertising space on the Web site where the content is made available, and a portion of the revenue is returned to the content provider.

This pattern of resource exchanges suggests that companies can use Resource Theory to uncover business opportunities. Companies can look for opportunities presented by novel resource exchanges, leveraging the infrastructure of the Internet to add value to the exchange process. For example, the Internet makes it possible for two parties to carry out a nonmonetary exchange that provides value for each, while still providing revenue to a third party.

Classmates.com illustrates the opportunity for new forms of resource exchange afforded by the Internet. The site lets users connect with other graduates from a particular school. The classmates can use the service, free of charge, to exchange contact information. For a fee, a user can view the personal profiles posted by classmates about their lives since graduation. The site developer also provides advertising space to other companies, trading **eyeballs,** or site visitor exposure to ads, for money. Exchange capabilities such as those developed by Classmates.com have resulted in new products and in new business models that we will examine in subsequent chapters.

Chapter Summary

Marketing can be described as a collection of activities intended to foster exchange. In this chapter, we have examined the role of the Internet as an environment for commercial exchange. We began by developing a framework to

---

BOX 2-2

'Net Knowledge

DESPERATELY SEEKING STATUS

Resource exchange via the Internet doesn't always take forms that follow the rules of civilized societies. In February 2000, the Web sites of Yahoo!, Buy.com, eBay, Amazon, CNN, Datek, and eTrade were overwhelmed by millions of "pings" to the servers that hosted their sites. These mysterious pings, used to determine whether a computer system is present on a network, converged on the servers from locations around the world. Unable to manage the floods of traffic, the businesses were forced to temporarily cease operations, resulting in revenue losses estimated as high as $1.7 billion.

In Toronto, a 15-year-old watched the mayhem he had created from a computer in his bedroom. Mafiaboy had launched the distributed denial-of-service attacks to prove his "skilz" as a hacker, using "warez" borrowed or pirated from more talented, "leet" hackers to break into 75 different computer systems. He then instructed the computers to send—in the case of the Yahoo!, attack—more than 3.5 million messages per minute to the company's servers.

Mafiaboy was not alone in his quest for status. Despite the destructive nature of the attacks, several other "script-kiddies" claimed responsibility, seeking to enhance their reputations in the hacker underground. In the end, Mafiaboy's boasting, in chat rooms and on a wire-tapped phone, led the FBI and the Royal Canadian Mounted Police to his bedroom door. Once again, the Mounties got their man.

---

describe the presence of four key perspectives in the environment—buyers, sellers, policy makers, and technology developers. Buyers and sellers comprise the central exchange environment, and their interactions result in bidirectional exchanges. Policy makers and technology developers exert an indirect influence on the central exchange environment; their activities alter the nature of the digital business environment.

Relationships between people serve as the vehicles for making exchanges happen. We described relationships in terms of their goals, their characteristics, and their participants. Relationships serve goals of decreasing uncertainty and reducing costs, as well as providing direction for meeting needs. They are bidirectional and meaningful, and they involve multiple activities and interaction over time. Relationships may be formed between people within and between each of the four perspectives in the digital business environment.

Relationships also exist between the resources that people exchange. People conduct exchange processes to obtain desired resources. We applied Resource Theory to describe the relationships that may exist between six types of resources: money, information, services, goods, status, and love. Exchanges are more likely to occur between more similar resources than between dissimilar resources. Implications of resource theory for uncovering business opportunities in the digital environment were discussed.

Resource Theory guides our understanding of how people trade or exchange resources in order to obtain needed resources. With our exchange framework, we can incorporate the idea of resource exchanges between people in the marketing environment, and we can describe the types of exchanges that are possible by considering the reasons for why the exchange relationships may exist.

Bits & Bytes 2.5
The average number of Internet activities by individual users is 7.2.
(*Source:* Internet and Society report, from the Stanford Institute for the Quantitative Study of Society.)

Combining Resources and Relationships: Looking Ahead

When the four perspectives—buyers, sellers, technologists and policy makers—are integrated into a single model, we arrive at the general exchange framework shown in Figure 2.8. This framework lays out the different relationships that characterize many aspects of business, and the role of the Internet as a technological force in the development of business strategy. In the remaining chapters of this textbook, we will use the framework to integrate the different factors that affect the success of business activities that involve the Internet.

In the next four chapters (Section II), we will take a closer look at each of the four perspectives in the exchange environment of the Internet. The environment creates opportunities and poses challenges for growth and success that are unique to each perspective. This uniqueness is due to differences in the goals that motivate the exchanges between perspectives.

CONTENT MANAGEMENT

USEFUL TERMS

- ADA
- B2B
- B2C
- bricks-and-mortar
- brochureware
- C2C
- central exchange environment
- clicks-and-mortar
- concreteness

- EFT
- encryption
- exchange processes
- eyeballs
- framework
- intelligent agents
- order tracking
- particularism
- personalization
- pure-players

- relational exchange
- Resource Theory
- resources
- shopping bots
- shopping carts
- transaction
- Web accessibility
- Web site posting

REVIEW QUESTIONS

1. Distinguish between the concepts of exchange and transaction.
2. What four key interest groups may be involved in exchanges in the digital business environment?
3. What goals do relationships address?
4. What are the four basic characteristics of relationships?
5. Explain the difference between "particularism" and our reinterpretation to "personalization."
6. Explain how the pattern with which resource exchanges were undertaken on the Internet follows the basic predictions of Resource Theory.
7. How does the Internet influence our traditional view of the business environment?
8. From a business perspective, what are the benefits provided by intelligent agents?
9. The key role of buyers and sellers is to create the exchange environment. What is the key role of policy makers and technology developers?

WEB APPLICATION

Keeping Tabs on Trends: Site Content Comparison

Your ability to carry out business strategy can be affected by your customers and by your competition. In addition, the environment in which you implement business activity can be affected by policy decisions and technological developments.

As a tool for refining and implementing business strategy, the Internet is an information resource of huge power. Of course, you have to be able to harness that power by identifying information sources that provide relevant and accurate material. Given the ease with which anyone—not just experts on topics—can post information on the Internet, it's possible to see large differences not only in opinions, but also in the reported facts and statistics that lead to these opinions. As a result, it is necessary to be familiar with a subset of sites that can give you comprehensive and trustworthy intelligence.

1. As a simple illustration of how widely information can vary, use the Internet to get estimates of online advertising revenue since the commercialization of the Internet took off in 1995. Try typing the phrase, "estimates of online advertising revenue" into any of the major search engines (e.g., Google, Lycos, AltaVista). How many results did you get? Hundreds, probably! Which should you believe?
2. One strategy is to turn to a respected source that aggregates information, like Nua Online Surveys (www.nua.ie). For instance, examine the following sets of data, available on the Nua site. These data are published by four major business research firms: Forrester, Jupiter, ActivMedia, and Yankee Grop. (MM stands for millions.)

	ActivMedia	Forrester	Jupiter	Yankee Group
1996			$301MM	$220MM
1997	$400MM	$500MM	$940MM	$630MM
1998	$1,700MM	$1,000MM	$1,900MM	$1,200MM
1999	$4,700MM	$1,750MM	$2,460MM	$1,850MM
2000	$11,200MM	$4,100MM	$4,400MM	$2,200MM
2001	$23,500MM	$5,600MM	$5,800MM	$3,800MM
2002	$43,300MM	$8,100MM	$7,700MM	$6,500MM

Who is most optimistic about growth in advertising online? Who is least optimistic?

One way to understand the differences between the estimates is to visit the Web site for each company and try to learn how the data was collected. Is each research house measuring "revenue" in the same way as the others?

In addition, you can look for estimates from other sources to try to develop a consensus. For instance, the Interactive Advertising Bureau (www.iab.net) reports advertising revenue of nearly $3 billion dollars for the first half of 2002. If we assume that revenues will continue at the same pace, whose estimate appears most likely to be matched by actual ad spending at the end of the year?

3. Develop a set of sites that provide information and statistics for a particular market or industry for each of the following groups:
   a. competitors
   b. customers
   c. technology developers
   d. policy makers

Is the information you have acquired for each group consistent
   a. within the group?
   b. across the groups?

What conclusions can you draw about the nature of the business or industry based on your analysis?

Concepts in Brief

1. Digital business strategy can be guided by using a framework to organize people and their goals in the online environment.
2. The framework describes the relationships that exist between buyers and sellers as the central exchange environment.
3. Buyer-seller relationships are characterized by direct influence of one party on the other, and by their bidirectional nature, as both parties carry out exchange processes.
4. The central exchange environment is influenced by the indirect participation of policy makers and technology developers.
5. All parties may develop relationships to achieve their exchange goals.
6. Relationships address goals of reducing uncertainty, dependence, and cost.
7. Relationships also share four characteristics: **R**eciprocity, multiple **A**ctivities, **M**eaning, and **P**rocess.
8. Objects of exchange are called resources, and can be classified into six sets: money, information, goods, status, services, and love.
9. People may trade between any two resources, and the likelihood of an exchange is a function of the perceptual distance between two resources.
10. The Internet may affect what gets exchanged, and how, by changing the availability of resources and the perceptions of distance between resources.

Thinking Points

1. How is the concept of a framework useful for understanding the implications of the Internet environment for business activity?
2. Why is it necessary to distinguish between the concepts of exchange and transaction?
3. How is the exchange/transaction distinction useful for describing the development of a relationship between two parties?
4. Using the framework developed in this chapter (see Figure 2.8), develop examples of exchange processes for each of the four key parties (e.g., business-customer, business-technologist).
5. How can we use Resource Theory to explain and predict exchange over the Internet?
6. What unique influences does the Internet environment exert on exchange processes?

ENDNOTES

1. These conclusions are drawn from a March 2000 survey of 1548 U.S. consumers by BrandForward, Inc. A similar conclusion is reached by Greenfield Online, based on an April 2000 survey of 3000 respondents, in which 43% expressed highest comfort levels with clicks-and-mortar retailers.

2. Kraut, et al., "Internet Paradox: A Social Technology that Reduces Social Involvement and Psychological Well-Being," *American Psychologist*, September 1998.

SUGGESTED READINGS

1. *Resource Theory: Explorations and Applications*, by Uriel G. Foa, John M. Converse, and Edna B. Foa (San Diego: Academic Press, 1993).
2. *The Hacker Diaries: Confessions of Teenage Hackers*, by Dan Verton. (McGraw-Hall/Osborne; Berkeley, CA, 2002).
3. "The Once and Future Craftsman Culture," by Les Alberthal. In *The Future of the Electronic Marketplace*, edited by Derek Leebaert (The MIT Press: Cambridge MA, 1998, pages 37–62).
4. "A Store as Big as the World," by Walter Forbes. In *The Future of the Electronic Marketplace*, edited by Derek Leebaert (The MIT Press: Cambridge MA, 1998, pages 63–90).
5. "Advertising in an Interactive Environment: A Research Agenda," by Eloise Coupey. In *Advertising and the World Wide Web*, edited by David W. Schumann and Esther Thorson (Lawrence Erlbaum Associates: Mahwah, NJ, 1999, pages 197–215.)
6. *Internet Culture*, Parts One and Two, edited by David Porter (Routledge: New York, 1996.)

LEARNING LINKS

Competition

www.aeaweb.org/RFE/EconFAQ.html
www.commerce.gov/

Consumers

www.inside.com/default.asp?entity=AmericanDemo
www.bls.gov

Technology

firstmonday.org/issues
www.virtualchase.com

dmoz.org/News/By_Subject/Information_Technology/Internet/Headlines_and_Snippets/
www.ittoolbox.com/

Policy

jurist.law.pitt.edu
www.ilpf.org/groups/bib4_15.htm

Hackers

www.hackers.com
www.cultdeadcow.com
www.2600.com

The Framework
In-Depth

Perspectives on Digital Business

Buyers, sellers, technology developers, and policy makers all play vital roles in the digital business environment. In this section we take an in-depth look at each of the four perspectives represented in the exchange framework of Chapter 2. The overarching goal of this section is to help you understand how the Internet affects the activities of individuals in each perspective. As a general objective, it is important to understand when, how, and why the Internet fosters or inhibits exchange processes within and between each perspective in order to recognize opportunities and pitfalls for business activity.

In Chapter 3 we consider the impact of the Internet environment on the exchange activities conducted by consumers to obtain resources. Companies can identify new product and customer opportunities by understanding the types of resources sought by buyers, and make those resources available with the Internet. Problems in taking advantage of opportunities can be reduced by knowing how the Internet affects consumption processes, such as information processing and decision making.

The Internet affects how businesses function. In Chapter 4 we consider the influence of the Internet from the business's perspective. For instance, the Internet can provide benefits obtained from changing the structure of a business, such as emphasizing the importance of different types of personnel. In addition, the Internet alters the processes for business activity, both within and outside the organization.

Technological advances resulted in the creation of the Internet. For digital business, however, it is the ongoing interactions between people who develop technology and the other perspectives in our framework that influence business activity. In Chapter 5 we look at the impact of technology on the exchange activities that take place between perspectives in the Internet environment.

Businesses' actions are governed by regulatory policy. Because the Internet is a new and novel environment for commerce, many regulatory issues are undecided, while still others are unknown. It is therefore important for businesses to understand how policy decisions are made, and to be able to recognize the factors that create situations that necessitate regulation. Public policy in the Internet environment is the focus of Chapter 6.

CHAPTER

3

How Does the Internet Affect Buyer Behavior?

Focus and Objectives

The focus of this chapter is on the relationships that exist between shoppers and the consumption environment of the Internet. Building on the framework for resource exchange presented in Chapter 2, we consider the effects of the Internet environment on buyer behavior. Demographic and psychological characteristics of online shoppers provide a basis for assessing the impact of the Internet on the ways in which people conduct exchange relationships to acquire money, goods, services, status, information, and love.

Your objectives in studying this chapter include the following:

■ Develop familiarity with characteristics of typical online shoppers and their consumption activities.

■ Understand how the Internet affects consumption behaviors.

■ Recognize the facilitating and inhibiting effects of the Internet environment on peoples' ability to carry out resource exchanges.

■ Identify opportunities for business activity based on knowledge of resource exchange theory.

Casting a Wide Net

"Too far away. Not bad, but has young kids. Definitely not! Way too old! This is promising . . . likes sushi. Oh wait – this is good, 'Be the center of my universe.' This guy could have potential. Bookmark him . . . "

Jocelyn is looking for a soulmate, although she would settle for someone who is "romantic, thoughtful, and enjoys a quiet evening, a roaring fire, and

---

a good bottle of wine." The attractive, vivacious, single mother of two grown boys has invested years of Saturday nights on endlessly long blind dates, looking for Mr. Right. Now she has decided to turn to the Internet, in an attempt to weed out obvious mismatches before committing to an evening of awkward conversation.

She's not alone. Online matchmaking is one of the fastest growing services on the Internet. While many companies marketing traditional goods and services had difficulty luring traffic to their sites during the dot-bomb era, matchmaking sites grew in size and number. Matchmaker.com, for instance, claims 3 million members, with over 500 million pages accessed by site visitors each month.[1]

What's the attraction? Jocelyn and the millions of other members of online dating services are enthusiastic about the benefits of online versus off-line searches for a partner. "You get to screen a lot of profiles, based on what you want. That, alone, can be hours of entertainment. Plus, there's the security of knowing that your personal information only gets passed on if you choose to let someone know who and where you are. That's great because if you start e-mailing someone and then discover that he's a jerk, you don't want to have to worry about him stalking you via e-mail. You can ask the service to dump any further e-mails from him to you," says Jocelyn. In addition, some services screen e-mails to eliminate correspondence that contains profanity or inappropriate language. "Besides," Jocelyn adds, "I'm in Dallas, where the dating competition is tough enough if you're a drop-dead gorgeous 21-year-old, impossible when you hit 30, and lethal when you hit 40 if you're not an heiress. I need all the edge I can get."

The edge is honed by services that use matching systems to indicate the potential for a successful relationship. These systems collect information from hopeful suitors about likes and dislikes, as well as the intensity of these preferences. This information is not made available to people searching through profiles, but it is used to determine, for instance, whether Soulful Spring Chicken is a likely prospect for Luv2Dance.

Other benefits of looking for love online include the ability to cast a worldwide net, as well as savings in time and money. Access to tens of thousands of singles' profiles can be had for free, for a monthly subscription fee, or on a per-prospect basis.

And Jocelyn? "I haven't met Mr. Right yet, but I have met several really nice guys, who have turned into very good friends. I'll keep looking!"

The popularity of online dating services highlights two trends in the development of the Internet as a business environment. One trend is an increase in the variety of goods and services marketed online. As recently as the mid-1990s, Internet-based shopping consisted mainly of computer equipment and software, and books. Today, it is possible to search for—and find—virtually any item that exists in the traditional marketplace, as well as a host of newly spawned goods and services that reflect our fascination with and adoption of this new "marketspace."

A second trend is the growth in numbers of online shoppers from many demographic profiles. Today, people of many backgrounds and interests are using the Internet as an essential tool for all aspects of consumption. Their use of the Internet is shifting from using the technology mainly to obtain information about goods and services to an increasing emphasis on purchasing these goods and services via the Internet. The rapid and widespread acceptance of the Internet as a marketplace has resulted in more online shopping than predicted by many business researchers. The trend toward a wider range of products and the trend toward a wider range of shoppers are interlinked, feeding off each other. More products lure more shoppers, and more shoppers provide more business opportunities.

A Changing Culture of Exchange

As in traditional markets, buyer behavior on the Internet is far more than just buying products that satisfy wants. Consumers can search for information about companies and their products, communicate with businesses and with other people who have similar consumption goals or experiences, and even establish online communities and organizations devoted to praising or criticizing the activities of a business. One of the key differences between traditional shopping activities and consumption with the Internet is the role that the Internet itself plays, as an influence on the nature of buyer behavior.

A More Demanding Shopper: Heightened Expectations

The Internet is a vast source of information about things we can consume. We expect information to be readily available, from businesses' Web sites, from other buyers' posted experiences, and from shopping comparison and ratings sites. Digital communications, as through e-mail, also increase our expectations about the addressability and accountability of businesses. **Addressability** refers to the ability to reach out and touch someone, via the Internet. Web sites often post contact addresses with which shoppers can obtain further information and assistance from the company in making a purchase decision. **Accountability** is the burden placed on the seller to undertake responsibility for the satisfactory completion of an exchange. Dissatisfied customers can initiate communications about the product experience with the company, and with other shoppers, through complaint sites, bulletin boards, and discussion lists.

The global, borderless nature of the Internet has also changed our expectations of what we can buy, where we can get it from, and what it should cost. As a worldwide catalog of things to get, the Internet opens up consumption opportunities from far-flung places to which people did not have access prior to the Internet. In addition, the relatively low costs to present products and services on the Internet, compared with setting up a traditional, physically bound, storefront means a wider range of products available to purchase. Finally, in the economic world of supply and demand, as more of an item becomes available, its cost decreases. As a result, buyers may often expect to pay less for a product purchased online. The graph in Figure 3-1 indicates that while cost is an important factor in online shopping, being able to find items easily and saving time are the two biggest perceived benefits of the Internet as a marketplace.

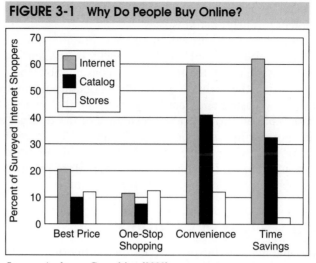

FIGURE 3-1 Why Do People Buy Online?

Source: Andersen Consulting (2000).

A Different Way to Consume: New Opportunities For Exchange

Remember resource theory from Chapter 2? The Internet can influence the types of exchanges that are carried out by making it possible to get resources that are less readily available in traditional marketplace settings. For example, imagine how difficult it would be to find out what other people with tastes and values similar to yours thought about a particular product, such as a new car. Short of polling friends and neighbors, getting these opinions could amount to carrying out a full-scale research project! On the Internet, however, this information is readily available through bulletin boards and newsgroups. As a result, the Internet environment influences the types of exchanges people make, and the types of relationships formed to carry out these exchanges.

The rapidly changing pace of the environment for digital business—in terms of technology and people's response to technology—makes it important for companies to understand how to anticipate and adapt to likely changes in buyer behavior. In this chapter we will look at characteristics of online consumers, and at different segments of shoppers in the online marketplace. We will also take a look back at how the "typical" online shopper has changed, and why. Doing so will help you evaluate future trends and opportunities for business and the Internet.

Bits & Bytes 3.1

One of every five kids, aged 2 to 17, with Internet access from home, used the Internet in July 2002.
(*Source:* Nielsen/NetRatings)

To begin, we look at who is shopping online, and what they are buying.

Who Are the Online Buyers?

In the "old" days of the Internet—the mid-1990s—the typical online shopper was a man in his mid-30s, with a professional job, college education, and an annual income of $58,000. As people have become more comfortable with the Internet, and as the Internet has developed into a user-friendly marketplace, the profile of an online shopper has become very similar to the profile of an average offline shopper. By mid-2001, women outnumbered men as online shoppers, and the average household income of an online shopper had dropped from $62,000 in 1996 to $49,800.

But what does it mean to be an "average" buyer? The increasing variety of shoppers on the Internet means that businesses have to understand their target markets and how the shifts in patterns of Internet use within these markets may affect business strategy. We can examine the impact of the Internet on people and their shopping behaviors with **descriptive research.**

Describing Online Shoppers

Descriptive research relies on demographics and psychographics. **Demographics** are useful for answering questions such as, "Who is buying on the Internet?" and "How frequently do people complete online transactions?" and "What products are most likely to be purchased via the Internet?" **Psychographics,** a combination of demographics and psychological dimensions that reflect peoples' beliefs and opinions about consumption-related activities, can be used to obtain insights about when people might use the Internet to make purchases, and for what types of purchases.

To illustrate the difference between demographics and psychographics, consider Jocelyn's description of her ideal date. "He'd be between 35 and 45, at least five-foot ten. Good sense of humor, sensitive, but not wimpy. He also has to be a decent conversationalist, so a college education is good. I want to be treated well, so he'd better have a good job! Romantic is an absolute must, and he has to be a good person—good values. He would also have to be in shape, and like water-skiing."

Age, education and occupation are examples of demographic variables. Preferred activities, like water-skiing and working out, as well as beliefs and personal values, are examples of lifestyle and attitudinal information that can be assessed with psychographic measures. All of these types of variables can be used by marketers to develop profiles of consumers for different products and marketing activities.

With the Internet, companies can accumulate information about *what* their customers purchase. This information is a **behavioral measure,** because it reflects what customers *do*. In addition, asking a site visitor to register with a store provides an opportunity to gather demographic information, such as gender, age, and occupation. Both of these tactics are common in offline environments, as well as on the Internet. On a less obvious level, however, the Internet is also a source of information about shoppers' lifestyles and activities. Businesses can track what visitors looked at, for how long, and how frequently, and they can use this behavioral information to understand and predict a shopper's interests and needs. With this type of behavioral data, it is possible to build a profile of a shopper that is a rich composite of demographic and psychographic information (Figure 3-2). This profile can then be used to customize the set of products offered to each visitor. We will take a closer look at how businesses can

FIGURE 3-2 Describing Online Buyers with Demographic and Psychographic Variables.

Demographic	Psychographic	Behavioral
Age	Religious values	Number of purchases
Education	Social values	Type of purchase
Income	Personality traits	Quantity purchased
Gender	Activities and interests	Frequency of site visits
Marital status	Views and opinions	Length of site visits
Occupation		Type of products searched
		Sequence of products searched

gather information about consumers in Chapter 9, when we examine the effect of the Internet on marketing research.

Recent research has provided us with descriptions of Internet shoppers, in varying levels of demographic and psychographic detail. Ongoing surveys of Internet use are one source of this information. For instance, the Pew Internet & American Life project at *www.pewinternet.org,* surveys Internet users to gather information about the impact of the Internet on many aspects of behavior, including consumption. Many commercial research firms also publish data about Internet uses and users.

Another source of descriptive information about buyers is obtained from academic researchers, who integrate demographics with psychological features to develop profiles of Internet consumers. This type of psychographic research is often conducted with a goal of being able to predict longer-term changes in consumption patterns and reactions to product offerings on the Internet.

Market Segmentation and the Internet: Applying Psychographic Theory

Because it may not be cost-effective or feasible to develop marketing strategies for each unique consumer, companies often look for groups of customers who make up **market segments** that are good targets for marketing activity. A goal of descriptive research is to identify the variables and potential customers who define a desirable target segment. The importance of descriptive research for identifying online segments is evident in a study that applied psychographic theory to examine the attitudes of online shoppers toward buying on the Internet.[2] The researchers used measures of computer literacy and of lifestyle factors to develop the eight categories of online shoppers shown in Figure 3-3.

Based on surveys sent to more than 20,000 Internet users, the researchers concluded that the psychographic data indicates marketing opportunities in each of the segments, except the Fun Seekers (surfing for entertainment), the Technology Muddlers (confused by technology, but not motivated to learn), and the Shopping Avoiders (impatient with delayed product delivery).

In the other segments with sales potential, the psychographic measures provide insights into the different business activities that would be needed to encourage online shopping in each segment. Shopping Lovers are sources of word-of-mouth, good for community-building, while Adventurous Explorers make good opinion leaders.

FIGURE 3-3 **Psychographic Bases for Segmentation Suggest Options for Business Activity.**

Understanding Segments Using Psychographics

Shopping Lovers 13%

Adventurous Explorers 10%

Fun Seekers 14%

Technology Muddlers 22%

Suspicious Learners 11%

Shopping Avoiders 18%

Fearful Browsers 12%

In contrast, Suspicious Learners might benefit from increased computer and Internet knowledge, while Fearful Browsers need reassurance about transaction security. Business Users would benefit from activities that increased the convenience of online shopping.

As more and more people flock to the Internet in search of goods and services, the importance of segmenting online shoppers has increased. Suppose you sell science fiction books, and you know that the vast majority of Internet users are men in their 30s, with some postgraduate education and a fascination with all things technological. Sound familiar? This profile described the online consumer in the early 1990s. From the science fiction marketer's point-of-view, the universe of online shoppers was a perfect target market—one that needed no further segmentation.

Today, however, the variety of online shoppers makes it important to be able to distinguish between different groups of potential customers according to characteristics that motivate their consumption and describe their online activities. By segmenting online shoppers into groups that share demographic, psychographic, and behavior patterns, businesses can direct their efforts to subsets of the entire online population who are receptive to the product.

As the variety of online buyers increases, the importance of several market segments also increases. These segments are not new to companies, but they are new in terms of their potential value for Internet-related marketing activities. For instance, seniors—typically defined as people aged 55 and older—were slow to adopt the Internet. As hardware and software became increasingly user-friendly, however, seniors recognized the advantages of the Internet for communications, information, and shopping.

In the next section, we'll take an in-depth look at three online market segments in the United States, and their growing importance for companies. Two of these segments are based on the demographic variable of age: seniors and teens. The third segment, the Hispanic minority, is based on ethnic and racial descriptors.

> **Bits & Bytes 3.2**
> In September 2002, the number of people online around the world topped the 600 million mark.
> (*Source:* nua.com, using data compiled from various sources.)

Market Segments Online: Targets of Opportunity

Being able to know whether a group of people is a good target for your business activity is an important goal of market segmentation. Off-line or online, the same basic criteria for effective segmentation apply. First, can you define the segment? Which people from the general market for your product are in the segment, and which are not? What variables indicate that people in the group are similar to each other, and less similar to people outside the group? This criterion is called **identifiability.** Second, are there enough people in the segment to make it worth investing your marketing effort? That is, does the segment display **sufficiency**? Third, can you reach the people in the segment to sell to them? Does the segment display **accessibility**? A huge, clearly defined segment of people with one foot longer than the other, with a strong desire to purchase different sized shoes in a pair might be just the segment that your online odd-sized shoe company has been dreaming of. If, however, this collection of oddly sized consumers all live, say, on Tuvalu (see Chapter 1 for a refresher) without Internet access, you may need to rethink your marketing plan.

Each of the following segments shares several important characteristics for online business activities. They are growing segments in online consumption, with growth rates faster than other possible target markets. In addition, the segments can be clearly defined by straightforward application of a demographic variable. Finally, each segment has a high percentage of people with Internet access.

Selling to Seniors

The United States is an aging nation. As the Baby Boomers, born between 1945 and 1965, celebrate their 65th birthdays (between 2010 and 2030) the number of older Americans will swell to more than 70 million by 2030 (Figure 3-4). In 2000, 1 percent of the U.S. population was over 65. That number will climb to make up 20 percent of the population in 2030.[3] In addition, seniors are living longer than ever. In the last century, the average life expectancy increased by 30 years. As a result, the senior segment is an important group of buyers to understand.

Although older Americans were slower to hop on the Internet than younger Americans, their presence indicates recent rapid adoption, and widespread acceptance of the medium for a range of activities. More than 14 million seniors (aged 55 and older) were active online in 2000, with estimates of 22 million, or 36 percent of the senior population, online by the end of 2002. In addition, seniors "surf the 'net' " frequently, with 76 percent online daily, according to eMarketer's eRetail Report for 2000.

FIGURE 3-4   Americans Are Living Longer and Growing in Number.

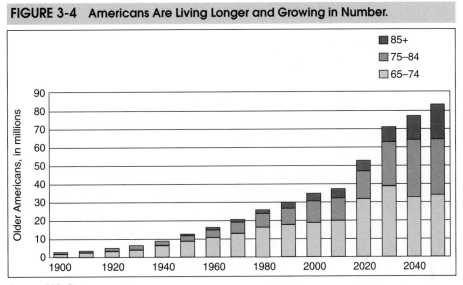

Source: U.S. Census.

In contrast to younger online segments, seniors surf with a purpose. Healthcare information sites are a popular destination, as are travel sites. In addition to searching for information, seniors also spend money online. A survey conducted by Zona Research found that 42 percent of seniors had purchased online, compared with 39 percent of all adult Americans. In addition to buying 80 percent of all luxury travel, seniors shop online for books, computer hardware and software, clothing, and compact discs.

American seniors are a lucrative target segment, even given their potential longevity. It is estimated that the 50-plus population controls 77 percent of U.S. financial assets. With savings from retirement planning and grown children out of the home, seniors are also able and willing to spend more money than other age groups. Purchases with discretionary income on the Internet are nearly three times higher for seniors than across all online shoppers, according to Zona Research.

The Internet is a good fit with the unique characteristics of the senior segment. For instance, access to communications, information, goods, services, and entertainment on a global scale offset diminishing mobility. Online resources for seniors, such as *Suddenly Senior*, an online magazine shown in Figure 3-5, and retired.com, a portal targeted to—yes, you guessed it—retired seniors, use the Internet to leverage the size, stability, and purchasing power of the senior segment for marketing targeted products.

High-Tech Teens

Remember those Baby Boomers—the largest bulge in the population? Many of them had children, and many of those children are now teenagers. More importantly for businesses, those teens have access to the Internet, and they are learning how to be shoppers. Marketers are interested in the teen segment because the ability to create

FIGURE 3-5 Online Portals Target the Retiree Segment with Consumption Opportunities.

favorable opinions and brand loyalty in consumers at an early age increases the lifetime value of the customer to the marketer. **Lifetime value (LTV)** is the total amount of profits that, discounted over time, result from sales to a customer.

Recent surveys indicate that 91 percent of American teens have access to the Internet, whether from school, home, library, or a friend's house. The chart in Figure 3-6 shows the ways in which over 6,700 teens surveyed by a commercial research firm spend their 12 hours a week online.

Notice that in Figure 3-6, online shopping does not appear as a popular activity. In spite of access and interest, teens are not big spenders on the Internet. Why not? One explanation is that many teens don't have access to credit cards. Popular teen sites, such gURL.com, provide a way for companies to create product and brand awareness without requiring a purchase.

Teens' inability to buy with a credit card does not diminish the value of the segment to businesses. Many teens use the Internet as a way to collect information about potential purchases, by looking at competing sites and by using price comparison sites. Jupiter Media Metrix reports that 89 percent of teens have not made an online purchase, but that 29 percent have researched a product online before buying it off-line. This behavior means that companies can use the Internet to build brand awareness and influence attitudes, in conjunction with off-line business activities. In addition, prepaid cards are increasing in popularity. These cards enable teens to buy online, securely and without parental oversight, and without going into debt. The

FIGURE 3-6 Sub-segments In The Teen Market Suggest Different Business Opportunities.

Source: Digital Market Services, January 2002.

acceptance of prepaid cards, like Visa Buxx, is predicted to send online teen spending in the United States and Europe as high as $10.6 billion in 2005, compared with $483 million in 2000.

American teens are technologically savvy. They have access to computers in school, and classes in "keyboarding" are standard electives as early as sixth grade. The high penetration of personal computers into homes also provides teens with hands-on computer and Internet opportunities. It is not surprising that teens are interested in influencing and purchasing high-tech products. Data from a survey by InsightExpress of 300 students lets businesses identify likely purchases, and the extent to which teens will make the decision to buy (Figure 3-7). Of the teens surveyed, 40 percent stated that they will pay for their high-tech purchases themselves.

FIGURE 3-7 Teens Exert Strong Influence Over Their Personal Technology Purchases.

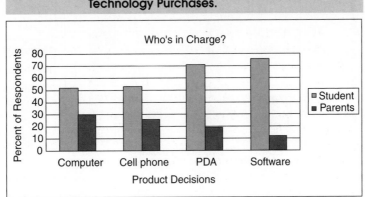

Source: InsightExpress, July 2002.

The Hispanic Segment

Although they are the third largest ethnic group on the Internet, Hispanics in the United States are the fastest growing minority, second only to African Americans. In 2002, the general online population in the United States increased by only 3 percent, while the Hispanic population jumped 13 percent to 7.6 million users.

Businesses are interested in this segment not just for its size and growth rate. The Hispanic population is a uniquely accessible segment with purposes for Internet use that differentiate them from other ethnic segments. For instance, 55 percent of Hispanics online in the United States access Web content in Spanish. For marketers, this behavior enables targeted marketing through Spanish-language portals, such as YupiMSN.com, a company operated by TelMex and Microsoft. The YupiMSN portal is a collection of Spanish-language sites, including a community site and a women's-interest site.

The targeted portal can also offer features that directly address the buying needs of the segment. For example, YupiMSN's concierge service fosters online shopping and shipping from the United States to Latin America. The service provides a way for site visitors to make purchases and have them delivered to Latin America, at a lower cost than a traditional courier service.

The Hispanic segment differs from other ethnic segments in its widespread adoption of technology products, such as PDAs and digital satellite television. As shown in Figure 3-8, Hispanics exhibit higher levels of ownership of several types of home media devices.

These types of characteristic purchases reflect an underlying emphasis in the Hispanic segment on quality of life. This emphasis is also observed in Internet-related activities. Many Hispanics who participated in a Pew Internet Life survey indicated that Internet access improved their quality of life, providing closer connections with

FIGURE 3-8 **Hispanics Buy More Home Technologies Than Do Other Ethnic Segments.**

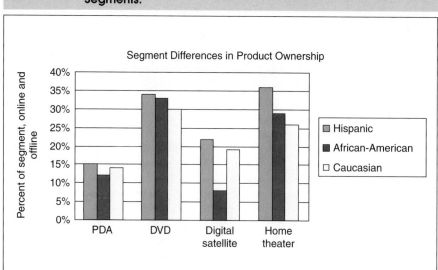

Source: Spring 2002 Ownership Report, The Home Technology Monitor.

loved ones, and access to resources that fulfilled personal objectives. For example, benefits obtained from the Internet were financial management (noted by 33 percent of respondents), shopping (37 percent), health information (41 percent), and the ability to pursue hobbies (51 percent).

What Do Shoppers Acquire Online?

Now that we know who the buyers are—at least in general descriptive terms—it is time to take a closer look at what they consume in the online environment, and how the Internet affects their consumption. We can organize our study of consumer behavior by using the six categories of resouces for exchange that we met in Chapter 2.

Keep in mind that buyer behavior is not just about *buying* things. Consumption can occur in many ways that cannot be described by the exchange of money for a product. The exchange-related behaviors that people carry out in order to consume resources can provide opportunities for marketing activity far beyond the simple selling of goods and products to meet needs. We are interested in understanding the ways in which resources have meaning for people, and how companies can use the Internet to create and encourage meanings that motivate online exchanges.

> **Bits & Bytes 3.3**
> Moms are online, too. American mothers spend even more time online than their teenagers—16 hours and 52 minutes per week, on average, compared with 12 hours and 17 minutes for teens.
> (*Source:* Digital Marketing Services, an AOL subsidiary, May 2002.)

The following sections are focused on pairs of resources. The resources in each pair can be exchanged with each other, and with resources in other pairs. We look at each resource to understand how it can be consumed via the Internet, and how the Internet affects the opportunities for exchanging it with other resources.

Money and Information Online

As one of the six basic resources in Foa's Resource Theory, money is characterized by its position, relative to the other resources, as the least person-specific resource. That is, money is universal; it can be acquired from a wide number of sources, without changing its inherent value. It can also be traded to others, in exchange, perhaps, for other desired resources. Economists refer to this readily exchangeable quality as **fungibility.** Given its fungible nature, money is a basic cornerstone of online exchange.

The other resource in this pair is information. Information of an almost infinite variety is widely available via the Internet. Sports, current events, weather, fashion, and health are all frequently searched topics on major search engines. Although many sources of information are free of any monetary cost, many sites can—and do—develop revenue streams based on charging visitors to access their content. Fees in exchange for content can be charged in several ways. For instance, a one-time fee may provide ongoing access, as is common with many dating sites. Alternatively, a site may require a fee each time a source of information is accessed (e.g., PeopleFinder.com and knowX.com charge the customer each time a search is conducted prior to providing detailed search results). Other sites provide information on a subscription basis, charging for content on a set time unit (e.g., per month, per year). Many pornography sites charge fees based on the amount consumed, as in minutes used within a site. Internet Service Providers (ISPs) also commonly use this set-up. Regardless of the payment form, the exchange of money for information is common on the Internet.

We are used to *getting* information as a resource, but the Internet makes it possible to acquire many other types of resources by *giving* information. Many Web sites provide content in exchange for visitors' information. For instance, Yahoo! requires a visitor to complete a registration survey prior to setting up a customized MyYahoo! page. A person who wishes to use the service must provide information about gender, occupation, area of specialization, job title, zip code, and language. While this information is used to deliver targeting content to the user, it is also a valuable source of visitor information for the marketer. Accumulated registrations provide demographic information that may be used to refine and further develop the portal product, enhancing its appeal within old markets and creating interest in new markets.

When information can be given up in order to get something, whether a service, like MyYahoo! or access to Web content, visitors' personal information becomes a resource that can be traded, much like money. In the following sections, we'll take a closer look at the nature of money and information online.

The Nature of Money

In order to carry out online transactions that involve money, businesses need a digital form of cash. Several different ways to implement online monetary exchanges already exist. For example, the "old-fashioned" use of credit cards is prevalent. In addition, some companies have introduced payment forms and money transfer that involve **cybercash,** or **digital cash.** These are forms of money that can be stored in online accounts and transferred digitally to other online accounts. As Figure 3-9 indicates, each type of money has advantages and disadvantages that may influence its adoption by online shoppers. The central idea is that the form of money on the Internet is often quite different from money forms available in traditional, physical marketplaces; there is no physical form of the money, as there is with cash, checks, and credit cards.

One issue for online commercial activity is whether the form of money affects its meaning to shoppers. To illustrate the idea that the form of money may affect its meaning, think about what happens when you go to a casino (not, of course, that we are recommending that you do so in order to verify this example), or play a friendly game of poker. In many cases, you exchange money for chips in order to begin playing. One advantage of the chips is that they facilitate play; it is easier to make bets and collect winnings with only a few categories of value (e.g., red chips, blue chips, white chips), than it is with all different denominations of cash. But is this the only reason for chips?

Another effect of the changed form—from money to chips—is that it separates the meaning of money from its actual, physical nature. As a result, it may be

FIGURE 3-9   Forms of Electronic Money Differ in Advantages and Disadvantages

	Electronic Checks (e.g., eCheck, NetCheque)	*Smartcards and Stored Value Cards (SVC's)*	*Electronic Cash (as electronic tokens or notational money) (e.g., eCash, CyberCoin, NetCash)*	*Person-to-Person Payment Systems (e.g., PayPal)*
Pros	Familiar form for consumers Readily transferred across networks for automatic crediting and debiting	Integrated processing chip enables multiple functions (e.g., as credit, debit, or cash cards) Not limited to online commerce	Customer anonymity (Digicash) Security through encryption Ready transferability	Immediate transfer to payee Record of transations
Cons	Expensive and time-consuming to process Primarily used only in the U.S.	Security concerns (e.g., broken encryption, counterfeit cards) Unclear regulation	Requires foresight; customer must stock electronic wallet Some forms do not protect anonymity	Security concerns e.g., fraud) Some systems place limits on transfer amounts

psychologically easier to part with chips, in placing bets, than to part with cash. What does the separation of the meaning of money from its physical nature mean for buyer behavior online?

Spending Money Online   Getting and using money online may differ from offline behaviors in several ways. First, the difference in tangibility may affect shoppers' buying behaviors. That is, because it is possible to negotiate exchanges and carry out transactions without ever seeing the money, or physically handing over a check or credit card, the value of the resource may be less salient than in other exchange environments. As a result, online shoppers may find it less painful to pay for things online than in a traditional environment.

Researchers have found that people often have systems of **mental accounting,** in which they establish internal, cognitive accounts that reflect a budget plan. In general, unexpected hits to the budget are more likely to be viewed as undesirable events than are budgeted, planned for debits.

We can extend these ideas to the online environment. First, people may be more willing to part with money when it is made less tangible, as with digital transfers (Figure 3-10). Second, some types of transactions may benefit more from the online transfer of money than other types. When the transaction is desired, people may prefer to enjoy the actual act of the transaction—giving up the money is not painful. In contrast, when the transaction is not desired, it may be better to be able to make the payment in a digital form, rather than in a very salient, physical form.

Making the act of paying less tangible may increase the likelihood and frequency of similar transactions, as well as the customer's satisfaction with the exchange. The popularity of online bill payment services is due to increased efficiency, but also to the ability to avoid writing a check, stamping, and mailing the payment. Some bill

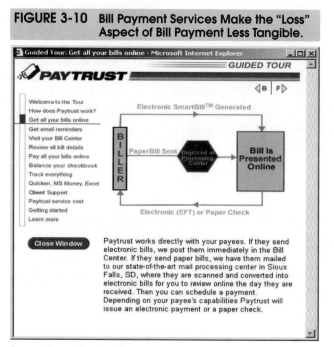

FIGURE 3-10 Bill Payment Services Make the "Loss" Aspect of Bill Payment Less Tangible.

Source: Reproduced with permission PayTrust, Inc. Copyright 2003. All rights reserved.

companies even offer **e-bills,** digital copies of bills that can replace the unwelcome envelopes that arrive all too often in our mailboxes.

Getting Money Online   To this point, we have considered issues of how people might transfer money online, and how their willingness to use money in a transaction might be helped or hindered by characteristics of the online medium. Equally important, however, are some of the novel ways in which the Internet environment makes it possible for people to get money.

Although some of the original "surf for cash" sites, such as AllAdvantage.com, have disappeared from the Internet landscape, there is no shortage of replacements. These sites offer users payment in exchange for viewing ads, or for visiting Web sites. In general, they make their money from advertisers, who pay to get their information on your computer screen. Some of the more popular sites to offer this exchange of money for viewing behavior are coins2cash.com, paidforsurf.com, and spedia.com. Primarewards.com enables people to accumulate points for visiting sites. These points can be "cashed in" for credits at online venders, such as Amazon.com. Other online opportunities for getting money are offered by sites that specialize in contests and sweepstakes. One of the better-known of these types of sites is iWon.com, a portal-type site that offers members the chance to win large cash prizes while viewing information provided by advertisers.

Yet another opportunity for consumers to get money on the Internet is provided by companies like goZing.com, who pay site visitors for completing surveys. Such sites act as marketing research consultants, posting surveys and gathering responses on a variety of topics. This type of site use, combined with the increasing frequency of

'Net Knowledge

MONEY FOR NOTHING?

An innovative business approach makes it possible for people to surf the Internet and make money while doing so. For example, a company can use a site to register users who wish to benefit from **net-surfing,** moving through Web sites in search of interesting or useful content. Users provide some personal demographic information and agree to accept advertising content on their screens while using the Internet. Their surfing behaviors are tracked and recorded. Users are compensated for the advertising they choose to view, and their viewing selections are tracked and recorded. If users sign up other users, they get a percentage of the revenue received by the other users.

The businesses behind these types of sites make money in several ways. One is by combining the user's demographic profile with those of others who register for the service. That information serves as a user database that can be made available, for a price, to interested companies. In addition, the Internet usage patterns of registered users can be aggregated as marketing research data and sold to interested companies. In short, the user obtains a resource by providing a service—Internet usage behavior—that would not be possible without the existence of the Internet environment.

similar, information-based ways to obtain money on the Internet, underscores the importance of understanding the role of information as a resource.

Information as an Online Resource

Many types of information can be obtained from the Internet (Figure 3-11). The variety of uses of information on the Internet can be simplified by classifying information into one of two categories: (1) information that is consumed for its own sake; or (2) information that is used as a means to an end. To illustrate the first category, think of Web sites that provide sports information, entertainment, and news. In the second category, consider sites that enable people to make informed decisions about purchases or other activities. The distinction between the goals of information use is important for businesses because different goals can suggest different opportunities for influencing buyer behavior. For instance, a person who visits espn.go.com to check on football rankings might find a link to a review of sport utility vehicles. If the visitor goes to the linked site, this type of **incidental exposure**—unsought-for advertising that can help build brand and product knowledge in a person's memory—may affect decision making in this product category during future vehicle shopping, even though it may not be relevant right away.

In contrast, a shopper who goes online to get information about the best type of sport utility vehicle for her purposes might visit several consumer sites, as well as auto dealerships online. This type of **directed information search** provides businesses with the chance to display product information in a format that best influences buyer decision making. Companies can often decide whether—and how—they wish their product to be presented in a comparison site.

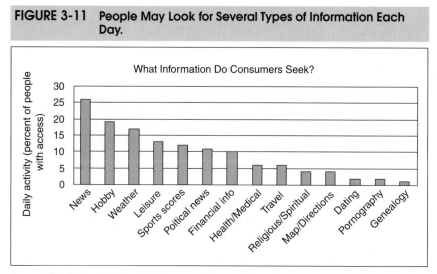

FIGURE 3-11   People May Look for Several Types of Information Each Day.

Source: Pew Internet Project, 2002 survey data.

How Do People Use Information?   Researchers in the area of cognitive psychology have developed **information processing theory** to explain how people use information. By applying this theory to buyer decision making, we can better understand how to influence incidental and directed information use. Think of how a computer works. First, you give it some input: a series of commands. Next, the computer processes the commands internally. Finally, the computer provides you with some output.

In a very simplistic sense, people work the same way. Given some input, such as an ad, we process that input by integrating it with the related information we have stored in memory. Based on that processing, we create some output, perhaps in the form of a decision to make a purchase. Of course, people are not dependent on external input, as are computers. Sometimes a decision is reached based simply on knowledge we already had in memory. The focal part of the sequence for information processing theory, however, is what happens internally, and how that processing affects the decisions that consumers make.

Decision making is described by three stages: (1) information search, (2) information evaluation, and (3) postchoice processes. Each aspect of information processing for decision making is important for developing a thorough understanding of how information available from the Internet, or through similar types of interactive, digital environments, may be received and interpreted by online shoppers. Figure 3-12 depicts a simple, stage-based model of information processing in decision making.

Searching for Information Online   There is a lot of information on the Internet. The amount of information, as well as the variety of search engines that can be used to weed through the information, can provide an online shopper with larger numbers of things to consume than would be available in a marketplace-based search. Thus, the Internet can facilitate information search.

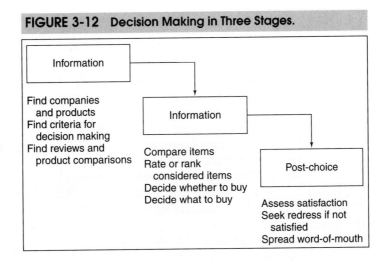

FIGURE 3-12   Decision Making in Three Stages.

The Internet can also make search difficult. The ability to obtain large amounts of seemingly relevant information may strain peoples' processing ability, and lead to **information overload.** Information overload occurs when people get too much information; the sheer amount of information can be overwhelming. This situation may result in a poorer quality decision, as is shown Figure 3-13.

So what's a seller to do? The Internet is big. You want your company and product to be found, but how?

Search engines and **intelligent agents** are two ways in which people can specify characteristics of the information to be returned from an automated search. These types of tools represent a range of abilities to customize search. Search engines (e.g., Google and Lycos) use a variety of methods to search through and index Web

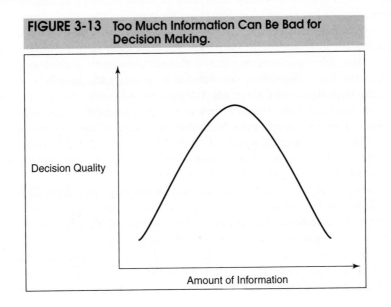

FIGURE 3-13   Too Much Information Can Be Bad for Decision Making.

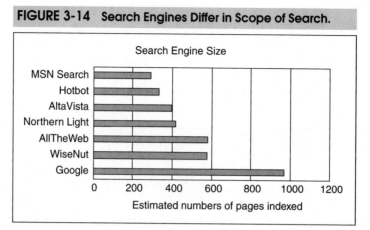

FIGURE 3-14 Search Engines Differ in Scope of Search.

Source: searchengineshowdown.com, March 2002.

pages. As the chart in Figure 3-14 illustrates, different search engines vary widely in the scope of their searches, based on the number of Web pages they have indexed, or noted in their databases. Intelligent agents (e.g., Firefly) perform a similar, automated search, but they often build on the capabilities of search engines by incorporating knowledge of user preferences to conduct searches with greater detail and precision.

Information Evaluation Online   Once the shopper has a set of information to consider, the next stage of the decision process is to evaluate the possible choices. In the evaluation stage, the buyer compares the options and applies some criteria to determine which option is most suitable for the goal of the decision.

Web retailers can incorporate comparison capabilities into their sites. For example, Microsoft's eShop is an online collection of many retailers, including Blue Nile, Eddie Bauer, ToysRUs, and Amazon. Shopping tools on the site enable customers to compare information about a product across brands and vendors, and to specify searches for comparative information on particular features, such as price ranges and return policies. Assisted comparison shopping provides consumers with desired information in a structure that reduces the effort needed to evaluate the brands.

The importance of a clear, easy-to-understand format applies not just to comparisons of products across venders, but also within a single vender. The online air travel industry provides examples of several different types of formats. For instance, the major travel sites—Travelocity, Expedia, Orbitz, CheapTickets, and LastMinuteTravel—each provide search results in a display that organizes results by flight and some combination of features, including airline, flight times, and price.

Orbitz.com touts its "exclusive matrix display" as a benefit for search-weary travelers. Similar to the other travel sites, Orbitz' display provides a brand/attribute matrix that includes flights organized as rows in the matrix. Features of each flight, such as price, airline, travel times, and origins and destinations, are arranged as columns. Recognizing that customers place differing amounts of importance on these features, Orbitz also enables visitors to request that the matrix be displayed so that the feature they say is most important is displayed in the first column of the matrix.

Postchoice Processes Online: Satisfaction and Word-of-Mouth All aspects of the decision process, including searching for and evaluating information, as well as the actual transaction, may affect postdecision processes, such as satisfaction with the outcome. The Internet can affect buyers' feelings of satisfaction, and of confidence in their decision processes.

Companies use the Internet to track customers' perceptions of the buying experience, and to facilitate the spread of positive word-of-mouth. Online surveys and requests for feedback via e-mail can keep businesses on top of customer perceptions. **Online communities,** forums provided by companies within their sites to encourage customer interaction, can foster the spread of word-of-mouth.

Some sites such as BizRate.com, are designed to collect customer feedback about online shopping experiences across retailers. These sites have several functions. One function is to provide feedback to the company about aspects of site design and function that may lead to dissatisfied consumers. A second function is to provide a ratings site that can be used as a shopping guide by online shoppers. These sites also provide customers with an opportunity to vent frustration, rather than spreading negative word-of-mouth.

These aspects of information and its use affect peoples' ability to acquire and use other Internet-based resources. In each of the remaining resource pairs we will examine, information plays a role. For example, when we think of goods or services as forms of resource that can be obtained in the Internet environment, information about these resources is often a shopper's primary way of evaluating the quality or desirability of a possible purchase.

Bits & Bytes 3.4

The first e-mail message from an American president was sent on March 2, 1993 by Bill Clinton.

(*Source:* The Internet Index, #1)

Getting the Goods (and Services) via the Internet

As the Internet continues to increase in popularity as a commercial medium, the amount and variety of goods and services available through the Internet also grows. Many things that can be obtained through the Internet have been developed outside the recognizable boundaries of traditional marketing institutions. For example, the development of the MPEG music compression capability (MP3) has made it possible for people to obtain music in a digital format from the Internet, sometimes by trading music files with other music aficionados.

This person-to-person opportunity for exchange underscores the idea that a product is not just something that must be acquired through an exchange with a marketer, as the result of a transaction of financial resource. The Internet can enhance and inhibit people's ability to effect exchanges of products, not only by making new types of products possible, but also by creating new relationships for carrying out exchanges.

The Nature of Goods and Services Online

Although they are lumped together as "products," goods and services are different. One simple difference for many people is that goods tend to be tangible, while services tend to be less tangible. That is, goods are things you have, and services are events that happen to you. In the following sections, we'll take a look at how the nature of goods, and of services, affects and is affected by, online marketing. In addition, we will examine two roles of the Internet in marketing goods and services. In one role, the Internet is a source of goods and services. In another role, the Internet is a means for conducting marketing activity that influences consumption of off-line goods and services.

More About Goods . . .   Goods are classified as search, experience, and credence goods. People are usually able to understand the benefits of **search goods** through their attribute descriptions. In contrast, the benefits of **experience goods** can only be evaluated after you have had a chance to try them out (e.g., swimsuits). **Credence goods** are items for which quality cannot easily be assessed, even after consumption. For some credence goods, such as wine, quality can be based on the advice of other, more knowledgeable shoppers.

One difference between online search goods and off-line search goods may be a shortened time between the decision to acquire the good and the consumption of the good. This means that search and experience may often be more closely related for online goods than for physical goods. As a result, people may store in memory more information about their overall evaluation of a product than about the specific attribute values that describe the product. From a business perspective, this means that advertising designed to trigger retrieval of attribute-specific information (e.g., a brand's warranty) may be less effective for online search goods than for off-line search goods.

Experience goods provide a challenge for quality assessment, both online and off-line. In both cases, difficulty stems from the need to provide shoppers with a situation in which the benefits of the product can be sufficiently understood. For example, in a physical environment, such as a clothing store, the clothing can be tried on, and the effect on appearance or comfort analyzed. In a virtual environment, however, sensory knowledge of the experience is limited. Even with new technologies that provide simulations of users to try on clothes, the tactile sense that tells you if the clothing is comfortable is missing.

Many people shop for experience goods by trying the item first in an off-line setting, and then using the Internet to obtain the good when it is needed subsequently. This approach is popular for durable goods, where the characteristics of the product are consistent and predictable over time.

Credence goods provide a unique set of opportunities for online buyers and sellers. Credence goods depend on the formation of a set of beliefs about the quality of a product. As a result, simply being able to obtain information about the good, or even trying the good may not be enough to lead a person to believe that he or she can confidently assess the quality of the good. An expert's recommendation can influence the evaluation process.

Relying on the expertise of other consumers to gauge the quality of a credence good is made easier by the Internet environment. For instance, Amazon provides reviews of books on their site so that you can see whether other people, whose reading tastes resemble yours, thought a book was good. In addition, online vineyards often provide expert recommendations about wine selections. For instance, winestuff.com offers visitors the opportunity to "Ask the wine geek" about wines via e-mail.

More About Services . . .   We describe services in terms of three characteristics: inseparability, heterogeneity, and perishability. **Inseparability** refers to the idea that the service cannot be separated from its consumption, or from its provider. Unlike goods, which can be produced, stored, and then consumed, a service does not really exist until it is consumed. **Heterogeneity** refers to the variation that may exist because a service is performed by different people in different places at different times. **Perishability** stems from the intangible nature of services and reflects the idea that services cannot be stored in warehouses. Services that are underconsumed at the time they are produced are a loss to the provider, unlike goods that can be stored for later sale.[4]

The Internet has the potential to change the influence of each of these characteristics for services that can be obtained online. For example, the types of buyer-oriented services that are available through the Internet are often sufficiently automated that their consistency is high, decreasing heterogeneity. An automated tax preparation advisory service can rely on a database of accumulated expertise that may be greater than the ability of any single provider. In addition, the ability to automate the provision of many online service offerings (e.g., through intelligent agents) means that **online services** often do not face the same concerns of overconsumption and underconsumption as services that exist in the physical marketplace, decreasing issues of perishability and separability.

Goods and Services Available Online

Rapid growth in the service sector is driven by familiar and novel opportunities for online products. Some examples of familiar items include news services, such as the customized content available through portals like Yahoo! and America Online, as well as stock and financial services (e.g., eTrade). Other services include online education and professional services, such as tax and accounting applications. In addition, companies have begun to investigate the potential of online customer service, for goods and services purchased in online or traditional outlets.

Bits & Bytes 3.5
Of the £140 million ($220 million) spent online in Europe during 2002, almost 50 percent was on pornography.
(*Source:* Jupiter Media, October 2002.)

Some of the services that have acquired an online presence would not be possible without the development of other, entirely new services that enable their existence. For example, Internet service providers (ISP's), such as Earthlink and AOL, have formed and grown as the result of high demand for Internet access and functionality. These services are termed **Internet services,** and they are focused on providing access to the Internet. Another area of product opportunity due to the commercial development of the Internet is that of **Web services.** Web services are the set

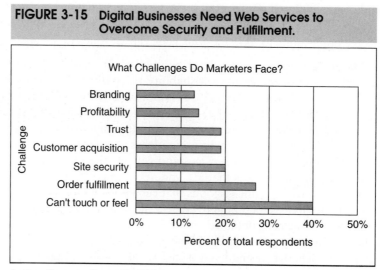

FIGURE 3-15   Digital Businesses Need Web Services to Overcome Security and Fulfillment.

Source: Forrester Research, 2001.

of activities and processes focused on the development, deployment, and maintenance of Web-based applications.

The existence of Internet services and Web services makes many buyer-oriented online services possible, because they provide the basic infrastructure for aspects of online business-to-consumer (B2C) exchanges. The importance of Web services to online business activity is illustrated in Figure 3-15.

Online Information for Off-line Goods and Services

The Internet is often used as a tool for business activities that encourage and facilitate off-line sales of goods and services. Companies use the Internet to provide information about products, to influence customers' awareness of brands, and their attitudes toward brands, and to provide incentives, such as coupons, to purchase a product.

Research indicates that the number of online shoppers who say that their opinions of brands, and their purchase behaviors, have been changed by information they received online has grown each year since 1998. From 14.4 million shoppers in 1998, the number has grown to 40 million. The impact of online information on brand opinions is important, because it is linked to changes in purchase behavior. A Dierenger Research Group survey indicated that opinion change led to purchase change in 60 percent of purchase decisions. The link between opinion change and purchase switch gets stronger as the amount of Internet experience increases.

The Internet also influences off-line purchases. A study conducted by comScore Networks examined the relationship of online advertising to off-line purchasing. Using information about previous purchasing history and data collected from visitors to Nestlé Purina's dog food site in November 2002 (Figure 3-16), the researchers demonstrated the power of Web-based brand exposure. Banner ads on the site increased brand awareness for Purina, as well as purchase likelihood.

FIGURE 3-16 Banner Ads on an Informational Site Boost Brand Awareness and Purchase Intent.

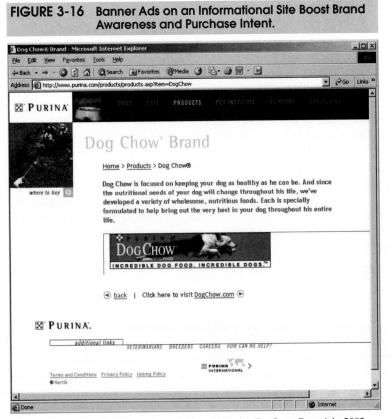

Online marketing can also boost consumption of off-line services. Travel services, such as Travelocity and Expedia, offer travelers the opportunity to find the best prices on travel and lodging. Because travel is a perishable item from the seller's point-of-view, online travel reservations services provide an opportunity to sell off airline seats, cruise ship staterooms, and hotel rooms at discounted prices, as the deadline for consumption nears.

Status and Love on the Internet

The last two categories of resources that people obtain from the Internet, status and love, are each characterized by internal, psychological descriptions, unlike the first four categories. **Status** is based on the evaluation of others about the relative esteem, prestige, or regard of an individual. Status refers to the rank or evaluation of one person, relative to a comparison group of peers. **Love** is characterized by relationships that have as a primary goal the shared satisfaction of emotional needs. These relationships include marriages and friendships, and community and social organizations. In contrast to status, which is self-focused, love is based on caring for someone else.

InSite

WWW.RATEME.BIZ: DESPERATELY SEEKING STATUS

Did you ever wonder how others see you? If the thought of being rated on your appearance by people you don't even know—and probably never will—appeals to you, then rateme.biz may be for you. The site was developed in conjunction with an online dating service, thus combining aspects of status and love.

The rating process is simple. Register to become a member, upload a photo (presumably of you), and then submit your photo and profile to the rating game.

Although the process is simple, the outcomes are not for the faint-of-heart! Members who are brave enough to be rated are scored on a scale from 1 ("Urgghhh)) to 10 ("Yummy"). A photo can be rated by anyone who visits the site, and an average rating appears only after a rating is made. In other words, you have to rate a profile in order to see how your opinion compared with everyone else's.

The Nature of Status and Love Online

Scarcity and **exclusivity** are often the motivating factors behind status. In economic terms, scarcity refers to the idea that the supply of a resource would not be sufficient to meet the demand for the resource if the resource were available free of charge. In human terms, scarcity means that we tend to accord status to people who demonstrate an ability to obtain larger amounts of limited, desirable resources than we do. Exclusivity reflects limits placed on membership in a group; keeping people out to enhance the status of members.

More About Status . . .   The Internet influences how people maintain or increase status by enabling them to obtain scarce resources, and by providing ways to indicate exclusivity. In terms of scarcity, the environment may make it easier for people to acquire resources that serve as a basis for obtaining status. For example, the Internet has created an opportunity for new goods and services, creating in the process, a new class of Internet millionaires.

The Internet makes it possible for people to get information online that enhances their status off-line. In addition, the Internet enables people to present information about themselves online that supports, creates, or reflects a status-worthy image. Web sites can be developed to present personal information that promotes and maintains a desired image, consistent with exclusivity. People can invent new selves, managing the impressions of themselves that they create for others, in order to acquire status.

The highly technical environment of the Internet can provide a way to get status by demonstrating high levels of skills in using the environment, as we saw in the case of hackers in Chapter 2. The Internet also provides an opportunity for gaining status by contributing to the online environment, as through sharing software programs, tips, and other forms of useful information.[5]

FIGURE 3-17   Different Combinations of Dimensions Offer Marketing Opportunities.

THE ANATOMY OF LOVE

Dimensions →	*Characteristic Relationships* →	*Internet Applications*
INTIMACY The feeling of love for someone else, rather than the feeling of being "in love." Generally reflects deep liking and trust.	**FRIENDSHIP** High intimacy combined with low passion and commitment indicates a friendship of limited duration. High intimacy and high commitment indicate a more lasting friendship.	**SUPPORT GROUPS** High perceived intimacy, low commitment and passion. **eMAIL, GREETING CARD SITES** Foster intimacy and commitment with online communication.
PASSION The feeling of being "in love," an arousal state. Generally reflects high levels of uncertainty and anxiety about whether the love is reciprocated.	**ROMANTIC LOVE** High intimacy and passion, but low staying power. **INFATUATION** Passion by itself.	**ONLINE ASTROLOGY** Foretelling the future may allay uncertainty in early, passion-only relationships.
COMMITMENT The desire to nurture a relationship, often by doing things that please the other person. Generally reflects doing what is necessary to maintain the relationship, putting the other person's needs first.	**"PUPPY LOVE"** Passion and commitment, but without intimacy. **CONSUMMATE LOVE** All three dimensions present.	**BUY-A-SPOUSE SITES** Foreign nationals seek commitment-only marriages to emigrate to the U.S. **ONLINE DATING** Looking for consummate love.

More About Love . . .   Resource Theory states the exchanges can occur between any pair of resource categories. At AmericanSingles.com, theory meets marketing in a list of benefits for members that includes the following selling point:

> *"Putting a price on love—it's a great deal:*
> *Contact 1,000 potential soul mates for less than the price of a couple*
> *of theater tickets!"*

The Internet is a rich source of marketing opportunities that include love as a resource for exchange and consumption. These opportunities become more evident when we consider the different forms in which love can exist. Figure 3-17 summarizes the key dimensions of love, as well as several Internet applications.

The Internet can serve as a way for people to initiate relationships of different sorts, and as a way to develop different types of relationships. Business opportunities arise from the ability to provide goods and services related to finding or nurturing relationships, from gathering information from site visitors, and from providing advertising to visitors in exchange for love-related content.

CHAPTER SUMMARY

In this chapter, we have focused on the interaction between shoppers/buyers and the Internet environment. Following an overview of online buyer demographics, and of trends in the relative importance of online buyer segments, we looked at the things that people consume online.

Consumption was organized by the six categories of resource theory described in Chapter 2: money, information, goods, services, status, and love. We examined the role of the Internet as a medium for enabling people to acquire each type of resource online, and as a means for influencing shopping behaviors offline.

With the Internet, companies can enable online consumption, and they can facilitate offline consumption. In both situations, customers' ability to get resources from the Internet that help them reach their consumption goals offers novel opportunities for business action. Consistent with the prediction of resource theory that less personal and more concrete resources tend to be exchanged, we saw that early commercial uses of the Internet focused on exchanges of money and information, while later exchange opportunities included goods and services. Widespread acceptance of the Internet, and its adoption as a feature of everyday life, has also created business opportunities that enable resource exchanges that promote status or provide love.

CONTENT MANAGEMENT
USEFUL TERMS

- accessibility
- accountability
- addressability
- behavioral measure
- credence goods
- cybercash/digital cash
- demographics
- descriptive research
- directed information search
- e-bills
- exclusivity
- experience goods

- fungibility
- heterogeneity
- identifiability
- incidental exposure
- information overload
- information processing theory
- inseparability
- intelligent agents
- Internet services
- lifetime value (LTV)
- love
- market segments

- mental accounting
- netsurfing
- online communities
- online services
- perishability
- psychographics
- scarcity
- search engines
- search goods
- status
- sufficiency
- Web services

REVIEW QUESTIONS

1. How does the Internet influence the types of exchanges that are carried out?
2. What factors can explain the appeal of the Internet as a virtual marketplace for shopping?
3. Discuss the differences between demographics and psychographics.
4. What is the profile of the average Internet user? How has this profile changed since 1998?
5. How does the Internet separate the form of money from its meaning? Why might this separation affect online spending?
6. What is one advantage of using the Internet to search for information? What is one disadvantage?
7. What is information overload, and how is it relevant for information search on the Internet?
8. What different categories of goods are available to Internet shoppers?
9. What three dimensions can be used to differentiate services from goods?

10. How does the Internet change the ways in which we describe goods and services?
11. How does the Internet affect off-line sales of services?
12. How does the Internet environment enable people to acquire status? Love?
13. What marketing opportunities arise from the ability to provide love and status online?

WEB APPLICATION

Who Are You? Understanding Customers with SRI

The VALS Survey is a tool that enables online assessment of shopper types. VALS stands for Values And LifeStyles. The original VALS survey was developed in the 1970s, as a way to understand consumer behavior with personality traits, attitudes, opinions, and values.

A redesigned version of the survey provides results that classify a person into one of eight different segments. The segments are organized with two dimensions: (1) primary motivation, and (2) resources. The primary motivation reflects the person's goal for consuming, while the resources dimension captures the person's perceived ability to attain the goal.

1. Try it yourself. Go to http://www.sric-bi.com/VALS/presurvey.shtml. Answer the questions, noting the difference between the psychographic measures and the demographic measures.
   What type of person are you? Did the results surprise you?
2. One challenge that companies face is to understand what resources people want to consume, and how. The VALS Survey describes different types of people. Look at the descriptions of the segments. Which segments do you feel would be most likely to be open to online shopping? How about providing information online, in exchange for something? Which segments do you believe would be resistant to online consumption? What are the likely demographic descriptors of these segments? How would you attempt to change their attitudes?
3. Make a list of five people you know. Next to each name, write the two VALS categories that best describe that person, that is, the primary motivation and the resources. Next, write two or three types of resources (e.g., information, goods, services) that you think each person would be likely to consume from the Internet.

If your list people are willing, have each of them take the VALS Survey and tell you the resulting VALS classification. In addition, ask them to rate the likelihood that they would consume each of the things that you predicted.

How accurate were your predictions? What did you learn from your mistakes about what makes shoppers tick?

CONCEPTS IN BRIEF

1. Buyer behavior is more than just buying products that satisfy wants.
2. The Internet has heightened buyers' expectations about companies' accountability.
3. The borderless scope of the Internet provides shoppers with many new opportunities to consume different types of resources.
4. Online shoppers come from all walks of life, and their variety is increasing each year.
5. We can describe online shoppers with descriptive research in the form of demographics, psychographics, and behavioral measures.
6. Three rapidly growing online segments are seniors, teens, and Hispanics.
7. People consume all types of resources online, creating opportunities for exchanges that extend beyond trading money for goods and services.
8. Personal information that can be used by companies can be a form of currency that online shoppers can use to obtain other resources.

9. Businesses can use the Internet to influence how customers make decisions, by facilitating information search, comparison, and evaluation processes.
10. The Internet creates marketing opportunities for resources that emphasize psychological dimensions, like status and love.

THINKING POINTS

1. Profiles of Internet users are often based on data aggregated from a number of sources. What issues does this aggregation raise for marketers who attempt to use these data for segmentation and forecasting purposes?
2. Demographic variables can provide a broad description of customers in a marketplace. Why is it often desirable to augment demographic insights with analysis of psychological factors?
3. Why is it necessary to describe Internet users? That is, why are they likely to differ from people who do not use the Internet for getting goods and services? What are some of the implications of these differences for online business activity?
4. The Internet can facilitate or inhibit people's resource exchanges by affecting the types of resources, types of exchange processes, and types of relationships that are available. What are some types of exchanges that exist in a digital business environment that do not exist in traditional commercial environments? What aspects of the resource exchange differ most markedly? How?
5. The Internet provides people with new consumption opportunities, as well as new ways to conduct exchanges and transactions (e.g., digital cash). How might the novelty of the Internet environment influence the ways that people evaluate goods and services? What are some of the advantages and disadvantages of this novel environment for online shopping?
6. What do the differences between goods and services suggest about the relative ease with which people might adopt the Internet as a source of goods, versus services? That is, services are often perceived as more highly variable in quality than goods. How might the provision of services via the Internet affect this type of perception?
7. Foa's Resource Theory suggests that resources that are more similar to each other are more likely to be viewed as reasonable candidates for exchange. What are some types of resource exchanges that can be facilitated with the Internet, using the Internet to minimize perceived distances between resources?

ENDNOTES

1. Data about site traffic was obtained from www.matchmaker.com.
2. http://www.byu.edu/news/releases/archive01/Jul/internet.htm
3. Reference material was obtained from the U.S. Census and from the American Association of Retired Persons Web site, at http://research.aarp.org.
4. Think about getting a haircut. Inseparability is present because the service cannot exist without the stylist, and it does not exist for you until your hair is actually cut.

   Have you ever had a haircut you didn't like? The interaction between the skills of the stylist and the unique characteristics of your hair results in service heterogeneity. In addition, whether or not anybody walks into the salon on a day that it is open, the owner incurs the costs of having the stylist available. If more people come in than can be clipped, and the salon owner turns them away, then revenue potential is lost. Hence, perishability is reflected in the underconsumption or in the overcapacity demand for the stylist's efforts.
5. Based on research reported in "Conspicuous Contributions: Signs of Social Esteem on the Internet," a doctoral thesis by David Neice at the Science and Technology Policy Research, University of Sussex, Brighton, UK (2000).

SUGGESTED READINGS

"Some Consequences of Electronic Groups," by Lee Sproull and Samer Faraj, and "Netiquette 101," by Jay Machado. In *Internet Dreams*, edited by Mark Stefik (The MIT Press: Cambridge, MA, 1997).

"Consumer Behavior in the Future," by Jagdish N. Sheth and Rajendra S. Sisodia. In *Electronic Marketing and the Consumer*, edited by Robert A. Peterson (Sage Publications, Inc.: Thousand Oaks, CA, 1997).

"Evaluating the Potential of Interactive Media Through a New Lens: Search versus Experience Goods," by Lisa R. Klein. *Journal of Business Research,* 41 (1998), pages 195–203.

"Kiddie Kash," by Rebecca Vesely. *Business 2.0,* (May 1999), pages 24–26.

"Social Impact of the Internet: What Does It Mean?" by Robert Kraut, Sara Kiesler, Tridas Mukhopadhyay, William Scherlis, and Michael Patterson. *Communications of the ACM,* 41, 12 (1998), pages 21–22.

LEARNING LINKS

Examples of Resources for Exchange

Money

www.home.iWon.com
www.primarewards.com
www.coolsavings.com

Information

www.dealtime.com
www.bizrate.com

Goods

www.uniquesports.com
www.cruisingoods.com
www.earthlygoods.com

Services

www.wunderground.com
www.irs.gov
www.hrblock.com

Status

www.aeroplan.com/en/offers/news_prestige.jsp
www.carvalu.com/symbol.asp
www.bizrate.com

Love

www.personals.yahoo.com
www.amomslove.com
www.technologyreview.com/articles/wo_jenkins100402.asp?p=3

Self-Assessment (e.g., Personality, IQ, Entrepreneur)

www.2h.com
www.od-online.com
www.sri.com

Online Dating

www.singlec.com (Christian site)
www.catholicsingles.com
jewishmatch.com
astralhearts.com
www.fitnessdate.com
www.veggiedate.com
www.animalpeople.com

CHAPTER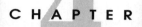

How Does the Internet Affect Businesses?

Focus and Objectives

This chapter is focused on the relationship between businesses and the Internet environment. Characteristics of business activity online are described, and the influence of the Internet on the nature of business activity is considered in terms of its effect on company structures and processes. The Internet is described as an environment that creates challenges and opportunities for companies. Business responses to challenges are addressed by considering ways in which companies can identify opportunities to meet strategic objectives, given customers' goals for resource exchange.

Your objectives in studying this chapter include the following:

- Develop familiarity with characteristics of companies involved in e-commerce.
- Understand the implications for businesses of differing levels of Internet integration into business activity.
- Recognize potential effects of the Internet on the ways that companies organize themselves for business, and on the processes for business action.
- Identify major sources of challenges and opportunities for businesses in the Internet environment.

It *Is* All Fun and Games

Computing technology has changed not only the way we work, but also the way we play. From board games like Risk and Monopoly, we moved to video games, like Pong, Pac-Man, and Space Invaders. The development of home gaming consoles by Atari, Nintendo, and Sega brought the entertainment into our living rooms, and introduced the whole family—young and old—to Mario and Zelda. By the end of the 20th century, computer-enabled gaming had gone mobile with the popularity of the Game Boy, and similar handheld devices.

CHAPTER 4   *How Does the Internet Affect Businesses?*   **87**

Like peas and carrots and peanut butter and jelly, computer-based gaming and the Internet seemed made for each other. By the end of 2001, gaming companies had developed the technologies to connect gaming consoles to the Internet with high-speed, dial-up modems. This made it possible for gamers to download games from Web sites and interact with games via the Internet, instead of using programs stored on cartridges and CD-ROMs. Still, something was missing.

Video games place players in virtual environments, where they interact with game characters and attempt to survive a host of challenges. In each case, the characters—with the exception of the gamer—are merely the creative products of some very clever software programmers. They aren't real. With the Internet, the prospect of creating different environments and situations in which gamers could play against each other became more than just a dream. The Internet enables players to communicate with each other, sending information between many players as they maneuver in the shared, virtual environment.

At present, the most popular online game in the United States is Sony's EverQuest. More than 430,000 players from around the world cough up $13 each month to play the game. Sony also charges for the software required to be able to play. Gamers like the person-to-person, real-time interactivity of EverQuest, as well as the ongoing, ever-changing nature of the game.

Massively multiplayer online gaming (MMOG) is predicted to become the next big thing in the gaming industry. Video games reaped $9.4 billion in 2001 (beating Hollywood's total box office take by more than a billion dollars). With the major gaming consoles—Xbox, Playstation, and Gamecube—ready for online play, analysts forecast revenues of over $2.5 billion by 2006 just for online gaming in the United States. Companies are hard at work developing ways for gamers to participate in online games with PDAs and cell phones. Mobile gaming is also anticipated to be a lucrative market, with estimates of revenues worldwide as high as $2.8 billion by 2006.

The history of computer-based gaming illustrates many of the challenges faced by marketers who attempt to integrate the Internet into their marketing activities. In the early years of video games, several attempts to sell games and consoles failed; consumers simply couldn't understand how to use the product. Similarly, some early online companies went bankrupt because their targeted customers were not far enough along the Internet learning curve to understand the benefits offered by the company and product. Remember Webvan, from Chapter 1? Shoppers just weren't comfortable with the idea of buying groceries online.

As the video gaming industry evolved, the companies making and selling the games had to adapt to stay competitive. For example, Sega, the company that produced the DreamCast gaming console, shifted its focus from hardware to software. Sony added an online product, EverQuest, to its traditional inventory of consumer electronics. Similarly, the Internet has made it necessary for many different types of companies to reinvent themselves in order to stay in business. Some companies have shed their off-line presence to move online, while others have incorporated capabilities of the Internet into their standard marketing practices.

For marketers, the Internet is a new and rapidly changing environment for selling goods and services. It is nearly impossible to ignore the growing popularity of the Internet for business applications. Business periodicals and newsletters devote much column space to the benefits of using the Internet to conduct business; Internet services are touted in television, radio, and print media; Web sites are increasingly replacing more traditional promotion activities; and new companies with the .com suffix appear daily. These are only a fraction, however, of the total population of companies who operate within the Internet environment. Many companies make use of the Internet for aspects of marketing other than to sell goods or services online.

Bits & Bytes 4.1

The first video game was created in 1958, at the Brookhaven National Lab, a U.S. government research facility. The game—video tennis.

(*Source*: Office of Scientific and Technological Information, U.S. Department of Energy)

In this chapter, we will examine the impact of the Internet on buying and selling from the business perspective. What does the availability of the Internet mean for developing business strategy, and the actions needed to implement the strategy? How do the relationships that exist, either directly or indirectly, between sellers and buyers, technology developers, and policy makers, affect the formulation of effective strategy? The ability to answer these questions will provide you with the insights needed to develop appropriate goals for organizations who wish to incorporate the Internet into business strategy, and to understand the characteristics of business activity that use the Internet to achieve goals.

We begin with a general characterization of businesses in the central exchange environment of the Internet. Then we consider the effect of the Internet on the ways that companies carry out their business activities.

Businesses in the Digital World

Several descriptors can be used to characterize the types of companies that conduct business activity in the Internet environment. We will look at three of these descriptors to get a bird's eye view of the marketing environment: (1) .com versus traditional companies, (2) types of products sold online, and (3) types of customers online.

A Company Focus

As a simple descriptor, we can divide the business world into .com companies and non-.com companies. We can complicate this description by recognizing that many .coms are **pure-player** companies; that is, all of their transaction activities are conducted via the Internet. Ebay and Amazon are examples of pure players—companies with no physical world, brick-and-mortar retail presence. Between the two extremes of all-online pure-players and all-off-line bricks-and-mortars are many .coms with an off-line presence, such as Gap.com and Walmart.com.

We can describe the extent to which a company relies on the Internet to carry out buying and selling activities with two concepts. The first concept is a **continuum of electronic commerce** that captures the range of levels of involvement of a company in electronic commerce (e-commerce) activities. The second concept, **netcentricity,** is a measure that quantifies a company's involvement in e-commerce as a function of online activities.

An Involvement Continuum for E-Commerce

The e-commerce continuum provides a way to describe companies in terms of their adoption of e-commerce. The continuum consists of four stages, in which each successive stage reflects the increasing pervasion and influence of e-commerce on the company's activities. The continuum is presented in Figure 4-1.

In Phase I, involvement with e-commerce is limited to familiarity with the Internet, and use of the Internet, by the company's employees. Phase I is characterized by little or no formal expectations on the part of the company of how tasks will be conducted using the Internet. Instead, the Internet is used on the employees' initiative, to facilitate coordination and communication through e-mail. Typically, a company has passed through Phase I when most of the senior employees regularly use the Internet.

Phase II reflects a shift from internal, company use of the Internet to an external, consumer-oriented focus. In this phase, the company uses the Internet as a way to communicate features and benefits of its products or services. A company has passed through Phase II when its Internet presence is more than a **brochureware** presentation of the company, in which company literature is simply reproduced on the company's Web site.

Moving from maintaining an online presence to actually completing transactions online reflects a Phase III level of business involvement on the Internet. In Phase III, typical accomplishments include the ability to use the Internet's interactive capabilities to complete sales and to provide online service. A company that has passed through the third stage has integrated the consumer orientation of Phase II with internal processes used to effect transactions, building on the employee acceptance of e-commerce in Phase I.

In the final phase, the integration of e-commerce in the business is complete. At the end of Phase IV, the company's core processes are linked with e-commerce applications (Figure 4-2). For example, a company might carry out its business activ-

FIGURE 4-1 **A Four-phase Description of Involvement in E-Commerce.**

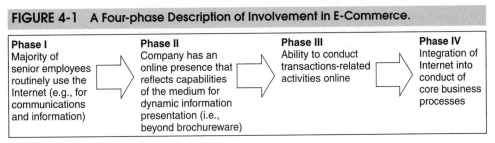

Phase I	Phase II	Phase III	Phase IV
Majority of senior employees routinely use the Internet (e.g., for communications and information)	Company has an online presence that reflects capabilities of the medium for dynamic information presentation (i.e., beyond brochureware)	Ability to conduct transactions-related activities online	Integration of Internet into conduct of core business processes

Source: Adapted from Zona Research, 1997.

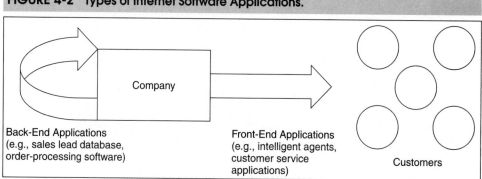

FIGURE 4-2   Types of Internet Software Applications.

Source: Adapted from Zona Research, 1997.

ities in a traditional manner, with the exception of developing a Web site from which customers can obtain product information and order products. The software and technological capabilities that make these activities possible are referred to as **front-end applications.** In addition, the company might decide that there are benefits to using the Internet to complete other business activities, such as maintaining databases of customer queries for sales leads, and coordinating budget development and activity. These types of e-commerce applications—invisible to the ordinary customer— are called **back-end applications.**

In general, smaller companies tend to move more rapidly through the continuum. This effect occurs because smaller companies are often more flexible in structure, and they can adapt to change more readily than larger companies.

Of course, being in a later stage is not necessarily more desirable than being in an earlier stage. For some types of companies, a Phase II presence may be the best level of e-commerce involvement (e.g., an ice cream shop). For other companies, competitive competency may only be achieved through complete integration of e-commerce into all aspects of business function (e.g., a digital music provider).

Netcentricity: Quantifying E-Commerce Involvement

Another way to characterize the impact of the Internet on the ways that companies do business is by looking at the company revenues. Netcentricity is the percentage of revenues due to online activity as a portion of the total revenues earned by a company. It is used as a way to quantify the extent to which a company has adopted e-commerce— especially Phase III in the continuum—as a way of doing business. In the aggregate, we can look at netcentricity to determine which types of companies and industries tend to move most quickly toward online activity, and to compare the extent of such activity. The graph in Figure 4-3 is based on reports of netcentric activity by 375 companies across several industries.

A Product Sales Focus

While describing companies as .coms or not-coms provides some descriptive information about the impact of the Internet on the formation of new companies, it is an incomplete description. Many companies have **multichannel strategies** that combine Internet capabilities with traditional marketing methods to achieve marketing goals. These

FIGURE 4-3 Netcentricity Differs Widely, Depending on Business Type.

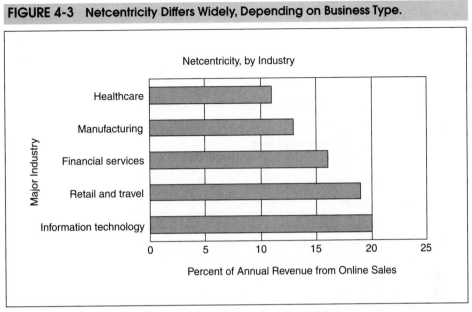

Source: InformationWeek Research E-Business Agenda Study, June 2002.

companies may get revenue from Internet-based transactions, in addition to sales in off-line stores. We can segment companies by the types of products or services they emphasize to see what sells on the Internet. The chart in Figure 4-4 shows the main categories of goods and services that provide revenue through Internet-based transactions.

FIGURE 4-4 A Product Focus Illustrates Differences in Online Retail Demand.

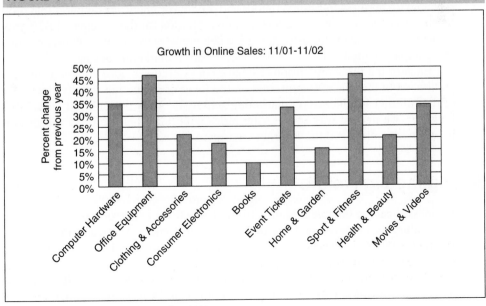

Source: comScore Networks, November 2002.

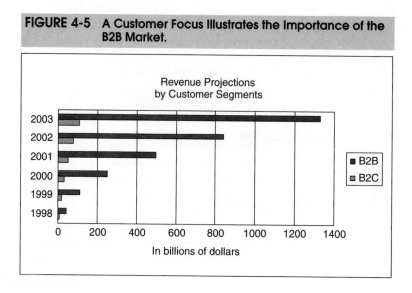

FIGURE 4-5   A Customer Focus Illustrates the Importance of the B2B Market.

A Customer Focus

The product focus emphasizes online sales of goods and services to individual consumers. For example, a company might emphasize a **business-to-consumer (B2C)** approach, such as selling a product or service to a single person who will be the end user of the item (e.g., compact discs from Buy.com). Of course, this approach leaves out a very important segment for marketing—the business consumer. A company may have a **business-to-business (B2B)** focus that targets sales of products or services to organizations that will use them for conducting aspects of their business operations.

Business-to-business transactions are big business. As Figure 4-5 shows, the revenue potential for business-to-business goods and services dramatically outpaces that projected for the business-to-consumer segment. A major reason for the anticipated B2B growth is the need to develop the infrastructure for e-commerce activities. We will take a closer look at the impact of the Internet on business-to-business marketing in Chapter 13.

Each of the three dimensions we have considered provides complementary information about the role of the Internet on the focus of marketing activity. Because much of the Internet's influence on marketing activity may not be centered on online sales, however, we need a way to describe more generally the nature of the interaction between marketers and the Internet environment.

Seeing the Big Picture

Businesses can be complex. Many different functions and processes make it possible for products to be developed and delivered to customers. As we saw in Chapter 1, the Internet influences aspects of each function of e-commerce. Figure 4-6 illustrates the primary flow of business activity.

The Internet creates challenges and opportunities for businesses. Reacting to challenges and taking advantage of opportunities often requires companies to make

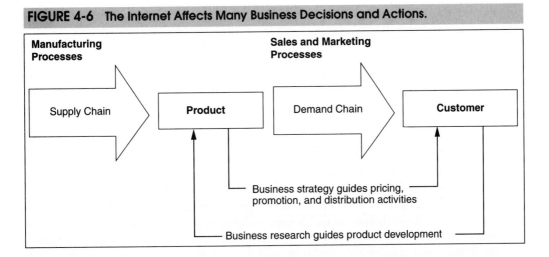

FIGURE 4-6   The Internet Affects Many Business Decisions and Actions.

changes to the ways that they operate. In traditional approaches to business, the need to alter business activity often results from an inability to control one or more of five factors. These factors, often called the five C's, consist of **Company**, **Channels**, **Customers**, **Competition**, and **Conditions**. These factors are ordered by the decreasing influence of the company; that is, a manager is likely to have the most direct influence on his company, but far less control over general conditions, such as the rate of technological development. As Figure 4-7 illustrates, businesses have the most direct

FIGURE 4-7   The Internet Necessitates Adaptive Business Activity.

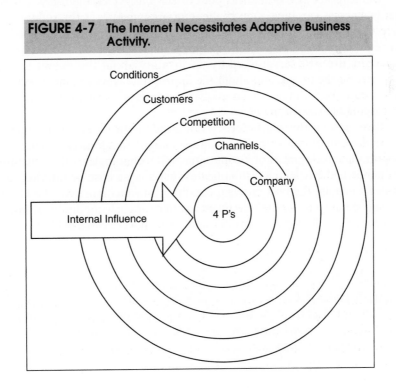

control over the components of commercial activity that provide customers with a purchase opportunity: product, price, place, and promotion.

In the Internet environment, adapting to change is a bit more complex. Not only must businesses deal with the same five factors that have always made business strategy an inexact science, now they must manage an additional influence—that of the Internet itself. The Internet changes the ways that the five factors affect marketing activity. The marketer must be able to recognize the implications of these changes, and to adapt marketing strategy accordingly.

The Internet Affects Market Conditions

General market conditions, such as economics, politics, and climatic conditions, influence business activity. In the Internet environment, business activity is most directly affected by the climate of the central exchange environment. Recall that in Chapter 2, we examined the influence of technology and public policy on the exchange environment that exists between buyers and sellers. We can think of these groups as influences on political and economical conditions that, in turn, affect the activities of businesses. (To this point, weather and climatic conditions seem unperturbed by the popularity of the Internet.)

The Internet was not developed with an eye toward facilitating commercial transactions, or for carrying out any of the activities typically associated with business exchange. As a result, companies need to know how to use the technologies of the Internet, adapting business practices to make effective use of the structure and function of the digital environment.

The Internet also influences policy decisions, which themselves affect the actions that businesses can take. One challenge for companies is the relatively undeveloped state of policy specifically directed toward use of the Internet in general, and as a venue for commerce. Issues for Internet policy, such as taxation, fraud, fair access, and copyright, are still surrounded by uncertainty about the extent to which they are concerns for the public, and about the appropriate ways to manage the situations that they create. For commerce, an evolving regulatory structure creates challenges for developing business strategy.

Research on the characteristics of good environments for e-commerce underscores the importance of policy and technology.[1] In addition to political agendas that support the development of e-commerce, and technological infrastructures that enable e-commerce, the research also indicates that a large base of Internet-savvy citizens is needed to create the best growing conditions for e-commerce. The United States was the only country to be ranked in the top tier for each condition, although the United Kingdom, Canada, Japan, Australia, and Sweden were close behind.

Bits & Bytes 4.2

Online retailers trimmed the average cost to acquire a customer from $29 in 2000 to $14 in 2001. Marketing costs per order also dropped, from $20 to $12.

(*Source*: Shop.org and The Boston Consulting Group, June 2002)

The Internet Affects Customer-related Issues

Next to conditions, companies have the least direct control over their customers. Wanting them to buy a product does not insure that they will. The Internet can be used to influence buyer behavior, and it can also complicate such attempts. For instance, the Internet is a way to provide desirable information about a company's goods and services. Of course, the competition has the same opportunity. As a result, shoppers are able to compare information across manufacturers and merchants with lower search costs than are encountered in many off-line, traditional marketplaces. As we saw in Chapter 3, the information that consumers obtain may influence the attitudes they hold about brands, products, and companies. In addition, it may affect the behaviors they carry out, such as word-of-mouth, and purchasing. In general, more knowledgeable consumers tend to be more demanding consumers, in terms of product quality and service.

These results are important even for businesses with little or no e-commerce involvement. Suppose that you are an automobile dealer with absolutely no interest in the Internet. You are determined to sell cars the way you have always sold them: big holiday sales, year-end inventory clearance, and tooth-and-nail negotiations between customer and manager. Unless you have a pool of customers equally determined to buy cars in the same way that you have always sold them, you may have a problem. Anybody can post information on the Internet, given the skills and equipment. This means that information about your product can be made available to consumers in ways over which you have no control. As a result, you must react to the effect of this information on your customers.

Consumers often research products online and then buy them off-line. In contrast to off-line shopping, online shopping requires consumer willingness to accept technology. Concerns with transaction security and delayed delivery lead many people to use the Internet for comparison shopping, but not for buying.

Knowing what customers want (e.g., simple, secure transactions) and being able to provide it increases the likelihood that online shoppers will become online buyers. For many businesses with an online storefront, loyalty and repeat purchases are necessary to offset the costs of doing business on the Internet. **Customer acquisition costs** reflect the amount of money needed to create awareness, interest, and purchase of a good or service. This cost tends to be higher for first-time purchases of a product, because repeat purchases eliminate the need to create awareness and interest. As a result, businesses work to create satisfaction and loyalty.

To foster consumer loyalty, businesses can use the Internet to provide information and services related to a product. With the Internet, customer support does not necessarily require interpersonal, interactive communications. Companies can provide information about a host of typical issues in the form of **FAQs,** or frequently asked questions (Figure 4-8).

The Internet Affects Competitive Activity

The Internet has changed the nature of competition by affecting aspects of business activity that are based on information flows: (1) product development; (2) benefits of cooperation, versus competition; and (3) strategies for product consumption.

FIGURE 4-8   FAQs Enhance Loyalty with 24/7 Customer Assistance

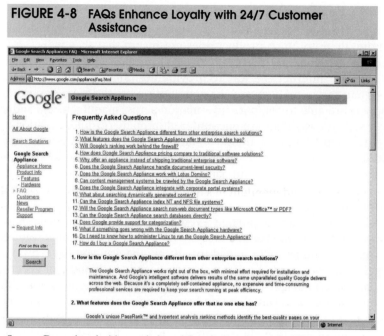

The Pace of Product Development

The effect of the Internet on the pace of business activity—and on many aspects of day-to-day productivity—has introduced the idea of Internet time into our vocabulary. **Internet time** reflects the increased speed with which many types of tasks can be completed using the Internet. It also reflects the changes to expectations of what people can be expected to accomplish, given the capabilities of the interactive medium. People are expected to do more, and to do it better and faster, with the information and communications capabilities of the Internet.

This increase in performance expectations is illustrated by increasingly shorter intervals between product introductions in Internet-related industries. In the computer industry, for example, prior to the widespread adoption of the Internet by businesses, new models were introduced at an average rate of one model every 18 months. Expectations on the part of management and consumers have changed; to remain competitive, a company must now unveil a new model every 4 months. This increased pace is due in large part to **information acceleration:** an increase in the rate at which information can be compiled and transmitted via the Internet.

Internet time creates challenges for businesses in maintaining product quality and product differentiation. Shortened horizons for planning and producing new products mean that less time is available for product testing. Combined with the speed with which product information can be communicated and new product benefits can be observed, the shorter intervals between product introductions may result in decreased differentiation between products in a product category. As a result, the speed of product introductions needed to remain competitive can increase the importance of developing and maintaining a differential advantage, as well as the difficulty of accomplishing the differentiation.

The Power of Cooperation

The Internet environment also affects the benefits of cooperation for supply and demand chain activities. With the Internet, companies can find new sources of components for product manufacturing, and they can create and manage distribution-related relationships, including transportation, warehousing, and promotion. Prior to the widespread adoption of the Internet, a greater number of companies tended to work independently to develop their processes, product, and markets.

As technology and communications capabilities have progressed, the value of being completely independent has decreased. Internet capabilities enable businesses to develop **strategic alliances** between companies that might previously have competed for the same pool of customers. For example, the merger of America OnLine and Time Warner was a strategic alliance that eliminated the need for direct competition between the two companies in the online content market. Another example of a strategic network of allied companies is Orbitz.com, the travel reservations site. Several major airlines cooperate to provide consumers with access to the flight information of all the participating airlines through one site. This type of **strategic network** provides Orbitz partners with a competitive advantage over airlines that are not in the network, because Orbitz partners get customer exposure through the site, and they are assured that their fares will be displayed in all searches by travel customers.

The Potential for Novel Product Strategies

A third influence of the Internet environment on competition stems from the opportunities that arise in making products available for consumption. That is, with the Internet, a competitor can make the same product offering, but provide it in a way that differs from the traditional means of product consumption. A competitive challenge exists if the new form of consumption is preferred by a significant proportion of current customers. For example, online trading, such as that popularized by E*TRADE and Ameritrade, provides consumers with the same service as that provided by Merrill Lynch: consumers can trade stocks. The difference is in the form of the service; the online firms enable consumers to complete their trades via the Internet. Once again, the competitive challenge enabled by the Internet underscores the importance of developing a defensible differential advantage, based on a clearly defined market segment.

The Internet Affects Channel Behavior

For many companies, the Internet provides a new way to move goods to customers. In some cases, as with digital goods, the Internet itself can be used as a distribution channel. In other cases, the Internet can be used to coordinate aspects of distribution, including inventory control and shipping scheduling.

The Internet can change traditional structures for distribution. For some types of companies and products, the Internet enables businesses to eliminate middlemen, a process known as **disintermediation.** For instance, customers have rapidly adopted the

Internet for booking travel reservations, thus eliminating the need for many travel agencies. For other products, however, additional steps may need to be included to enable products and services to be sold through the Internet. Adding middlemen to the distribution process, termed **reintermediation,** is often observed in the Internet environment when new participants are used to manage the transmission of distribution-related information.

Companies must determine the appropriate channel structures. In addition, they must also be able to meet the challenges created by the change from old channel relationships to new ones. New channel members must be identified and relationships forged in a way that does not hinder the flow of products from company to consumer.

Many businesses have adopted a multichannel approach to reaching customers. While some companies integrate an Internet channel for sales into their traditional channels, such as retail stores and catalogs, other companies use the Internet for a subset of marketing activities designed to create customer awareness and build a brand. For instance, Maytag, the manufacturer of many household appliances, does not sell its products on the Internet (Figure 4-9). It does, however, use its Web site to provide product information and to help potential customers locate retailers from whom they can buy appliances online or off-line.

For some companies, issues of channel management reflect concerns about maintaining good relationships with existing channel members. We will take a closer look at how the Internet affects the balance of power in channels in Chapter 11.

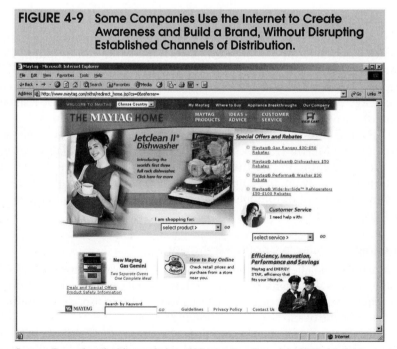

FIGURE 4-9 Some Companies Use the Internet to Create Awareness and Build a Brand, Without Disrupting Established Channels of Distribution.

Source: Reproduced with permission of Maytag, Inc. Copyright 2003. All rights reserved.

The Internet Affects Business Structure and Function

With its boundary-less nature and ease-of-use, it's no surprise that the Internet has had a profound effect on how businesses operate. In some cases, companies have shifted from traditional, bricks-and-mortar set-ups to entirely virtual organizations. Egghead.com, for instance, began software sales through mall stores in 1984. Given the digital nature of its main product, however, the move from malls to the Internet in 1998 seemed inevitable. Although the company went bankrupt in 2001, its purchase by Amazon gave it new life as a software pure-play.

Incorporating the Internet into business activities affects two aspects of business life: (1) the structure of a business, and (2) the culture of the business. How much the Internet affects each aspect is related to the extent of e-commerce involvement; putting up a Web site to promote a brand has far fewer implications for employee culture than does creating an entirely virtual company.

Internet Effects on Business Structure

The Internet has changed *where* people work, and *how* people work. The ability to communicate instantaneously and easily over distances has increased the number of employees who work away from the business's physical site, a practice known as **telecommuting.** As Internet adoption has increased, so has the number of telecommuting employees. The results of a 2001 study commissioned by AT&T reported that 28 millions Americans work away from the office—a 17 percent increase over 2000. This number was projected to grow as high as 137 million by the end of 2003, according to estimates by GartnerGroup, a research firm.

Bits & Bytes 4.3
Seventy-two percent of teleworkers say they get more done at home than in the office. In addition, teleworking reduces absenteeism costs by 63 percent.
(*Source:* AT&T 2000 survey)

The Internet also increases the ability of company employees to coordinate activity across the different functions (e.g., marketing, sales, engineering, and accounting). Being able to communicate directly and efficiently with people in other functions eliminates the need for many traditional hierarchies intended to oversee and control the flow of information from one person to another. That is, while hierarchies, or chains of command, served an important cost-reducing function previously, the Internet can make such structures potentially less efficient than structures that foster direct communication between employees. This effect is reflected in changes to *how* employees work

Many businesses have shifted to the use of teams, called platforms, for product development and marketing. The **platform approach** consists of cross-functional teams of employees, in which team members are empowered to make significant decisions about many aspects of the product. In addition, the team is given the responsibility for overseeing the processes that must be completed to produce a product that can be marketed successfully. This responsibility results in the hand-in-hand coordination and reliance of all team members.

This coordination often has two related effects. First, it increases the need for effective access to team-based digital applications for completing work activities. For example, Chrysler's ability to develop its new automobile models using shared, networked applications has been an important factor in the company's ability to move from concept to production and distribution more quickly than the competition.

A second influence of the Internet on the environment in which marketers operate is the increasing importance of integrating and managing knowledge in the workplace. **Knowledge management** is the framework and processes with which an organization gathers, stores, analyzes, and disseminates information pertaining to its strategic goals. The ability to integrate, store, and communicate information in shared databases, such as market research about consumer needs, means that information can be entered by one person, but accessed by many. As a result, rather than each organizational function operating independently, the functions can be coordinated and processes can be standardized to create efficient processes for acquiring and sharing information that result in decreased errors (e.g., through flawed data entry). Of course, the flip side to this benefit is that if an error is entered, its impact may be large (and negative), because it is widely distributed.

Making the Business Work

So how do companies manage the change from physical to virtual organization, given the changes in where and how employees work? The Internet and its influence on company life has caused managers to look at who they hire, how they expect their employees to operate, and the types of tools available for getting the job done.

The Internet enables businesses to conduct online interviews to gauge whether a potential employee is well suited for a particular job. For instance, Fitability Systems provides online surveys that assess a candidate's personality characteristics, record, and track the candidate's responses to an online survey with questions designed by the prospective employer, and communicates the results of the candidate's responses to the employer (Figure 4-10). This type of service can streamline the hiring process, and reduce the employer's costs to recruit qualified employees.

Companies can also use the Internet to guide the interaction between team members. For example, companies can use **workflow software,** designed to streamline business processes that rely on document sharing and communications between business functions. At Lawrence Livermore National Laboratory, for instance, the use of an Internet-based workflow system call Zephyr resulted in time savings of up to 90 percent. It also created substantial cost savings and improved product quality. In addition, the lab's ability to pay suppliers more quickly increased the number of vendors willing to work with the lab, thus creating competition and the potential for additional cost savings.

Workflow software is one tool for helping employees get the job done. Another tool is the personal computer. Some companies, including Ford Motor Company and Delta Airlines, have introduced programs that provide employees with the computing equipment, such as PCs and laptops, to work anywhere, anytime. By

FIGURE 4-10   Online Interview Software Helps Companies Make Good Hiring Decisions.

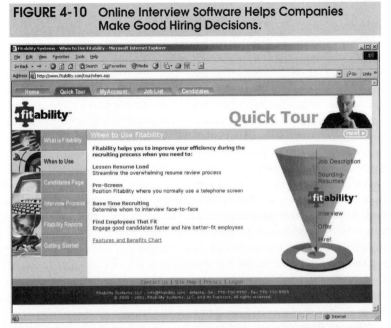

Source: Reproduced with permission of Fitability, Inc. Copyright 2003. All rights reserved.

combining the equipment with Internet access to the corporate site, Delta sought to increase productivity and job satisfaction—both important aspects of company culture.

Internet Effects on Business Culture

Businesses moving toward a virtual organization face the challenge of creating a shared culture among employees. After all, it's hard to get to know your fellow employees when they are working from locations around the world. In addition, creating and fostering company values can be difficult.

Many companies use the Internet to address some of the very challenges it creates. Open communications via e-mail decrease the isolation of telecommuters. In addition, e-mail and instant messaging (IM) often decrease the formality in communications that occur in hierarchically structured workplaces. **Instant messaging** is the ability to communicate in text form between two computers, or other Internet devices (e.g., PDAs, cell phones) in real time, creating the ambience of an online chat. The ability to communicate readily and informally can increase a sense of company community.

Some companies use the Internet to create online, company-oriented communities for employees. These communities are often accessed through **intranets,** private networks within companies, to which access is typically restricted to employees. Intranets can provide a range of company information, from health benefits and payroll deductions to the schedule for the organization's softball team.

'Net Knowledge

NET, WORKING

Intranets are local area networks that use the fundamental structure of the Internet to move information from place to place, but which are internal to the organization. These corporate networks provide managers with a means of disseminating information efficiently through the levels of the organization. Intranets can be used to facilitate data transfer across functions in the organization, streamlining traditional business practices. In addition, the communications capabilities of intranets can be used to foster interaction between employees. The form of these interactions may be hierarchical, with information flows upward or downward. They may also be horizontal, as through interactions between employees at the same level or rank.

Intranets are typically established to maintain the ability to carry out networked communications within an organization. The protected, proprietary nature of corporate intranets is reflected in the efforts made by companies to develop networks that cannot be accessed by outside parties. The techniques for enhancing network security often involve the use of firewalls. **Firewalls** serve as barriers that block unauthorized access to a site on a network.

In some instances, however, businesses may find it advantageous to allow an outside party some level of access to an intranet. **Outside intranetting** occurs when an organization provides access to the corporate intranet to a third party—someone outside the company. Outside intranetting is used when the interaction between members of the organization and the third party work together to accomplish a specific objective. For example, a company might provide a consulting engineer with access to its intranet to facilitate communications between marketing researchers and company engineers about the optimal design of a new product.

When businesses need to allow access to information by a set of users in distant locations, they can set up extranets. **Extranets** are wide area networks that operate much like the Web. They enable businesses to overcome network limitations of size and distance that exist with intranets. Extranets can be designed so that access to the network can be protected, as with a password. They can be used for a range of business applications, such as linking suppliers and customers.

While the Internet creates new marketing opportunities and greater efficiencies in business processes, it also introduces new challenges for employee management. The results of a study by Websense, Inc., an employee management firm,[2] suggest that 25 percent of polled employees feel an addiction to net-surfing. Of 305 employees surveyed in the study, 67 percent said they had surfed the Internet at work for personal reasons. The biggest blow to productivity was dealt by online shoppers (24 percent), while news (23 percent) and pornography (18 percent) took second and third place.

The potential for decreased employee productivity due to Web surfing has led many businesses to institute employee surveillance programs to monitor Internet-related activities. **Employee Internet Management software,** or **EIM,** was a $63 million

---

InSite

WWW.INTERNALMEMOS.COM

An article in Forbes.com, on September 26, 2002, asked the question, "Will e-mail kill Wall Street?" The premise behind the question is that e-mails are a trail of information and conversation that can be damaging to a company's reputation and that may even be used as evidence in legal cases. The ease with which e-mail can be copied and forwarded has led many companies to institute e-mail policies that guide e-mail use.

Policies, however, are not always followed. The Web site, www.internalmemos.com, is a collection of e-mails and corporate memos sent via the Internet that have been made publically available by employees of the represented companies. The e-mail collection is a wide-ranging—and very revealing—look at the operations and

reasoning behind some well-known and lesser-known companies. Companies with e-mail representation on the site include eBay, MTV, AT&T, and Atlantic Records. Some of the posted memos contain information about company policy, others serve to guide employee expectations about future staffing needs, while still others provide an often-surprising and potentially embarrassing view of business communications.

Submitting an internal memo is simple. The site contains an online form that enables the e-mail receiver to submit the message to the internalmemos.com site anonymously. While some correspondence can be viewed for nothing, other e-mails can only be viewed with a paid subscription, available on a monthly basis.

---

business in 1999, and is expected to grow to a $562 million industry by 2004, according to International Data Corp.

The Internet Affects Business Activity

Most of us, as consumers, are aware of many ways in which businesses use the Internet to tell us about their products. E-mail, banner ads and pop-up ads, Web site addresses on packages, and television ads are just a few of the more common approaches. While the Internet has changed buyer behavior, it has also changed seller behavior. From the conception and manufacture of new products, to producing, pricing, and promoting them, the Internet affects each element of the marketing mix, and many aspects of business strategy.

We have seen some ways in which the Internet affects marketing mix decisions—with more to come in subsequent chapters. For instance, product development is influenced by Internet time. In addition, pricing decisions are influenced by the ready availability of price comparisons, and the ease with which pricing information can be distributed over the Internet.

Strategic decisions about "place," or where to sell a product, have led many companies to alter channel strategies, and to undertake fundamental changes in retail operations. Some bricks-and-mortar companies, such as The Gap, have adopted multichannel strategies, while other companies have moved, like Egghead.com, to a pure-player, online presence.

Promotion decisions have also been affected by the rise of the Internet. Businesses develop Web sites, banner ads, and e-mail campaigns to create awareness, provide information, build brand images, and foster brand loyalty.

Recall that businesses have the most direct control over the mix elements. Businesses can incorporate the Internet into an overarching business strategy by managing and leveraging its influence on each element of the mix. Recognizing and adapting to less controllable factors, such as customers, channels, and competition, combined with understanding mix opportunities, is necessary for an effective business strategy.

Bits & Bytes 4.4

A study of Web addiction provided results to indicate that the average employee surfs sites that are not work-related for a total time of more than one full day each workweek.

(*Source:* Harris Interactive, 2002)

CHAPTER SUMMARY

In this chapter, we examined the role of the business in the exchange environment of the Internet. We began by considering several dimensions with which business activity in a digital environment can be described, including a product category focus and a customer focus (i.e., business-to-consumer [B2C] versus business-to-business [B2B]). In addition, we used the concepts of e-commerce involvement and netcentricity to develop additional insights into the relationship between businesses and the online environment.

Businesses must adapt to the Internet environment. The changes that companies make often reflect challenges to the effectiveness of previous marketing strategy. We looked at five different sources of challenges, and at the impact of the Internet on each source. These source, known as the five C's, are **Company**, **Channels**, **Competition**, **Customers**, and **Conditions**.

Business activity is affected not only by what happens outside the company, but also by changes within the company. To further our understanding of the Internet as an influence on business activity, we considered its effect on the ways companies structure themselves to take advantage of Internet capabilities. Moving toward virtual organizations often requires companies to make changes to the processes by which employees do their jobs, and to the ways in which company culture is created.

Companies are used to adapting. Businesses make changes to products, and to the way they are presented, based on shifts in customer preferences and on developments in technology that enable the production of products that satisfy wants and needs. This is the essence of the marketing concept. The Internet, however, not only introduces opportunities for product changes, but for changes to the processes for conducting business activity. These changes are not limited to the facets of business that are visible to customers; the Internet may affect the basic processes by which companies operate to produce and distribute goods and services.

Looking Ahead

In Chapters 3 and 4, we have looked at the characteristics and activities of the two main sets of people in the central exchange environment: buyers and sellers. These groups exert a direct, bidirectional influence on each other. In Chapters 5 and 6, we will continue to examine the relationships that exist in the business environment of the Internet, by looking at the influence of technology and policy on the exchange environment of buyers and sellers.

CONTENT MANAGEMENT

USEFUL TERMS

- back-end applications
- brochureware
- business-to-business
- business-to-consumer
- continuum of electronic commerce
- customer acquisition cost
- disintermediation
- Employee Internet Management (EIM)
- extranets
- FAQs
- firewalls
- front-end applications
- information acceleration
- instant messaging
- Internet time
- intranets
- knowledge management
- multichannel strategy
- netcentricity
- outside intranetting
- platform approach
- pure-player
- reintermediation
- strategic alliances
- strategic network and telecommuting
- workflow software

REVIEW QUESTIONS

1. How is a pure-player company different from a traditional company?
2. Why is the predicted revenue potential greater for the business-to-business approach to online sales than for the business-to-consumer?
3. Distinguish between front-end and back-end applications.
4. Discuss the four phases of the continuum of e-commerce.
5. What is netcentricity?
6. How does the Internet environment affect the way that companies organize themselves for business activity?
7. How are intranets different from extranets?
8. What five factors have been traditionally considered to be outside the realm of businesses' control?
9. Discuss the ways in which the Internet environment changes the approach to adapting to the five C's.
10. Describe the changes to company structure and culture that the digital environment may necessitate or enable.

WEB APPLICATION

Assessing Adaptivity: Tracking Company Change on the Internet

Times are changing, and companies are following suit. One way to see the impact of the Internet on business is by tracking the way that companies present themselves online. From early, simplistic presentations of brochureware to slick, interactive, multimedia communications, many company Web sites have evolved into Web-savvy marketing vehicles.

Businesses examine trends and changes in marketing communications with a method called content analysis. Content analysis involves taking a longitudinal, over time look at communications content to examine changes to company objectives, strategies, and capabilities. With the Internet, we can track changes to Web sites with archives of Web sites.

The Wayback Machine is an Internet archive that contains collections of digital material. In essence, it's a digital library in which we can compare Web pages from different points in time. The site, www.archive.org, contains more than 10 billion pages. To see how the Internet has affected what companies do, and how they do it, complete the following table, indicating whether or not the Web site has the indicated features. Some good sites to examine are buy.com, Amazon.com, and eBay.com. These sites have a longer history than many sites, and thus provide a good overview of change.

	Company					
Year	Privacy Policy?	Online Payment?	Shopping Cart?	Online Contact Capability?	Online Help?	Sales Tax Calculation?
1996						
1997						
1998						
1999						
2000						
2001						
2002						
2003						

1. What did you notice about the company's presentation of its material? Did the site content change in function? In appearance?
2. An asterisk (*) next to a date indicates that on that date the Web site content was updated or altered. For the company you have examined, was there a regular pattern of updates? If not, how would you describe the timing of the updates—frequent or infrequent?
3. Was the pattern of updates related to the extent of change to site content? That is, did content change dramatically in single updates, or bit by bit, over a series of updates?
4. Look at your notations over the years. At what point in time did technological capabilities, like online payments and shopping carts, appear?
5. Similarly, how closely in time did online transaction ability and the privacy policy occur?
6. In terms of changes to core content, has the company become stable, or do updates still result in large changes to what and how information is presented?
7. What does your conclusion to the preceding question suggest about the strategic objectives of the company, vis-à-vis its Internet strategy?
8. Complete the table for two key competitors of the company you did first. Do any changes to Web site content appear at similar points in time? What factors might explain any observed pattern of updates?

CONCEPTS IN BRIEF

1. As a rapidly changing environment for commercial activity, the Internet spurs company change, in structure and organization, and in strategic focus and implementation.
2. The extent to which a company depends on the Internet to carry out its business processes can be described with a four-phase continuum of e-commerce.

3. Although some companies are well-suited for total e-commerce involvement, other types of companies may be better served by more limited investment in Internet-related activities and capabilities.
4. Reliance on the Internet as a source of revenue is described as netcentricity.
5. Companies can be described in three ways: (1) by netcentricity, (2) by types of products sold online, and (3) by the end customer (i.e., B2C versus B2B).
6. Much of the Internet's influence on business cannot be simply measured in terms of online sales.
7. All aspects of business processes that move products through the demand chain to the consumer can be influenced by the Internet.
8. The Internet affects factors that businesses cannot control, but to which they must adapt. These factors are the 5 C's: conditions, customers, competitive activity, distribution channels, and company structure and function.
9. All aspects of the marketing mix may also be influenced by Internet characteristics.
10. The types of business activities that companies can undertake are affected by the companies' adjustments to Internet influences on company organization, culture, and functioning.

THINKING POINTS

1. The marketspace can be described in terms of company type (e.g., pure-player vs. hybrid), product focus, or customer focus. Why are three different descriptions possible? How might the conclusions a business could draw about the online marketplace differ, depending on the perspective adopted?
2. What factors might affect the desirability of moving toward greater e-commerce involvement, as characterized by the four-phase continuum of involvement? That is, what characteristics of companies are likely to provide the greatest benefits from increasing integration of e-commerce into business practices?
3. The Internet can influence changes to business structures and processes. Consider the implications of adopting either a proactive or a reactive approach to implementing structural and procedural changes. What are the potential costs and benefits of each approach?
4. Business activity must adapt to changes in each of the five C's. How does the Internet environment necessitate adaptation? That is, what are possible effects of the Internet on each factor, and how might these effects create a need to adapt?
5. How can the Internet be used to facilitate adaptation to each of the five C's?
6. What changes might an employee experience in the nature of daily activities as a business moves toward an online presence? How might different uses of the online presence by the company influence employee participation in company culture?

ENDNOTES

1. These conclusions are based on the results of a study that were published in November 2002. The study was conducted by Booz Allen Hamilton for the Office of the e-Envoy and the Information Age Partnership of Great Britain.
2. As cited by Cyberatlas, August 21, 2002.

SUGGESTED READINGS

1. *21 Dog Years: Doing Time at Amazon.com*, by Mike Daisy (The Free Press: New York, 2002).
2. *Making the e-Business Transformation*, by Peter Gloor (Springer-Verlag: London, 2000).
3. *dot.bomb*, by j. David Kuo (Little, Brown & Company: Boston, 2001).
4. "Work Remade: An Electronic Marketplace Inside the Corporation," by David Braunschvig. In *The Future of the Electronic*

Marketplace, edited by Derek Leebaert (The MIT Press: Cambridge, MA, 1998, pages 177–205).

5. "Get the Right Mix of Bricks and Clicks," by Ranjay Gulati and Jason Garino. *Harvard Business Review, 78*, 3 (2000), pages 107–114.

6. "Evolution of the Marketing Organization: New Forms for Turbulent Environments," by Ravi S. Achrol. *Journal of Marketing, 55*, (October 1991), pages 77–93.

7. "Twelve Themes of the New Economy," and "The Internetworked Business at Work," in *The Digital Economy*, by Don Tapscott. (McGraw-Hill: New York, 1996).

8. "The eCommerce Engine: How It Works," by Mohanbir Sawhney, Alicia Neumann, Kim Cross, Mark Leon, Sean Donahue, and Carol Pickering. Edited by Jeffrey Davis. *Business 2.0*, (February 2000), pages 1–12.

LEARNING LINKS

Tracking Change in Content

www.archive.org
www.faqs.org/faqs/

Company Organization

www.fitability.com
www.websense.com/company/news/companynews/02/040102c.cfm
www.networkmagazine.com/article/NMG20010125S0011/1

www.fastcompany.com/online/51/sgodin.html

Company Adaptation

www.businessweek.com/smallbiz/news/coladvice/book/bk990625.htm
www.rapidinnovation.com/articles/10principles.pdf
www.squarewheels.com

Technology and the Digital Marketplace

Focus and Objectives

In this chapter we examine the Internet environment from a technological perspective. In addition to creating the possibility for digital business, technology developers often work hand-in-hand with companies to produce products and services that enable and enhance commercial activity. To understand the nature of the relationship between technologists and digital business, we briefly discuss the history and technological characteristics of the Internet. Then we examine the influence of technology on the relationships that exist in the exchange environment of the Internet.

Your objectives in studying this chapter include the following:

- Develop familiarity with the basic structure and terminology of the Internet.
- Understand the technological implications of the Internet as a communications channel for the end user.
- Learn the primary types of Internet access and their associated demographics.
- Recognize and understand the impact of technology on the Internet experience of the end user.
- Identify the implications of Internet technology for buyers and for sellers.

How Do You Get Your Pizza?

Pizza is popular. In the United States, pizza is the second most ordered entrée in foodservice. It is estimated that the typical American family will eat pizza

30 times a year, and that fewer than 4 percent of the population do not go out for a piece of tomato pie.

Pizza has a long history, beginning in Naples, Italy. The first pizzeria, established in 1830, baked pizzas in an oven lined with lava from Mount Vesuvius—conveniently located nearby in the Bay of Naples. The restaurant, Antica Pizzeria Port' Alba, is still open today.

Port' Alba was not the only pizzeria for long. Italian immigrants brought their pizza recipes with them to the United States, and Gennaro Lombardi opened the first pizzeria in the country in 1905, in New York City.

Pizza went nationwide after World War II, when soldiers returned from Italy with tales of bravery, warfare—and pizza. People's fondness for pizza is responsible in large part for the 5,200 percent growth in oregano sales between 1948 and 1956. As the pizza craze spread, the variety of pizzas expanded: from Neapolitan to thin crust, hand-tossed, pan, stuffed crust, and many more.

There are many ways to get your pizza . . . and about as many options as there are styles of pizza. There's always the old standby; go to the pizzeria. If you're Queen Margherita of Italy, however, hobnobbing with the riffraff isn't your style, so pizza delivery is the only way to go—even in 1889. Pizza delivery took off after the telephone became widely available. In the 1980's, the rapid growth of pizza chains was abetted by the ability to call up for carry-out or delivery. Domino's Pizza, for instance, operates solely on a carry-out/delivery basis.

The Internet opens up new opportunities for satisfying your pizza cravings. Some sites, created by serious pizza enthusiasts, offer up virtual pizza: digitized two- and three-dimensional images of pizzas. If that's not enough to quell your hunger pangs, some purveyors of pizza have introduced the Internet as a channel for ordering pizza for take-out or delivery.

One of the first companies to provide online ordering was Pizza Hut, in 1994. Although online ordering isn't available everywhere, Pizza Hut's site does provide coupons and a store locator, complete with driving directions. When online ordering can be done, hungry customers customize their pizzas with selections of crust style and toppings combinations. Payment, with a delivery charge, is due when you receive the pizza, but before you eat it.

Taking the Internet/pizza connection one step further, a Chicago company, Malnati's, has installed Internet kiosks in high foot-traffic locations from which customers can order deep dish pizza—a company specialty. Customers pay for their orders online, and specify desired delivery time and location.

Other forms of online access to pizza include mobile orders placed from cell phones and PDA's. In addition, pizza portals aggregate brands of pizza and customer demand, providing consumers with the opportunity to pick and choose efficiently, based on personal preferences for pizza and pizza delivery timeframes (Figure 5-1). For pizza marketers, the online option can cut costs per order by reducing employees' phone time, and it can create efficiencies by facilitating efforts to sort and combine deliveries.

How high can demand for pizza go? In this case, the sky is *not* the limit. In May 2001, cosmonauts in the International Space Station made history as they

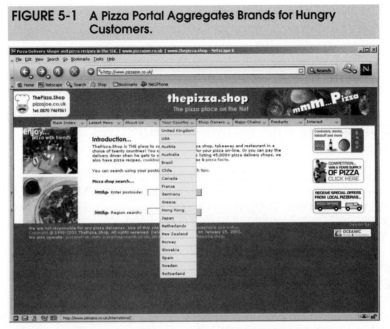

FIGURE 5-1   A Pizza Portal Aggregates Brands for Hungry Customers.

Source: Copyright 2003 by ThePizza.Shop. Reproduced with permission. All rights reserved.

ate the first pizza in outer space. The pizza, produced by Pizza Hut, was redesigned to withstand the rigors of space travel. Unfortunately for present residents of the space station, online ordering is not yet available in their area.

Much like pizza, the Internet has gained popularity and acceptance and grown rapidly. So rapidly, in fact, that it is easy to forget that the Internet of today is vastly different from the Internet of just 10 years ago. The technologies that have resulted in the arrays of networks and the software that make the networks useful are changing daily. The pace of these changes underscores the importance of recognizing the influence of technology on business activity that uses the Internet.

Despite the fact that the Internet was not developed for business purposes, it has been quickly adopted for commercial use. In order to facilitate business applications on the Internet, technologists have focused attention on the development of hardware and software that augment present capabilities and present new opportunities. For instance, Pizza Hut's online ordering facility processes customer requests using sophisticated database software that results in the delivery of a customized pizza. In addition, mapping software is used to guide customers to store locations. Technological developments such as these create the Internet environment in which marketers and consumers interact. As a result, it is important to understand the basic technology of the Internet, and the potential extensions of its abilities to business activity.

In this chapter, we will begin with a brief look at the nuts and bolts of Internet technology. This is a very complex area, and a discussion of the history, challenges, and techniques that reflect the development of the present-day Internet is far beyond the scope of this text. To keep things manageable, we will focus on the impact of technology on business practice, and explore ways in which future technological development may alter current business activities.

The Technology that Makes the Internet Possible

A common description of the Internet is that it is a "network of networks." Of course, networks existed long before the Internet was begun. Most of us are familiar with a number of different applications of networks, such as television and radio networks, and networks of friends and acquaintances.

What Is a Network?

The importance of a network becomes clear if you stop and think about what a network does. Typically, a **network** is a set of connections between otherwise discrete, separate entities—like people or computers. People throughout history have joined together in communities, in which networks of human interaction convey social values, daily events, and plans for activities that foster the well-being of the individual within the community, and the community within the larger environment.

Businesses have long counted on networks of customers to spread favorable word-of-mouth about products. These **referral networks** are often a fast, efficient means of communicating information. Suppose that one customer tries a product, likes it, and recommends it to two friends. Then these two friends try it, like it, and each recommends it to two more friends. Next, the friends of the original friends try the product, like it, and . . . you get the idea. The number of people who may potentially be exposed to word-of-mouth information about the product grows rapidly. This phenomenon is often described as **viral marketing,** because the pattern of communication reflects the pattern with which an especially contagious virus might move through a set of interacting hosts.

The Internet is an important tool for viral marketing. Research conducted in 2001 by Burson-Marsteller, a public relations firm, indicates that 10 percent of American Internet users are **e-fluentials.** E-fluentials are people who influence others' Internet-related behaviors. In off-line environments, word-of-mouth tends to be spread from one person to two other people. E-fluentials disseminate information to an average of 14 people. In addition, people are four times more likely to seek the advice of e-fluentials on business and technology issues than of average users.[1]

Bits & Bytes 5.1

E-fluentials share positive experiences with an average of 11 people, but they share negative experiences with an average of 17 people.

(*Source:* Burson-Marsteller Public Relations, 2001.)

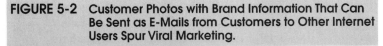

FIGURE 5-2 Customer Photos with Brand Information That Can Be Sent as E-Mails from Customers to Other Internet Users Spur Viral Marketing.

Source: Reproduced with permission of PictureMark, Inc. Copyright 2003. All rights reserved.

The underlying concept behind the viral marketing technique is that people will interact with other people (Figure 5-2). The speed with which the information is disseminated depends on the nature of the network that exists between the people. The ultimate number of people exposed to the information depends on the size of the network. Although viral marketing describes a single direction of information flow in a network, networks are often characterized by repeated interaction between network members. This ability to interact and build relationships of ongoing exchange contributes to the value of the network.

The size of the network also contributes to its value as a means of communication. To illustrate the relation between size and value, think about a very simple network between two people. The number of conversations that occurs between the two people is just one. If you add one more person to the network, you have the possibility of three conversations. Things get even more interesting if you add a fourth person, because now there can be six conversations. The basic idea is that the more people you add to the network, the greater the value of the network as a means of transmitting information. In addition, the value of each additional person increases, because the number of conversation links introduced by the new person is greater than the number contributed by any prior entrant to the network. These ideas are illustrated in Figure 5-3, and are often referred to as **Metcalfe's Law.**

A Network of Computers

The idea of networking computers into what we now recognize as the Internet gained interest (and government funding) in the 1960s, even though widespread implementation

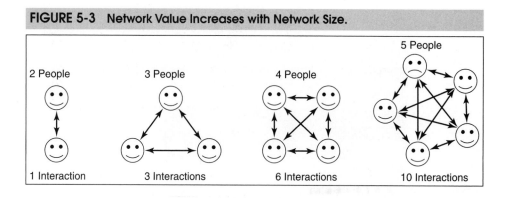

FIGURE 5-3 Network Value Increases with Network Size.

and adoption of the technology as a medium for business did not occur until the 1990s. The value of a network of computers through which scientific advances could be communicated lay in its ability to make computing resources, as well as research results, quickly and widely available. This meant that resources did not have to be duplicated, thus saving time and money.

The value of a network can only be fully realized if all of the points connected by the network communicate in the same language. For the Internet, two aspects of communications "languages" are relevant. One is the way in which information is translated into a common tongue for all computers, and another is the way in which the information is moved between the networked computers, or the **Internet protocols (IP).**

A Digital Language

The information being transmitted over a computer network is encoded in a **digital format.** This format is an alternative to sending a physical instance of an item (e.g., a sweater) or a physical analog of an item (e.g., a photo of a sweater). With a digital transmission, binary computer code transforms information into digital ones and zeros that, in unique combinations, serve as symbols for their physical counterparts. For instance, a 1 is represented as a 1, but the number 2 is a 10, while 3 is a 11. Applied similarly to letters, these combinations of 1's and 0's can be represented in a computer as the presence or absence of electrical signals. While the earliest efforts to digitize information focused on letters and numbers, current techniques enable fast digitization of graphical images, such as photographs and pictures, as well as auditory signals, such as voices or music.

Information stored in a digital form is stored in **bits.** Digitization enables rapid transmission of bits across computer networks. Digital information is available through many sources. For example, digital cell phones and televisions transmit information. The same information can also be transferred over a computer network, such as the Internet. Figure 5-4 describes how images are digitized for transmission.

Moving Bits with Packets

Being able to digitize information means that a symbol or a whole idea, such as an image, can be broken up into parts. The bits are divided into **packets** (also known as

FIGURE 5-4   The Nature of Digital Information.

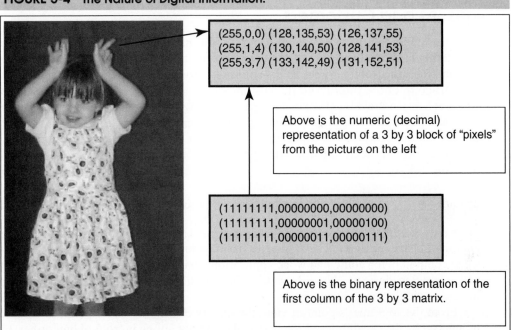

(255,0,0) (128,135,53) (126,137,55)
(255,1,4) (130,140,50) (128,141,53)
(255,3,7) (133,142,49) (131,152,51)

Above is the numeric (decimal) representation of a 3 by 3 block of "pixels" from the picture on the left

(11111111,00000000,00000000)
(11111111,00000001,00000100)
(11111111,00000011,00000111)

Above is the binary representation of the first column of the 3 by 3 matrix.

datagrams), which are then sent out across the network. The network consists of many possible paths a packet could take, and the packets that make up a single message might travel by very different routes. The packets wind up in the right place, and are reassembled in the proper order, because each packet leaves the originating computer with the Internet address from which it came, and the Internet address to which it should arrive.

How do the computers on the network all know how to correctly read the address information, so that they can forward the packets properly? This problem is addressed by Internet protocols that enable computers to "talk" with each other. These protocols are agreed-on standards for encoding and transferring information. **TCP/IP** stands for Transfer Control Program/Internet Protocol. The Internet protocol (IP) contains the address information that tells a computer where to send the packet. The network protocols are standards for communication between computers on the network.

Bits & Bytes 5.2
The domain name business.com was bought in 1997 for $150,000. It was sold in 1999 for $7,500,000.
(*Source:* Hobbes Internet Timeline at www.isoc.org)

Internet Technologies: Connecting Businesses and Customers

With the ability to digitize information and to transmit it over a network, we have the foundation of the Internet. For businesses, however, this is only the beginning. Getting information to customers requires data to travel from the company across the major infrastructure of the Internet to the customer's computer. The customer relies on an **Internet Service Provider (ISP)** to connect to the Internet. Each of these aspects of the process—personal computer, connecting service, and infrastructure—can affect the quality of the consumer's experience in receiving the commercial information. The three primary technological components for online communication are shown in Figure 5-5.

The User at the End of the Channel

Over the years, the cost of technology has decreased and the capabilities of computing equipment have increased. These changes have made it possible for people to buy personal computers for home and work applications that would have been unimaginable just a few decades ago . Note, however, that the likelihood of owning a computer increases with income. (Figure 5-6).

From the consumer's point of view, the quality of the Internet experience is most influenced by the capabilities of the personal computer sitting in front of him or her. In terms of hardware, **resolution** (clarity of screen images), **memory** (amount of computer storage), **processing speed** (rate at which the computer processes information) and **sound** (quality of audio data) affect the Internet experience. For software, usage issues include the user-friendliness of the software, such as how easy the software is to install and learn to use. In addition, software concerns revolve around flexibility, or the extent to which the software makes it possible for the user to manipulate and produce content.

Businesses can work jointly with software developers to make it easier for customers to have the intended online experience. For instance, the Bose Corporation, a manufacturer of high-quality home entertainment systems, worked with Macromedia, the developer of software such as Flash and ColdFusion for Internet applications, to develop SoundAdvisor(sm) (Figure 5-7). SoundAdvisor(sm) is an interactive, online

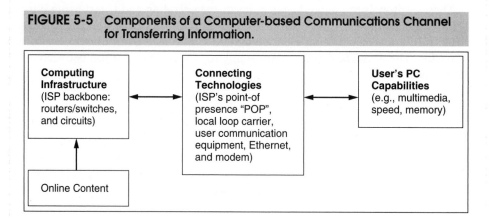

FIGURE 5-5 Components of a Computer-based Communications Channel for Transferring Information.

Computing Infrastructure (ISP backbone: routers/switches, and circuits)

Connecting Technologies (ISP's point-of presence "POP", local loop carrier, user communication equipment, Ethernet, and modem)

User's PC Capabilities (e.g., multimedia, speed, memory)

Online Content

FIGURE 5-6   At-Home Computer Access Is Related to Income.

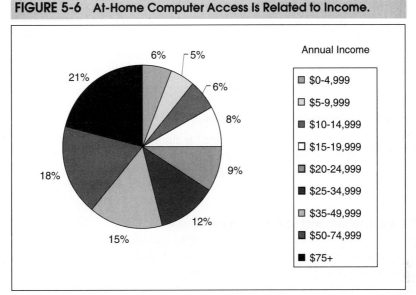

Source: www.ntia.doc.gov, 2001.

FIGURE 5-7   Partnerships Between Business and Technology Can Provide User-Friendly Internet Introductions to Products and Services.

tool that helps a customer create a floor plan to decide placement of home entertainment components. The customer can readily obtain the software needed to run the application by installing a Flash plug-in. A **plug-in** is a piece of software that interprets the information in a streaming file and communicates it in a recognizable form to the user's computer. Plug-ins with basic playback capabilities are often available free of charge to users.

Access to Computer Communications

The quality of the Internet experience for the end user is also influenced by the technologies that bring the digital content to the desktop computer. For this purpose, two different classes of technologies are important: the equipment that transmits the content, and the service that provides access to the Internet.

Internet Access Is Affected by Equipment

The hardware options that enable a user to connect to the Internet differ in terms of connection speed and reliability. Many people connect to the Internet from home with a **dial-up modem.** Modems connect computers to the Internet through telephone lines. They vary widely in the speed with which they can transfer data. Speed is measured in **bits per second**, or **bps**, and it takes approximately 10 bits to transfer a single text character. This means that a modem that transfers data at a speed of 28.8 kbps (*kilo*bits per second) can send a page of text in around two-thirds of a second. The range of modem speeds typically used to access the Internet is from 14.4 kbps to 56.6 kbps.

Businesses have to be careful when designing Web sites to recognize the speed with which visitors can download information from the site. Sites that are dense with graphics or animation may take longer to download than users are willing to wait, given the constraint of modem speed. The results of a survey conducted by ActivMedia suggest that $4.35 million in online revenue is lost each year to marketers whose sites frustrate potential customers. These results are explained in terms of the **"eight-second rule"**—people are willing to wait 8 seconds for a page to download, but no longer!

Other connection options tend to be more expensive than modems, and they are not available in all areas. These options include **ISDN** lines, **DSL** lines, **cable,** and **wireless** (e.g., satellite) options. These technologies enable the user to transfer data from the Internet more quickly, and with fewer glitches in data transfer, than with standard modem technology.

Internet Access Is Affected by Service

The Internet operates much like a relay, or the Pony Express of the 1800s; data packets are transferred from computer to computer until they reach their destination. Connecting to the Internet works similarly. Users gets access to the Internet through Internet Service Providers (ISPs), who allow the users to connect to their computers to other computers on the Internet. Many users connect to the Internet through national service providers, such as America Online and Earthlink. These companies not only provide Internet access, but also a host of other services, including instant messaging and Web site development tools. The table in Figure 5-8 indicates the popularity of national service providers.

FIGURE 5-8   Most Users Access the Internet Through National Service Providers.

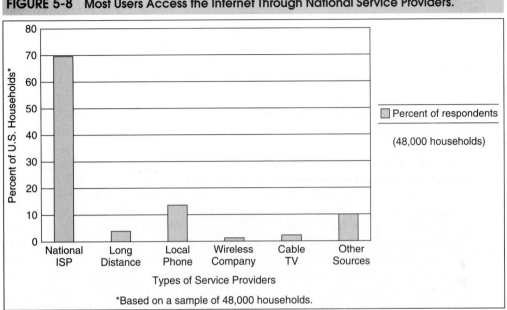

Source: www.ntia.doc.gov, 1999.

The Outside World

Internet service providers enable users to receive and transmit information from their own computers to other computers connected to the Internet. The computing infrastructure that makes possible the transfer of massive amounts of information every second depends on the availability of acceptable bandwidth. **Bandwidth** describes the speed with which information can be sent over telecommunications lines. It is measured in bits per second (bps). High bandwidth is similar to a large pipe: more stuff can be sent through it. The large amounts of bandwidth needed to connect the many Internet computers together are available from **backbone providers,** such as Sprint and MCI. These companies not only provide bandwidth, they may also run the services needed by many companies to carry out their Internet activities. These backbone providers are strategically located near areas of high bandwidth infrastructure (e.g., Washington, D.C.).

Bits & Bytes 5.3
The estimated 7 million wireless gamers in the United States are predicted to grow in number to more than 71 million in 2007, making gaming a very serious business.
(*Source:* IDC, via CyberAtlas 2003.)

Putting It All Together: From First-Mile to Last-Mile

New and more complex ways to put different types of data online are introduced frequently. Some of these technologies include the ability to transmit voice data digitally, the ability to provide video conferencing, and programming advances that make possible animated banners and streaming audio and video. **Streaming media** are audio and picture files that are transmitted continuously, upon request, to a user's computer. This transmission format avoids the need to download and store space-consuming files on the user's computer. Collectively, these technologies that provide an engrossing, interactive experience for users are termed **rich media.**

Boosting Bandwidth With Broadband

A concern for all parties who use rich media is the need for sufficient bandwidth to enable the transmission of the different types of data. This concern affects the consumer, because it is influenced by the type of computer and the speed of Internet access needed to carry the data the "last mile." As more and more companies incorporate rich media into their marketing strategies, the need to have access to sufficient bandwidth in order to make the digital technologies available to consumers places emphasis on the "first mile." Bandwidth characteristics and capabilities are often called **broadband.** The importance of bandwidth is reflected in the efforts of many companies to develop broadband strategies that guide media development and dissemination.

Growth statistics in broadband sectors illustrate the importance of adequate bandwidth for consumers. While Internet access through dial-up providers, such as America OnLine, grew only 2.2 percent in 2001, broadband providers, such as DSL and satellite, grew rapidly, increasing 12.6 percent and 24 percent, respectively. Leichtman Research predicts that over half of American households will have broadband access by 2007. This growth means that more people than ever will have the ability to receive commercial information in rich media formats. Broadband access also creates new product opportunities, such as streaming movies to a customer's computer on demand, or providing online tools for creating digital scrapbooks.

Media Convergence and Business Opportunity

The content viewed by a user on her computer is made available by the development of digital communications technologies that in turn rely on the computing infrastructure. This process reflects the convergence of objectives and abilities in three key industries: content, communications, and computing. The convergence of abilities creates opportunities for products and services. For instance, LikeTelevision.com takes television programs and converts them to high-quality, online digital videos (Figure 5-9). This convergence of Internet and television, along with computing software database applications, provides subscribers with access to a huge, searchable online library of video content.

Putting Technology in Its Place: Back to the Framework

The effects of technology in the Internet environment can also be examined through the relationships between elements of the exchange environment. Three components of the set of relationships in the business context of the Internet are presented in Figure 5-10.

FIGURE 5-9 Digital Technologies Create Media Convergence and Business Opportunities.

We will consider the effects of technology on the central exchange environment that exist between buyers and sellers. In addition, we can examine the relationships that exist between technologists and businesses, and between technologists and customers.

Technology and the Central Exchange Environment

We begin by considering the nature of the effect of technology on the central environment for exchange. This effect is illustrated by the two arrows in Figure 5-10 that drop from the technology node to the arrows that connect buyers and sellers.

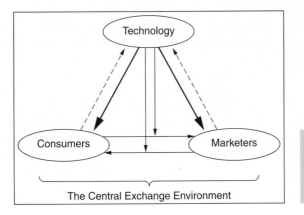

FIGURE 5-10 Technology Relationships with Buyers and Sellers Create and Influence the Central Exchange Environment.

Enabling the Exchange

Technology can influence the relationship between exchange agents in two different ways. First, technology can enable the exchange, by making it possible for the two agents to communicate. For example, with the Internet, a consumer can conduct a worldwide search for a particular product, establish contact with a vendor on the other side of the globe, negotiate an exchange, complete the transaction, and arrange delivery. Without the Internet, any or all of these activities might be impossible.

Changing the Exchange

Second, technology can affect the nature of the exchange between the two agents. Suppose that the scenario we just considered could occur without the Internet. For example, an explorer—like Columbus—could sail from Europe to India in search of spices, conduct the negotiation and transaction, and bring the spices home. With the Internet, however, characteristics of the exchange can change dramatically. At a minimum, the time and human effort to conduct the search can be reduced. In addition, errors in the process may be reduced—like tripping over the New World in route to India. As a result, even when the Internet does not determine whether an exchange relation can exist, it can influence the nature of the relationship.

Bits & Bytes 5.4

Technology start-up companies are alive and well. They make up almost two-thirds of all start-ups, and they receive the most funding from venture capitalists. (*Source:* VentureOne, 2002.)

The Nature of the Environment

At the heart of the Internet's effect on exchange relationships is its ability to foster interactivity. In the Internet world, interactivity is the glue that keeps users in the online environment. Interactivity is the extent to which two or more entities can act on each other, causing changes in activities or behaviors, in real-time.

Technology and Interactivity

Computing technologies provide the means by which buyers and sellers can connect in the Internet environment. A **computer-mediated environment** is a link between agents that is characterized by information technology (e.g., the computer) and interactivity (i.e., the ability to restructure the information environment).

Because the information technology imposes a computing environment between the two people in the communication, we can distinguish between the effects of person interactivity and machine interactivity on the nature of the relationship. When we think about an interaction between two people, such as a salesperson and a consumer, we can describe the nature of the interaction in terms of **person interactivity.** That is, we can consider all of the signals and content transmitted by each person as a way to facilitate understanding of what is being communicated. When we put a computer in the center of the communication, we introduce the possibility for **machine interactivity**.

FIGURE 5-11 Web Demos Can Guide New Visitors Through Site Features.

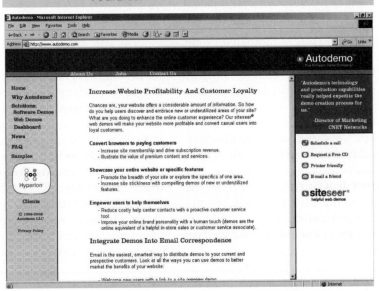

Source: Reproduced with permission of Autodemo, L.L.C. ©2003. All rights reserved.

Machine interactivity refers to the nature of the relationship between one of the agents and the computing environment. If a consumer has difficulty interacting with the computer environment and withdraws from the effort, a marketer's attempt to create an exchange relationship may be in vain. Web demos provide a technological means for introducing site visitors to the site's content and capabilities. As Figure 5-11 illustrates, Autodemo's animated demonstrations provide clients like Amazon and Yahoo with several different opportunities to heighten their customers' interest and consumption.

The person-machine relationship may also affect the nature of the relationship that develops between the two human agents. In this sense, the computing environment moderates, or changes, the human relationship. As a result, the computer-mediated environment moderates the central exchange environment. Although it sounds complicated, the underlying notion is straightforward; the technology of the Internet environment may influence the ways that people interact through the Internet. The trickier part, for businesses and for researchers, is trying to figure out how to predict the nature of the Internet's influence.

Making Technology Invisible

One factor that may affect the extent to which the computer-mediated environment moderates relationships and influences individual behavior is the salience of the computing environment to the user. That is, if the environment is unusual, unexpected, or necessitates changes to ordinary patterns of behavior, then it may occupy a more central position in a person's thoughts and actions. Because the Internet is

---

InSite

BE A KNOW-IT-ALL: WWW.HOWSTUFFWORKS.COM

Why do some passes in football go right where they should, while others take the wrong course? How does a copying machine work? Why does pulling up on a zipper close it? How does the Internet create opportunities for identity theft?

If you've ever had a question that you couldn't get answered, or if you were too self-conscious to ask, try www.HowStuffWorks.com. From the mundane to the utterly esoteric, the site contains information, analysis, advice, and diagrams to enlighten and entertain visitors.

The site was developed by an engineer named Marshall Brain (yes, really). Its popularity grew rapidly, as did the range of content. From its inception, the site has expanded to include thousands of topics. An advertiser's dream, the site pulls in over 4,000,000 unique visitors each month. HowStuffWorks has received awards for its content from *Time Magazine*, Yahoo!, and *Scientific American*, among others. The HowStuffWorks concept has been spun off in several directions, including the site, www.HowBizWorks.com.

---

a relatively novel environment for many people, it may receive greater attention and affect the nature of communications between agents more strongly than might other communications environments. As the Internet becomes a more typical venue for consumption, the effects of the technical environment on interaction may become less pronounced.

Consider the response of very young children to communications technologies. The immediate reaction of a toddler when handed a telephone with Grandma on the other end tends to be that of fascination with a new, talking toy. The next reaction is a perplexed look, and a desire to get Grandma out of the receiver. A similar "how-do-they-do-that?" concern is raised when children acquire sufficient cognition to express curiosity about how the little people get into the television. Invariably, however, the novelty of the telephone and television as communications media decreases with familiarity (and age), until the technology is taken for granted and the medium is simply a vehicle for conveying and acquiring information.

One goal for developing technology is to make it easy for people to experience the computer-mediated environment without the technology creating a barrier to the experience. Meeting this goal occurs when the salience of the technology is reduced, and the perceived experience of the environment is increased. In laymen's terms, this simply means that the objective is to make the communications experience via the Internet just like being there—wherever "there" may be. The screen in Figure 5-12 shows examples of virtual worlds created by Electronic Arts for their computer games.

To create computer-based environments that are the next best thing to being there, we need to understand the factors that affect perception of the environment. **Telepresence** is a concept developed to reflect the combined influence of technological factors and personal experience in the perception of the computer-based environment.

FIGURE 5-12   Reducing the Salience of Technology Creates an "Out-of-This-World" Experience.

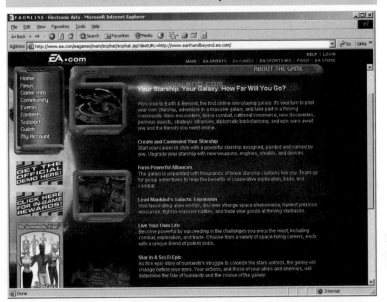

Source: Reproduced with permission of ElectronicArts, Inc. Copyright 2003. All rights reserved.

Telepresence in the Moderated Environment

The literal meaning of telepresence is reflected in its roots. "Tele," from Greek, means far off, while "presence" refers to nearness. A more complete description of telepresence is credited largely to Jonathan Steuer, who defined telepresence as "the extent to which one feels present in the mediated environment, rather than in the immediate physical environment." In other words, the perceived distance between the person and the environment being perceived is reduced or eliminated when telepresence is high.

In Steuer's description of telepresence, vividness and interactivity are two dimensions on which technological factors influence a person's perception of the environment. **Telepresence vividness** is "the ability of the technology to produce a sensorially rich, mediated environment." **Telepresence interactivity** is "the degree to which the user can influence the form or structure of the environment." Figure 5-13 illustrates the relationship between the two dimensions of telepresence, and the factors that create vividness and interactivity.

Vividness increases with **sensory breadth** and **sensory depth.** That is, the more senses that are involved in the perception of an experience, the more vivid the experience is perceived to be. For example, a mediated environment designed to convey information about a farmer's market would have greater sensory breadth if you could not only see the fruits and vegetables, but you could also touch and smell them. Sensory depth refers to the quality of the sensory experience, that is, the ability of the environment to convey the intensity of the sensory experience. In an online farmer's market, greater sensory depth would be achieved if the environment could

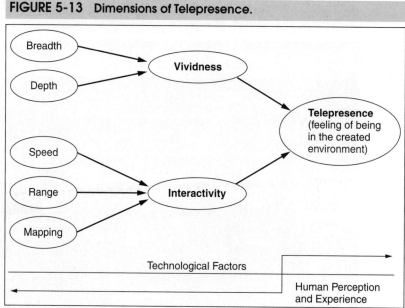

FIGURE 5-13 Dimensions of Telepresence.

actually provide the smell of fresh produce, rather than relying on words to convey the experience. Higher levels of vividness increase the reality of the perceived experience.

Interactivity is enhanced by three factors: speed, range, and mapping. Each of these is influenced by technological capabilities. **Speed** refers to rate at which the user's input affects the structure or form of the environment. For example, clicking on a menu of options in a Web site provides a new screen display. The faster the new screen appears, thus demonstrating the user's impact on the environment, the higher the level of perceived interactivity.

Range describes the size of the set of actions that a user could carry out to affect the nature of the mediated environment. Greater range is related to higher interactivity. A Web site that enables the user to pick and choose among several options or formats for viewing information would create stronger perceptions of interactivity than a "one-size-fits-all" graphical display.

The third factor that influences interactivity is mapping. **Mapping** refers to the extent to which the user's actions in modifying the environment correspond to changes in the environment. Early computer games required the user to work in a textual mode, typing in verbal commands to move through virtual rooms. Technological advances have made it possible to guide a virtual person through seemingly three-dimensional spaces by moving a joystick or by turning a wheel in the desired direction of travel. The improved match between the user action and movement within the environment increases perceived interactivity.

For businesses, the technological developments that increase interactivity and vividness can be tailored to create environments that increase the likelihood of telepresence. Telepresence is particularly important for marketing goods and services for which it may be difficult for customers to physically visit a location. For instance,

FIGURE 5-14   Virtual Tours Reduce Time and Effort Costs for Buyers and Sellers.

Source: Reproduced with permission of TimandAmyHudson, Inc. Copyright 2003. All rights reserved.

vacation travel destinations and house hunting can be "tried out" with online, virtual visits (Figure 5-14).

Communications in Place and Time

The concept of telepresence captures the idea that people respond to situations, or environments, differently depending on the extent to which the environment is perceived to be distant or near. For businesses, forms of communications can be characterized as environments that differ in perceived distance. For instance, a salesperson may be standing right in front of you, or he may communicate with you by telephone.

We can consider the Internet, as well as traditional environments, as differing not only in terms of physical distance, but also in terms of time. The table in Figure 5-15 classifies technologically created communications environments by place and time. For each dimension, synchronicity indicates no distance, while asynchronicity indicates at least some distance.

An interesting characteristic of the computer environment of the Internet is that it is closer to a real-world, face-to-face encounter with another person than are many other forms of traditional marketing communications. One impact of technology on the business environment has been to bring the interaction between agents in

| FIGURE 5-15 Time and Place as Dimensions of Communications Media. |||

| | Place ||
Time	*Synchronous*	*Asynchronous*
Synchronous	Face-to-face Internet	Telephone Live television broadcast Live radio broadcast
Asynchronous	Notes Phonemail	Mail (letters, brochures) Pre-recorded television Pre-recorded radio

the exchange environment full circle. Prior to the Internet, the most sensorially rich, interactive environment between buyers and sellers existed in local marketplaces, with face-to-face interactions. Even though the Internet cannot provide exchange agents with the full complement of sensory stimulation, its potential for telepresence is greater than that of other media. In addition, shortcomings in sensory richness may be compensated by the ability of the Internet to facilitate a sense of being there—even when "there" is thousands of miles away (Figure 5-16).

The Technology and Business Relationship

The effects of Internet technologies extend beyond their influence on the central environment for exchange. The relationship between technology and business affects the types of business processes carried out by companies, as well as the types of products

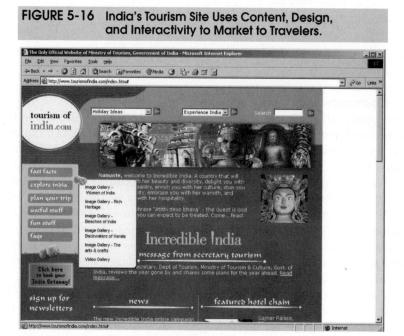

FIGURE 5-16 India's Tourism Site Uses Content, Design, and Interactivity to Market to Travelers.

Source: Copyright 2003. All rights reserved.

and services that can be provided. Technology is a basic force in determining the nature of the Internet environment; its effects serve in some ways to facilitate commercial efforts, and in others, to inhibit them.

Technology Benefits Business Activities

Internet technologies can increase the speed and cost-effectiveness of business processes. Two main categories of commercial applications illustrate the facilitating effect of technology: research processes and transaction-oriented applications. Both of these categories reflect the central importance of information to the business organization.

For research processes, the Internet enables businesses to gather information for primary and for secondary marketing research. Information from prospective customers can be collected from online focus groups, chat rooms, and online surveys. Secondary data can be acquired from published data, as well as through online databases. We will look at the use of the Internet for marketing research in greater detail in Chapter 9.

The technologies of the Internet also make it possible for businesses to provide information, to customers and to other business partners. For example, affiliate programs and technologies that enable businesses to provide targeted advertising lure customers to Web sites. In addition, content management technologies can be used to create online catalogs of goods and services designed to meet the needs of targeted segments. Online shopping is aided by virtual shopping carts and tax software that readily computes taxes based on the destination for the purchases. Product configuration software allows shoppers to customize products from an array of options, such as buying a personal computer from Dell. With a purchase decision made, technologies for money transfers streamline online transactions for marketers and consumers. All aspects of the process may be tracked, recorded, and used for future, personalized business activity by means of data-mining software.

Technology Creates Challenges

While technology can facilitate exchange, it also raises issues for online business activity when technology is misused. Of particular importance for businesses is the potential for unauthorized access into databases and network systems. For example, businesses must manage concerns associated with the protection of consumer information online, such as credit card numbers and social security numbers.

Many companies store transaction-related information. If the information, such as a set of credit card numbers, is stored in a plain text file on a computer, it is readable by anyone with access to the computer. One solution is to encrypt the file.

Encryption is a software technique that enhances security by coding messages so that they cannot be read by anyone who does not have the ability to decode the message.

Cryptographic methods have existed for thousands of years. Roman soldiers in Gaul used secret codes to communicate with commanders in ancient Rome, developing battle plans and arranging logistics of supplies and legion movements.

The fundamental idea behind cryptography is much the same today as when it was developed. A message is encoded using a cipher, which is a set of rules that explains the

'Net Knowledge

BUILDING SECURITY WITH BIOMETRICS

Fingerprints are often the clues at the scene of a crime that lead to a criminal's downfall. The value of fingerprints for identifying villains lies in their uniqueness to a particular individual—and the difficulty of removing them.

Advances in technology are increasing the value of fingerprints, and other personal, biological identifiers. Expanding their reach from crime to consumption, biometric technologies are breaking new ground. **Biometrics** refers to the use of distinctive human characteristics, such as fingerprint, voice, and retinal patterns, to "measure" a person's identity.

The need for biometric technology has increased with the spreading use of the Internet as a commercial environment. Companies who conduct transactions online with consumers they never see need to be sure that the person providing a credit card number is really the person authorized to use the card. In addition, services that use the Internet to store and transfer sensitive, personal information—such as financial and health data—need to be able to control access to the information.

A variety of biometric technologies exists for the digital environment. For instance, suppose you want to insure that no one else can use your computer. One method to control access is with a computer mouse that only allows computer access when it recognizes your individual palm print. You scan and register your palm print with a central, secure database. When you place your hand over your mouse, your palm pattern is matched with the stored, scanned pattern, and access is granted. Similar applications exist for facial image, voice pattern, and fingerprint recognition.

transformation of the information in the message. The encoded message, or cipher text, can only be decoded by someone who knows how the information was altered.

As applied to the Internet, encryption is a little more complicated. While many forms of encryption are available, one of the more prevalent forms of Internet applications of cryptography involves the use of an algorithm and a key. The algorithm and key work together as a cipher to produce the encoded text.

Encryption addresses issues of security and privacy by limiting access to the information in a message only to people who have the right key. In addition, some forms of encryption can be used to verify the identity of the message sender, thus enabling authentication. A message encrypted with a private key is similar to a digital signature; if the message recipient is confident that only the sender has access to the private key, then the message must have come from the sender.

The methods used to secure private information can make it difficult to transfer information between businesses involved in the transaction (e.g., the selling company and the credit card institution). The potential for communications difficulty underscores the need for standard protocols that facilitate secure information transfer. In 1997, a consortium of major businesses and credit card companies, including Microsoft, Visa, MasterCard, and Netscape, introduced **SET (Secure Electronic Transaction).** SET uses encryption and decryption methods to protect credit card information transferred through any online network.

The Technology and Customer Relationship

Customers in the Internet environment are also influenced by and interact with technology. As a general description, technological influences on buyer behavior can be classified as issues related to accessing the Internet, and issues related to using the Internet's content.

Accessing the Internet: Interface Capabilities

The Internet user population has shifted from its early base of scientists and computer technologists to a broader base of mainstream users and commercial applications. The shift has created a need for technical development intended to create user-friendly interfaces between computers and the people who use them. Researchers who address this aspect of technology development typically work in the area of **human factors,** or **human-computer interface (HCI).** Much of the work conducted by researchers in this area deals with issues of machine interactivity, with an objective of decreasing the difficulty with which people can make use of computer technologies.

Using the Internet: Resource Discovery

Technology development has also been focused on problems that arise when consumers attempt to use the Internet as an information resource. A key issue is resource discovery. **Resource discovery** refers to the results of the cognitive and behavioral processes people use to find information, to store and retrieve acquired information, and to customize information, using online resources.

Internet technologies make available vast information resources for consumers. Although information availability can facilitate the acquisition of desired information, the sheer mass of information to be searched can make the hunt for useful information difficult. As we learned in Chapter 3, users can be overloaded with information, to the detriment of decision quality.

Search technologies can assist people in sifting through information include search engines and intelligent agents that gather information and organize it for comparison. In addition, search capabilities have been advanced to include **natural language processing,** in which computer software is developed to recognize ordinary commands and syntax. Natural language capabilities make it easier for people to interact with computers to find information.

Extending the Internet's Reach: Mobile and Peer-to-Peer Opportunities

Technological developments make it possible for people to access the Internet via cell phones and PDAs, in addition to personal computers. While the development of hardware has increased Internet opportunities, software advances have created the possibility for peer-to-peer information exchanges. Both of these areas offer new ways for people to consume via the Internet.

M-commerce (*mobile* commerce) describes the activities associated with the buying and selling of goods and services using portable computing devices. With the widespread development of the cellular communications infrastructure, and the dramatic decrease in the cost of cellular service, people are not tethered to their personal computers for Internet access.

Businesses have acted on the mobile opportunities. Companies provide graphical advertising information designed for the small screen displays of cell phones and PDAs. They also use **short-messaging service (SMS)** to send e-mails to customers' phones, to notify them of special offers. **Location-based service** is a newly developing technology that will enable phone users to get information about services and activities in the vicinity. For instance, a traveler can access information about nearby restaurants, or travel assistance, even when lost. With mobile Internet access, people can shop, communicate, and even participate in online auctions with location flexibility.

Bits & Bytes 5.5

Men may be more mobile than women, at least in terms of cell phone and PDA Internet access. Men comprise 72% of mobile access surfers, while women are the remaining 28%.

(*Source:* comScore Networks, Inc., August 2002.)

For example, eBay customers can take advantage of wireless rebidding, developed by InPhonic. The service uses text messaging on a digital cell phone to let consumers know when they have been outbid in an auction. It also enables them to place bids, to get back in the game.

Advances in **peer-to-peer (P2P)** technologies have also opened up new consumption opportunities. Peer-to-peer computing is the ability to move files from one person's computer to another person's computer, without depending on a central computer to "serve" out the files. Being able to share files means consumers can use their computers to store and provide content that may be desired by other users. For instance, music that can be digitized and stored on a computer can be copied by another audiophile, provided the host computer shares access.

Peer-to-peer technology has received a lot of attention from businesses. Companies view P2P as a way to create community among customers, who create peer groups for different types of products. Peer-to-peer platforms also create commercial opportunities that leverage the customer-to-customer (C2C) nature of exchanges. Remember viral marketing? Fostering new exchanges between peers can spread the reach of a marketing communication.

One example of a company who implemented a P2P process for the Internet is Napster. Although the music-sharing company used a central server computer to store a database of digitized, compressed music files—called MP3's—the core ability to swap files between registered users illustrates a P2P platform for exchange. As we will see in Chapter 6, Napster's creative use of the Internet for file-sharing created issues for policy makers that ultimately resulted in the music company's demise.

CHAPTER SUMMARY

In this chapter, we considered the role of technology development on the nature of the Internet as an exchange environment. We started with the basics of networks and digital technology, and we characterized the transfer of data through the Internet to the end user as a computer-based communications channel. Three elements of the channel were described: personal computing capabilities, Internet access, and computing infrastructure.

We extended our examination of technology to include the relationships between the technological component of the Internet environment and other players in the environment. For instance, we looked at the influence of technology on the exchange environment that exists between buyers and sellers. Technology may function as a link that makes possible the interaction between exchange agents. In contrast, the technology influence may simply change the nature of the relationship that already exists between exchange agents.

The influence of the computer environment was characterized as the combination of technological factors that increase or decrease telepresence. These factors were described as the general dimensions of vividness and interactivity. The communications environment created by Internet technology was compared with traditional communications media to illustrate the importance of telepresence in creating communications environments that increase realism.

We also considered the relationships between technology and businesses, and between technology and customers. In each relationship, technology affects the types and quality of actions that can be conducted in the Internet environment.

CONTENT MANAGEMENT

USEFUL TERMS

- backbone providers
- bandwidth
- biometrics
- bits
- bits per second (bps)
- broadband
- cable
- computer-mediated environment
- datagrams
- dial-up modem
- digital format
- DSL
- e-fluentials
- "eight-second rule"
- encryption
- human factors
- human-computer interface (HCI)
- Internet protocols (IP)
- Internet Service Provider (ISP)
- ISDN
- location-based service
- machine interactivity
- mapping
- Metcalfe's Law
- m-commerce
- memory
- natural language processing
- network
- packets
- peer-to-peer (P2P)
- person interactivity
- plug-in
- processing speed
- range
- referral networks
- resolution
- resource discovery
- rich media
- sensory breadth
- sensory depth
- SET (Secure Electronic Transaction)
- short-messaging service (SMS)
- speed
- streaming media
- TCP/IP
- telepresence
- telepresence interactivity
- telepresence vividness
- viral marketing
- wireless

REVIEW QUESTIONS

1. What benefits are there to understanding the technological aspects of the Internet?
2. What is Metcalfe's Law, and how is it relevant for online communications?
3. In what ways does the nature of the Internet create unique opportunities for viral marketing?

4. What does TCP/IP stand for? Why is it important for the development and widespread adoption of the Internet?
5. What technological problem, often experienced by end users, may result in millions of dollars of lost online revenue?
6. How can technology influence the relationship between exchange agents?
7. What are the two main types of interactivity?
8. What are the two key dimensions of telepresence?
9. What are some advantages of Internet technologies for businesses?
10. What are some disadvantages of Internet technologies for businesses?

WEB APPLICATION

Getting Found on the Internet

1. *Search Engine Optimization*

   We all know that the Internet is big. How will prospective customers find your site, among the billion-plus pages that are out there? Many people search for products with one of the major search engines, like Google and Altavista. If, however, you type in a search term for a relatively common item, you're likely to get many hits. Suppose you sell running shoes of a particular brand. If a shopper types in "running shoes," it's possible that your brand might be listed low enough in the search result list that the potential customer never even sees it.

   So how do you get your site high on the lists of search engines? The following activities will help you understand the concept of search engine optimization.

   a. Go to each of the following search engines: www.google.com, www.altavista.com, and www.looksmart.com. At each site, type in "big red dog." Compare the results from each engine's search. What commercialized character appeared most often?
   b. What differences did you notice between the list formats of the engines? Which search engine appeared to take the most commercial approach? Why did you reach this conclusion?

2. *Commanding the Premium Position*

   Our next step is to understand how sites that appear early in a list of search results are able to command the premium position.

   a. Go back to each of the search engines. Which of the engines provides information about how to get a URL listed? What are the requirements for listing?
   b. Which of the engines does not enable users to submit sites?

   Some search engines work like spiders, crawling through the web of links that makes up the Internet. When the "spider" crawls through a site, it is looking for information that it can use to index the site's content, for inclusion in the search engine directory. As a result, it is important to understand what the spider is looking for.

   Web pages are coded into HTML, or hypertext mark-up language. At the top of each page, there are three tags that identify the page content. These tags are the Title tag, the Description tag, and the Keywords tag. The spider compares the information in the tags with the content of the page. If the keywords in the tags appear frequently in the content of the page, and early in the page, the site stands a better chance of being indexed by the search engine.

   To understand how companies use HTML tags, let's take a look at the HTML coding for the PictureMark business introduced in Figure 5-2.

```
<!DOCTYPE HTML PUBLIC "-//W3C//DTD HTML 4.0 Transitional//EN">
<!- - saved from url=(0023) - ->
<html><head><title>PictureMark - Put the Consumer in the Heart
of your Message</title>
<meta content="MSHTML 5.00.3315.2869" name=GENERATOR><!- -
Sample Meta tags - ->
```

```
<meta content="text/html; charset=iso-8859-1" http-
equiv=Content-Type>
<meta content="PictureMark- Picture Marketing Solutions for
Events and Fixed installations."
name=description>
<meta content="PictureMark, event marketing, photo, kiosks,
Photerra, Photo booths, FotoZap, picture marketing, customized
advertising, viral marketing, sponsorships, onsite photo
printing"
name=keywords>
```

As you can see from the source code, the company has titled its page, "Put the Consumer in the Heart of your Message." Using a title is good practice, because when a visitor bookmarks the site, the title becomes the label for the bookmark. As a result, companies can use the title tag to boost brand recognition.

The description tag contains information about the contents of the page. It's important to create a clear succinct description of your site, because many search engines provide this description with the site listing in the list of search results.

The keywords that you include in the Keywords tag will strongly influence your chances of improving search engine standing. Keywords should include terms that potential visitors might type in to a search and that are contained in your page. Notice how this company has used general terms, such as "photo," as well as specialized terms, like "viral marketing" and "picture marketing," to increase its odds of being found in user searches.

To see how effectively companies use meta tags, complete the following steps.

a. Choose a retail site online, and go to the home page for the site. While in your browser (e.g., Netscape or Explorer), pull down the View menu and click "Source." This action will display the source code for the site. Identify the three different tags.

b. Identify two competitors for the product sold in the retail site. Visit their home pages and look at the meta tag contents. How do the contents compare? Which site seems to have the best descriptors?

c. Test your conclusion by comparing search results for each of the three companies in one of the major search engines. Which company is listed most highly in the results? What differences in tag contents might account for the ranking?

CONCEPTS IN BRIEF

1. The development of technology has resulted in rapid and dramatic changes to the nature of the Internet as a commercial environment.
2. As a network of networks, the Internet facilitates the spread of marketing communications, through referral networks, viral marketing tactics, and influential consumers.
3. The bigger the network, the more influence it provides for businesses.
4. The Internet has achieved its size and influence because many types of information can be digitized, and because generally accepted standards enable the digital information to be shared widely.
5. Consumers' experiences with commercial information provided online are influenced by the technologies that connect the consumer to the content.
6. Companies work to provide content that is compatible with the computing capabilities of customers and their computers.
7. As Internet access moves toward broadband, opportunities to provide rich media content will be increasingly available to businesses.
8. Other business opportunities result from the convergence of computing, communications, and content entities.

9. The central exchange environment of the Internet is a computer-mediated environment that enables person interactivity and machine interactivity.
10. Increasing person interactivity and decreasing machine interactivity requires businesses to incorporate technologies that promote telepresence.
11. Telepresence enables businesses to use the Internet to create situations that simulate synchronicity in time and place.
12. Internet technologies provide businesses with new ways to reach customers, as with wireless commerce, and they provide customers with new ways to get resources, as with peer-to-peer (P2P) platforms.

THINKING POINTS

1. How does the concept of a network increase the value of the Internet as an outlet for business activity?
2. Standards, such as TCP/IP, have had a large influence on the development of the Internet. In addition to their positive impact, how might technology standards have a harmful impact on the development of the Internet as a commercial medium?
3. Describe a scenario that illustrates the role of the Internet on the experience of a person using a computer to access the Internet as a mediating effect.
4. Consider the likelihood of telepresence in each of the following environments: telephone, television, radio, and Internet. How might the experienced telepresence differ in each environment? Why?
5. For what types of situations might a business want decreased telepresence? (*Hint:* The Internet might be a distraction from the product focus.)
6. What benefits does the Internet provide businesses with its ability to mimic communications that are synchronous in time and place and communications and asynchronous in time and place?
7. Consider the link in the framework that describes the relationship between technology developers and policy makers. What are the implications for differences in the power that each entity has in the relationship? That is, what might be the effect of a situation in which technological developments are constrained by policy objectives, and vice versa?
8. How does P2P technology pose challenges for businesses? What does it mean for companies' control over all aspects of the business strategy? What opportunities does it create?
9. What changes to marketing activities might be necessitated by the widespread adoption of m-commerce? What are the implications for promotions, transactions, and customer service?

ENDNOTES

1. From a June 2001 study conducted by Roper-Starch.

SUGGESTED READINGS

1. *Peer-to-Peer: Harnessing the Power of Disruptive Technologies,* edited by Andy Oram (O'Reilly and Associates: Sebastopol, CA, 2001).
2. *Mobile Commerce: Opportunities, Applications, and Technologies of Wireless Business,* by Paul May (Cambridge University Press: Cambridge, 2001).
3. *The Essential Guide to Mobile Business,* by Ingrid Vos and Pieter De Klein (Prentice Hall: Upper Saddle River, NJ, 2002).
4. "Internetworking: Concepts, Architecture, and Protocols." In *Computer Networks and Internets*, by Douglas E. Comer (Prentice-Hall, Inc.: Upper Saddle River, NJ, 1997).

5. *Every Student's Guide to the Internet*, by Keiko Pitter, Sara Amato, John Callahan, Nigel Kerr, Eric Tilton, and Robert Minato (McGraw-Hill: New York, 1995).
6. "Defining Virtual Reality: Dimensions Determining Telepresence," by Jonathan Steuer. *Journal of Communication, 42*, 4 (1992), pp. 73–93.
7. "Thriving on Technology Change." In *Now or Never*, by Mary Modahl (HarperCollins Publishers, Inc.: New York, 2000).
8. "Cyber Crime," by Ira Sager. *BusinessWeek*, (February 21), 2000.

LEARNING LINKS

Wireless m-Commerce

www.epaynews.com/statistics/mcommstats.html
www.mcommercetimes.com
www.business.com/directory/internet_and_online/ecommerce/mobile_commerce_m-commerce/

Types of Technologies

www.openp2p.com
www.perceptualrobotics.com

crypt2000.hypermart.net/Course/see.htm
stat.tamu.edu/Biometrics/

Applications of Technologies

visualroute.visualware.com
partners.storefront.net
www.merchantanywhere.com
www.picturemark.com
www.referralware.com
www.precisebiometrics.com

CHAPTER

Policy and the Digital Marketplace

Focus and Objectives

This chapter is focused on the role of the policy perspective for digital business. The recent development of the Internet, combined with its novel nature, raises issues for policy makers that are unique and often not well understood. In this chapter, we review the history and nature of public policy, and we consider several policy-related issues in the Internet environment. The overarching goal of this chapter is to describe the role and scope of policy, and to delimit areas that may be affected by regulatory decisions, thus influencing what businesses can do.

Your objectives in studying this chapter include the following:

- Identify the primary regulatory agencies that affect digital businesses and how they operate.
- Understand the implications of previous policy decisions for regulation of digital business activity.
- Recognize major issues for policy makers from the buyer and the seller perspectives.
- Identify likely types and outcomes of regulation for business activity on several major issues.

Peer-to-Peer Piracy?

In 1998, a 19-year-old college student in Boston had an idea. What if online music files, called MP3s, could be collected into a giant, online index, to which Internet users could add their music file listings and search for files stored on other users' computers? What if you made the indexing software easy to download and use?

Shawn Fanning acted on his idea, and Napster was created. Within months, the music-sharing program was a success. The peer-to-peer (P2P) platform that enabled files to be swapped between computers made it possible for billions of music files to be indexed, stored, and traded. The set-up was simple: register with Napster and provide your catalog of music files to Napster's servers. Specify a file you want to find, and Napster searches its database, and provides a link to another member's computer, from which you can copy the file.

Not everyone was happy with Napster and its success. Record labels, companies that produce and distribute recorded music, felt threatened. Why, they worried, would consumers buy CDs if they could copy files for free? The trade organization that represents the five largest record companies, the Recording Industry Association of America (RIAA), decided to do battle against what it viewed as digital piracy.

The RIAA argued that Napster encouraged its users to make copies of music files available to other users, in violation of copyrights held by the record labels. In its brief to the court, the RIAA argued that "sharing" wasn't really the service that Napster was providing. "The truth is," the brief states, "the making and distributing of unauthorized copies of copyrighted works by Napster users is not 'sharing,' any more than stealing apples from your neighbor's tree is 'gardening.'"

The battle raged in court for months. Napster's membership grew dramatically as users raced to build music collections, fearing that Napster would be shut down. While the RIAA held to its copyright infringement position, Napster tried an assortment of different defenses. For instance, the fledgling company claimed that its service enabled users to "space shift," moving music from purchased CDs to the computer, and that it was merely a technology for sharing, just like a VCR—that no actual copies of music files were ever stored on its servers.

To the dismay of Fanning, Napster, and millions of loyal members, the courts disagreed with Napster's defense. Napster ceased operations in July 2001.

As Napster's tale illustrates, the Internet creates new business opportunities and models, but also challenges for policy makers. The court's decision to shut down Napster reflected the acceptance of the argument that laws and policies developed for traditional, analog media, like records, cassette tapes, and videotapes, just weren't right for digital media, like MP3s. Digital media are different; they offer the ability to make copies that are just as good as the original, and to distribute them worldwide, via the Internet.

Even though it shares many characteristics of other media, the Internet—with its global reach and rapid, interactive transmission—has the potential to create new situations that are not clearly addressed by existing policies. In addition, where existing regulation does apply to the Internet, policy makers must address the issues that the sheer size and scope of the Internet raises for policy enforcement. In this chapter, we will look at the role of public policy in the business environment of the Internet. We will begin with a brief description of what public policy is, and where it comes from. Then we will consider the issues for policy that result from the various exchange relationships in the Internet environment.

Bits & Bytes 6.1

CD sales dropped 7 percent in the first half of 2002, according to research conducted by the RIAA.

(*Source:* RIAA, 2002.)

Who Makes Internet Policy?

With the Internet, "Who is responsible for developing policy?" is more easily asked than answered. Some types of policies that set guidelines or standards for behavior are established by government agencies in the United States, such as the Federal Trade Commission and the Food and Drug Administration. When approved by Congress, these policies become laws that regulate buying and selling activities in the United States. In addition, states can make their own laws to regulate e-commerce, provided that the legislation does not conflict with federal law.

Of course, the Internet exists well beyond the boundaries of the United States. Other countries establish laws that regulate e-commerce and other online activities within their borders. In addition, international laws regulate online buying and selling. Countries form alliances, called **intergovernmental organizations(IGOs).** These IGOs formulate policies that all nations in the organizations agree to uphold. For instance, the World Trade Organization (WTO) has 135 member countries. In 1998, the WTO issued its Declaration on Global Electronic Commerce. The declaration was the forerunner for setting policies related to the online sales of goods and services between member nations.

Other organizations establish policies that affect Internet activities, but that do not have the force of law. For example, several groups have been instrumental in shaping and directing the development of the Internet. The Internet Society (ISOC) is an international organization that develops, reviews, and implements network policy. For instance, task forces and boards within the ISOC determine which standards and protocols will be used by all networks that want to be connected to the Internet.

Another group that formulates and implements Internet policy is the Internet Corporation for Assigned Names and Numbers (ICANN), an international, **nongovernmental organization (NGO).** An NGO is a nonprofit organization of members who reside in two or more countries. As we saw in Chapter 1, ICANN is responsible for managing the administration of the Domain Name System. ICANN also creates top-level domain names, and develops policy to resolve domain name disputes.

In the following sections of this chapter, we will take a closer look at how regulatory policy is developed and applied to the Internet in the United States. Going back to our broad framework, we will examine the role of policy with regard to the central exchange environment, and on buyers and sellers. We will also look at alternatives to government-imposed regulation, such as industry self-regulation.

The Government and Regulatory Policy

The government's regulatory policies are carried out by federal agencies (Figure 6-1). These agencies are created through acts of Congress. The commissioners who guide the agencies' efforts are appointed by the executive branch of the government (i.e., the president). These agencies implement laws enacted by the legislative branch of government (i.e., the Congress). When attempts to enforce legislation are not successful, the agencies may pursue legal sanctions, getting the judicial branch of the government involved.

Aspects of Government Policy

Public policy is the system of laws and regulatory measures related to a particular topic that are developed by a government or its agencies. For commercial activity, public policy exists for two main reasons: (1) to protect consumers in the marketplace, and (2) to provide a fair environment for commercial activity among businesses. These goals can be described as the more general objective of maintaining a balance between the interests of consumers and the interests of marketers.

Policies guide behavior. They can be established after something goes wrong, in order to correct a problem, or to insure that the same thing won't happen again. Policies can also be developed before a problem occurs, when there is indication that a problem is likely to happen.

Regulatory policy is an important component of the business environment. It can affect the type and quality of resource that can be exchanged, by restricting or enabling the types of products and services that can be offered (e.g., weapons). In addition, regulatory policy can influence the way in which the exchange is conducted (e.g., prescription drugs). As a result, the impact of regulatory policy on business activity can be substantial. Policy makers can determine the success or failure of a company or even an industry through the effect of regulatory action on the exchange environment.

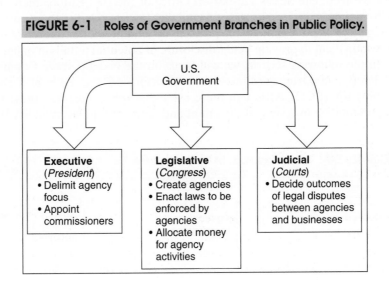

FIGURE 6-1   Roles of Government Branches in Public Policy.

Public policy also affects the marketing environment by fostering the development of infrastructures—like the Internet—that enable exchange relationships to occur. For example, the development of a nationwide communications network was facilitated by regulatory policies that enabled widespread access to telephone service (i.e., through the Communications Act of 1934) and to television (e.g., through the Rural Electrification Act of 1936).

Agencies and Their Activities

Public policy is executed by a variety of government agencies. Agencies are created by Congress to oversee and implement legislation in specific areas of interest. The president appoints the commissioners who run the agencies. Although many of these agencies' activities involve enforcement of existing laws, other activities address issues that reflect the underlying spirit of the legislation. For example, an agency may institute a program of consumer education to try to protect consumers from developing incorrect beliefs that could lead to detrimental effects of product use. In sum, agencies are responsible for making sure that policies are carried out. Their activities may be reactive, as when they respond to violations of legislation, or proactive, as when an agency attempts to forestall a potential problem.

The sequence of policy activities shown in Figure 6-2 is reflected in several Internet-based situations. For instance, when several consumers complained that they had not received their earnings for participating in a car leasing program, the Federal Trade Commission (FTC) began an investigation. After determining that the company's business was a pyramid scheme, the FTC took the case to court. A federal court ruled against the company. The Web site was shut down, the defendants were barred from any other multilevel marketing activity, and they were ordered to pay $2.9 million to their customers.

Policy activity can also be initiated by the agency. For example, the Securities and Exchange Commission (SEC) became concerned about online trading when a series of television ads made trading look glamorous and profitable, with little mention of the risks involved. The SEC's 125-person Office of Internet Enforcement inspected Web sites of online brokerage firms and found that few provided adequate disclosure of risk. The agency sought to remedy the problem by sending a letter to each online brokerage, requesting them to provide better disclosure of potential pitfalls in online trading.

In the following section, we will focus on the Federal Trade Commission (FTC), the Food and Drug Administration (FDA), and the Federal Communications Commission (FCC). Although there are many other agencies, these three provide a representative overview of the intent and scope of regulatory policy that affects the

FIGURE 6-2   Illustrative Path of Policy Actions.

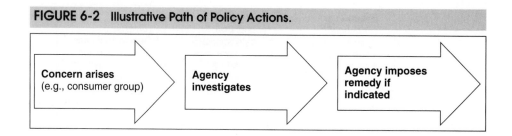

Concern arises
(e.g., consumer group)

Agency
investigates

Agency imposes
remedy if
indicated

commercial environment. The FTC regulates the operation of markets, the FDA regulates the products sold in the markets, and the FCC regulates the means by which information about commercial opportunities is disseminated (Figure 6-3). For the Internet, these agencies focus on how things are exchanged (FTC), what things are exchanged (FDA), and the arena in which exchanges occur (FCC).

The Federal Trade Commission

As its name implies, the FTC is directly concerned with the regulation of the exchange environment. Its overarching goal is to create a smoothly operating environment for trade. To this end, the FTC works to enforce antitrust laws designed to foster competition and fair trade. In addition, the FTC enforces laws that protect the interests of consumers in the marketplace.

The FTC also has two primary nonenforcement interests. First, the FTC conducts research on the effects of trade practices on consumers and competition, and it makes the results of the research available to interested parties. As a result, the FTC can influence the development of policy, as well as its implementation. In addition, the FTC develops and provides educational programs intended to provide information for consumers and for companies about deceptive or fraudulent business practices.

Issues have arisen that reflect each of the agency's mandates. For example, the FTC has scrutinized Amazon.com's practice of using its Alexa division software to monitor users' travels through Web sites for possible privacy concerns. In addition, the agency has assessed the timeliness of eToys' shipping, and decided to file suit against Toysmart.com for attempting to sell customer data when it guaranteed that it would not. In its nonenforcement arena, the FTC has published a proposal on the applicability of the law for advertising and selling on the Internet, and commissioned research on online privacy policies.

The Food and Drug Administration

The FDA regulates products such as food, cosmetics, drugs, and medical devices. The agency's mandate is consumer protection. The FDA was formed through the Federal

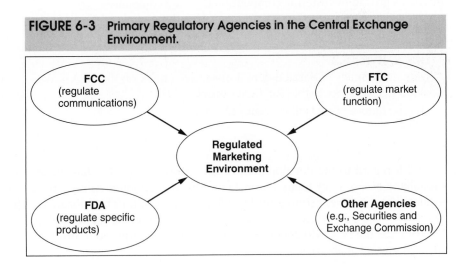

FIGURE 6-3   Primary Regulatory Agencies in the Central Exchange Environment.

Food, Drug and Cosmetic Act of 1938 to exercise oversight over the production, distribution, and sales of its focal products to insure that the products are safe, and that appropriate types and amounts of information for their safe use are available to consumers.

The oversight responsibility of the FDA extends to the way that businesses can advertise their products on the Internet. For example, the FDA can, and has, taken formal action against companies that post misleading information on their Web sites. In 1999, the FDA teamed up with the FTC in Operation Cure.All, an effort to combat fraudulent and illegal claims by online marketers of healthcare products. The FDA site includes a form with which consumers can report unlawful sales on the Internet, as well as information intended to help customers buy medical products online safely. By mid–2001, Operation Cure.All had resulted in 22 arrests, 12 product seizures, and 11 product recalls.

Although the FDA has not proposed a regulatory policy designed specifically for the Internet, its actions are consistent with the enforcement of legislation designed for print media. The multimedia nature of the Internet, however, presents the FDA with the issue of whether different types of legislation are needed.

The Federal Communications Commission

The FCC was formed in 1934 as a result of the Communications Act. The commission is responsible for regulating communications in the United States and its possessions (e.g., Puerto Rico) that are conducted via wire, radio, television, satellite, and cable. An important goal of the commission is to develop and implement regulatory programs that result in the effective coordination and operation of the different types of communications systems.

The Internet is, in many respects, a convergence of several separate communications systems. The FCC must make decisions about whether regulation would help or hinder the development of the Internet as a medium characterized by converging communications technologies. Historically, the deregulation of telephone equipment, and the absence of regulation of phone service—beyond basic service—may have spurred the Internet's growth by fostering competition between companies.

Bits & Bytes 6.2

Irate audiophiles initiated a denial-of-service attack on the RIAA Web site that made the site inaccessible for 4 days in July 2002.

(*Source: BusinessWeek* Online, August 12, 2002.)

With regard to the development of the Internet, the FCC has made the issue of broadband access a key focus. For instance, the agency conducts research to gauge the availability of different sources of broadband access in different locations. The results of research and other forms of public input are used to guide the formulation of policy. For instance, the FCC will decide whether ISPs will be required to offer access to high-speed Internet capabilities.

InSite

WEB RADIO WOES: WWW.KPIG.COM

Prior to 1995, KPIG-FM was a small, commercial radio station in Freedom, California, with an equally small—but very devoted—base of listeners. The location is a rural farming community, with a passion for pigs. KPIG used this passion to create its brand image, providing a widely varied playlist enriched with pork-related tidbits.

In 1995, KPIG became the first commercial station to simultaneously Webcast its content. The international audience grew rapidly, swelling to more than 200,000 listeners a month by mid–2002. Listeners appreciated the music mix, as well as the community-building appeal of Web-based extras, like the Swine Line (724-PORK), the Pig Squeals bulletin board, and the HamCam, giving listeners an "eye-on-the-sty" with live views of DJs at work.

The Digital Millennium Copyright Act of 1998 created a roadblock for KPIG and other Web radio stations in the United States, by requiring Webcasters to pay royalties to record companies and musicians on music broadcast—in addition to the royalties they, and their off-line counterparts, pay to songwriters and music publishers. Copyright Arbitration Royalty Panels (CARP), overseen by the Copyright Office, initially set the royalty rates, basing them on the number of songs played times the number of listeners. The first 10,000 "performances" incurred royalties of .0014 cents each, dropping to .0007 cents for each additional performance.

For KPIG, and for many other small stations without sizeable advertising revenues, the costs to Webcast were formidable. KPIG stopped its Webcasts in mid–2002, crediting the royalty costs for the halt. By late 2002, policy makers in Congress had approved a bill allowing small Webcasters to negotiate a different royalty structure, and KPIG was back on the Web. Although the debate about royalties continues and is likely to result in further changes, KPIG plays on.[1]

Applying Policy to the Internet

We can understand the effects that policy might have on aspects of marketing online by using the framework introduced in Chapter 2. Recall that in our framework, technology and policy exert an indirect influence on the central exchange environment. We can see this effect by considering the implications of the Telecommunications Act for the policy-buyer-seller triad, shown in Figure 6-4.

In 1996, Congress passed the Telecommunications Act. Because the act revamped policies pertaining to interstate communications networks, such as telephone and cable services, responsibility for implementing and enforcing the legislation fell to the FCC.

The Telecommunications Act addresses several aspects of how the Internet is likely to develop. For example, the act has as a key objective the provision of **universal service.** This means that any American who desires access to the Internet should be able to get it. In many cases, universal service is implemented by making sure that schools and libraries have access to telecommunications services. The policies associated with the

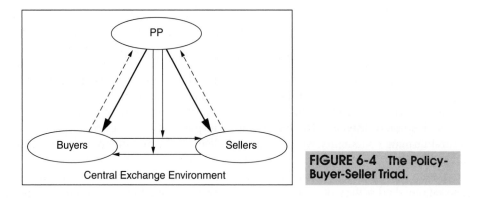

FIGURE 6-4 The Policy-Buyer-Seller Triad.

act have implications for business activity that involves the Internet. These implications extend to market function issues via the digital network of the Internet, and to consumer protection issues in Internet use.

Policy and the Central Exchange Environment

The goal of providing universal service so that everyone has access to the Internet reflects an effect of policy on the central exchange environment. The two center arrows in the Figure 6.4 reflect this effect. Widespread access to the Internet means that how people use the informational content, as in online resource exchanges, will become increasingly important for policy makers. Information-related policies may originate from either customer or business actions, and policy decisions may affect customers or businesses' behaviors directly, or the exchange environment indirectly.

One issue for policy makers is how people will use the information that is available on the Internet. Will businesses adhere to legislation that currently affects the way that product information can be presented, so that it is not misleading? If not, then the FTC and other agencies must determine whether different enforcement policies are needed for the Internet environment, or even whether entirely new regulation is indicated.

Businesses' actions that deceive or harm customers may result in investigation by a government agency. If the results of the investigation suggest that regulation is desirable, the agency may propose regulation that affects either a business directly, or the exchange environment, more generally. Similarly, consumers' use of Internet-based information may lead policy makers to assess the need for regulation. For instance, the potential exposure of children to adult-oriented material, or to controlled products (e.g., alcohol and tobacco) may lead to the imposition of regulation that restricts the manner in which these products can be offered via the Internet. These situations are represented by the arrows that originate with buyers or sellers, travel through policy makers, and back to the central exchange environment.

Universal Service and the "Digital Divide"

One concern for policy makers has been whether the Internet is a resource that is capable of creating a society of "haves" and "have-nots." That is, does the Internet provide benefits or create opportunities for users that cannot be obtained by nonusers?

The polarizing effects of the Internet, which suggest that people with access tend to be characterized by demographics such as higher income and educational attainment have created a situation termed the **digital divide.** One objective of the Telecommunications Act was to reduce the socioeconomic gap between people with access to the Internet and people without access to the Internet, by making access widely available, as in libraries and public schools.

Access Issues for Universal Service

Regulation designed to guarantee universal access must address two separate issues: access and capacity. **Access issues** focus on *who* will be able to use the Internet, while **capacity issues** focus on *how* these people will be able to use it. That is, access refers to whether a person can connect to the Internet, while capacity refers to the capability of the user's equipment to dictate the form of the information encountered by the user. These terms illustrate the concern that Internet access does not always mean full ability to use the Internet. Even if everyone has Internet access, thus implying universal service, differences in computing capacity mean that people will experience the Internet environment differently.

Bits & Bytes 6.3
In the United States, 78 percent of middle school and high school students use the Internet.
(*Source:* Pew Internet Project, 2002.)

Capacity Issues for Universal Service

Because capacity affects the computer-mediated environments in which consumers will obtain and process information—particularly for sites that rely heavily on graphics to communicate with consumers—the effects of different types of information environments on knowledge and decision behavior must be assessed prior to introducing regulatory policy. In addition, capacity issues mean that Internet regulation will have to be flexible enough to compensate for differences while still accomplishing regulatory goals.

Information Use and Internet Regulation

The issues for policy raised by capacity concerns tend to focus on how people will use information from the Internet. Information use issues fall into two categories. First, how will people's information-related behaviors be affected by the Internet? Second, how will these behaviors differ, if at all, from the behaviors typically observed in other information environments (e.g., radio and television)?

These categories are both important because policy makers have to determine whether regulating information on the Internet can be accomplished by simply transferring existing legislation, or whether entirely new policies must be developed. The task for policy makers is complicated. Even though current laws that regulate the provision of information, such as advertising, apply to the Internet, policy makers still must determine whether the Internet is more like radio, or television, or both, or neither. Different media have different restrictions, and it is not clear which restrictions are most appropriate for the Internet environment. As one former FTC Commissioner, Christine Varney, has noted, "[c]yberspace clearly represents a convergence of several technologies: telephones, broadcast media and other media. Any advertising on the Internet is subject to current law on deceptive or fraudulent advertising. But whether cyberspace should be considered more analogous to print or broadcast media remains to be seen."[2]

Understanding Internet Effects on Information Use

The wide variety and escalating amount of information available on the Internet suggests that policy makers will pay increasing attention to regulatory concerns in the environment as time goes on. At present, the Internet is relatively unrestricted. Businesses can operate proactively to recognize and curtail actions that may be harmful to customers. Failure to self-regulate effectively may lead to increased agency scrutiny and restrictive regulatory policy. Functioning proactively means that businesses have the same goals of understanding information use on the Internet as policy makers.

The Internet can influence information in several ways. For instance, the ready availability of information about a vast number of products may influence buyers' knowledge bases for product choices, including their perceptions of and attitudes toward goods and services. Because it affects the amount of information used to make decisions, this effect may lead to information overload, and perhaps to decreased decision quality.

In addition, the interactive nature of the Internet environment may influence the type of information that shoppers include in decisions. For example, being able to easily acquire jazzy graphics and animated simulations may lead a consumer to disproportionately include information about a product that is offered in this form. Alternatively, long download times for a graphically intensive Web site may cause a consumer to ignore relevant information. (Remember the eight-second rule?)

Finally, the novelty of the computer-mediated environment may influence information use by serving itself as a persuasive characteristic of a decision situation. This situation occurs when a consumer incorporates an evaluation of the computer-mediated environment into a decision about a product, even though the evaluative information is completely irrelevant. The computer-mediated environment serves as a peripheral cue that may influence the product evaluation, or even the consumer's comprehension of the product's capabilities—even when the computer-mediated environment has no informational value.

Bits & Bytes 6.4

In April 2003, the .edu domain—previously used only by 4-year colleges and universities—was expanded to include a wide range of educational organizations, including ballet schools and mortuaries.

(*Source:* Yahoo! News, February 12th, 2003.)

These potential influences of the Internet on information use are described in the table in Figure 6.5. In the table, each concern is reflected as a level in which the Internet environment interacts with information use. At Level 1, the effect of the environment is least obtrusive, meaning that observed behaviors will tend to be more similar to behaviors observed with information use in traditional media. At Level 3, the interactive environment is highly obtrusive, and behaviors are predicted to differ most from those observed in traditional media.

The policy issues associated with universal access and information use reflect proactive efforts by government agencies, such as the FCC and the FTC, respectively, to understand and avert problems before they happen. In other areas, however, problems have already surfaced. In the next section, we will consider several policy issues that influence the nature of the direct exchanges between buyers and sellers.

FIGURE 6-5   The Internet Environment Influences Information Use.

INTERNET INFLUENCE ON INFORMATION PROCESSING	DESCRIPTION	KEY LOCUS OF EFFECT	SAMPLE THEORETICAL ISSUES	POSSIBLE OUTCOMES/ BEHAVIORS
LEVEL 1 **Minimal**	Internet enables information provision, but does not influence its form or content	On *amount* of information acquired and used in decision making	Information overload; strategies for information acquisition and use	Objective decision quality may decrease, even though subjective perceptions of quality increase; frustration; decreased knowledge of key attributes
LEVEL 2 **Moderate**	Internet influences construction of form and content of information display	On *form* of information display used in decision making	Information display restructuring; information evaluation	Ignore information that takes too long to acquire/ download; develop incorrect product category knowledge
LEVEL 3 **Extensive**	Internet influences information processing as a persuasive attribute independent of form and content	On *content* of information acquired and used on decision making	Attitudes and persuasion (e.g., peripheral cues; subjective norms)	Focus on vivid but peripheral cues, with decreased message comprehension; peer pressure leads to decreased or inaccurate product knowledge

Source: Adapted from Cook, Don L., and Eloise Coupey (1998), "Consumer Behavior and Unresolved Regulatory Issues in Electronic Marketing," *Journal of Business Research,* 231–238.

Policy and Exchange Relationships in the Digital Business Environment

When situations arise in the exchange environment that create the potential for regulation, policy makers must consider several issues before deciding on the nature of regulation. First, they must evaluate the costs and benefits of regulation. Who will be harmed—and how badly—if regulation is not enacted? In addition, will the benefits of regulation that will be experienced by some segment of society, such as consumers, outweigh the potential costs of restriction to another segment (e.g., businesses)?

A second issue for policy makers is the extent to which a behavior should be regulated. For instance, too much regulation within an industry may squash innovation and decrease the appeal of the industry for potential entrants to the market, potentially reducing product variety and quality for buyers, as well as competition between sellers. On the other hand, too little regulation might place consumers and smaller companies in jeopardy, at the hands of large corporations.

Once the extent of regulation is decided, policy makers must figure out the nature and the form of the regulation. Regulatory policy is best designed when it has benefits for businesses, thus reducing enforcement and compliance hassles, as well as being readily understood by customers, thus increasing its efficacy.

The issues faced by policy makers as they decide whether to impose regulation, to remove regulation, or to do neither are summarized in Figure 6.6.

The issues in the following sections arise from the nature of the Internet as an environment for commercial exchange, and they jointly affect buyers and sellers. To simplify discussion of the issues, however, they are grouped as issues that more directly affect the well-being of consumers, and issues that more directly affect the activities of businesses.

Issues of Consumer Protection

Many of the laws and regulations that guide businesses' actions in exchange relationships with consumers are designed to address three main public policy goals: to eliminate some

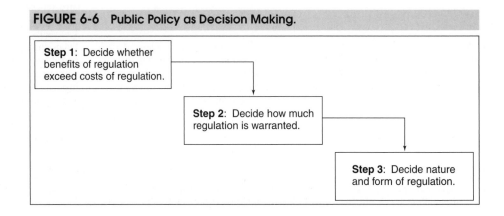

FIGURE 6-6 Public Policy as Decision Making.

Step 1: Decide whether benefits of regulation exceed costs of regulation.

Step 2: Decide how much regulation is warranted.

Step 3: Decide nature and form of regulation.

undesirable behavior, to protect some segment of society from harm, or to provide information necessary for making informed decisions. The laws and regulations currently in place were developed for businesses acting within the traditional media of print, radio, and television. Policy makers must determine how these laws apply to the Internet. Some of the difficulties in developing or extending and applying regulatory policy to the Internet can be seen by looking at concerns with advertising on the Internet, forms of online fraud, and concerns about privacy.

Advertising Regulation and the Internet

In general, as suggested by the quote from former FTC commissioner, Christine Varney, legislation for traditional media are applicable to the communications medium of the Internet. Regulation of advertising takes three forms. These forms are product regulation, audience regulation, and method regulation.

Product regulation imposes restrictions on advertisements for products that have the potential for negative effects on consumption. For instance, alcohol and tobacco products are restricted in terms of where they can be advertised, and when. Both tobacco and alcohol must include health warnings. The Cigarette Act of 1971 states that cigarette ads can be placed in print media, but not on any electronic forms of communication.

The Internet provides regulatory challenges in the way that information about regulated products can be promoted. Web sites that serve as virtual communities to promote lifestyles can be vehicles for indirect promotion of products and brands. Early examples of these sites included Budweiser's online radio, KBUD, and an entertainment guide site, Circuit Breaker, sponsored by the company that manufactures Lucky Strike cigarettes. Visitors to the Circuit Breaker site who noted they were smokers in their registrations were sent free, promotional tee-shirts.[3]

Audience regulation has a goal of protecting vulnerable consumers, such as children. While much of the regulation is self-regulation, voluntarily undertaken by the advertising industry, legislation does exist that regulates when certain types of ads can be aired on broadcast media to reduce children's exposure. In addition, regulation restricts the amount of advertising that can occur on television shows directed at children.

How do these regulations apply to the Internet? The Internet is not a typical broadcast medium. Its content can be accessed at any time. In addition, the Internet is not a passive medium, like radio and television. The audience interacts with the medium, collecting information and determining the amount and timing of exposure to Internet content. As a result, the time-based restrictions for traditional media do not transfer well to the Internet.

These issues are illustrated by Web sites that operate as branded environments. **Branded environments** provide entertainment and information linked to merchandise. For instance, a site produced for child visitors might contain product spokescharacters that interact with kids, and online games and activities designed to keep visitors in the site. Policy makers face the challenge of determining which forms of interaction are appropriate, communicating the guidelines and restrictions, and enforcing the regulations.

Method regulation is focused primarily on the prevention of deceptive advertising practices. For example, marketers may not lie about the quality or performance of their products. This restriction applies quite straightforwardly to the Internet.

A concern arises, however, with how to enforce the regulation. The ease with which a business can post information, and change posted information, accompanied by the vast amount of information on the Internet, makes enforcement by federal agencies a mountainous task.

Another issue related to deceptive advertising is based on communications that do not explicitly make false statements, but which have as a result the creation of an inaccurate perception or belief by the consumer. As with more extreme forms of deception, the intent of existing legislation applies readily to the Internet. Of concern, however, is whether the nature of the Internet medium can contribute to the formation of incorrect beliefs.

The way that search engines may list results illustrates this issue. When consumers look at search engine results, a reasonable conclusion is that results with higher rankings have more relevant content. On several search engines, however, rankings—or even simply getting included in the search—can be purchased. The process by which a site or URL can pay for placement or inclusion is called **paid placement.** Search engines often list results with paid rankings as "Featured Sites," or "Recommended Listings." Because some consumers may incorrectly believe that these listings reflect relevancy, the FTC has advised search engine companies that they must indicate whether they practice paid placement.

Fraud and the Internet: Online Transactions of Goods, Services, and Money

Concerns with how to regulate the way marketers advertise their wares have increased as reports of fraud on the Internet have escalated. The National Consumers League has tracked reports of fraud related to Internet exchanges since 1996. They note a consistent increase in reported frauds over the years. The top five reported frauds in the first half of 2002 were auctions (87 percent), general merchandise (7 percent), Nigerian money offers[4] (5 percent), computing equipment/software (1 percent), and work-at-home offers (.5 percent). The amount of reported losses totaled $7,209,196, with an average loss of $484 per victim. The chart in Figure 6-7 shows the percentage of victims by age.

Most of the reported frauds originated when consumers obtained the initial information about the exchange opportunity from a Web site (92 percent). Far smaller percentages of fraud stemmed from initial e-mail contact. Keep in mind that these statistics may reflect only a fraction of actual online fraud incidents; some people may just take their losses without taking any action. It is also important to note that the reported incidents cannot always be verified. As a result, these numbers may be very low, relative to actual instances of fraud, and the reported instances may overestimate the occurrence of fraud. Difficulties in obtaining accurate figures of problems are faced by agencies, such as the FTC, who often use information from consumer groups to determine whether to initiate regulatory reviews of individuals, companies, or industries.

The global nature of the Internet contributes to the difficulty in tracking online fraud. Agencies in 17 countries created the econsumer.gov Web site to encourage consumers to report commerce-related fraud that crosses national boundaries. Complaints may be filed online, and the material consumers provide is added to

FIGURE 6-7 Older and Younger Consumers: Fewer Victims, or Fewer Reports?

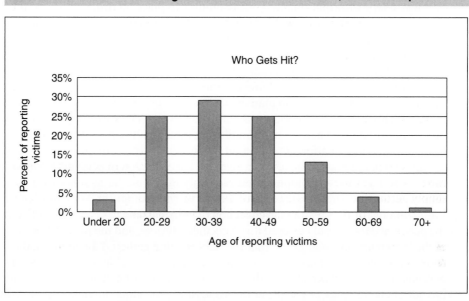

a database maintained by the FTC. The agencies that represent member countries may use the database to track fraud trends and companies with unsavory practices. There is no guarantee for the complainant, however, that a complaint will be addressed at the individual level.

Fraud and the Internet: Manipulating Behavior

Online fraud is not limited to purchases. The Internet makes possible unique forms of fraudulent activity, including **pagejacking** and **mousetrapping.** Pagejacking occurs when a consumer is diverted from an intended Web site to a Web site masquerading under a misleading meta tag. A **meta tag** is the hidden text on a Web page that tells a search engine what the contents of a Web page are, and how to index them. Once in the unintended site, a visitor can be "mousetrapped," unable to get out of the site with browser commands (e.g., "Back," "Forward," or "Close"). Pagejacking and mousetrapping are used for several reasons. Pagejacking can increase visitor numbers so that advertisers are willing to pay more for banners on a site. In addition, the pagejacking site may be paid by advertisers for each visitor to the site. Similarly, a mousetrapped consumer may be exposed to multiple advertisements during efforts to get out of the site. The site owner may be paid by advertisers for ad exposure.

These types of practices can be lucrative. In October 2001, the FTC won a case against a site developer who registered domain names using common misspellings of popular names. Visitors who mistakenly entered one of these sites were mousetrapped and bombarded with advertisements. The site developer was ordered to pay nearly $1.9 million back to his victims, partially offsetting the estimated $800,000 to $1,000,000 a year he received from advertisers.

Protecting Consumer Privacy

When you type information into your computer to place an order, and send it to a Web site, how do you know who will have access to that information? When you browse the Internet, looking for a perfect gift for Mother's Day, how do you know whether your search has been electronically watched? These concerns are related to the more general issue of privacy on the Internet.

Many organizations collect information about us on a routine basis. For example, Internet service providers who manage user accounts gather personal data. Companies from which we purchase goods and services also collect various types of consumer profile information. When we use e-mail on company networks, systems administrators have access to information about e-mail traffic, and to the content.

In the United States, public policy restricts the collection of personal information and the creation and use of computerized files only in the public sector—for government-related activities. The Privacy Act of 1974 and the Computer Matching and Privacy Protection Act of 1988 restrict the collection of personal data in several ways. For instance, the personal data can only be used for a specified purpose, and the person who is the focus of the data must be made aware that the data is being gathered. In addition, the government is not allowed to make the personal information available to anyone else. This type of regulation makes it possible for the government to collect and analyze information that provides benefits to society, while at the same time protecting the rights of the individual. The U.S. Census is an example of public sector collection of personal data.

To illustrate the reason for concern, suppose that you subscribe to an online health information service. To access the service, you type in an identifying password that can be linked back to your registration information. While you are searching for information about health-related topics of interest to you, a record is made of the areas of the Web site that you visit. This record is known as a **clickstream.** Who might be interested in acquiring this information from the health site? An insurance company might benefit from information about you as a potential policyholder that indicates whether there are health problems that might make you a poor insurance risk. In addition, an employer could make use of private, personal health information to decide whether to hire you. These situations, though extreme, underscore the reason for concern about Internet privacy.

Internet technology can be used to track users' search behaviors and preferences for a variety of reasons. Not all of the uses of tracking technologies threaten privacy. For example, cookies are often used to facilitate communication between a user and a Web server. A **cookie** is information in a text file that is sent to the user's browser (e.g., Netscape) by a Web server. The cookie can be used to store information, such as a user's registration and password for a particular site. The Web server can then read back this information when the user wants to return to that particular site. The user benefits by not having to retype all of the identifying information. Cookies can be used for online ordering systems, to remember what items a customer has selected. They can also be used to provide customized site displays (e.g., just news and sports scores from MSNBC.com). Businesses also use cookies to track how many unique visitors have been to a particular Web site.

The information obtained from cookies can provide companies with information about customers' habits and preferences, including which ads a user is exposed to, and which ads a user acts on (i.e., **click-through**). This information enables businesses to tailor promotional information. In some cases, however, there is the potential for

'Net Knowledge

CRUMBLING COOKIES

While some cookies can be useful, providing marketers with information used to customize and personalize content just for you, others can result in annoying intrusions on your privacy. Fortunately, it's easy to control which cookies you want to allow on your computer, and which you want to keep out.

The major browsers, Netscape and Internet Explorer, both provide information about cookies and their potential effect on your privacy. They also let you examine the cookies stored on your computer, and customize your management of cookies.

If you use Netscape, cookie management capabilities are on the Edit menu, under Preferences. The Privacy and Security option lets you choose Cookies, under which you can select your cookie acceptance policy. Not sure what the right policy is? The browser also provides information about privacy, and lets you see what cookies are currently lurking on your hard disk. In addition, you can get detailed information about the cookie, including the name of the cookie and its expiration date, as well as the domain to which it provides information.

With Internet Explorer, cookie control is found on the View menu, under Privacy Report. You can choose to block all cookies or no cookies, or you can deal with them on a one-by-one basis. It's also possible to import a privacy file that lets you customize your own cookie policy. After assessing the situation, implement your policy using the Settings option.

abuse. Information believed by consumers to be confidential may be transmitted to other vendors, or made available for uses unanticipated by the consumer. Internet users can disable cookies, but in many cases they may not be aware that cookies exist, or have the technical knowledge to change the browser settings to disable them.

The FTC investigates situations in which violations of privacy may have occurred, or in which they have the potential to occur. In 1998, the **Children's Online Privacy Protection Act (COPPA)** was passed. The law, which went into effect in April 2000, requires Web sites that obtain information from children to follow a set of rules vetted by the FTC. These rules require sites to obtain parental permission before transferring information obtained from or about a minor to a third party. In addition, children's sites must post privacy notices, and allow parents to prohibit the sale of personal information about a minor that was obtained for internal company use. The law mandates a fine of $11,000 per violation.

With regard to protecting the privacy of adults, the FTC has taken a watch-and-wait approach, focusing on investigation and observation. Their policy has, in effect, been to maintain the *status quo* of no regulation, letting companies and industries devise their own standards for privacy. A study commissioned by the FTC and released in May 2000, indicated that of sites with more than 39,000 unique visitors a month, only 20 percent protected consumers' privacy. The FTC recommended to Congress that privacy legislation be adopted. Until legislation is passed, companies must develop effective forms of self-regulation to protect consumers.

Bits & Bytes 6.5
The FTC notes that most of the top 100 online companies state their privacy policies on their sites.
(*Source:* www.ftc.gov)

Privacy and Self-Regulation

Our economic system operates under the fundamental economic premise that businesses should be allowed to grow and operate as freely as possible. This concept, known as a *laissez-faire* approach, translates literally from French as "to let do." Putting the concept in action translates functionally into the idea that fewer restrictions on the way that companies do business will result in a healthy, strong economy.

Internet self-regulation has been a key force in efforts to reassure consumers that their privacy is protected. Companies issue privacy statements that outline how they will use information provided by consumers. In addition, organizations such as the Better Business Bureau Online (BBBO) and TRUSTe act as digital "seals of approval" to increase consumers' confidence in online exchanges of information (Figure 6-8).

The TRUSTe program is a nonprofit organization that reviews the privacy statements of participating companies to insure that they meet goals of disclosure and informed consent. Companies are required to make available to site visitors a privacy statement that explains what information will be collected, how it will be used, and to whom the information will be available. Companies whose privacy statements meet the TRUSTe criteria can post the TRUSTe approval on their sites. When companies widely accept voluntary review processes of organizations like TRUSTe,

FIGURE 6-8 **The Better Business Bureau Online Issues Site Seals to Reassure Consumers About the Privacy and Security of Online Exchanges with BBBO-approved Companies.**

they effectively create a standard for behavior that benefits businesses as well as consumers.

A different approach to self-regulation is illustrated by the development of technologies that enable Web users to determine whether a site's privacy policy is adequate. For example, the **Platform for Privacy Preferences (P3P)** is a software agent that is stored on the user's computer. When the user goes to a Web site using an application that has the P3P capabilities, the agent scans the site's privacy policy and provides the user with information about the site's privacy policies. As Figure 6-9 illustrates, installing the P3P capability is straightforward.

One reason to adopt self-regulatory practices is often to forestall government regulation. In the case of privacy, companies may face a difficult task of reengineering information systems to meet data management requirements that could be imposed with legislation. For instance, companies could be required to provide **subject access.** The concept of subject access is not new; introduced to public policy with the Fair Credit Reporting Act (1970), subject access means that any person for whom personal information is amassed has the right to examine the information. Given the amounts of information that may have accumulated in online databases, however, the challenge of figuring out how to reconfigure information systems to enable subject access is a daunting one for many companies.

Issues of Market Function

From businesses' perspective, three policy issues of strong interest are taxation, liability, and copyright. For taxation, we will consider the issues related to whether, and how, Internet purchases should be taxed. For liability, we will examine several issues that

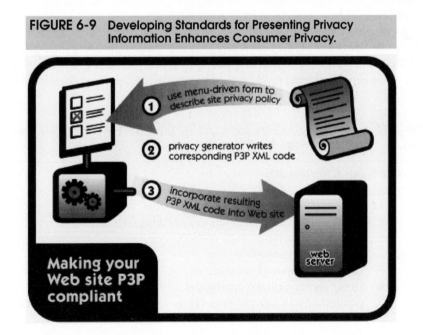

FIGURE 6-9 Developing Standards for Presenting Privacy Information Enhances Consumer Privacy.

1. use menu-driven form to describe site privacy policy
2. privacy generator writes corresponding P3P XML code
3. incorporate resulting P3P XML code into Web site

web server

Making your Web site P3P compliant

focus on the marketer's responsibility in Internet-based exchanges. For copyright, we will look at concerns created for marketers by the digital nature of the Internet.

Taxation

Policy on taxation in the business environment of the Internet involves business taxes and sales taxes. **Business activity taxes** are assessed on companies in accordance with the tax policies of the company's location: a cost of doing business. **Sales and use taxes** are assessed on customers' purchases according to the shopper's location.

For the Internet, tax policy is complicated in both situations, but for the same reason. The key question faced by policy makers is "Where is the company located?" Is a virtual presence, as at the end-user's desktop computer, the same as a physical presence in the downtown shopping center? How the question is answered often depends on who is providing the response.

Business Activity Taxes   When a company opens a store in a local shopping mall, the company is required to pay the business taxes appropriate for the locale. This may include taxes for the town or city, as well as for the county and state. If the company opens another location, taxes must be paid in that new location, in addition to the taxes for the first location.

Now, what happens if the company opens a virtual storefront in an online mall? Off-line marketers have argued that online merchants should be taxed as if the business had a physical presence, or **nexus,** at the point of online presence. Carried to an extreme, this means that an online marketer would have "stores" at every unique location from which its Web site was accessed! Taking the other extreme, some online vendors have argued that they do not fall within taxation guidelines; hence, they should be exempt from the tax regulations that apply to marketers in traditional environments. Legal scholars have outlined a physical presence nexus test to guide the determination of tax jurisdiction. The bases for physical presence are presented in Figure 6-10. Note that any one of these bases could be used by a state to establish a tax nexus for a company.

For policy makers, developing policy on taxation means balancing the need to keep the fledgling Internet economy growing, while upholding the rights of marketers in the traditional, off-line marketplace. Remember that one goal of market-related policy is to keep the playing field fair and competitive? One concern with the absence of a

---

FIGURE 6-10   Businesses Should Carefully Consider Tax Implications of Business Activities.

What Builds A Tax Nexus?

In the taxing state. . .
1. Renting office or warehouse space
2. Holding or attending trade shows and taking sales orders
3. Using a Web server
4. Maintaining an inventory
5. Licensing software to licensees
6. Hiring agents, including contractors
7. Conducting activities that promote the name, market share, or customer relations

uniformly applied tax policy is that it potentially creates an unfair competitive advantage for companies who conduct their transactions online. Going back to our policy-buyer-seller triad of Figure 6.4, we can see how a situation in which off-line businesses' complaints of unfairness could lead to the imposition of tax policy that in turn affects the buyer-seller exchange environment.

Sales/Use taxes   The topic of whether Internet purchases should be taxed in the same manner as off-line purchases is of interest to customers, as well as to competitors. For many shoppers, buying products from the Internet is a better option than buying off-line, because tax policy for the Internet is sufficiently murky that often no taxes are levied. For businesses, keeping the Internet free from tax policies applied to off-line transactions means that online retailers have an implicit competitive advantage, in terms of price. Of course, as online sales grow in number and amount, states face the prospect of losing increasing amounts of tax revenue.

States' tax revenues from transactions take one of two forms. A *sales tax* is applied at the point of purchase, based on the amount of purchase. It is collected by the seller. In contrast, a *use tax* may be levied when a consumer makes a purchase out-of-state for consumption within her home state. Use taxes are self-assessed. Not surprisingly, they are rarely paid.

The nature of the Internet creates problems for determining how sales/use tax policy should be applied. States pass their own tax laws, as do locales within states. This means that there are over 30,000 separate tax jurisdictions in the United States. At a minimum, transactions that occur within a state are subject to the tax laws of that state. For the Internet, however, which tax law applies? The law of the state in which the customer lives? The law of the state in which the home office of the vendor is located? Or the law of the state from which the order was processed and shipped?

For situations in which the online transaction is between a vendor and a customer in the same state, the state tax laws apply. A common practice for Internet vendors is to tell customers to add on the appropriate tax percentage if the purchase will be delivered within the state. Some off-line businesses have argued, however, that all purchases should be taxed at the appropriate rate of the state in which they are delivered, regardless of the source of the product or the location of the company. Countering this, some online businesses have taken the position that the state laws of the customer do not apply. In this approach, the delivery is characterized as simply a post-transaction transfer of the product, rather than the actual transaction phase of the exchange process.

Another issue for tax policy on transactions is whether the online vendor should be *responsible* for collecting the appropriate taxes for the state to which the product will be delivered, similar to physical marketplace vendors. Online businesses have operated in a manner more like catalog merchants; in general, customers are entrusted with the responsibility for determining the appropriate tax amount, and including it with payment. Off-line businesses that feel that this practice creates an unfair advantage for online businesses would like to see regulation enacted that would require the online vendors to collect the sales tax.

These are complicated issues, and there is no reason to believe that a regulatory solution will be any different. The Advisory Committee on Electronic Commerce, created by the Internet Tax Freedom Act of 1998, provided a report to Congress in March 2000 that grappled with some of the issues. The committee members recommended a permanent ban of taxes on Internet access, and an extension of an existing moratorium on new Internet taxes. In November 2001, President Bush signed legislation extending the moratorium until November 2003.

The moratorium does not limit the ability of local jurisdictions to apply existing taxes to Internet sales. Of concern for digital businesses is how to actually implement the calculation of taxes, given the wide variety of different tax structures. Tax collection software, like Velosant's Taxware Sales/Use Tax System, can automate the tax process (Figure 6-11). The software calculates the tax, based on the mailing or billing address, provides the customer with the charge, and forwards the tax information to the appropriate tax authority—all in real time, without slowing down the transaction or burdening the vendor.

Liability and Jurisdiction

The geographic vagueness of the Internet does not limit confusion to tax policy. It also influences policy-related concerns about businesses' **liability.** For example, if a customer purchases a product through the Internet, and the product is unsatisfactory or causes harm, where does the customer turn? The Internet creates an issue of **jurisdiction.** In a legal sense, jurisdiction refers to the authority of a court to hear a case. Suppose that the customer decides to take legal action. Similar to the concern for company location in taxation, the issue is where the business is located. Does a virtual presence mean the same thing as a physical presence? Is the seller liable wherever the buyer is, or in the place of the corporate headquarters?

For digital businesses, jurisdiction may be determined by whether the company's online presence is intended to serve the market in a particular state. This intention is reflected by the nature of the Web site. Sites can be **passive sites,** simply providing information about a company and its products that could be accessed by anyone, anywhere. Alternatively, sites can be **interactive sites,** actively soliciting business. Precedent-setting court cases have ruled that a passive site is not sufficient to confer jurisdiction of one state over an e-business in another state.[5]

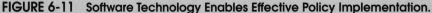

FIGURE 6-11 Software Technology Enables Effective Policy Implementation.

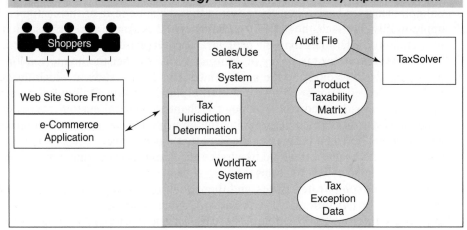

Source: Reproduced with permission of Velosant, LP. Copyright 2003. All rights reserved.

A company can attempt to influence jurisdiction if a lawsuit is filed against it. Many Web sites contain information about their terms of use, including legal notices, privacy policy, and a **forum selection clause.** This clause specifies a location intended to determine jurisdiction for legal actions. Information about the forum selection, as well as other site use agreements, is typically provided through links at the bottom of the site's home page.

Another set of policy issues related to liability concerns businesses' responsibility for verifying customer information. For instance, is a company responsible for the harm done to someone who misrepresents himself to obtain a restricted product, such as an underage consumer? On the Internet, it can be difficult to verify the age or identity of a customer. In a face-to-face exchange, the seller can assess the age of a prospective buyer. In addition, identity can be checked by requesting a driver's license, photo identification, or by matching a signature on a charge slip to the signature on the credit card.

In the digital business environment, these protections are not available to companies. Even when a business adheres to the regulations that guide sales of any product, verification is difficult. This difficulty facilitates online credit card fraud by consumers, estimated at $400 million in 1999. Credit card fraud is particularly pronounced for products that can be consumed directly from the Internet, such as software, reaching rates as high as 30 percent.[6]

Businesses can use fraud detection systems to combat credit card fraud. For instance, neural network systems compare stored profiles of fraudulent transactions with new transactions to determine the apparent legitimacy of the transactions. Because these programs can cost many thousands of dollars, however, they are used by fewer than 5 percent of online sales sites. Online businesses use low-tech methods to verify transaction authority, such as checking the e-mail, phone, and home address provided by a customer.

Protecting Proprietary Property in a Digital Medium

A third issue for policy makers and businesses is that of how to protect their proprietary material in the Internet environment. Businesses invest time, money, and effort in the development of products and services, and in promoting them, as through developing company name recognition and brand equity. The digital nature of the Internet makes it possible for companies to provide products and information that can be digitized, such as software, music, and books, through Web sites. In addition, many processes for creating off-line or online products are digitized, such as software to publish e-books and to develop inventory database capabilities. Finally, aspects of promotion such as trademarks, service marks, and trade dress may also be digitized to provide a business with an online presence.

The same characteristics that make it possible to become digital, however, also make easy the unauthorized reproduction and use of the digital product, process, or promotional feature. As a result, an important area of policy for marketers is that of **digital rights management (DRM).** Digital rights management refers to the processes and systems that are used to protect intellectual and creative property that can be presented in a digital form. Rights can be legal or transactional in nature. A **legal right** is obtained by either an inherent copyright—you wrote it, it's yours—or through a procedure, like applying for a patent or a trademark. A **transactional right** is obtained when ownership is transferred, as with selling a screenplay to a movie studio.

Although rights management laws developed to protect the creators of similar products in off-line contexts apply to the Internet, policy makers are faced with the need to determine how best to enforce the laws in the digital business environment.

As we saw in the Napster case at the beginning of the chapter, concerns raised by businesses in the music industry illustrate the challenges that Internet technologies pose for copyright enforcement. For example, **MP3** is a technology that enables digitized music to be stored in a format that compresses it to a small fraction of its initial, digitized size. This compression technique facilitates the ability to store and transfer music on the Internet—a capability refined by Napster and rapidly adopted by millions of music fans. Organizations that provide MP3 files or that make it possible to obtain MP3 files through their Internet systems have been sued by the Recording Industry Association of America (RIAA), on the basis that the copyrights held by record labels are violated when pirated music is made available free of charge. The resolution of these lawsuits will create precedents for the development and application of regulatory policy on copyright and intellectual property.

Important legislation for rights management was enacted under the **Digital Millennium Copyright Act of 1998.** The act protects digital rights by prohibiting the making and selling of products or services that can be used to circumvent technologies that protect copyrighted material. The act also provides a "safe harbor" for Internet Service Providers (ISPs). The "safe harbor" clause protects ISPs from liability for copyright infringement if subscribers use the ISP service to get or swap copyrighted materials.

Bits & Bytes 6.6

The longest domain name on the Web:
www.tax.taxadvice.taxation.irs.taxservices.taxrepresentation.taxpayerhelp.internalrevenueservice.audit.taxes.com.

(*Source:* www.inktomi.com/webmap/.)

Internet Legislation

The major regulatory activities that have affected the online exchange environment between buyers and sellers are summarized in Figure 6-12. As you can see, policy that specifically focuses on the Internet is both relatively recent and scarce. Reasons for the dearth of Internet legislation include the newness of the medium for business activity, and the expectation that existing legislation will address many situations that arise in the digital business environment. Government agencies have tended to take a wait-and-see approach, emphasizing the importance of industry self-regulation.

CHAPTER SUMMARY

Issues of public policy for the Internet tend to raise more questions than can be answered with a simple attempt to apply existing policy to the digital business environment. The number of unanswered questions about whether and how to regulate business on the Internet suggests that an emphasis on policy will be an active force in the development of the central exchange environment for the foreseeable future.

FIGURE 6-12   A Timeline of Regulatory Policy for the Internet.

Legislation	Description
Electronic Signatures in Global and National Commerce Act 2000	Gives electronic signatures same legal standing as handwritten signatures. Recognizes e-commerce as legally binding.
Electronic Funds Transfer Act 1999	Prohibits providing inaccurate or insufficient information in an electronic funds transfer.
Anticybersquatting Consumer Protection Act 1999	Protects registered trademark holder from domain name piracy.
Children's Online Privacy Protection Act 1998 (Effective April 2000)	Regulates collection and use of personal information from and about children.
Digital Millenium Copyright Act 1998	Establishes ISPs as "safe harbors;" prohibits technologies designed to circumvent copyrights.
No Electronic Theft Act 1997	Establishes copyright infringement liability — without economic gain — for value greater than $2500.
Telecommunications Act 1996	Mandates universal access for schools and libraries; deregulates aspects of competition between telecommunications providers.
Electronic Communications Privacy Act 1986	Defines limits to interception of electronic communications.

One way to understand what issues might provoke the attention of policy makers is to consider the nature of the agencies responsible for developing and enforcing Internet-related policy in the United States. To this end, we looked at the role of the Federal Trade Commission (FTC), the Food and Drug Administration (FDA), and the Federal Communications Commission (FCC) in developing the policies that regulate the digital business environment.

Another means by which we can anticipate future regulatory action is by understanding the forces that guided policy development in the past, and by comparing them to forces that characterize the present environment of interest. A brief overview of the sources of policy was presented to illustrate a shared and persistent emphasis on the importance of maintaining an equitable balance between a competitive environment for businesses, and a safe, yet fulfilling, environment for consumer activity. The interests of the FCC and the FTC were examined in terms of the policy issues of universal access and information use, respectively.

The process of developing policy for the digital business environment of the Internet was described as a series of three steps: weighing the costs and benefits of regulation, determining the extent of regulation, and deciding the form of the regulation. These issues were used as the implicit basis for considering several issues for Internet-related policy. Among the issues covered were topics of consumer protection, including advertising, privacy, and fraud. In addition, issues related to market function and the competitive environment were addressed, including taxation and liability, and the role of jurisdiction. Attention was also focused on the issues associated with digital rights management, and the protection of a company's intellectual property and investments.

CONTENT MANAGEMENT

USEFUL TERMS

- access issues
- audience regulation
- branded environments
- business activity taxes
- capacity issues
- clickstream
- click-through
- cookie
- Children's Online Privacy Protection Act (COPPA)
- digital divide
- Digital Millennium Copyright Act of 1998
- digital rights management (DRM)

- forum selection clause
- interactive sites
- intergovernmental organizations (IGOs)
- jurisdiction
- *laissez-faire*
- legal right
- liability
- meta tag
- method regulation
- mousetrapping
- MP3
- nexus

- non-governmental organizations (NGOs)
- Platform for Privacy Preferences (P3P)
- pagejacking
- paid placement
- passive sites
- product regulation
- public policy
- sales and use taxes
- subject access
- transactional right
- universal service

REVIEW QUESTIONS

1. What is the role of public policy in the Internet environment?
2. What are the main sources of policy for the Internet?
3. Describe the basic mandates of the FTC, FDA, and FCC.
4. Explain the *laissez-faire* approach to regulating businesses and the implication of this approach for the nature and development of Internet-related policy.
5. Discuss the difficulties of market regulation. Specifically address the balancing act of promoting consumer protection and fair competition.
6. What issues did the Telecommunications Act address?
7. What is the digital divide?
8. How does the Internet influence information use?
9. How can public policy be characterized as decision making?
10. What specific problem faced by policy makers makes taxation in the Internet environment a complicated issue?
11. What are the three forms of advertising regulation?
12. How are cookies used?
13. What approach has the FTC taken with respect to privacy protection?
14. How does the TRUSTe program increase consumer confidence in online information exchanges?

WEB APPLICATION

The Path of Policy

It's hard to predict the future, but businesses need to prepare for possible changes to regulatory and legislative policies that may affect their business activities. In many cases, the best predictor of what's likely to happen in the future is what has happened in the past.

Applied to Internet policy, this means that areas that have received disproportionate attention by policy-setting entities may continue to be the focus of attention in the future.

For instance, privacy — particularly where kids are concerned — is a mainstay of policy focus. In addition, fraud and tax issues crop up frequently.

You can get a better idea of the trends and issues before government lawmakers by tracking the progress of legislation introduced to Congress. One site that lists pending and approved legislation, making it easy to see what's happening, is maintained by the Center for Democratic Technology, an organization that reflects the relationship between policy makers and technology developers.

1. Go to the legislation section of the CDT site, at www.cdt.org/legislation/.

Note that legislation is organized by topic, such as "junk mail," "domain names," and "privacy."

2. Choose three topics. Now, go to each topic and take a look at the path of policy. Which areas showed the earliest signs of legislative interest?

Look at each session of Congress available for that topic. In which area/s does legislation appear to move most rapidly? Most slowly? What are some plausible explanations for the rate of passage?

Legislative policy issues are often influenced by the characteristics of the administration (i.e., the power held by Republicans or Democrats in Congress, and the presidency). Compare the types and rates of legislation introduced under the Democratic, Clinton administration (through 2000) and under the Republican, Bush administration (2000 to present). What differences do you see? What do these differences suggest for digital business activity?

CONCEPTS IN BRIEF

1. Policy that guides and governs the development and functioning of the Internet comes from several sources, including government agencies and nongovernmental organizations.
2. Regulatory policies of the United States are carried out by federal agencies, like the FTC and FDA.
3. For commercial activity, public policy exists to maintain a balance between buyers' rights and sellers' rights.
4. For the commercial environment of the Internet, public policy exerts an influence on the activities of consumers, businesses, and the central exchange environment.
5. The Telecommunications Act of 1996 mandated universal service, affecting the exchange environment by broadening access to the Internet and reducing the "digital divide."
6. Policy can be proactive, as with efforts to educate consumers about the ways in which the Internet may affect aspects of information use.
7. Major areas of consumer protection with regard to the Internet include privacy and advertising, as well as various forms of online fraud.
8. The Internet poses challenges to policy in that existing regulations may not transfer easily to the new medium, and because the digital medium creates novel policy situations.
9. For businesses, policy issues include the challenges of self-regulation, as with privacy policy, as well as concerns about taxation, liability, and digital rights management.
10. The global scope of the Internet, combined with the technological capability to reproduce and distribute perfect copies of original creations, poses huge challenges to managing digital rights.

THINKING POINTS

1. Suppose that no policy-making agencies monitored or regulated the Internet. What are some of the implications of a completely uncontrolled environment for businesses and for their customers?

How might the effects of an unregulated digital business environment differ from the likely effects of an unregulated marketplace?

2. The Telecommunications Act was written, in part, to attempt to reduce the digital divide. Will legislation that mandates access to the Internet be sufficient to reduce the chasm? Why, or why not?

3. What characteristics of the Internet environment may affect the way that people acquire and use information?

4. Are the policy concerns raised by the Internet as a source of information different from information-related concerns in other business environments? If so, how are they different? What implications do the differences have for the way that companies present information in the online environment?

5. Internet influences on information processing range from minimal to extensive. Consider the ways in which the extent of the Internet's effect on information processing might be related to the type of product (or, more generally, resource) that is being examined.

6. What characteristics do the policy concerns of taxation and liability share, with regard to the Internet?

7. What are the pros and cons for businesses that are associated with different forms of possible tax regulation? Of liability regulation?

8. What are the costs and benefits that policy makers must consider in determining whether business activity on the Internet should be regulated to protect consumers' privacy?

ENDNOTES

1. Sources include www.KPIG.com, washingtonpost.com, ZDNetUK News, and techTV.com.

2. Quoted in *The Los Angeles Times*, Business Section, page 1, May 21, 1995.

3. Both companies have removed these sites from the Web.

4. The Nigerian money offer typically takes the form of an e-mail, in which the author claims to be a Nigerian civil servant who needs to get a large sum of money out of the country. The sender requests the recipient's help, as an overseas partner, with a bank account to which the monies can be transferred. When the recipient provides his or her bank account number to effect the transfer, the money in the account is stolen. Other versions of the scam exist, but the outcomes are similar—people lose their money.

5. For example, *Bensusan Restaurant Corporation v. King*, 126 F.3d 25 (2d. Cir. 1997), as discussed in *Cyberlaw*, by Ferrera, Lichtenstein, Reder, August, and Schiano. Thomson Learning, 2001.

6. Data reported in *PC Week Online*, December 13, 1999, citing research by Meridien Research, Inc.

SUGGESTED READINGS

1. "Privacy, Surveillance, and Cookies," by Larry R. Leibrock. In *Electronic Marketing and the Consumer*, edited by Robert A. Peterson (Sage Publications, Inc.: Thousand Oaks, CA, 1997).

2. "Interview with Christine Varney," with D. C. Denison. In *World Wide Web Journal, 2,* 3 (Summer), 1997.

3. "Privacy in the Digital Economy," by Don Tapscott. In *The Digital Economy* (McGraw-Hill, Inc.: New York, 1995, pages 271–284).

4. "Universal Service and the Telecommunications Act: Myth Made Law," by Milton Mueller. *Communications of the ACM, 40,* 3 (1997), pages 39–48.

5. "Avoiding Misuse of New Information Technologies: Legal and Societal Considerations," by Paul N. Bloom, George R. Milne, and Robert Adler. *Journal of Marketing,* 58 (January 1994), pages 98–110.

LEARNING LINKS

Government Agencies with Internet Function Oversight

www.ftc.gov
www.fda.gov
www.sec.gov
www.fcc.gov

Intergovernmental Organization (IGO) Links

www.eConsumer.gov
europa.eu.int

www.inta.org
www.oas.org

Nongovernmental Organization (NGO) Links

www.w3.org
www.isoc.org
www.isoc.org/internet/law/trade.shtml#e-com
(for international law issues)
www.cdt.org

Integrating the Perspectives

The Digital Business in Context

In the first two sections, we considered characteristics of the Internet environment, and of the different perspectives of people engaged in exchange-related activities in the environment. In this section, we put the parts together, integrating the Internet environment with aspects of business activity, in order to understand how the nature of the Internet influences strategic business thinking. This section is intended to provide a general characterization of the impact of the Internet on aspects of the commercial environment, and on business activity within this environment. As such, it serves as the basis for more focused discussion in subsequent chapters.

In Chapter 7, we examine the nature of the Internet as an environment for business. We use **population ecology,** a biological theory developed to explain the growth of groups of organisms—like companies and industries—to describe aspects of competition and cooperation for digital business.

In Chapter 8, we build on the theoretical basis of population ecology to consider ways in which the Internet affects the strategic business activities that companies undertake to obtain a competitive advantage. For example, the Internet creates opportunities for new goods and services, as well as new business models for selling them. Aspects of these models are discussed.

7

The Evolution of Digital Business

Focus and Objectives

In this chapter we examine the impact of the Internet on business goals and activities. We use a theoretical perspective called *population ecology* to provide a basis for discussing the influence of the Internet on business. Concepts from population ecology are used to describe competitive and cooperative behaviors. We also consider ways in which businesses structure their organizations and activities to promote effective competition in the digital business environment.

Your objectives in studying this chapter include the following:

- Recognize the key forces that drive change in the digital business environment.
- Understand the application of population ecology to business in the Internet environment.
- Identify the major strategies for competing in a product-market.
- Identify the primary characteristics of the Internet ecology.
- Understand the Internet's potential for influencing value chain activities and market structures.

A Toy Story

Kids like toys. Parents like convenience — and happy kids. eToys combined these elements to create the world's first online toy store, started in 1997. The idea was simple. Use the Internet to provide a huge array of toys for purchase in a helpful and hassle-free manner, any time, delivered to your door.

The idea caught on quickly, aided by aggressive marketing to the "mom" demographic to create brand awareness. eToys used nationwide advertising

---

169

campaigns on television and in print media that highlighted the ability to shop pleasantly and peacefully from home. Strategic agreements with AOL, The Gap, Rosie O'Donnell, and Visa also gave eToys lots of visibility.

The concept of an online toy store appealed to investors, as well as parents. Venture capitalists poured millions into the company, and the initial public offering (IPO) in 1999 added to the company's coffers. In the first day of trading, eToys shares were offered at $20, but rose rapidly to nearly $80. This money enabled eToys to expand its product assortment, its sales and marketing activities, and its customer base. eToys started with 1,000 different products. By early 2000, that number had topped 100,000, with many specialty toys from small manufacturers not represented in large, off-line toy stores. In an effort to maintain its advantage as the first, and best-known, online toy store, eToys spent lots of money on advertising and promotion; marketing and sales expenses for 1999 reached $120.5 million. It worked: customers flocked to the site, more than 1.7 million of them in 2000.

Despite its pioneer position in the online market for toys, eToys was not able to lock out the competition. Other online efforts, such as ToySmart.com and Toytime.com caused eToys to increase its spending on sales and marketing. Keeping customers satisfied with timely fulfillment also proved to be costly. eToys started with a small, in-house distribution system, but the rapid increase in orders over the 1998 Christmas season led to an outsourced solution.

Another headache soon made its presence felt—Toys R Us. The major off-line toystore made its move to the Internet in 1999. The toysrus.com site leveraged its brand recognition to cultivate first-time online shoppers, its financial resources to offer competitive prices, and its physical locations to facilitate product returns. In its first holiday season online, toysrus.com beat eToys in customer visits, and in the average order amount: $134 for toysrus.com, compared with $127 for eToys. The two companies were in a neck-and-neck race for market share, handily beating the other competition.

Fortunately for eToys, Toys R Us was not prepared for its success. Unfortunately for eToys, neither was it prepared for its own success. Both companies suffered from slow site performance, due to the volume of business, and distribution problems that resulted in irate customers and unhappy kids when toys did not arrive—as promised—by Christmas.

Toys R Us solved their problem with $100 gift certificates to disappointed customers and the decision to outsource their online presence to Amazon. eToys ramped up its efforts and investments in in-house distribution centers, placing an even greater financial burden on the company, which had yet to turn a profit. Poor fulfillment drove off customers, while poor sales and higher-than-expected expenses to acquire other product lines, like party supplies, alarmed investors. The problems were reflected in the price of eToys' stock. By May 2000, shares had dropped 92 percent from their October 1999 high of $84.25—all the way down to $7.09.

By the 2000 Christmas season, the Toys R Us/Amazon alliance was paying off nicely, while eToys was struggling to stay afloat. In January 2001, eToys laid off 700 of its 1,000 employees. In March, the company filed for bankruptcy and sold its inventory to KB Toys, the chief off-line competitor of its archrival, Toys R Us.

Does the saga of eToys mean that online companies just cannot compete with off-line companies that move online? It's clear that many factors contributed to eToys' meteoric rise and equally spectacular flame-out. What is less clear is whether the problems could have been avoided. The newness of the Internet as a business environment, coupled with the obstacles faced by a pure-player, with no off-line presence to fall back on, might have been insurmountable in any event. eToys' history does, however, illustrate the importance of understanding the context in which the company will operate, including the challenges posed by competitors and the nature of customer demand. This chapter is guided by the deceptively simple question, "What aspects of the Internet lead to fundamental changes in the digital business environment?"

The Internet has been described as a revolution by researchers and many writers in the popular press. Typically, a revolution implies a change to the existing order: old ways are overthrown, and new ways define practice. Changes may be evident in several forms. First, we can look at the effect of the Internet on the *structure* of the marketing environment. Very generally, what does the marketplace look like when the Internet plays a role? Second, we can study the effect of the Internet on the *forms* of business activities that can be carried out. For instance, here we might ask the questions, "What features of the Internet lead to changes in the business environment that enable new business activities?" and, "How can businesses use the Internet to accomplish traditional strategic objectives in new ways?"

The Caveats of Change and Constraint

The fast pace of technological development, and of people's adoption of the technology, means that what we know and how we use the Internet to develop business strategy may quickly become outdated. In order to make effective use of the Internet as a business tool, it is important to adopt a perspective that recognizes that the business environment is affected—and even defined—by changes and constraints. This means that rather than learning specific facts, formulas, and theories based on their applications in well-defined, static situations, it is important to know how the concepts work well enough to transfer them to situations that can change quickly and dramatically.

Key Forces in a Changing Business Environment

Recognizing changes in the business environment can be accomplished by understanding the forces that create change (Figure 7-1). One such force includes the advances in technology, in terms of hardware and software. In addition, peoples' reactions to technology development may also lead to new relationships in the business environment. For instance, increased ease of communication among customers may lead to the formation of new referral networks and brand communities. Finally, the changes to the types of interactions between companies and their customers that are made possible by the Internet may result in regulatory policies that affect the market structure. The Children's Online Privacy Protection Act illustrates this situation.

Making a Big Picture Bigger

In any environment that is characterized by rapid and dramatic changes that affect the activities that can be undertaken by inhabitants of the environment, it can be helpful to

FIGURE 7-1 Key Components of an Evolving Business Environment.

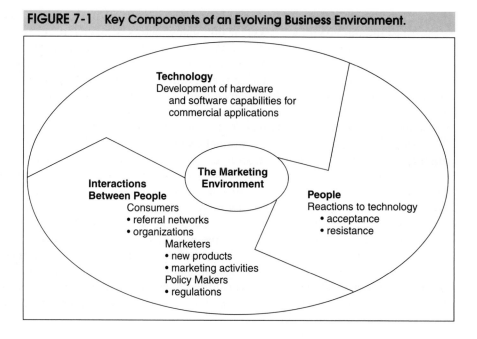

have a big picture to serve as a guide for organizing the issues. The exchange environment framework in Chapter 2 described the relationships between businesses, customers, and policy and technology developers; and it provided an overview of the possible interactions that create an exchange environment.

Now we are ready to use that framework to examine business relationships within the broader context of the Internet. Our goal is to understand the forces that affect the business activities of organizations, fostering or hindering business growth in the online environment. In the next section, we will use a basic population ecology model to characterize the environment created by the Internet and its effect on business activity.

Bits & Bytes 7.1
In 1999, online toy sales grew by nearly 1,000 percent, while total toy sales grew by 8.6 percent.
(*Source:* NPD Group, Inc. and MediaMetrix 2000)

A Population Ecology Approach to the Digital Business Environment

Population ecology is a science developed to provide a systematic explanation of the environmental factors that determine characteristics of a population, such as its size, distribution, and rate of growth. Although biologists use population ecology to talk about organisms, such as plants and animals, many of the concepts that describe change in organic, biological environments are readily applicable to the technological environment of business and the Internet. (And not just because computers can have bugs, too.)

In population ecology, **biotic potential** is the growth in the population that we would expect to observe if the environment was characterized by optimal growing conditions. Arthur Boughey,[1] one of the earliest proponents of population ecology, provides a good description of biotic potential. In terms of bugs, he notes that if a certain type of bacteria divided every 20 minutes, in 1 $\frac{1}{2}$ days, the entire planet would be a foot deep in bacteria. A day later, it would be over our heads.

This example makes two key points: First, with optimal environmental conditions, a population can grow very quickly. Second, the notion of biotic potential is more of theoretical interest than actual fact—reassuring when you think about the bacteria. Most environments are not optimal for unchecked growth; they are constrained. Constraints to growth tend to take two forms: **natural circumstances,** such as the availability of food, and **cultural conditions,** such as a societally imposed limit on numbers of children in a family. These constraints are jointly termed **environmental resistance.** The point at which the amount of resistance leads to a halt in growth of the population defines the **carrying capacity** of the environment for that population. Figure 7-2 depicts the relationships between growth rate, environmental resistance, and carrying capacity.

Population Ecology and Industry Growth

Applied to the business world, the Internet constitutes a virtual ecology, in which different types of industries coexist as the populations. For example, we can think of the domains represented in the Domain Name System as a simplistic classification of species: commercial, educational, military, and so on. If we focus on the commercial domain, for example, different industries serve as the species populations. Each organi-

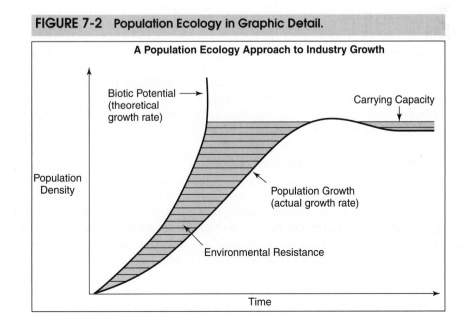

FIGURE 7-2 Population Ecology in Graphic Detail.

A Population Ecology Approach to Industry Growth

Biotic Potential (theoretical growth rate)

Carrying Capacity

Population Density

Population Growth (actual growth rate)

Environmental Resistance

Time

zation, or company, in the industry is analogous to the individual organism in the species population description of population ecology.

Of particular interest are the factors that sustain, encourage, or inhibit the ability of an industry to flourish and grow, given constraints of the Internet ecology. For example, think of the constraints that might create environmental resistance to the growth of an industry. One might be the limits imposed by available technologies. Companies who offer sophisticated and graphics-intensive Web-site hosting are affected by this constraint when the target market for their services lacks access to the type of computing equipment needed to experience the services as intended.

Another constraint might be the regulations imposed by policy makers on the types of activities that companies in a particular industry may conduct. For example, several tobacco companies registered Internet domains with the hope that publicizing and advertising their products would be possible on the Internet in ways that are not possible in other media, such as television. While regulatory policy for the Internet is still developing, the FTC has warned the tobacco industry that restrictions in other media will apply to the Internet.

> **Bits & Bytes 7.2**
> After its initial public offering, eToys market capitalization, a measure of company worth, exceeded $7.7 billion, compared with $5.6 billion for Toys R Us—even though eToys had fewer than 1 percent of the amount of annual sales made by Toys R Us.
> (*Source:* NPD Group, Inc. and MediaMetrix 2000)

Environmental Constraints to Industry Growth

The constraints of technology and policy are analogous to the two types of constraints in biological settings. We can think of impediments to industry growth due to technology as natural circumstances, and constraints due to policy, as determined, imposed, and enforced by societal agencies, as cultural conditions (Figure 7-3). In the case of technology development, the constraint is a function of the availability of the resource, rather than its desirability. In contrast, the application of policy is determined by society's perception of its need and value.

Natural Constraints to Growth

In the case of natural circumstances, we can use concepts from population ecology to understand the nature of the factors that limit growth by introducing another distinction between the factors. Population growth can be limited by factors that are **density dependent** or **density independent.** Both types reflect constraints imposed by the demand on limited sets of resources. A constraint due to density dependence occurs when the number of organisms in the population affects growth. For example, an industry may be unable to continue to grow when the market for its product becomes saturated; that is, the limited pool of possible buyers is exhausted. In addition, a production-side constraint may curb industry growth when supplies needed to produce the product are unavailable.

FIGURE 7-3 Two Types of Constraints Affect Industry Growth in the Internet Environment.

Natural Circumstances	*Cultural Conditions*
• *Supply-side* (technological capabilities) - Density dependent (high competition for necessary production materials) - Density independent (low availability of necessary materials, without competition) • *Demand-side* (buyers) - Density dependent (high competition for consumers) - Density independent (market is saturated, for all competitors)	• *Territoriality* (niche behaviors between competitors) - Patents for intellectual property - Product/process standards • *Regulatory policy* (influence of social norms) • *Emigration* (shift to alternative product focus)

While both of these situations involve constraints due to limited resources, the first case is density dependent, and the second case is density independent; if the supplies exist for no one, then the size of the industry makes no difference to its growth.

Other examples of density independent constraints on industry growth include seasonality and the presence of cycles in consumption. Seasonality leads to often-predictable variations in the amount of consumption from a product category. Market researchers noted dramatic shifts in Internet consumption during the 1998 and 1999 holiday seasons, particularly in the toy industry. Shoppers moved away from browsing and online research activities, and toward heavier online shopping. Spikes in buying behavior were a key factor in eToys' decision to beef up its product line, as a way to increase sales throughout the year, rather than just at Christmas.

Cycles appear to be less predictable in occurrence, but they can exert a substantial effect on the revenues of a company. For instance, bell bottoms and fur coats have both experienced a recent revival in popularity.

Cultural Constraints to Growth

A second set of factors that act as constraints are cultural conditions. These character-istics are behavioral attributes of the individual groups in the population that affect the overall size of the population. Cultural conditions differ from the density depen-dent and independent constraints we have examined in that they are self-imposed, rather than being dictated by the physical environment or the supply of available resources.

Because cultural conditions often reflect conscious decisions of population mem-bers to behave in approved ways, these characteristics are particularly useful for describing the effects of the Internet environment on the activities and behaviors of companies. Many business activities in the online environment reflect constraints due to behavioral attributes that are closely related to aspects of strategic planning. For instance, competition may lead one industry member to develop strategies that define territories that can be defended against other companies. Patents to guard intellectual property, such as new product technologies, and the development of a standard for a process or application are ways that companies protect their ability to compete within the industry. These types of behaviors also serve as constraints on the behavior of other industry members, thus potentially limiting growth.

As Figure 7-2 suggests, the actual growth rate of a population—or an industry—slows down as the number of companies within the industry increases. This change in rate results from competition between industry members. This competition is for the resources, such as supplies and customers, which are necessary for the continued existence and growth of companies in the industry.

Competition within industries has been an important focus of business research, and a fact of life for many companies. In the following section, we will take a closer look at the strategies companies use to compete in the online environment.

Competition in Markets: Strategies for Success

The concepts of population ecology have been applied in business to provide a conceptual basis for explaining and predicting the success of competing firms as they move through the product life cycle (PLC). For example, marketing researchers[2] have used the stages of the PLC—introduction, growth, maturation, and decline—to develop a set of descriptive strategies for success that integrate a company's characteristics with more general characteristics of the industry. Understanding the benefits of each strategy is useful for predicting the types of companies that are likely to succeed in different stages of the PLC in the Internet environment.

In this approach, several aspects of population ecology are central. First, population density is a key factor in the intensity of competition; the more competitors in the market, the greater the demand on resources (e.g., customers). Second, the concept of market niches serves as the basis for selecting a competitive strategy. A **niche** is the combination of resources and environmental conditions, including competition, with the ability to sustain growth of one type of company.

Internet portals illustrate the value of a niching strategy. Portals are Web navigation hubs, such as Yahoo! and Lycos. Early portal strategies focused on being general—combining content and capabilities that would appeal to broad audiences. The strategy worked well for Yahoo! The portal increased its traffic totals by more than 50 percent in 1999. This rapid growth made it difficult for other, smaller portals to compete effectively. As a result, second-tier hubs such as Disney's Go.com and Excite.com shifted their strategies to develop competencies in specific areas. Go.com focused on entertainment and recreation, and Excite.com promoted itself as the Web's "leading personalization portal."

The research on population ecology and competition, combined with anecdotal evidence from the Internet environment, suggests that different strategies are appropriate for different types of companies at different stages in the development of the product market. In new markets, characterized by low population density and weak competition, successful organizations are likely to be smaller, more specialized companies who can use their small size and focused skills to exploit a market opportunity and create a **first-mover advantage,** as eToys attempted in the online toy market. This advantage is created when the first significant company in a market is able to gain an edge (e.g., protected technology, market penetration) over subsequent competitors, given its early entry.

Companies with these characteristics are described as **specialists.** For instance, Dialpad.com is known for it core offering, Internet **telephony,** the ability to transfer voice data over the Internet (Figure 7-4). Although it competes with large telecom services, such as AT&T and Verizon, to offer long-distance phone service, Dialpad's focus on its Internet competency has provided brand name recognition among consumers, and staying power in the competitive Internet telephony industry.

For more established markets, in which more is known about the likelihood of a product's success, and about the different markets for the product, companies who have expanded the specialized capabilities of the early market entrants tend to be the most successful. Success depends on the ability to capitalize on the experience of pioneers in the earlier niche, generating enough resources to expand to compete in the present niche. For instance, Toys R Us used it physical presence and lessons learned from eToys' experience to forge a successful online presence in alliance with Amazon. Companies with these expanded sets of capabilities are described as **generalists.** Yahoo! capitalized on its early, focused, successes to develop broader capabilities, as by acquiring GeoCities and Broadcast.com.

In the later stage of the cycle, population density and competition are high. Because most of the types of organizations that could enter the market have already done so, the amount of environmental change is relatively low. As a result, successful businesses in this type of market tend to have the broad-based industry presence to be able to flexibly redirect their capabilities to exploit a particular competency or a need of a specific segment. As a result, they tend to be generalists, but with some characteristics of the early niche specialists. In the case of Internet portals, existing

FIGURE 7-4 Dialpad Specializes in Internet Telephony, Competing with Generalist Telecom Companies Like AT&T and Verizon.

sites used their resources to refocus, specializing on particular market segments. New portals in the market will have to be able to take on the giants, like Yahoo!, and provide evidence of differentiating capabilities to pull traffic.

Competition, Niches, and the Internet Ecology

The population ecology model of market evolution can be used to describe and explain the nature of market development when the Internet is a factor that influences the nature of the business environment. In a simple sense, we can look at the Internet as the source of a new product-market; innovative products, and the companies that spawn them have been created to take advantage of the opportunities offered by the Internet ecology. In a more complex sense, however, we must also look at the effect of the Internet on the nature of competition in existing product markets.

Types of Product-Markets

As a new product-market, the Internet constitutes an embryonic niche. Early entrants into the market tend to fit the Lambkin and Day profile: smaller companies with specialized capabilities. The rapid proliferation of Internet start-up companies in the late 1990s, and the vast amounts of venture capital that underwrote their endeavors, was encouraged by low population density and competition, and a belief that high profit potential existed in the Internet niche. For example, eBay, the online auction company, provides a service that would not have been feasible prior to widespread adoption of the Internet as a means for communication and commerce. Another example is that of Cisco Systems, the company that produces the systems components known as *routers* that enable the Internet to transfer packets of information. The Internet is the reason for Cisco's existence.

For established product-markets, the Internet provides an opportunity to develop a competitive niche, differentiated on the basis of technological savvy. Companies such as Amazon and eToys entered the Internet market early. They developed online competencies that earned them brand awareness, despite the fact that in both cases, the core product was not new—books for Amazon and, as the name hints, toys for eToys.

As skills and technologies develop, and as knowledge of them is shared, barriers to market entry in the Internet environment are lowered. Many long-established companies have begun to shift parts of their marketing efforts to the Internet. Some, like IBM, have begun to offer products and services specifically focused on the use of the Internet for business applications. For these companies, the Internet creates the product-market. For other companies, like Barnes and Noble, and Toys R Us, the Internet is just another outlet for selling what they have always sold. In both cases, the companies are generalists, with a broad base of resources that can be applied to take advantage of their follower status in the Internet ecology.

The entrance of established generalists changes the nature of the competitive environment. For example, in April 1999, Toys R Us announced plans to invest $80 million in its e-commerce activities, supplanting pure-player eToys to become a dominant force in the online toy marketplace. Toys R Us sought to achieve its goal of being the market leader by 2000 by emphasizing convenience: online purchases could be returned to any Toys R Us store. The strategy was successful. During the holiday shopping season, MediaMetrix reported growth in site visits of 93 percent for eToys, compared with 277 percent forToys R Us.

The graph in Figure 7-5 shows the competitive strategies companies can choose as a function of the life cycle within a product market. Companies like Cisco and eBay are specialists, who got their start in an online environment characterized by low competition and high uncertainty. Many of the clicks-and-mortars who have leveraged their off-line capabilities for online advantage are generalists, like Barnes & Noble and Toys R Us.When the market becomes stagnant, successful companies look for new opportunities, as through developing spin-off companies or new, focused divisions within the parent company. For instance, Sony has maintained its core focus on electronics, but it has moved aggressively to compete in the gaming market with its PlayStation console and interactive, online game, EverQuest.

Business Ecosystems

The integration of the Internet with traditional business activities means that the types of business structures that have existed over time may evolve into forms that reflect adaptation to the new environments for commerce. Population ecologists have found that competition for resources and the structure of populations tend to be systematically related. Competition for resources leads to interaction between different populations in the environment, in order to determine the allocation of the resources.

FIGURE 7-5   Life-cycle Stage and Competition Guide Strategic Activity.

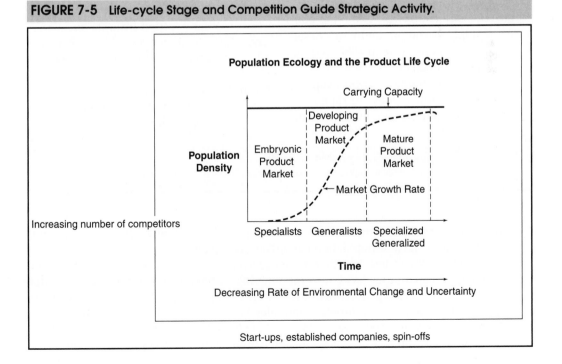

InSite

REINVENTING BUSINESS: WWW.CISCO.COM

You're sitting in front of your computer in one room, and you'd like to communicate with your spouse, sitting in another room in a nearby building. It's time to come up with a dinner plan, and e-mail seems like the fastest way to communicate. Unfortunately, your two computers, both connected to the Internet, cannot communicate with each other; they are on different networks. You decide to. . .

    a. Walk over to chat

    b. Yell, loudly, to communicate

    c. Develop a way to connect the networks

    d. Skip dinner

    Leonard Bosack and Sandra Lerner faced a similar dilemma while working at Stanford University. The husband and wife team merged their problem-solving abilities to develop a router that would allow two computer networks to communicate. Stanford was happy, and the couple decided to start a company to sell routers. Cisco was begun in 1984, and the first router shipped out in 1986.

    With an infusion of venture capital, the company grew rapidly. So rapidly, in fact, that it outgrew its ability to manufacture ordered routers. The solution? Outsourcing. Cisco took orders and specifications for its products, and provided the custom order to its manufacturers. In many cases, the product was never touched by Cisco hands.

    As Cisco continued to grow, more manufacturing capacity was needed. Because satisfying customer requirements was a cornerstone of Cisco's corporate strategy, the need for quality control of a wide range of product configurations grew complex. Again, Cisco found a solution. Rather than getting their manufacturing partners to use Cisco manufacturing systems, Cisco developed a network of control systems that tracked product quality, regardless of how the product was manufactured. These control systems communicated process and inventory data to Cisco, enabling the company to manage its partners for maximum returns.

    Cisco has profited from its business savvy, reaping financial benefits of nearly $2 billion dollars in 2002.[1] It has developed its Internet Business Solutions Group to provide consulting for companies who wish to emulate Cisco's business ecosystem approach.[2]

---

[1]Bosack and Lerner also profited; they cashed out in 1990 for $170 million.

[2]Sources for this section include www.pbs.org, www.cisco.com, and *Optimize Magazine*, November 2001.

Interaction may lead to interbreeding, creating a new, genetically different, population. In many cases, the new population has a resource advantage.

    Similar types of interbreeding have occurred in the digital business ecology. This mingling of capabilities has led to the blurring of boundaries of the industries that comprise the business populations of the Internet. For example, Microsoft is known primarily for its software development and sales. However, they also offer a travel service, Expedia, and an Internet browser, Internet Explorer. While their products and services are clearly linked by the software competency, the nature of the products and services they offer crosses the boundaries of traditionally defined industries. The merger of Time-Warner and America Online provides another example. Time-Warner, an entertainment conglomerate, is a content provider. AOL provides the service for content delivery. The interbreeding of these corporations results in a relationship between divisions of the previously independent companies that provides them with a competitive advantage over the other population members of the two industries in which they developed. The emergence of these interbred industries has resulted in hybrid business structures, termed **business ecosystems.**

An effective ecosystem leverages the unique and complementary abilities of its partners. For instance, an ecosystem in the automotive industry might include a company that specializes in information technology solutions for supply chain applications and customer support software, as well as the more traditional manufacturers, suppliers, and dealers of automotive parts and vehicles.

The Internet increases the opportunities for developing business ecosystems, as well as the value of these ecosystems. By increasing the geographic reach of any ecosystem partner, and by decreasing the costs of communication and collaboration, the Internet makes it possible to include partners in the ecosystem based on merit and ability, rather than location convenience.

Strategic Alliances

The concept of business ecosystems is closely related to the idea of **strategic alliances.** The technological and communications capabilities of the Internet have made global competition a reality for many industries. To succeed in the global economy, companies often enter strategic alliances, like the partnership between Amazon and Toys R Us. The goal of a strategic alliance is to combine complementary resources to enhance the ability of the allied companies to compete more effectively in their markets. While business ecosystems may arise as informal patterns of communications between companies, strategic alliances tend to reflect intentional partnerships between organizations. Strategic alliances also tend to share common goals, while business ecosystems reflect the potentially diverging goals of the ecosystem companies.

Strategic alliances take many forms, from formal mergers to informal partnership agreements. This approach to competition is termed **strategic network competition.** Strategic alliances differ from business ecosystems in that the companies in the strategic alliance remain independent entities, while components of the business ecosystem are organized under a parent company. The graphic in Figure 7-6 illustrates the array of strategic alliances that existed in a subset of the Internet environment from 1998 to 2001. Notice how businesses create alliances that extend across industries to enhance their competitive capabilities.

To this point, we have used a population ecology approach to build a general description of the environment created when the goals of business activity interact with the capabilities of the Internet. This environment is a virtual ecology, complete with factors that can constrain or encourage the growth of populations, or industries, within the environment. In the following sections, we will consider the impact of the online environment on what businesses can do to meet their strategic goals.

FIGURE 7-6 Strategic Alliances Provide Competitive Advantage Through Industry Interbreeding.

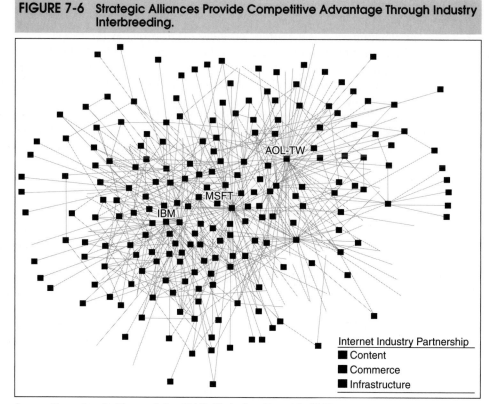

Source: Reproduced with permission, Valdis Krebs, Inc. Copyright 2003.

Constraints and Technological Innovation

One of the most obvious—even defining—features of the digital business ecology is that it is virtual; that is, it exists, but not in the ways that we typically expect a concept based on physical description to exist in the physical world. Take, for example, the idea of a virtual storefront. We know that in the physical world, a storefront is a real entity with goods, salespeople, and checkout counters, in which we can touch, smell, see, hear, and, depending on the product, even taste the wares. In a virtual storefront, the physical environment shifts to a digital environment. Our use of senses to perceive the experience is currently limited to—at best—seeing and hearing product information.

The importance of the shift from a bricks-and-mortar world to a bits-and-bytes world raises issues for digital business. For example, virtualization can be characterized as one of a set of environmental characteristics. These characteristics may serve as factors that influence environmental resistance to industry growth. That is, some factors may operate as constraints on the ability of a particular industry to grow in the Internet ecology. In contrast, other factors may create opportunities for growth that cannot be found in other environments.

To illustrate the nature of the Internet as a source of constraints and opportunities for populations, consider the Internet as a medium for electronic communications.

While such a view oversimplifies the array of differences that sets the Internet apart from traditional marketing media, such as television, radio, and print, it underscores the novelty of the evolving business environment.

Bits & Bytes 7.3

Hewlett Packard created an employee portal with 170 services for its employees worldwide. The benefits? Better communication, streamlined processes, and $15 million cost reduction.

(*Source:* EarthWeb IT Management, April 2002)

Redefining the Marketplace

As a means for electronically transferring information between buyers and sellers, the Internet has changed our ideas of what constitutes a marketplace. On a general level, conducting business activity with the Internet has created a shift from a physical transaction space to an information-defined transaction space. In a traditional marketplace, buyers acquire information about goods and services, often from direct, hands-on examination of the products and through face-to-face conversations with the seller. In an Internet-created marketspace, however, the environment changes. Remember telepresence, from Chapter 5?

Environmental Constraints in the Digital Business Environment

In the digital business environment, the customer's acquisition of product-related information is separated from the product itself; typically, a computer enables the exchange of information between the buyer and the seller. The buyer receives information about the product and may even be able to observe a real-time use of the product to obtain a vicarious experience, but hands-on trial is not possible. In this situation, the virtual environment can be viewed as a constraint, creating environmental resistance that limits the growth of companies that rely on physical product experience. Companies whose products rely on sensory experience in modalities that cannot be offered digitally may find it difficult to persuade shoppers. Some examples include perfume manufacturers and bakeries, whose success may depend on shoppers' experiential reactions to the product.

Of course, there are cases where the product can be experienced on a trial basis over the Internet, as with software packages, but this opportunity is limited to products and services that can be digitized. For these types of companies, the digital environment may create opportunities for promoting and disseminating the product. For physical products, companies attempt to create virtual experiences to overcome experiential constraints in selling nondigitizable products online. Clothing retailers who use online simulations to provide consumers with the experience of "trying on" a garment are a noteworthy example. For instance, Lands' End offers My Virtual Model, shown in Figure 7-7.

Shoppers can customize a virtual model and use the model to assess clothing appearance and fit. This capability moves the product from being an experience good closer to

FIGURE 7-7 My Virtual Model Addresses a Technological Constraint to Product Experience.

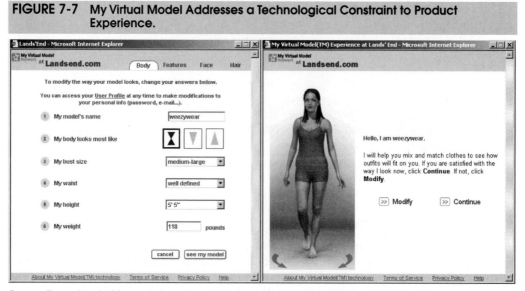

being a search good, because the visual representation of the product's features on the customized mannequin can be evaluated without having to actually try on the garment.

Cultural Constraints in the Digital Business Environment

Businesses online can encounter constraints that are not created simply by the nature of the environment. Remember the cultural factors that affect survival and growth? These factors stem from the members of a population, rather than from the environment itself. An example of a cultural factor in the Internet environment is the set of expectations people hold about the nature of an experience, such as learning about a product. These expectations serve as a cultural constraint on the interpretation of a virtual product experience. For instance, a customer who has always purchased medicines at a local drugstore, where a licensed pharmacist provides information about dosage and side-effects, may be reluctant to purchase from an online pharmacy that provides a searchable database of medicine-related information—even when the amount and quality of information is the same.

Environmental constraints and cultural constraints may join forces to influence the success of an organization in the virtual environment. For example, the quality of the experience can be compared to the effects of situational factors in a marketplace—an environmental constraint. In a traditional business environment, a customer's perceptions of the situation may be affected by characteristics of the environment. Atmospherics, such as lighting, music, and temperature, have been shown to influence product evaluations. In addition, interactions with salespeople can enhance or detract from the perceived quality of a product.

In the digital environment, however, the nature of customers' interactions with the business environment is different due to the unique characteristics of the environment.

The environmental constraints of the virtual ecology may interact with the cultural constraints imposed by people's experience with traditional environments to affect their perceptions of the virtual product experience. Thus, while off-line and online businesses may share features at a general level, it is important to understand how the situational differences may influence exchange behaviors at more specific levels.

To illustrate the idea of interaction between types of constraints, think about shopping for clothes on the Internet. We have already discussed the environmental constraint imposed by the limits of the digital environment, as well as businesses' efforts to overcome the constraint through simulated garment modeling techniques. A cultural constraint may also be in effect for online clothes shopping.

Many people like to shop with others, such as friends or family. The opinions of others serve as a gauge by which the shopper measures the benefits of a purchase and reduces his uncertainty about the purchase. Shopping in an online environment, however, is often a solitary experience: a customer, a computer, and a distant, digital Web site. As a result, the environmental factor and the cultural condition may operate together to create a barrier to online clothing purchases.

Technology developers have worked to reduce or eliminate this barrier. **Shared browsing,** or **cobrowsing,** enables two or more people, operating from separate computers, to shop together, viewing the same item and exchanging opinions though the online medium. Microsoft was one of the first companies to offer a shared browsing service (Figure 7-8). Subscribers to the MSN 8 software service can look at sites simultaneously, as they chat via Microsoft Messenger.

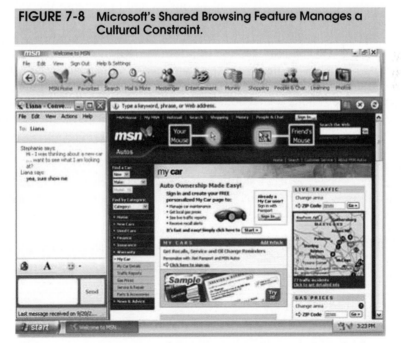

FIGURE 7-8   Microsoft's Shared Browsing Feature Manages a Cultural Constraint.

Source: Reproduced with permission of Microsoft, Inc. Copyright 2003, all rights reserved.

Internet Effects on the Structure of Digital Business Activity

We have used concepts from population ecology to describe effects of the Internet ecology on aspects of business activity. Now we turn our attention to the way that the environment influences the structure of companies as they carry out their business activities. We continue, however, to use population ecology as a guide. The application is straightforward. Populations are structured in ways that enhance their ability to exist and to grow. The environment in which a population exists consists of factors that enhance or impede growth. Thus, the Internet environment affects the ways in which populations, or industries, will structure themselves in order to succeed.

The Internet Ecology and the Value Chain

The **value chain** is a popular concept for describing the set of activities that an organization undertakes to move its products from development to the market. If you think of the process as a sequence of links, the basic idea is that each link provides an opportunity to increase the value of the offering to the end purchaser (Figure 7-9). Increased value may occur when processes can be sped up to make the product available more quickly. Value may also be added if new technologies enable the production of a higher quality product, or a product that costs less. As a result, the way that a value chain is structured can create competitive advantage.

The environment is an important factor in the development of a value chain with a competitive advantage. It can create opportunities for change that enable a company to maximize its use of resources and to increase the value of different links.

Consider the development of a single product, from an idea to a saleable item. The increased availability and use of information communication technologies, such as those that make up the Internet, can influence each stage in the path of the product from design to distribution to disposal. Input from customers about product needs can be readily obtained, stored, tracked, analyzed, and interpreted via the Internet. Negotiations with suppliers and with distributors can be conducted with greater speed and information sharing. As a result, adjacent steps in the value chain—the flow of materials and services in route to market—may be integrated and made more efficient.

These changes reflect a shift from a physical value chain to a **virtual value chain,** in which information is a primary factor.[3] The information-related activities that affect

FIGURE 7-9 Each Link in a Value Chain Is an Opportunity for Adding Value.

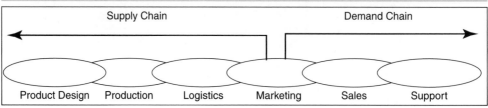

Supply Chain   Demand Chain

Product Design   Production   Logistics   Marketing   Sales   Support

each link of the value chain include collecting, structuring, integrating, analyzing, and disseminating information. Each of these activities can be conducted for separate links in the value chain, thus creating a wealth of opportunities for changing the ways that value is created. As Figure 7-10 indicates, each intersection of a link and an information activity provides an opportunity to enhance a business process. In addition, the set of process opportunities under a particular link creates new product opportunities. For instance, the ability to gather information via the Internet created new search engines as new products. The ability to distribute digital information via the Internet as products, such as books, software, and music, affects channel structures and logistics. The ability to disseminate information via the Internet affects promotional aspects of marketing activity, as well as sales and support processes.

Adapting to the new, information-defined environment can lead to adaptations in the types of market structures used by a company for all aspects of moving goods and services through its value chain—from manufacturing the product to marketing the product. In the next section, we will look at two types of structures.

Bits & Bytes 7.4
Lands' End credits My Virtual Model, introduced in 2000, with a 26 percent increase in new sales in its first year of use.
(*Source*: eCommerceTimes.com, November 5, 2002.)

FIGURE 7-10 **As an Information Resource, the Internet Provides Process and Product Opportunities Through a Virtual Value Chain.**

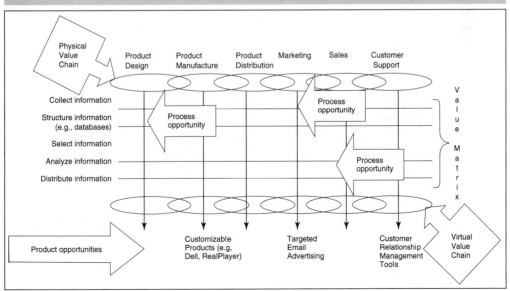

Source: Adapted from Rayport and Sviokla, "Exploiting the Virtual Value Chain," *Harvard Business Review,* November–December, [1995].

Two Types of Market Structures

Two basic types of market structures tend to reflect the characteristics of most economic activity related to the production and distribution of products: hierarchies and markets. A **hierarchical structure** is illustrated by a company that uses a vertically integrated approach to the value chain. For example, Hewlett-Packard's laser printers require specialized integrated circuitry. To insure a steady and timely supply, HP acquired the manufacturing capability to produce its own circuits.

A hierarchical structure tends to be adopted for products that are complex and that require specific components that are not widely available from a pool of suppliers. In other words, the products have a complex **product description** and high **asset specificity.** These constraints have historically tended to make it advantageous to integrate vertically, to insure the ready availability of parts and processes. In a hierarchical structure, managerial decisions control product movement through the value chain. In terms of population ecology, this structure may enhance the ability of the company or industry to survive and thrive in its environment.

In a **market structure,** the flow of the product through the value chain is coordinated and determined by the market forces of supply and demand. At any point in the chain, the buyer of a product component or process compares the appropriate options available from a variety of sources and selects the option that provides the optimal combination of desired benefits. A market structure is viable for products with simpler product descriptions and low asset specificity. For example, consider a large hotel with a need for a constant supply of clean towels. The laundry service needed by the hotel has low asset specificity: any service will do, provided the towels are cleaned in a timely manner. In addition, the needed service has a simple product description and its purpose can be readily communicated: use detergent, get the towels clean. As a result, the hotel can pick and choose from among a variety of service providers in a market structure to take advantage of price and performance. The ability to obtain the service in a market economy reduces the dependence of the hotel on any one laundry, thus relaxing an environmental constraint. In addition, the market economy may result in more competition for the cleaning job, potentially increasing the quality and reducing the cost of the service for the hotel.

A Shift from Hierarchies to Markets?

The digital business may enable industries to shift from hierarchical structures to market structures. The increasing sophistication of information technologies means that complex product descriptions can be communicated more effectively than with previous communications capabilities. For example, a company can demonstrate the nature and function of a complicated piece of machinery to a potential buyer via an online, virtual simulation—an impossible achievement with a fax machine. Even when the communication could be effectively completed face-to-face, the online environment may be cheaper and more efficient. The technology reduces difficulties associated with communicating information about a complex product, and the costs associated with trying to coordinate business activities with organizations outside the traditional, vertically integrated structure.

The technologies of the Internet ecology also change the impact of the asset specificity constraint. Advances in technology make it possible for companies to develop

'Net Knowledge

CRUNCHING COMMUNICATIONS COSTS

Many companies use **virtual private networks** (VPNs) to transmit data from one corporate site to another, using the distributed nature of the Internet. To be effective, a VPN must provide secure transmissions, without ability to copy or corrupt transmitted data. They must also be able to verify sender and recipient, so that transmitted information can be trusted. An advantage of VPNs is that they do not rely on dedicated lines. The use of flexible connections reduces costs through efficient use of network resources.

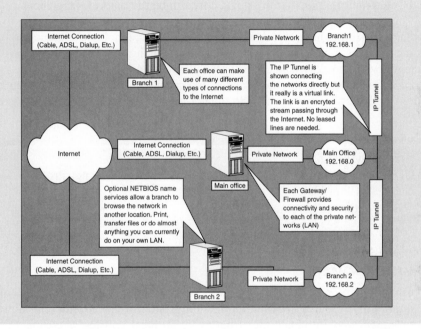

flexible production capabilities. This means that more companies can become involved in the manufacture of highly specific product components, reducing a company's need to depend on a narrow set of suppliers. The information technologies of the Internet also make it possible to reduce the coordination costs of matching up buyers and sellers. We will look at the ways in which businesses coordinate their activities in market-type structures in greater detail in Chapter 13, when we consider the role of the Internet on business-to-business activity.

Evolution of the Digital Business Environment

We have seen how the Internet ecology may lead to a shift in the ways that industries structure their activities, from hierarchies to markets. The shifts may occur in stages, and the length of the stages may depend on the nature of the industry. Going back to ideas from population ecology, we can describe the process as one of evolution;

companies will adapt to the changing nature of the environment in order to thrive, and the changes will occur over time, reflecting the dynamic, constantly changing nature of the environment.

The evolution of structures in the digital business environment has been described as a three-stage process: an initial, biased stage, a subsequent unbiased stage, and a final personalized stage. To illustrate the idea of stages, consider the development of electronic airline reservations markets. United Airlines was one of the first airlines to enable travel agents to book reservations electronically—provided the bookings were on United flights. American countered with a system that enabled agents to search all flights. Of course, American's flights were at the top of any list! Subsequent regulation—largely a result of complaints by other airlines—sought to restore competition by reducing bias in the electronic markets. At this point, a true, unbiased market was achieved.

In recent years, electronic systems have become available to customers, without having to go through a travel agent. In addition, the technologies that underlie the electronic markets have developed to a state in which personalization is possible. For instance, with Travelocity, an online travel planning and reservations service, a customer can specify dates, desirable fare ranges, and specific airlines. These preferences can be stored, and information "pushed" to the host computer when the criteria are met.

> **Bits & Bytes 7.5**
> Of 436 large organizations surveyed, 81 percent had Internet Protocol VPNs in place, as of July 2002.
> (*Source:* InStat/MDR, February 2003.)

CHAPTER SUMMARY

In this chapter, we looked at the ways in which the interaction of technology with business goals creates a dynamic, new environment for commercial activity. This environment may influence the structure of business entities, as well as the types of activities they carry out.

We adopted a population ecology approach to characterize the nature of this digital business environment. Concepts associated with population ecology were used to describe the types of constraints that might be expected to the development of industries within the Internet ecology. An important aspect of the model is to characterize the nature of competition between organizations, and the role of the Internet in creating opportunities and strategies for success in the digital business environment. We examined the impact of the Internet on the formation of strategic alliances to enhance competition. We also considered the influence of the Internet on the business activities reflected by value chains.

Using population ecology and market evolution to guide our examination, we looked at possible changes to market structures in the evolving business environment, and we considered characteristics of the environment that may facilitate or impede these changes. Differences between markets and hierarchies were discussed, and characteristics of industries that affect the emphasis of a market structure in the digital business environment were described.

CONTENT MANAGEMENT

USEFUL TERMS

- asset specificity
- biotic potential
- business ecosystem
- carrying capacity
- cobrowsing
- cultural conditions
- density dependent
- density independent
- environmental resistance

- firstmover advantage
- generalist
- hierarchical structure
- market structure
- natural circumstances
- niche
- population ecology
- product description
- shared browsing

- specialist
- strategic alliances
- strategic network competition
- telephony
- value chain
- virtual private network (VPN)
- virtual value chain

REVIEW QUESTIONS

1. Describe the key forces that create changes in the digital business environment.
2. How is the science of population ecology relevant to the study of business and the Internet?
3. What two types of constraints impede industry growth?
4. Distinguish between the concepts of density dependence and density independence.
5. What role do ecological characteristics play in the Internet environment?
6. Discuss the role of specialists and generalists at different stages of the PLC.
7. Describe the effects of industry interbreeding in the Internet ecology.
8. How is the digital environment for business different from the off-line environment for business?
9. What factors might influence the shift from a hierarchical structure to a market structure?

WEB APPLICATION

Surviving in an Evolving Environment

We've seen lots of companies come and go on the Internet. What makes the ones who last successful? Some of the dot-coms that failed looked like winners, even to the experts who backed the start-up ventures with lots of capital. Remember Pets.com (*hint:* think sock puppet)? How about Webvan?

Picking the right strategy for a company involves more than just finding something that consumers want to buy, or providing a novel way to make a purchase. As many dot-coms have discovered, success requires being able to adapt to an environment that is constantly changing, both technologically and culturally.

Adapting business strategy to function profitably over the PLC can take very different forms, depending on company and industry characteristics. To take a look at how companies have adapted to meet environmental changes, go to www.archive.org and track the ways that companies have altered their approach over time. It is helpful to start with a couple of very successful entities, like eBay.com and Yahoo.com, and then compare characteristics with a couple of less successful efforts, like uBid.com and excite.com.

To gain additional insight into what works, take a look at some companies who started up, failed, shut down, and then revamped. What are the differences? What are the apparent lessons learned? Some sites to explore include Boo.com (through FashionMall.com), Furniture.com, and eToys.com. Use the following guidelines to direct your analysis.

1. Look at the Web sites at different points in a company's history. What are the key changes to the site

      a. in appearance?
      b. in functionality?
      c. in product offering?

2. Read the about-the-company information. Have there been changes to the strategic mission? If so, how do the changes appear to influence the Web presence?

3. Do the changes to business strategy reflect a PLC shift in strategy? That is, can you detect a shift from specialist to generalist, or vice versa, as a function of increasing online competition within the industry or category?

4. For companies within an industry, do the shifts seem to happen at the same point in time? How do successful companies compare with less successful companies in the speed and extent of implementing changes?

5. Has the company developed strategic alliances? With what types of companies is it allied? How do the alliances benefit the company's PLC strategy? That is, do they enable the company to be a specialist, or do they enhance its competitiveness as a generalist?

CONCEPTS IN BRIEF

1. The Internet affects the structure of the business environment, as well as business processes.
2. Key forces in the digital business environment are technology and people's reactions to technology, as well as the interactions between people in the environment.
3. A population ecology perspective characterizes changes to the digital business environment as the result of constraints to business and industry growth that stem from natural circumstances, like competition, and cultural conditions, like regulatory policy.
4. Companies adopt different strategies to manage competition within an industry. These strategies differ depending on the stage of PLC, across the industry, and the competition in the online environment.
5. The Internet has changed the focus and function of many companies by facilitating interaction between companies that operate a business ecosystem.
6. Relationships within an ecosystem are strategic alliances that enable sets of companies to compete against other companies, resulting in strategic network competition.
7. The types of industry interbreeding that lead to business ecosystems are often the result of efforts by companies to manage constraints to growth, such as the need for new technology, or new markets for products.
8. Companies also manage competition by leveraging the Internet as an information resource to add value to each link in the value chain.
9. Changes to value chain activities enabled by the Internet have made it possible for some conpanies to reduce their emphasis on vertical integration.
10. As the Internet continues to evolve as a digital business environment, business structures and activities will continue to adapt.

THINKING POINTS

1. What unique characteristics are available in a digital environment for business?
2. Discuss the evolution of the electronic marketplace from a population ecology standpoint.
3. How do characteristics of the Internet change the way businesses can attempt to create brand equity?
4. How can we utilize a population ecology model to explain and predict the nature of competition between organizations?

5. Why might early electronic markets tend to be biased toward a specific vendor?
6. What factors encourage the evolution of markets in the Internet environment to move from being biased to being unbiased?
7. The Internet enables companies to disaggregate the components of a product offering that create value for customers. Is this ability unique to the Internet?

ENDNOTES

1. Arthur S. Boughey, *Ecology of Populations,* (New York: The MacMillan Company, 1968).
2. Mary Lambkin and George S. Day, "Evolutionary Processes in Competitive Markets: Beyond the Product Life Cycle." *Journal of Marketing, 53* (July 1989), pages 4–20.
3. A detailed discussion of the strategic implications of the virtual value chain can be found in Jeffrey F. Rayport and John J. Sviokla , "Exploiting the Virtual Value Chain," *Harvard Business Review*, November–December (1995), pages 75–85.

SUGGESTED READINGS

1. *Digital Darwinism,* by Evan I. Schwartz (Random House, Inc.: New York, 1999).
2. "The Internet's Impact on Competition," in *Now or Never*, by Mary Modahl (HarperCollins Publishers, Inc.: New York, 2000).
3. "Evolutionary Processes in Competitive Markets," by Mary Lambkin and George S. Day. *Journal of Marketing, 53*, (July 1989), pages 4–20.
4. "Are You Next?" edited by Jeffrey Davis. *Business 2.0* (March 1999), pages 44–54.
5. *Ecology of Populations*, by Arthur S. Boughey (The MacMillan Company, Inc.: New York, 1968).

LEARNING LINKS

Business Ecosystems

business.cisco.com
www.line56.com/articles/ebiz_ecosys_index.asp
itmanagement.earthweb.com/ecom/article.php/1014411
www.systemtransformation.com/Org_Transformation_Articles/org_ecosystem.htm

Strategic Alliance Issues

business.cisco.com/prod/tree.taf%3Fasset_id = 83031&public_view = true&kbns = 1.html

business.cisco.com/prod/tree.taf%3Fasset_id = 57637&public_view = true&kbns = 1.html

Online Life-cycle Strategies

www.nichemarketresearch.com/market-niche.html
www.netgain.co.nz/library/what_soap.htm
www.website101.com/arch/archive03.html
www.sap.info/resources/RFILE215473cd67a6d08f3e.pdf

Strategic Planning for Digital Business

Focus and Objectives

Strategic planning enables companies to develop and maintain a competitive advantage in the Internet environment. This chapter is focused on describing and explaining the influence of the Internet on the need for strategic planning and the processes for conducting it. We review types of planning, including strategic planning across and within strategic business units. Then we focus on the role of the Internet in business planning to develop and implement business activity. In particular, we address business models that leverage characteristics of the Internet environment to enhance product characteristics, such as image, or revenue.

Your objectives in studying this chapter include the following:

- Know the different types of planning typically undertaken by businesses.
- Understand the factors that affect the development of a competitive advantage, and how they are related to aspects of business planning.
- Recognize characteristics of the Internet that help businesses identify opportunities and leverage resources to create a competitive advantage.
- Identify the effects of the Internet environment on the motivation, processes, and outcomes of strategic planning.
- Learn the characteristics of revenue-focused and product-focused business models for achieving strategic objectives with the Internet.

Evolution or Extinction?

Dodo birds were discovered on the island of Mauritius by the Portuguese in 1507. The birds provided amusement, and food. They were clumsy, dragging their bellies on the ground as they attempted to escape from the new predator—dogs and cats—that the explorers brought with them on their voyages. Though neither the Portuguese nor the Dutch, who subsequently colonized Mauritius, found the dodos particularly tasty, their pets were fond of the dodo's eggs. By 1681, the dodo was extinct.

The experience of the recording industry shares similarities with the dodo bird. Both had carved out existences that fostered survival and growth, given characteristics of the environment. Both were threatened by the introduction of new forces that changed their ability to function as they had in the past. For the dodo, explorers introduced predators, while for the recording industry, the Internet created the threat. The development of MP3 technology was worrisome, but it wasn't until widespread access to the Internet enabled easy copying and transfer of digital music tracks that the recording industry realized the extent of the threat to their profits.

In both situations, the speed with which the new threat spread through the environment made it difficult to respond effectively. The dodo's bizarre, belly-dragging shape needed to evolve faster than time permitted. For record labels and music retailers, the rapid penetration of the Internet, and the even more rapid adoption of peer-to-peer file sharing services, such as Napster, Morpheus, and KaZaA, threatened to make the old ways of doing business obsolete.

Both entities fought to survive. Dodos used their sharp, hooked beaks, and the record labels filed lawsuits. The dodo didn't win, but the Recording Industry Association of America did score some victories that bought them time to evolve.

Evolution on demand isn't easy. For the recording industry, avoiding extinction required a new business model to meet the old objectives. In 2002, several of the major labels decided to put thousands of songs online for 99 cents apiece. This decision required the industry to address concerns about cannibalizing CD sales and antagonizing distributors and retailers. Strategies for protecting downloaded tracks from unlawful copying and distribution still have to be developed.

Another strategic issue for the industry was the need to provide sufficient value to customers so that they would be willing to pay for music they had become accustomed to getting for free. Record labels had to cooperate to create a large enough online database of tracks to compete with free, peer-to-peer networks. Planning to cooperate required communication and compromise within and across record companies. By the end of 2002, the five largest labels had completed an agreement with Listen.com to offer more than 175,000 songs online through Listen's Rhapsody service. Weeks later, Pressplay introduced a subscription-based model, banking on its agreements with three of the labels in the Rhapsody stable to provide value through content.[1]

> Will the new business models work? The recording industry has developed new strategies to remain profitable in a digital world, based on adaptation to market forces and technological innovation. Now, all they need are paying customers.

As the experience of the recording industry illustrates, the Internet can create opportunities and challenges for business strategy. Old ways may become obsolete as new technologies offer customers new products, or new forms of old products. Technological advances can also increase the speed with which products can be developed and brought to market. These advances may also make it possible for consumers to become aware of new products, moving from trial to adoption more rapidly than before. These effects can mean that for many organizations the windows of opportunity, in which new products are envisioned, produced, and distributed, may become shorter. As a result, the importance of developing long-range and short-range plans for the way in which the organization will respond to the changing environment can be crucial for the success of the company.

The Internet can influence aspects of planning across all levels and functions of a business. Consider, for example, how the Internet has created new opportunities for products and services that have defined the focus and purpose of many companies, both small and large, and old and new. Amazon.com, an Internet retailer, entered the digital business environment to sell books. While the idea of a bookstore was not new, the concept of a virtual bookstore, in which shoppers can search databases of titles and reader reviews, order a book, and complete the payment part of the transaction online was novel. The opportunity for such a business did not exist until the technologies that comprise the Internet were available and accepted by a sufficient number of users to provide the online retailer with a viable target market.

In contrast, IBM, already well-known and respected as a force in the international market for business machines, targeted the market for electronic business solutions. Without giving up or cannibalizing any of its existing business avenues, IBM has devoted many resources, including time, money, and personnel, to developing name recognition in the rapidly growing and developing market for e-commerce.

The Internet can lead to an assessment and redirection of strategy, even for large, well-established companies that have no intention of marketing products online or of otherwise targeting electronic markets. For instance, a company that wishes to streamline its ability to produce and distribute its products more efficiently may revamp its strategy to emphasize products that can be more feasibly developed using Internet tools. In addition, strategic changes may occur at a more focused level, targeted toward changing the way that the business activities for a particular product line are carried out. Internet facilities, such as the availability of media buying information from online sources, and competitive research from online databases, can be used to develop business plans for traditional, off-line situations.

In this chapter we will consider the goals, processes, and outcomes of planning that integrates the Internet into business activity. We begin with a description of the different types of planning within an organization, to set the stage for a discussion of the effects of the Internet on planning. Then we discuss the influence of the Internet on the motivation, development, and execution of planning processes that result in a strategic plan and business model development.

Digital Business Planning: An Overview

Planning processes within organizations take different forms, depending on the purpose and focus of the planning effort. Strategic planning involves the long-term relationship of an organization to its environment,[2] in which decisions are made about the objectives and resources of the organization.

More formally defined, strategic planning is the process by which managers develop long range plans, implemented by shorter-range tactics, for the activities necessary to accomplish the goals of an organization. **Strategic planning** is important because it serves as the basis for effective decision making in many different areas of the organization. It is also the basis for decision making about a variety of different functions associated with moving the products of a company from design and production to the end consumer.

The process of strategic planning involves the within-organization analysis of fit between organizational resources and environmental opportunities. A strategic plan is designed to maximize the performance of a set of strategic business units. A **strategic business unit (SBU)** is the smallest unit within an organization that has responsibility and control over the determination and execution of the activities it will undertake to achieve its mission, and the resources needed to do so.

Planning Across Strategic Business Units

Strategic planning is intended to serve as a roadmap for activities designed to meet organizational objectives over an extended period of time. As information becomes available about the outcomes of completed activities, the strategic plan may be adjusted to accommodate changes to expectations and resources.

While strategic planning is intended to provide continuity of objectives and activities across and within units of the organization, the Internet may lead to shorter planning horizons. The ready availability of information with which to update expectations about market behavior, combined with the flip side—competitors are more able to learn what an organization is planning—may result in the need to adapt strategic plans with increasing frequency.

The benefits of strategic planning may become more pronounced as the Internet creates new opportunities for business products and practices in the central exchange environment. The Internet creates an opportunity to reassess strategic planning, as well as a way to develop and refine concepts and tactics associated with strategic planning. These opportunities can lead to strategic changes as dramatic as a redefinition of organizational mission or as subtle as a shift in the procedures used to share documentation within a company.

> **Bits & Bytes 8-1**
> Many off-line companies have protected their brand names online, by snapping up names in the .com, .org, and .net domain. Of the top 25 global brands, 15 already have an online presence.
> (*Source:* nua.ie, citing VeriSign, Inc.)

Planning Within Strategic Business Units

Within a SBU, managers translate the goals of the overall company into objectives for a specific business unit or product. Planning within the SBU is a process with two objectives. First, the process asks, "What resources do we have, and what is out there in the environment that lets us do something new that fits with organizational objectives?" Second, the process asks, "How should we do what we want to do, given the resources we have and the targeted market(s)?" For each question, the Internet may influence the relative emphasis placed on resources and opportunities. For example, in a smaller company with a single product focus, the Internet may create an opportunity to reach new markets for the existing product. Planning activities to tap into these markets may be desirable, given the limited resources of the company to modify the product or to develop other products.

In contrast, a larger company with a diversified set of products may capitalize on the technological capabilities available through the Internet for collaborative product design and production, in order to leverage existing resources for more efficient production. The enhanced resources, due to increased efficiency, may then be used to modify or develop new products.

Internet Effects on Planning

The Internet may influence the development of business planning in three distinct ways. First, it may lead a business to recognize a need for new planning. Second, the Internet may influence how a business conducts its planning activities, regardless of the reason for which they originate. Third, the Internet may influence the content of a strategic plan. That is, the interactive environment may suggest changes to objectives and activities.

Internet influences on strategy development may occur at any level of planning: across SBUs or within an SBU. The opportunity for these influences is depicted in Figure 8-1.

The Internet Affects Motivation for Planning

Rapid changes in technologies and Internet content present strategic challenges for businesses. For example, the rate of change to the central exchange environment of the Internet may lead to shorter windows of opportunity for introducing new products and heightened customer expectations about the rate at which new or modified products will be introduced. The strategic windows of opportunity decrease in length for three reasons. First, new technologies lead to new products, thus making old products more

FIGURE 8-1 The Internet Influences Three Levels of Business Planning.

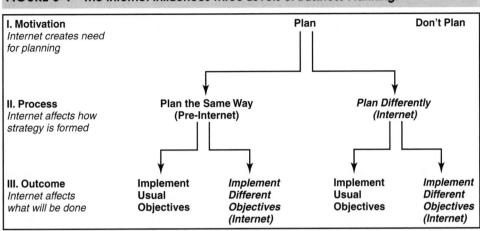

rapidly obsolete. Second, new technologies lead to faster communications among customers, thus speeding adoption rates and establishing product standards. Third, new technologies lead to increased product visibility across competition, thus reducing the time needed to develop a competitive product (and the competitive advantage of a novel product). These reasons reflect the impact of conditions, consumers, and competition, respectively, on the need for business planning.

To illustrate the effect of the Internet as a motive for strategic planning, suppose that you work for a company whose business mission is to provide music. The businesses of the organization are diverse, including concert production, instrument sales, and music recording sales. Your division is responsible for sales of recorded music. Your products, including cassettes and compact discs, have been popular since their introduction, but your research department has suggested that a new "compression technology" may make it possible to efficiently transmit music over the Internet. Although you are concerned that digital music may harm your company's sales of cassettes and compact discs, you feel that this is an opportunity that should not be missed.

This scenario reflects strategic planning motivated by environmental scanning. In this case, the environment includes the Internet and traditional formats for music recording sales. The mission of the SBU focused on music recordings may be redefined to emphasize a shift to the focus of core strategy on product type, even though the overarching mission of the larger organization is largely unchanged.

Bits & Bytes 8-2
As online business evolves, so do consumers. More and more people are subscribing to music sites, and shifting away from peer-to-peer networks. AOL Music averages 18 million visitors per month.
(*Source:* Wired.com, February 2002.)

The Internet Affects Processes for Planning

As noted in Figure 8-1, the second way in which the Internet may affect planning is by influencing the manner in which planning is accomplished. That is, by changing the nature of the processes for planning.

The Internet augments resources for planning and may influence the processes for planning in two ways: (1) by facilitating communications, and (2) by serving as an information resource. For instance, strategic planning may benefit from collaborative communications technologies available on the Internet to enable communications horizontally (within the SBU) and vertically (through organizational levels). Results of enhanced communications via the Internet may include faster planning cycles, more flexible plans, and increased cross-functional involvement in planning.

Web conferencing is an increasingly popular tool for planning. **Web conferencing** enables a set of people in different locations to communicate online as if they were in the same place. While early Web conferencing was limited to back and forth, typed-in comments, recent applications enable meeting participants to see and hear each other, and to share documents, presentations, and whiteboard capabilities for effective planning. Web conferencing can increase planning input and efficiency, and decrease planning costs.

As an information resource, the Internet can be used to glean intelligence about consumers and competitors. As we have already seen, this knowledge may affect the course of strategic planning by introducing new opportunities for achieving a competitive advantage in the marketplace.

The Internet Affects the Outcomes of Planning

The Internet may influence the focus and structure of the marketing strategy that results from the planning process. Characteristics of the Internet may enable businesses to carry out activities that would not be possible without the Internet, or to complete activities differently. In either case, the end result may be a shift in the objectives of strategic planning. For instance, the Internet may create an opportunity for a new product, or it may make an existing product obsolete.

As we saw in the vignette at the beginning of this chapter, the recording industry is concerned that the ability to download music from the Internet may eliminate demand for the dominant forms of its music product—compact discs and cassette tapes. To protect their profits in the marketplace, several of the larger record labels have agreed to let customers buy songs that can be downloaded from the Internet. Implementing this strategy requires the labels to shift their marketing efforts from selling collections of songs on compact discs to selling the concept of buying individual, digitally distributed songs. In addition, the option to use the Internet as a direct channel for distributing a label's songs requires the label to reconsider its traditional channel strategy, as the music retailers can be disintermediated. As a result, the strategic decision to develop an online music product necessitates rethinking the other mix elements of pricing, promotion, and distribution.

Change and Convergence Issues for Planning

In Chapter 7, we saw how companies adapt their business strategies to keep ahead—or at least apace—of changes in their industries. The Internet has changed the technologies available for conducting many aspects of business, and it has created new product opportunities. In addition to changing the marketing environment, the Internet has also changed the nature of the relationship between marketers and consumers within the central exchange environment. As the Internet continues to grow and evolve, so does the buyer-seller relationship.

Traditional approaches to marketing tended to reflect businesses' ability to leverage technology to "push" product offerings to customers. With the Internet, buyers gained the power of technology, and were able to push back at sellers. As we learned in Chapter 4, buyers are better informed about products, and they demand seller accountability, all due to the Internet's information and communication capabilities. As a result, an early phase of digital business emphasized the importance of targeting the **cyberconsumer,** for whom the Internet was a primary source of consumption.

As the novelty of the Internet as a consumption environment has worn off, the unidirectional buyer-seller relationship has changed to the bidirectional, reciprocal relationship introduced in the framework in Chapter 2. In addition, companies recognize that customers are likely to use both online and off-line resources for consumption, operating as hybrid consumers.[3]

The convergence of the online and off-line worlds, and the evolving relationship between customers and companies, underscore the importance of strategic planning that recognizes and acts on change—in the past, present, and future.

Strategic Planning Under the Microscope

Strategic planning is conducted with two chief objectives: (1) define the opportunities that exist in the environment, and (2) determine how best to leverage resources to capitalize on opportunities (Figure 8-2). Framed as questions, these objectives are "What should we do?" and "How should we do it?" The first question emphasizes the importance of planning, while the second question underscores the role of implementation.

Defining Opportunities: What Should We Do?

A fundamental goal for business strategy is to develop a means by which a company can perform better than its competition. "Doing better" may translate into faster growth, greater market share, or higher profits. Each of these measures of success, however, can be related to the concept of **competitive advantage.**

As a general characterization, a company that has a competitive advantage tends to have an ability to obtain profits that are higher than average, among the pool of competition. Competitive advantage can be created in several ways (Figure 8-3). For example, having a product or process that nobody else has—and which is superior and in

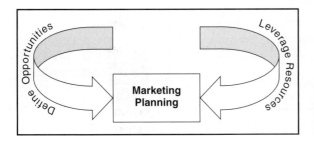

FIGURE 8-2   The Primary Objectives of Strategic Planning.

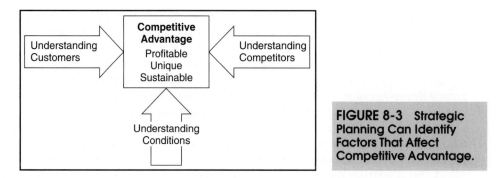

FIGURE 8-3 Strategic Planning Can Identify Factors That Affect Competitive Advantage.

demand—can provide competitive advantage. Amazon's patented 1-Click checkout system speeds the transaction process and creates a barrier to competition. Microsoft's ability to bundle its browser software with every computer it sells gives it a market penetration advantage over other browsers. In effect, a competitive advantage provides the business with a niche that fosters the success of the company in the environment.

The Internet and Opportunity

Identifying opportunities and developing strategic objectives requires asking the question, "How is the Internet going to change what companies do in my industry?" Answers to the question can differ in the nature and extent to which they affect strategic planning. For instance, the Internet might enable a company to provide product information online, while sticking to business-as-usual for all other business activities. In contrast, the Internet may necessitate a complete overhaul of traditional business models, as we saw with the music industry, including record labels and music retailers.

The difference in opportunities is shown in the pyramid in Figure 8-4. The pyramid describes increasing commitment to e-business, much like the continuum of

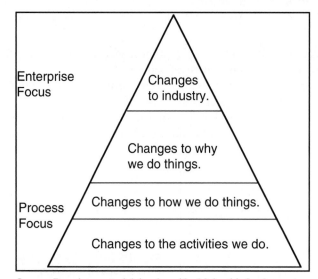

FIGURE 8-4 The E-Business Commitment Pyramid Outlines Strategic Opportunities.

Source: Based on material developed by Mohanbir Sawhney at www.mohansawhney.com.

e-commerce introduced in Chapter 1. The pyramid is also useful, however, for discerning ways in which the Internet creates opportunities for marketing activities, and the associated changes to marketing planning needed to realize the opportunities.

At the lowest level, the Internet may affect some of the activities carried out by a business, like providing brochures online, or posting FAQs to enhance customer service. The next levels reflect opportunities to streamline or augment business processes. While the changes may not alter the products or mission of the company, they can be an important component of business strategy. For instance, some car companies, such as Saturn and Honda, let customers design and order their cars online, increasing customer involvement with the brand to increase sales and loyalty (Figure 8-5). At the third level of the pyramid, the Internet can alter the nature of an industry. For example, the Internet made online gaming possible, creating opportunities for new products, as well as new venues for existing games. Sony's decision to enter the online gaming market with its subscription-based EverQuest game was a move into a new product-market for the electronics company that required strategic planning as well as marketing planning. At the highest level, a company's mission is defined by the Internet. For instance, Internet Service Providers (ISPs) and search engine companies only exist because the Internet exists.

Defining Opportunities with the Internet

The Internet is a source of market intelligence for defining opportunities, once they are identified. Researchers can acquire information directly from consumers about desired

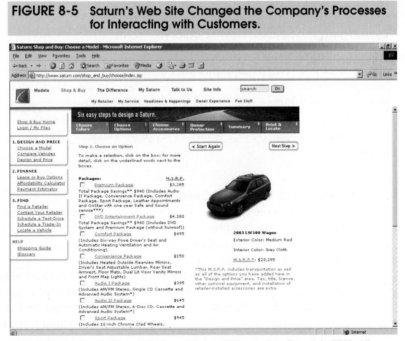

FIGURE 8-5   Saturn's Web Site Changed the Company's Processes for Interacting with Customers.

Source: Reproduced with permission of General Motors, Inc. Copyright 2003. All rights reserved.

product and service features, using e-mail and online survey approaches. In addition, information about consumers' preferences and attitudes can be gathered indirectly, through discussion groups and mailing lists.

Information about the competitive climate can be assessed by analyzing the product offerings and promotional material provided on the Internet by firms in product niches that are related to the product objectives of the company conducting the research. In addition, newsgroups, chat rooms, and online bulletin boards are often sources of evaluative information about the extent to which a company's approach meets consumers' needs.

Businesses can also use the Internet to assess trends and develop predictions about the nature of market conditions that can affect the efficacy of a strategy. Internet content, such as press releases, agency reports, and public and private sector databases, provides a range of ever-changing insights on the role of technology, the economy, and policy for business. We will examine ways to use the Internet for business research in greater detail in Chapter 9.

Bits & Bytes 8-3

Online consumers may pay for tunes, but not for content. Sixty-three percent of adults surveyed by Jupiter Research say there is no form of content they would be willing to buy.

(*Source:* Wired.com, March 2002, citing research presented at the Jupiter Media Forum.)

Leveraging Resources: How Should We Do It?

Once a business strategy is formulated, attention shifts to implementing it. At this level, the objective is to capitalize on characteristics of the digital business environment that serve as resources with which to develop an effective marketing mix. The goal of mix development is to provide value to the customer: to create a persuasive value proposition. Value can be derived from three aspects of the Internet: (1) its role as a source of content, (2) its ability to serve as a channel, and (3) its use as a form of communication.

The Internet as a Content Resource

The information-rich nature of the Internet means that it can be used as a resource in several ways. In one use, Internet content may be a product offering, when the product can be digitized (e.g., books, music). This use is closely related to the role of the Internet as a channel resource.

A second use of the Internet as a content resource is to develop and maintain information to guide product development. For instance, the data that result from marketing research can be collected, organized, and stored in internal databases that can be "mined" to provide insights for future product development or business activity, a concept we will revisit in Chapter 9. In addition, Internet technologies can be used to implement online product planning and design efforts.

As a third use, benefits related to the product offering—such as customer support and product information—can be provided online, even when the product cannot be offered in a digital form. This use of the Internet as a content resource can create **soft benefits,** or reasons for being loyal to a brand that are not related to the actual nature or function of the product. For instance, Web site content that leads a customer through the steps of how to install and use tax preparation software may create an advantage for the product by making the effort to learn a new package unacceptably high.

Companies are not the only source of content. Customer-created content, as enabled through online brand communities or by posting information to a product or company Web site, may create a positive buyer-seller relationship. We will examine the role of content as a factor in strategy implementation in Chapter 10.

The Internet as a Channel Resource

To illustrate the Internet's role as a channel resource, suppose that you have a company that produces a popular software product that is widely available in retail outlets. With increasing competition, however, it has been getting harder to maintain the profit margins your software used to provide. Pressure from the competition has forced your company to cut the price of the software, but the costs of producing and getting the product to the target markets have increased. What can you do?

You might conclude that the software product could be sold and distributed entirely through the Internet. This change in practice reduces packaging costs and shipping costs. Of course, these benefits must be weighed against the loss in sales and brand recognition for packages sold in retail outlets. Management feels, however, that by increasing advertising to make potential customers aware of the online availability of the software, issues of sales and brand exposure can be addressed. Thus, the change to the distribution element of the marketing mix is based on the determination of management that the benefits of the Internet as a distribution outlet outweigh the costs of a diminished presence in retail outlets. We will consider the channel implications of the Internet for digital business in Chapter 11.

The Internet as a Communications Resource

The Internet can be used as a vehicle for communications between a company and its target market. The multimedia, interactive nature of the Internet enables companies to develop promotional campaigns and to provide product-related experiences in ways that differ from the forms of communications typically seen in traditional media.

The novel characteristics of the Internet as a communications medium can be used to achieve strategic objectives, such as creating awareness, or attracting attention to a brand or product. In addition, the technologies that facilitate real-time, digital interaction between a company and a consumer can be used to foster relationship development. These types of relationships might include a salesperson-customer exchange, or a consumer-customer service exchange.

An important aspect of online communications is the content of the communication. The nature of the Internet, however, makes it possible to consider the effect of the content of a communication as separate from the effect of the manner in which the content is transmitted. This distinction is explored in Chapter 12.

To this point, we have reviewed the basic characteristics of business planning. We have also considered how the Internet can be used to define strategic opportunities and to provide the means with which to seize these opportunities. In the next sections, we will look at the way the Internet may influence processes for developing and implementing business strategy.

From Opportunity to Action: The Planning Pyramid

The strategic planning process within a business unit results in two key outcomes: (1) a set of strategic objectives, and (2) a business model to guide activities for achieving the objectives. At a basic level, the objectives answer the question, "What are we going to do?" The business model answers the question, "How are we going to do it?" Taken together, these two outcomes reflect the strategic phase of planning activity (Figure 8-6). The activities associated with the implementation of the marketing strategy are the nuts and bolts of business planning: managing mix elements and resources over time to reach strategic goals for moving products through the value chain to customers.

The Internet and Strategic Objectives: Understanding Opportunities

Several primary objectives of commercial activity are influenced by the increased emphasis on information in a digital business environment. These objectives include developing brand equity and fostering customer loyalty.

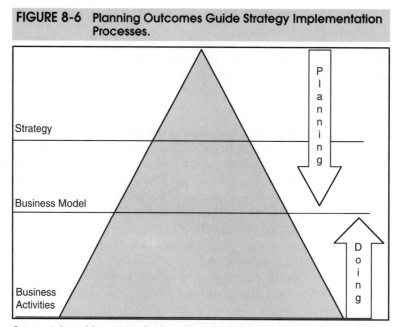

FIGURE 8-6 **Planning Outcomes Guide Strategy Implementation Processes.**

Source: Adapted from "An e-Business Model Ontology for Modeling e-Business," by Alexander Osterwalder and Yves Pigneur. *Proceedings of the 15th Bled Electronic Commerce Conference, Slovenia* (2002), pages 1–11.

Building Brand Equity

Brand equity can be very simply defined as the value of a brand name. While defining it may be easy, achieving it can be far more complicated. The Internet can play an important role in developing brand equity. **Cyberbranding** refers to strategies used to build brand equity using the Internet.

Businesses attempt to create brand equity by manipulating elements of the marketing mix, such as product characteristics and distribution strategies, to differentiate their brand from competing brands. In a traditional marketplace, mix elements work together to create perceived value on the part of the customer. The elements are viewed as dependent and inseparable—all part of a marketing and sales program for a particular product. As a result, brand equity typically results from an aggregate-level approach to creating value for the target market segment.

In an information-defined transaction environment, however, differentiating a brand through traditional combinations of mix elements may be less feasible than in traditional business environments. Consider the following example of a car purchase in each type of environment.

Traditional approaches to building brand equity typically explain equity as the result of an effective combination of three elements of a transaction: content, context, and infrastructure. Content refers to the product, or to information provided about the product. Context describes the setting, or environment, in which the transaction occurs. The infrastructure is the system or facilities that enable the product to be conveyed from the marketer to the consumer. For example, in an off-line setting, the content component of a car purchase would consist of the cars available for evaluation at a dealership. The context would be the dealership from which the car is to be purchased. The delivery of the car is facilitated by the infrastructure, which might consist of an inventory system that results in the selected car being available on site, or an ordering system through which the car is built at the factory and then delivered to the customer.

Now suppose that the customer wants to purchase a car from a vendor on the Internet. The content is no longer the physically tangible car, but information about the available vehicles. The context is not the face-to-face interaction with a salesperson at the dealership, but a series of electronic, on-screen communications. The infrastructure shifts from the organizational characteristics of the dealership to the computer and communications systems that enable the transaction.

In the traditional marketplace, the components are clearly distinct. Unless all of the components are present, however, there is no product offering to be consumed. In short, value is the result of the holistic availability of all three components. More simply, the whole really *is* greater than the sum of its parts.

Researchers note that in the Internet environment, the components can be separated so that each individual component can convey value.[4] This possibility means that businesses can attempt to create brand equity in new ways, with different combinations or implementations of components.

For example, Amazon Books, an online vendor, is comparable in its earliest online offering, books, to other book vendors in traditional marketplaces (Figure 8-7). In contrast, however, Amazon leverages the online context to provide access to its inventory in a customized form, tailoring the information provided to customers. This creates value in the form of a new benefit for customers. The databases of customer

FIGURE 8-7 Examples of Disaggregating Components for Differential Emphasis.

	Traditional Business: A–1 Bookstore	*Digital Business: Amazon.com*
Content	Product offering: books at specified prices	Database of inventory and product-related information
		Value opportunity: can be applied to other forms (e.g., tools and toys)
Context	Physical location of retail outlet	Online, digital format, searchable by user preferences
		Value opportunity: can be restructured to personalize presentation of product assortments
Infrastructure	Retail capabilities: space and equipment (e.g., warehouse, shelves, employees, cash register)	Internet
		Value opportunity: can be used for near real-time communication with consumers in remote locations

input and sales information also provide Amazon with the ability to obtain detailed and up-to-date information for inventory and distribution, thus streamlining and redefining infrastructure.

Fostering Customer Loyalty

Customer loyalty is closely related to brand equity. Developing loyalty to a brand, product, or company in information-defined environments can be accomplished by taking advantage of the ability to separate the value components. In an Internet environment, customers may develop loyalty to individual components, rather than to an aggregate notion of value for a particular brand, product, or vendor. For example, a company that distinguishes itself from its competition because its Internet presence provides customers with a tailored product search or simplified ordering or a faster delivery time has capitalized on context to develop a competitive advantage that encourages loyalty.

Aspects of the Internet that enable the development of loyalty require careful management. The ready availability of information over the Internet may diminish loyalty by making comparisons across brands quick, easy, and relatively cost-free. For example, online reservation services for air travel provide travelers with information about flights and fares for several airlines. Airlines must then rely on differentiation in content, or on other aspects of the offering, to encourage loyalty. To this end, airlines can differentiate through content, such as frequent flier programs and awards. They may also differentiate through context, as with online customer service, to increase loyalty to a particular vendor.

Building a Better Business Model

Think of all the products and services that are available for consumption. It is not surprising that there are also many ways that businesses attempt to create awareness,

---

InSite

BUILDING A BRAND, BIT BY BIT: WWW.AOL.COM

The ability to disaggregate the components of value also enables businesses to develop brand equity by creating combinations of components in novel ways, as through developing relationships with other vendors. To illustrate, consider the success of America Online. The content is a collection of news from national newspapers, and the infrastructure is a combination of widely available communications, goods, and services, not owned by the company. The success of America Online is the result of the creation of a valued context that enables users to customize the information they receive online. This context is America Online's brand, and the basis for the brand equity that the company enjoys.

---

demand, and loyalty for these items. It would be impossible to specify every possibility, much less study them. We can, however, describe the main elements of a successful business model, and examine the role of the Internet for each part.

Prior to the Internet, business models typically contained three necessary ingredients: a good reason for the consumer to buy the product (**customer benefits**); a way to produce and distribute the product (**delivery infrastructure**); and revenue from product-related transactions (**revenue streams**). With its ability to facilitate communication, the Internet makes an additional feature important for business models: a means for fostering buyer-seller relationships (**customer-company interaction**).

Creating Value with Customer Benefits

The digital business environment may affect the way that marketers create and communicate economic value to consumers. With the Internet as the vehicle for many business activities, the information provided electronically about the product takes on greater importance, and it may exert a critical influence on the success of the company.

We can describe product-focused benefits in terms of the extent to which they differentially emphasize one of three aspects of customers' perceptions of the product: *image*, *incentive*, and *improvement* known as the **3 I's** (Figure 8-8). All of these aspects contribute to brand equity. We will look at each of the 3 I's in the following sections.

Image   An image-based objective emphasizes business activities that enhance people's perceptions of the product or brand. Companies can use the Internet to build a brand image by increasing awareness and exposure to the item. An example of a technique that can accomplish these goals is a **link exchange,** in which two companies place logos or hyperlinks to each other's Web pages on their sites. Companies may also develop more formal arrangements that foster coexistence in the digital business environment. These arrangements include partnerships to cobrand products.

FIGURE 8-8   Product-focused Models: The 3 I's.

Model Type	Image	Incentive	Improvement
Objective	Enhance customers' perceptions of brand, product, or company	Reduce costs associated with product purchase	Create benefits in product performance or use experience
Internet Tactics	Use Web site to provide related information; create co-brands and alliances	Use Internet as channel, or to streamline processes (e.g., reduce delivery time)	Use Internet for customer support, including feedback, product customization, and product upgrades

A goal of cobranding is to identify a partner whose brand, when linked with yours, has the potential for increasing customer's perceptions of your brand. For example, Lycos, a search engine, and Barnes & Noble, a bookseller, negotiated a partnership for online presence. Lycos expected to benefit from the longstanding reputation of Barnes & Noble in the traditional marketplace, while Barnes & Nobles sought to gain visibility in the digital environment.

Image is also enhanced by Web site content. Content that lures users repeatedly to a site can also build brand image through exposure. In some cases, the content may be only tangentially related to the product, but the positive affect associated with the site may transfer to the brand. **Web site stickiness** describes the ability of a site's content to engage users' interest. For example, Mattel's Barbie.com site uses colorful images and interactive capabilities to provide an entertaining site visit (Figure 8-9).

Online brand building is important. Recent study results from Harris Interactive (2000) show that 20 percent of online shoppers type in the URL of a desired product, rather than searching the Web for information about the product category. The survey provides evidence for six categories of online shoppers. These categories are shown in Figure 8-10. "Brand Loyalists" know what they are looking for, and they go straight to sites where they can get it. They are the biggest spenders and report high levels of satisfaction with online shopping. In contrast, "Hunter-Gatherers" are comparison shoppers. This group tends to have shoppers in their mid–30s, married, with children. The "Hooked, Online, & Single" shoppers tend to use the Internet primarily to consume services, such as banking, investing, and entertainment. Both the Hunter-Gatherers and the Hooked segments constitute desirable markets and represent viable targets for brand building efforts. "Time-sensitive Materialists" are another viable target for brand building. These consumers look for convenience and time savings in online shopping. Creating a strong brand that reduces search and instills loyalty addresses these objectives.

The remaining categories exhibit fewer opportunities for online branding. Shoppers in the "Clicks & Mortar" category are concerned about the security of online shopping. They tend to look for product information online, but shop in traditional outlets. The "E-bivalent Newbies" are older, less interested in online shopping, and spend the least amount of time online.

FIGURE 8-9   Enhancing Product Image with Site Content.

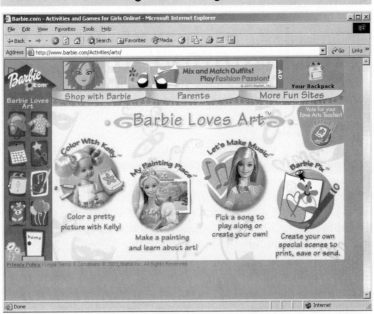

Source: Reproduced with permission of Mattel, Inc. ©2003 Mattel, Inc. All rights reserved.

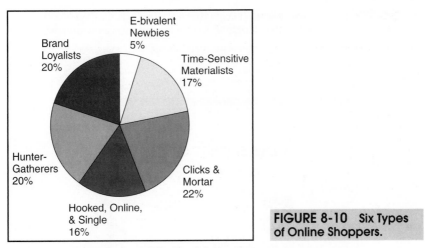

FIGURE 8-10   Six Types of Online Shoppers.

Source: Nua Internet Surveys, citing Harris Interactive (2000).

Incentive   The Internet can provide companies with ways to streamline production and distribution processes. In addition, the Internet can facilitate some forms of promotional effort, due to the ease with which content can be tailored and transmitted. These capabilities can mean that costs associated with product activities decrease. This reduced cost, when passed on to consumers, serves as an incentive to purchase the product.

Companies that wish to use an incentive-based approach can use the Internet as a resource for creating incentives in several ways. For example, a channel structure in which the Internet eliminates or reduces the number of middlemen can lower product costs for the consumer. In addition, products for which updates or changes can be distributed digitally can also provide cost incentives to consumers. For instance, patches and upgrades to software, and revisions to published content can be handled wholly through the Internet.

Another form of incentive is represented by promotional efforts that provide free samples, trial offers, and digital coupons and rebates to encourage consumers' interactions with a product. For example, iVillage.com, a navigation hub targeted to women, uses its Savings Center to provide information about coupons and incentives to visitors (Figure 8-11). Clicking on a coupon offer takes the visitor to a printable coupon for an advertised product. Other companies have followed this approach to lure first-time online customers, including the Home Shopping Network, which offered $15 off the first $20 purchase.

Yet another form of incentive is illustrated by clickrewards.com (Figure 8-12). The company provides a system that rewards customers with digital currency in the form of "clickmiles" for shopping at member sites. Users collect the clickmiles in an online account, and can spend them at a variety of online stores that have agreed to accept

FIGURE 8-11   Promotional Efforts Through Savings Center Provide iVillage Visitors with Purchase Incentives.

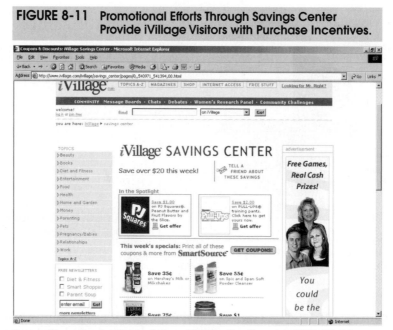

clickmiles in lieu of money. Businesses can use the ClickRewards service to attract customers, to reward repeat shoppers, and to gather information.

Improvement   The third product-focused approach is characterized by a business' efforts to enhance perceptions of a product by increasing the product value to customers. The changes, or improvements, to the product offering can be implemented in a variety of ways with the Internet. As we have already noted, Web site content can serve as an added benefit of a product. Another form of improvement is customer service, both before and after the transaction. Customer service on the Internet can be as simple as posting technical manuals and tips for product use, or as technologically involved as interactive, real-time, online communication between the user and a service representative. Dell Computer's e-mail support approach falls between these two extremes in terms of technological complexity and interactivity (Figure 8-13). When a customer e-mails a technical support representative, Dell's System Profiler can include details of the user's computer in the e-mail to streamline the process of directing and responding to the support issue.

These three product-focused approaches address different ways to enhance customers' perceptions of a product experience. In some cases, one approach may address multiple objectives, such as using online customer service to reduce costs (thus creating a price incentive) and to provide an extra product benefit.

Developing value through customer benefits may sometimes result in increased costs to the business. For instance, creating the capability to provide online live help to customers can be costly. Even though the feature adds value to the product, a company

FIGURE 8-12   The clickrewards.com Incentive Program Rewards Customer-Company Interactions.

Source: Reproduced with permission of clickrewards.com inc. Copyright 2003. All rights reserved.

FIGURE 8-13 Using Online Customer Support to Provide Value.

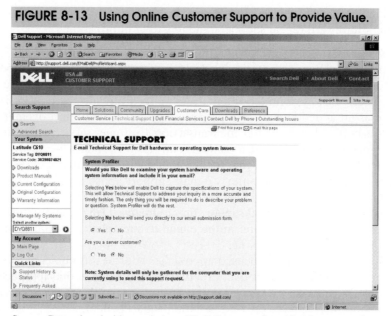

may elect not to increase the price of the product. Companies must determine the time frame within which the anticipated costs of implementing a product-focused model are acceptable, as well as the longer-term returns on investment.

Developing the Delivery Infrastructure

The infrastructure needed to move a product from concept to consumption includes the components of the value chain, including suppliers, manufacturers, and distributors. In addition, the infrastructure may operate using strategic alliances and partnerships. As we saw in Chapter 7, the rise of business ecosystems in the online environment is based on strategic networking between companies, as they attempt to leverage their strengths and outsource areas of weakness, all along the value chain.

A third aspect of the infrastructure is the set of assets that the company has at its disposal. **Firm-level assets** include **tangible assets,** such as manufacturing facilities, warehouses, and equipment. In addition, **intangible assets** are an important element of the delivery infrastructure. For instance, intellectual property can protect the processes for creating or distributing a product, contributing to the infrastructure. The ability to deliver a product is also based on **human assets,** such as skilled employees, or creative and highly able managers.

Online Revenue Streams

Revenue streams are designed to bring money into a company. The Internet enables companies to generate revenue with traditional models, and it has created the opportunity for several less traditional processes for making money. Similar to their off-line counterparts, however, online revenue models follow a predictable risk/reward pattern. That is, the less predictable a source of income is, the greater the potential for reward. In addition, higher rewards tend to be accompanied by higher performance expectations. Even on the Internet, TANSTAAFL![5]

Revenue from Transaction Models: Direct Streams   An obvious source of revenue is to sell something to someone: an exchange of one resource, such a good, a service, or information, for money. This model is popular on the Internet, as is clear from the variety of products advertised and the increasing numbers of online sales. **Merchant models,** including virtual "e-tailers" like Amazon, and clicks-and-mortar catalog vendors like Lands End, are transaction models between retailers and customers.

Manufacturer models are similar to merchant models, in that a transaction is made with a customer. In contrast, however, the source of the product is the manufacturer, rather than another, downstream channel member. The Internet has increased the viability of manufacturer models, given the ease with which manufacturers can communicate online with customers. Dell and Apple Computer both use a manufacturer model to sell online.

Another form of a transaction model is a subscription model, such as basing fees on the amount of a product or service that is consumed. For example, some ISPs base their rates on the number of minutes a user is connected to the Internet in a fixed time span, such as a month. A related model is based on user subscription to a service, such as a news-clipping service, or a business reports newsletter. In this model, the fee is usually based on a predetermined time for consumption (e.g., a 1-year subscription). For example, for $19.95 per month, movie buffs can rent up to three DVD movies from NetFlix, choosing from over 15,000 titles. Classmates.com uses a peer-to-peer approach to keep classmates in touch. For a monthly subscription fee of $3, members can create and access detailed personal profiles.

Revenue from Other Sources: Indirect Revenue Streams   The direct revenue streams share one characteristic: the customer is the source of revenue. Other forms of revenue models emphasize income potential from a source other than an end customer. Some of the revenue streams most often used in business models that incorporate an online component involve intermediary models, affiliate models, and advertising models.

Intermediary models serve as nodes in networks that link other agents in the central exchange environment. Intermediaries tend to take of two forms: brokerage models or infomediary models. Companies who use a **brokerage model,** such as Auto-by-Tel and Ticketmaster, make their money through commissions based on the sales of others companies' products. Their job is to facilitate the company's ability to connect with customers. Subsets of brokerage models are **auction models,** like eBay; **market exchange models,** like Orbitz; and **transaction fulfillment models,** like PayPal.

Infomediary models build revenue streams based on the collection and distribution of information, from companies and from customers. For instance, **targeted advertising models,** like Doubleclick, provide businesses with information about shoppers' consumption of banner ads. **Incentive/loyalty models,** like CoolSavings.com, collect visitor information to provide to businesses, in exchange for coupons.

An **affiliate model** operates by creating a partnership between two companies. This arrangement is a unidirectional form of linking—in contrast to a link exchange—in which the site that displays the link information can obtain revenue based on how site visitors use the link. The affiliate agrees to place information about its partner on the affiliate Web site. This information is often the logo of the partner company. The information serves to link the affiliate site to the partner company.

Affiliates make money from the arrangement when a visitor to the site acts on the link information. In some arrangements, the affiliate earns money when the visitor uses the link to go to the partner site. In other arrangements, the affiliate only benefits when the link results in a sale of the partner's product.

Affiliate programs not only provide revenue prospects, but also have potential benefits for increasing brand image and brand equity. For the company who offers the affiliate program, benefits are obtained from increases in sales and from image enhancement due to broader exposure. For the affiliate site, being associated with the partner company can improve consumers' perceptions of the affiliate company. The presence of a well-known company, in the form of a logo, on the affiliate site may increase consumers' trust in the affiliate company, as well as enhance perceptions of the affiliate's product or service. The positive or negative impact of a company or its product on the evaluation of another entity is called a **halo effect.**

Bits & Bytes 8-5

Word-of-mouth matters. In a 2002 study by Taylor Nelson Joffres, 98 percent of respondents said they would recommend a site that satisfied them. Only 1 percent would pass on word of a dissatisfying site.
(*Source:* Nua.ie, May 2002.)

Advertising models take several forms. In one form, Web site content serves as the lure for visitors. Through **content sponsorship,** a company can pay the site to have its logo displayed on the site with the sponsored content. Portal companies, like Yahoo! and iVillage, use content sponsorship models to offset the costs of procuring desirable content. On the Internet, sponsorship is often linked to site content; that is, a company may sponsor the provision of a particular form of content on a Web site. Sponsorships are typically based on a fixed payment agreement, in which the amount of revenue is tied to a length of time in which the sponsor will be acknowledged as a sponsor on the displaying Web site.

Another advertising model is the **classified ad model.** For instance, on Monster.com, prospective employers can pay to post a job opening, and they can pay to search Monster's database of posted resumes. There is no cost to post a resume, or to apply for an advertised

Net Knowledge

RISK AND REWARD IN INDIRECT REVENUE MODELS

Indirect revenue models operate by creating a relationship between two companies. The models differ in two ways: (1) by the behavioral commitment of the site visitor to the partner company, and (2) by the certainty, or predictability, of the revenues that will stem from the affiliate relationship. Look at the relationship between the nature of the commitment and the prospects for revenue in the graphic. The potential for revenue is related to the amount of revenue risk that the company assumes upon entering a particular relationship.

In the affiliate relationship, the potential for revenue is highest, because the programs are often structured so that higher commissions are paid for affiliate links that result in sales, rather than just looking. When revenue is acquired through fees to place a banner ad on a site, revenue potential is typically lower than for affiliate relationships. For content sponsorship relationships, revenue potential is often lowest, reflecting the lower requirements of site visitors, in terms of exposure and purchase-related behavior in the sponsor's site.

job through the site. Similar to the classified model, the **paid placement model** is another form of revenue stream based on advertising. As with most search engines, companies can pay to have their listing displayed prominently on the page of search results.

The revenue stream in an advertising model may often depend on visitor behavior. For instance, a company may enter an agreement in which the company's site allocates space for the advertising message of another company. This message is often called a **banner.** The company who displays the banner receives revenue based on **impressions,** or how many times the banner is viewed. Alternatively, revenue can be based on the types of behaviors of a visitor to the displaying site. For example, the advertiser may pay a set amount each time that a visitor clicks through the banner to the advertiser's site. In addition, banners can be constructed so that visitors fill out registration forms within the banner, thus providing sales leads to the advertiser without leaving the displaying site. The advertiser may pay for each lead the banner generates.

Selecting and Combining Revenue Streams   An effective business model may take advantage of more than one revenue stream. For example, CNET is a content site that provides news and reviews about technology products. CNET does not rely on sales to end consumers. The company began making money by charging other companies to place ads on its site. Now, the company also derives revenue from leads it provides when consumers are exposed to product information placed by a vendor on the CNET site, and then go to the vendor's site. CNET's purchase of an auction site also enables the company to get revenue from listing fees.

Cultivating the Company-Consumer Interaction

The fourth business model component reflects the importance of the Internet as a means of communication between marketers and consumers, and the central role of information in fostering the relationship. As we saw with the virtual value chain in

Chapter 7, information collected via the Internet can be used to create value for consumers in a variety of ways. For instance, registration and purchase data—as well as information gathered by infomediaries—can be used to create consumer profiles that serve as input in strategic marketing planning. In addition, knowledge of what consumers want and how they use Web sites to get it can help businesses personalize the consumption experience.

This ability to adapt to consumer needs and input reflects the idea of convergence between buyers, sellers, and technology that was discussed earlier in the chapter. The convergence of goals makes it possible for companies to customize the products and information that they provide. In addition, customers can also be active participants in the customization process. The ability to create custom portals, like MyYahoo!, can increase customer loyalty and reduce customer acquisition costs.

Chapter Summary

Strategic planning integrates business objectives with resources for reaching those objectives. Careful strategic development is important for creating a competitive advantage. A company's competitive advantage increases the company's prospects for long-term survival in the environment by leveraging resources of the company and the environment to capitalize on identified opportunities for growth, as through market share or profit.

In this chapter, we examined the role of the Internet on aspects of strategic planning. We considered the way that the Internet can be used to identify possible sources of competitive advantage. For example, the Internet environment may create opportunities for new products and services, or for new ways of making existing offerings available. In addition, the Internet serves as a tool for assessing the types of opportunities that may exist. Market research with the Internet can provide insights into customers' needs, competitors' actions, and broader environmental conditions.

The Internet affects the planning processes used to develop strategy. We considered the implications of the Internet on three aspects of strategic planning. The Internet may motivate planning, as when it presents new opportunities for growth. The Internet may also influence the processes by which a company conducts its planning activities. For instance, the networked nature of the Internet may facilitate communications between far-flung offices and divisions of a company, thus enabling broad participation and representation in strategy development. The Internet may also influence the strategy that results from the planning process. The Internet may affect the types of objectives delimited by the planning process, as well as the nature of the activities deemed appropriate for attaining the objectives.

The Internet can also affect the implementation of a strategy. Characteristics of the Internet can be used by companies as resources to be leveraged for strategic objectives. Businesses can use the Internet as a content resource, a channel resource, and a communications resource. The relative emphasis of each characteristic depends on the types of objectives that guide the efforts of management.

With a strategic plan in place, business models for the Internet enable companies to address product-related objectives and revenue-related objectives. Business models have four key components: (1) customer benefits/value proposition, (2) a delivery infrastructure, (3) one or more revenue streams, and (4) a way to manage the company-customer interaction. We considered two categories of revenue streams: (1) models that reflect an exchange relationship between a company and a customer (e.g., a sale), and (2) models that reflect the role of the Internet in relationships between companies as a way to influence subsequent company-customer interactions (e.g., leads, exposure). In the latter group, we examined the use of affiliate programs, banner and button advertising, and content sponsorship as Internet business models.

CONTENT MANAGEMENT

USEFUL TERMS

- 3 I's
- advertising model
- affiliate model
- auction model
- banner
- brand equity
- brokerage model
- classified ad model
- competitive advantage
- content sponsorship
- customer benefits
- customer-company interaction
- cyberbranding
- cyberconsumer
- delivery infrastructure
- firm-level assets
- halo effect
- human assets
- impressions
- incentive/loyalty model
- infomediary model
- intangible assets
- intermediary model
- link exchange
- manufacturer model
- market exchange model
- merchant model
- paid placement model
- revenue stream
- soft benefits
- strategic business unit (SBU)
- strategic planning
- tangible assets
- targeted advertising model
- transaction fulfillment model
- Web conferencing
- Web site stickiness

REVIEW QUESTIONS

1. What types of planning are used to guide business action?
2. Describe the differences between the goals and actions associated with each type of planning.
3. Describe the factors that can create a competitive advantage.
4. Why is a competitive advantage important for a company?
5. How might the Internet enable a company to develop a competitive advantage?
6. Describe three ways that the Internet can be used to identify strategic opportunities.
7. Describe three ways that the Internet can serve as a resource for achieving strategic objectives.
8. What are the three levels at which the Internet can influence strategic planning?
9. Identify and describe two primary classes of strategic objectives.
10. How can the Internet enable businesses to disaggregate the three components of brand equity to create value?
11. What are the 3 I's, and how are they related to strategic planning?
12. In revenue-based business models, what two groups of people are the main sources of revenue?
13. Describe three types of Internet-based revenue models (*Hint:* think ABC's).

WEB APPLICATION

Dot-com Decomposition: Taking Apart a Business Model

We've learned that a successful business needs a good business model. Moreover, a good business model has four key components: customer benefits/value; delivery infrastructure for the benefits;

a way to make money; and a way to foster the interaction between company and customer. Many early online efforts failed because they didn't adequately develop all facets of the business model. In contrast, companies who have succeeded have done so because they have addressed all four components.

This exercise is designed to help you identify ways in which companies implement the four components as part of a comprehensive business plan. Complete the following table by describing how each company put its business model into action. It's helpful to start with the company Web site to identify the value and benefits to consumers. Then, corporate financial information, such as the annual report, can be used to identify the key revenue streams, as well as strategies for developing the customer-company interaction and improving the delivery infrastructure.

When you have completed the table for each of the different types of online business, compare the results in each row. What differences do you see as a function of business type? The first company has been completed to serve as a guide for finishing the table.

Type of Business	Community	Portal	Retail
Name of Business	Classmates.com	Yahoo!	Amazon
Value/Benefits	Provides reunion tools for high school, military, and other directories		
Delivery Infrastructure	Pure-player set-up focuses on seamless, scalable service to a database of more than 19 million members		
Revenue Streams	Annual subscription fees, plus advertising		
Customer-Company Interaction Strategy	Leverages emotional/nostalgic ties to encourage repeat visits; incorporates new ways for people to interact (photos, profiles, interest groups)		

Concepts in Brief

1. In order to remain competitive, companies must be able to adapt to the evolving nature of the online environment for business activity.
2. Evolution is best accomplished by careful planning, which may take place at the overall company level, and/or within strategic business units (SBUs).
3. For strategic planning, the Internet can influence the motivation, processes, and outcomes of planning.
4. Developing a competitive advantage may involve the Internet as a way to define opportunties and leverage company resources.
5. The Internet can serve as a resource for a company in three ways: as a content resource, a channel resource, and a communications resource.
6. The Internet can be used to implement planning objectives, as by building brand equity and fostering customer loyalty.
7. Strategic objectives are met with a carefully thought-out business model. For Internet-oriented businesses, a complete model includes customer benefits, delivery infrastructure, revenue streams, and customer relationship management.

8. Revenue streams for online efforts can be direct, as from selling a product, or indirect, as by operating as an intermediary.
9. Revenue streams based on selling advertising differ in structure; revenue potential is typically related to the activity, or behavioral commitment, required of a consumer who sees an ad.
10. Many companies combine different types of revenue streams.

THINKING POINTS

1. In what ways can the Internet influence the amount of emphasis that is placed on company resources and market opportunities for strategic planning?
2. How can the Internet be used to identify strategic opportunities and to leverage resources to capitalize on these opportunities?
3. The Internet has influenced the nature of competition within industries. What does this impact of the Internet suggest for the ability of any company to develop a sustainable competitive advantage?
4. Consider the motivation for, and the processes and outcomes of, strategic planning. Does the Internet affect the aspects of strategic planning in ways that differ from the same aspects of planning in traditional business environments?
5. How does the Internet influence the ways that businesses can create value? Does the increased ability to create value by disaggregating value components have any disadvantages?
6. Why is it necessary to have a business model for digital business activity? What dot-com failures appear to have been the result of flawed or absent business models?

ENDNOTES

1. As reported in *BusinessWeek Online*, August 12, 2002.
2. Subhash C. Jain, "The Evolution of Strategic Marketing," *Journal of Business Research, 11* (December 1983), 409–425.
3. Researchers Yoram Wind, Vijay Mahajan, and Robert Gunther suggest that today's hybrid consumers are centaurs—half human, half-horse—harnessing human intelligence, emotion, and social needs with the informational power of the Internet to consume. Their characteristics and abilities underscore the importance of convergence marketing, strategies that leverage online and off-line marketing capabilities to enhance buyer-seller relationships. (Yoram Wind, Vijay Mahajan, and Robert Gunther, *Convergence Marketing: Strategies for Reaching the New Hybrid Consumer* [Prentice-Hall: Upper Saddle River, NJ, 2002]).
4. Jeffrey F. Rayport and John J. Sviokla, "Managing in the Marketspace," *Harvard Business Review*, (November–December 1999), pages 141–150.
5. There ain't no such thing as a free lunch.

SUGGESTED READINGS

"The Virtual Countinghouse: Finance Transformed by Electronics," by Daniel P. Keegan. In *The Future of the Electronic Marketplace*, edited by Derek Leebaert (The MIT Press: Cambridge, MA, 1998), pages, 205–240.

"Marketing in an Information-Intensive Environment: Strategic Implications of Knowledge as an Asset," by Rashi Glazer. *Journal of Marketing, 55* (October 1991), pages 1–19.

"What Makes Internet Business Models So Difficult," in *Now or Never*, by Mary Modahl (HarperCollins Publishers, Inc.: New York, 2000), pages 103–126.

"Commercial Scenarios for the Web: Opportunities and Challenges," by Donna L. Hoffman, Thomas P. Novak, and Patrali Chatterjee. *Journal of Computer-mediated Communication*, *1*, 3 (**<add year>**), pages **<add page numbers>**.)

"Managing in the Marketspace," by Jeffrey F. Rayport and John J. Sviokla. *Harvard Business Review* (November–December 1999), pages 141–150.

LEARNING LINKS

Business Model Components

www.theendoffree.com
www.mednetmedia.com/pdfs/whatsyouronli.pdf
www.clickz.com/design/freefee/article.php/2177381

Business Model Applications

www.wipro.co.in/enterprisesolutions/ebusinesssolutions/casestudies/crisil.asp
www.network-marketing-plan.com/online-business.html
howto.lycos.com/lycos/series/1,,6 + 35 + 97 + 23715,00.html
news.com.com/2100–1040–922435.html

Strategic Planning Examples

www.fda.gov/cdrh/strategic/strategic-future.html
www.greatconnect.com/transform/compete.htm

SECTION IV

Applying the Framework

The Internet and Business Activity

In this section, we focus on ways in which the Internet influences business action. Building on the previous section, this section illustrates the impact of the Internet as a tool for implementing strategic planning with business action. To this end, in Chapter 9 we examine the role of the Internet as a tool for conducting research and developing business intelligence. In addition, we consider the use of the Internet as a set of resources that affect business action. These resources are described as content, channel, and communication. The Internet enables businesses to provide information as content, to augment distribution as a channel, and to interact with customers to facilitate communication.

In Chapters 10 through 12, we look at the impact of the Internet on elements of business activity. In addition, we consider ways that the Internet—as content, channel, or communication—effects the actions of people in each of the four perspectives in the exchange environment.

Developing Business Intelligence with Online Research

Focus and Objectives

In this chapter, we focus on the role of the Internet as a tool for business research. The Internet serves as a source of information for identifying opportunities, and as a way to collect information. We review the stages in the research process, and consider the influence of the Internet on the activities associated with each stage. We also apply a framework for classifying data in business research using the Internet. We discuss the implications of Internet-based research for the objectives of understanding customer behavior and competitor behavior.

Your objectives in studying this chapter include the following:

- Recognize the benefits of the Internet for business research.
- Understand the difference between internal and external sources of data, and the role of the Internet in developing each source.
- Identify the five stages in the research process, and possible influences of the Internet in each stage.
- Understand the value of the presented framework for conducting business research with the Internet.
- Know the classes of Internet-based data sources and the dimensions that define them.
- Identify the risks (e.g., ethical breaches) and benefits of online research.

Getting to Know You

General Mills is the manufacturer of many well-known brands of food products. The Pillsbury Doughboy, Betty Crocker, and the Jolly Green Giant are all members of the General Mills family. The company's products feed families throughout the day. From Cheerios and Wheaties at the breakfast table, Progresso soups and Totino's pizzas at lunch, an afternoon snack of Bugles and Fruit Roll-Ups, to Hamburger Helper at dinner, and some Pop-Secret popcorn late at night, General Mills makes them all.

How does General Mills so accurately predict peoples' tastes? The answer lies in extensive market research. Throughout its nearly 150-year history, the company has tracked and analyzed the American palate. Using mall intercepts and phone surveys, General Mills has gathered insights into the complex love affair between people and their food, and how it's packaged. Research results led the company to develop two organic food brands, to revamp Betty Crocker—currently in her eighth iteration—and to offer a line of Cheerios brand products, among other things.

With the Internet, General Mills is able to collect even more information from its customers. For instance, the company used the Internet to conduct a taste test for a new Bugles snack flavor. Although the snacks arrived via snail mail, they came with a Web address and an invitation to sign up to take part in an online survey. The Internet approach worked well. Customers liked the comfort, convenience, and privacy of completing the survey at home. The company liked the savings in time and cost; time to field the study was cut from a typical 2-week time frame to mere days, and the cost dropped from $15,000 to $5,000.[1]

General Mills has been happy with its foray into online research. So happy, in fact, that it plans to move more and more of its market research to the Internet. The company had more than 60 percent of its research activity online prior to 2002, and it continues to seek out new ways to use the Internet to develop consumer insight.

For instance, in 2001, the company pushed its efforts to use the Internet to gain consumer insight by introducing a sample set of consumers to MyCereal.com. The site measured customers' individual taste preferences and health characteristics, thus accumulating a hefty store of descriptive information. Using a person's data, the site suggested ingredients and combinations for individual cereals; participants could mix their own cereals, delivered to the door for around $7 a box, plus shipping. Although the experiment in custom cereals was short-lived, it served the company's purposes, stimulating interest and increasing satisfaction with the company's other cereal brands. In addition, it provided a valuable database of information about preferred tastes and configurations of ingredients.

General Mills used the Internet to understand its customers, and their needs and wants. This knowledge enabled them to identify product opportunities, to test new product concepts, and to revamp business strategies for existing products. But do the methods used by General Mills work for other companies? Is there a risk of generalizing results from online research to preferences of purely off-line consumers? Does online research work for companies in different industries, or with a solely off-line presence?

In this chapter, we'll examine how companies can use the Internet to develop the business intelligence necessary to create a competitive advantage. For companies, information is a vital component for developing business strategy. Business intelligence is divided into two main categories: (1) developing insights into the market for a product, including customer demand; and (2) developing insights into the nature of competition for customers. First, we will consider how the Internet affects business research. Then we'll examine how businesses can use the Internet to carry out the research process, including the types of data that can be used to understand customers and competition in a particular target market.

Generalizing from General Mills: Benefits of Internet Intelligence

Businesses use online research to answer questions about business activities. For example, an organization may wish to determine the profit potential of a new product or market, to assess the quality of its present business strategy, or to track a particular problem with a product. Getting answers to the questions that initiate the research effort might depend on how the research is conducted, such as the methods for gathering the data, and on the types of data that are collected (e.g., surveys or clickstreams). Given the wide array of data that are available to businesses, it is important to understand the pros and cons of different data sources, and the issues involved in using them, to answer business questions.

> **Bits & Bytes 9-1**
> Understanding whether a site works is important. Market research to evaluate Web sites indicates that 50 percent of surveyed consumers are *less* likely to make a purchase after visiting a site.
> (*Source:* www.vividence.com, 2003.)

Internet Benefits for Business Intelligence

The Internet can be used to augment traditional research techniques and processes, and even to replace them (Figure 9-1). Its strengths as an information resource provide three primary benefits for business researchers: (1) the ability to gather related information across a wide array of sources, (2) the ability to update knowledge bases rapidly, and (3) the ability to use Internet technology to integrate the results of market research with decision-making processes.

Getting Information with the Internet

The research conducted by organizations is typically problem-oriented; the organization is focused on developing a strategy to maximize a limited set of resources, given

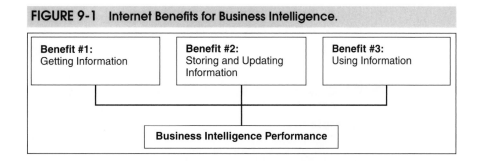

FIGURE 9-1   Internet Benefits for Business Intelligence.

a specified set of situational constraints. The Internet enables business researchers to collect data that serve as input for decision making. For instance, surveys and focus groups can be conducted online more quickly and often with lower costs than their off-line counterparts. General Mills estimates that its online survey research provides savings of 75 percent — in costs and in time — compared with off-line methods.[2]

The rapid acceptance of digital content has resulted in an increased demand for more and different types of online information. At the same time, the decreasing costs and heightened availability of software for digitizing and posting information have lowered the hurdles to putting information online. As a result, the information available on the Internet reflects a wide variety of interests, objectives, and budgets. For instance, information about companies and their product offerings, both online and in traditional environments, is readily available as input for developing competitive intelligence. In addition, the communication and publishing characteristics of the Internet mean that providing information is not just one-sided: consumers can also get into the act. For example, an unhappy passenger on United Airlines set up the untied.com site to collect the experiences of other passengers with the company (Figure 9-2). How might United's management use this source of information to guide business activity?

Online news groups and chat rooms are forums for people to express concerns with product performance, or company actions. They also enable customers to share tips about product use and alternative products. The many sources of information available via the Internet are a valuable asset for business research.

Keeping Information Current

Markets are dynamic. For instance, technological advances enable new product development. In addition, social changes may affect the desirability of existing products. These changes mean that consumers' tastes and preferences may also change over time, and that the length of time for the change to be evident in consumption patterns can vary widely across products. The challenge for business researchers is to be able to provide reliable, timely information as input for managerial decision making.

The Internet makes it possible to update business intelligence quickly. The availability of thousands of online databases means that business researchers can acquire up-to-date information about customers, competitors, and conditions that affect the business environment. The number of databases increases the business researcher's ability to assess the reliability of information. If information acquired from several sources leads to a similar conclusion, then the convergence reinforces the reliability of the information.

FIGURE 9-2 The Internet as a Public Forum and Source of Feedback.

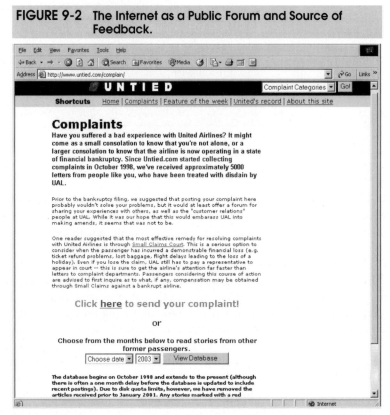

Putting Information to Work

Once the researcher has the information indicated by the research questions, the next step is to use that information for decision making. Information in business research can be obtained in many different ways and forms—from direct contact with respondents to automated search and retrieval from electronically managed databases. For instance, a **marketing information system**, often abbreviated as MIS, is the combination of people and procedures required to gather, organize, and integrate internal and external sources of information to meet the objectives of marketing strategy (Figure 9-3). Internal sources include data about transactions, sales leads, and customer service reports.

FIGURE 9-3 A Marketing Information System Integrates Many Sources of Intelligence.

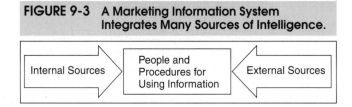

External information sources are typically the primary focus of business research. These external sources include information about customers, competition, and conditions that may affect the viability of business strategy. The Internet can be used to collect and store data that pertain to each component of business research. We will consider these components in more detail in the remainder of this chapter.

Getting Smart: How Is Business Intelligence Developed?

Most business search involves a series of stages that are used to answer two main questions: What do we want to know, and How are we going to learn it? In the research process, the first question involves defining the problem. To answer the second question, we develop the research plan, collect the data, analyze the data, and draw conclusions. The stages are shown in Figure 9-4.

What Do You Want to Know? Asking Questions

Business research begins with the specification of the research problem. For example, an organization that wishes to develop and market a new product may have a general research problem about the most desirable form of the product. This general question itself reflects a set of more specific questions. Who is the appropriate target market for the new product? What features should the product include? How different is the product from those available from competitors? Where do consumers purchase other forms of this product? Each of these questions can be addressed through research.

Asking the Right Question

The set of questions that creates a need for business research will differ from organization to organization, and over time within an organization. As a general description, however, the purpose of the research process is to provide information of three key types: **descriptive**, **diagnostic**, and **predictive**. For example, the question of where customers presently purchase similar products is descriptive. If the question is reframed to

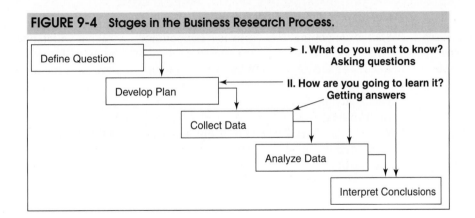

FIGURE 9-4 Stages in the Business Research Process.

ask *why* customers purchase at these locations, then the goal of research is to provide diagnostic information (e.g., the product is only available at that location). Finally, if the question is posed as, "How many customers are likely to purchase from our location?" the issue is one of prediction. Figure 9-5 provides examples of different questions that can guide online research.

The amount of available information, and the relative ease with which it can be incorporated into business decision making with Internet technologies, increases the need for a clear understanding and specification of the research question. The adage, "garbage in, garbage out," is particularly relevant for settings like the Internet, where large amounts of information can be obtained, often at low cost to the researcher. Even if collecting and incorporating data of questionable utility is relatively quick, easy, and cheap, the implications for decisions based on poor data can be very costly.

Data from the Internet can be used for a variety of research purposes, such as relationship development, competitive analysis, distribution channel analysis, and market analysis. In each of these situations, the Internet can provide business researchers with information and online tools that can be used to develop input for action-based decision making. For instance, information can be obtained for target market specification from comments of participants in discussion groups and e-mail lists. Direct contact with group members can be accomplished with Internet communications capabilities, enabling researchers to send questionnaires, conduct online focus groups, and complete interactive in-depth interviews.

Bits & Bytes 9-2

Trying to estimate the size of an online market in another country? The CIA's *World Factbook* provides population statistics, number of Internet users, and the number of ISPs in countries around the world.
(*Source:* www.cia.gov/cia/publications/factbook/.)

FIGURE 9-5   Research Objectives Ask Different Types of Questions.

	Descriptive	**Diagnostic**	**Predictive**
Research Focus	"What is happening?"	"Why is it happening?"	"What will happen in the future?"
Sample Question	"How is our site being used?" "Who is buying our product?"	"What is wrong with our brand image?"	"What is the market for a new product?"
	"Which banner ads generated the most site traffic?"	"How is our business strategy working?"	"What is the expected ROI (return on investment) for a new, online promotion?"

How Are You Going to Learn It? Getting Answers

Getting the answers to your research questions requires the development of the research plan, and then collecting, analyzing, and interpreting the data. In each stage, decisions have to be made about how to proceed.

Making Decisions About Research Plan and Procedure

With a clear set of objectives in place, the marketing researcher is ready to develop a plan for acquiring the information that will provide answers to the research questions. In this second stage, the researcher determines the type and amount of data needed for drawing conclusions with confidence. In addition, the researcher decides *how* to obtain the data. That is, will the research be conducted in-house, or is it desirable to outsource the research effort? Business managers consider company capabilities and resources, combined with the scope and nature of the proposed research, to analyze the costs and benefits of outsourcing research.

Outsources of Data   Commercial market research firms with Internet expertise provide a valuable service to many companies with an interest in the digital business environment of the Internet. The decision to have an outside firm do research, rather than conduct it within the company, may be based on several reasons. For instance, the complexity of the data available from the Internet, combined with the fast pace of commercial activity online, has led many companies to rely on external sources for data collection, analysis, and interpretation. Another reason for outsourcing marketing research is to protect customers. Auto-by-Tel, for example, felt that asking customers to provide information about their purchases might be considered intrusive. To avoid the potential backlash from irritating their consumers, the company hired an outside firm to conduct, analyze, and interpret its existing records.[3]

Some market research firms specialize in a particular type of data collection, while others offer a wide variety of capabilities. In addition, research firms differ in the ways in which they manage the knowledge obtained from data collection; some companies offer their services to companies that compete within an industry, while other companies will serve only one company in each industry sector. The selection of an external research firm should be based on information needs and marketing resources, and on the fit between company needs and characteristics of the research firm.

Types of Data   Business managers must also make decisions about the type of data to be collected. Two common dimensions for describing data are (1) primary or secondary, and (2) quantitative or qualitative. In the first case, is the research focus so specific to the company or product that the data collection must be planned and implemented from scratch, or are there other, existing sources of information that can be used to develop the intelligence? This situation reflects the difference between primary data and secondary data. **Primary data** is information that is being collected for the first time, in order to address the problem defined by the business researcher. **Secondary data** is information that was collected at an earlier time, often for a different purpose. Examples of secondary information include census data and databases that are designed and constructed to provide ongoing access to stored information, which may or may not be updated.

Both types of data can be obtained with the Internet. For example, a researcher can conduct an online survey to acquire primary data about peoples' perceptions of a proposed product. In addition, the researcher might access an existing online database to develop estimates of market size for the product.

Each type of data has its advantages and its disadvantages. Primary data is desirable, and often necessary, when the research question is so new, or sufficiently specific, that you are unlikely to find any previously developed data sets that are relevant. The chief advantage of primary data is that because you designed the research to address your objectives, the data you collect are more likely to be relevant, and thus to be useful for developing insights for decision making. The downside to primary data is that it has to be collected; the research instruments (e.g., surveys and interview formats) must be developed and administered; and the data collected and recorded. These efforts can be costly in terms of manpower and money.

Secondary data can reduce or eliminate issues of the time and money needed to prepare and administer data-gathering methods. All the available data in the world, however, will be of no use if it cannot be structured to address your research needs. The major drawback to secondary data is that it often is not sufficiently relevant to eliminate the need for primary research. That said, however, there are many locations on the Internet that provide a broad array of data about consumers and their consumption activities, both online and off-line.

The second way to describe data differentiates between qualitative data and quantitative data. In general, **qualitative research** tends to be open-ended, with the format and substance of the research encounter strongly guided by the participants. Data from focus groups and in-depth interviews are often the results of qualitative research. In contrast, **quantitative research** tends to be more structured, seeking answers to specific, well-defined questions from a representative sample of respondents. Surveys are often conducted to provide quantitative data that can be summarized with charts and numbers.

Deciding whether a research effort should be qualitative or quantitative depends on the research questions you are trying to answer. Qualitative research can provide unexpected insights and rich detail about consumers' attitudes and opinions toward products and brands. As a result, it is often used in the early, exploratory stages of developing a product concept. Once the concept has taken shape, questions about the specifics of the concept, such as, "How much should we charge?" and "What forms of shipping should we offer?" can be answered with quantitative methods.

Gathering Data

With a research plan developed, including the type of data to be used, the next step in the research process is to collect the data. The Internet provides business researchers with ways to gather primary and secondary data. The technologies that make up the Internet serve as tools for collecting primary data. These technologies differ in terms of whether the person providing the data is an active participant (e.g., answering a survey), or a passive participant (e.g., providing clickstream information). In addition, the technologies differ in terms of where the data is stored; whether it is stored on the user's computer (e.g., a cookie file), or whether it is on the server that hosts the Web site (e.g., a site's history of visitor activity). A third differentiating characteristic of data collection technologies is whether the data is collected at the level of the individual user or is aggregated, or combined, across a set of users.

The type of research question—descriptive, diagnostic, or prescriptive—often suggests the tools that should be used to collect the data. For instance, a business manager might want to know how many people visit the company's site, and when. This information can be obtained with software packages that track activity in a Web site through the server that makes the site available. This software creates a log file, which serves as a record of the type of activity that occurs within a Web site. **Log files** typically contain information about the files requested from a server during a visit. A log file may also contain the times that the files were requested, or **hits**, and how long the visit lasted. In addition, the software may record the last URL,[4] or Internet address, visited by the user, and the IP address of the user. By tracking the information stored in a log file over time, a marketer can gauge traffic to a company site, as well as which aspects of the site were most examined (i.e., through file access), and when site information was most highly in demand. Figure 9-6 is a typical log file.

Descriptive information can also be obtained from clickstream data. **Clickstream data** refers to the recorded sequence of clicks made by a consumer either within a site, or across a site. In contrast to log file data, which combines the information of all visitors to a site, clickstreams provide individual-level views of user movements. For instance, a researcher could track the number of clicks made by a visitor prior to making a purchase. By comparing this number with the minimum number of clicks required to move through the site with a goal of making the purchase, the researcher can assess the functionality of the site. This measure is called **first purchase momentum**, and it is calculated as

Required Clicks/Actual Clicks = First Purchase Momemtum

Clicks can also be used to diagnose the effectiveness of an online ad campaign. Businesses compare the number of click-throughs to the cost of buying banner exposure to determine whether the advertising investment paid off, in terms of attracting visitors to a site. This measure is called the **acquisition cost**. For instance, suppose you pay $20,000 to have a banner ad on a portal site displayed 1 million times. If 4 of every 1,000 people who see the ad actually click through, and come to your site, then your acquisition cost is

Banner(advertising cost)/Number of click-thoughs = Acquisition cost,or
$$\$20,000/(1,000,000/.004) = \$20,000/4,000 = \$5.$$

Of course, what you'd really like is for the visitors to become customers. You can track your sales success by examining the **conversion cost**: the number of visitors who become customers. This measure is calculated by simply changing the denominator in the formula we just used from click-throughs to actual sales.

Suppose, however, that you are interested in more than simply describing online consumer behavior; you want to know what people really like about your site, and why. Moreover, you'd like to know whether some changes you are thinking about making will lead visitors to become loyal customers, boosting your **retention rate**. To diagnose the strong and weak points of your site, and to predict which changes will improve loyalty, you may need to get information from consumers about their attitudes, perceptions, and preferences. Collecting data online can be accomplished by a number of methods, including direct assessment, as through online focus groups and surveys, and through indirect assessment, as through tracking newsgroups and chat rooms.

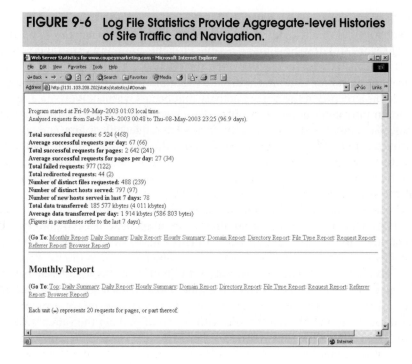

FIGURE 9-6 Log File Statistics Provide Aggregate-level Histories of Site Traffic and Navigation.

Putting It All Together: Making Sense of Data

With data acquired, the business researcher moves to the analysis and interpretation stage of the research process. Whether the data were obtained from online sources or off-line sources, the Internet can be used to facilitate the combination and analysis of data. As a tool for communication, the Internet enables business researchers to integrate data from multiple sources. In addition, software packages enable researchers to develop statistics with online data, and to update the statistics on a continuous basis.

The variety of information sources available for business research may necessitate data mining. **Data mining** is the use of often-sophisticated software tools to elicit patterns and impose order on sets of information. While data mining can be conducted on organized databases of information, it may provide greater explanatory benefits for information that has no readily apparent structure or organization. For example, a data mining algorithm that tracks through a 12-month set of user profiles provided by visitors to a Web site may uncover the interesting finding that the majority of visitors in the summer months are over the age of 55. If this finding is in sharp contrast to the higher numbers of 20- and 30-somethings that visit the site in the other seasons, then the company may want to consider changes to its promotional tactics to appeal more directly to the apparent audience, depending on the season.

Drawing Conclusions and Delivering Insights

Suppose that you have just been handed a research report on consumption patterns within targeted market segments for your company's Internet service product. The report notes a discrepancy between the projected consumption of the product in the target market segments and the actual consumption. The researcher concludes that the smaller-than-expected sales are due to inaccurate estimates of the target market in the previous year. How do you determine whether the conclusion is correct, and how do you protect yourself from misleading data?

You can reduce the possibility of being misled by incorrect data in several ways. First, balance data obtained from online and off-line sources. If possible, do not rely entirely on any single data source. The range and quality of data sources on the Internet can be used to determine whether the conclusions you have drawn from one set of data are supported by other data that address the same purpose. Second, assess the purpose and method of data collection, regardless of whether the data is from an online or an off-line source. Understand what assumptions have been made that may affect your interpretation of the data, and why the assumptions exist. Third, update your data frequently. Many online data sources focus on particular aspects of research, such as tracking electronic commerce in a specific industry sector. By keeping up-to-date with newly posted information, you can detect trends in behaviors that may affect your research conclusions.

As noted earlier in this chapter, the Internet population has expanded to mirror off-line population characteristics. In any situation, however, data gathered online should be interpreted in view of the fact that your respondents may represent only a subset of some possibly larger population. This subset may be different from the larger population, in that your respondents are the people who were willing to respond to the questions. Systematic differences between respondents and nonrespondents in the same, larger population would tend to indicate the presence of bias in the data.

Even when the preceding stages in the process are conducted in off-line, traditional environments, the Internet can be used to communicate the research report and to integrate and update feedback from different functions within the organization. The communications capabilities available with the Internet can be used to shorten the time required to produce and share iterations of the research results.

Bits & Bytes 9-3
Survey results indicate that 82 percent of companies with more than 500 employees use some form of Web conferencing to plan and coordinate activities.
(*Source:* IDC Conferencing Survey, 2001.)

Types of Online Data Sources

The characteristics of the Internet, such as its rich content and rapid communications technologies, make it important to consider the types of information that marketing researchers can obtain from the Internet. In this section, we will consider the characteristics of data sources for research, and discuss several approaches by which researchers can obtain data from the Internet, and the issues associated with each approach. This discussion expands on the second and third stages of the research process: designing a research plan and collecting the data.

Describing Data in Two Dimensions

We can use a framework for describing data, developed by Runkel and McGrath in the early 1970s, to better understand the differences between types of data, and the implications of these differences for appropriate research use. The Runkel and McGrath framework organizes the types of data available to a researcher by two key properties related to the situations in which the data were generated: (1) who recorded the data (data source), and (2) whether the person (or persons) who provided the data was aware that the data were being collected. Before we dive into the descriptions of these dimensions further, however, it is useful to having a working definition of what is meant by the term "data."

In the Runkel and McGrath framework, a **datum** is based on a single behavior by a respondent. (When two or more datums get together, we call them data.) Behaviors become data when two events occur. First, the behaviors are recorded by an observer. Second, the researcher interprets the recorded behaviors, thus giving them meaning. In other words, a behavior that isn't recorded and interpreted is just a behavior, and a behavior that is recorded but not interpreted is just information. This definition means that the development of data requires four things to occur: behavior, observation, recording, and interpretation (Figure 9-7).

Why do we care about the activities that create a data point? Each step on the data path is an opportunity for something to occur that changes how the ultimate data point might be interpreted. For instance, two researchers might observe a single behavior, but record and interpret it very differently. Similarly, a program that tracks visitor behavior on a Web site might have different thresholds for recording behaviors than another program with a similar focus. One program might track only behaviors that occur for a preset length of time (e.g., viewing a page for more than .2 seconds), while the other program might record every view, with no minimum times. The resulting log files might look very different, and give rise to different inferences about the value of a page's content. As a result, knowing and understanding the source of data is an important factor in evaluating the quality of business research.

Where Do Data Come From?

While the observation of a behavior may co-occur with its recording, the interpretation of the data can occur at a later point in time, and by a different person. In addition, the person who carries out the behavior, the respondent, may or may not be the same person who records the behavior. As a result, the framework's property of data source has three components—the respondent, the researcher, and the recorder. The source of the data is the person who observes and records the behavior of interest.

To illustrate the concept of data source, suppose that a city council wants to obtain information about the desirability of a new public parking lot. One way to get the data is to send out a mail survey to local residents. A respondent who fills out the mail

FIGURE 9-7 The Path of Events from Behavior to Data.

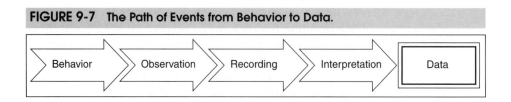

survey, essentially observing and recording her own responses, is one type of data source. Alternatively, the town could run a focus group. In this case, the researcher who moderates the discussion and records the behaviors serves as the data source. As a third approach, the city manager could comb through archived information about public sentiment toward similar proposals in the past. In this case, the person who recorded the responses in the past is the data source.

The data source dimension is important because it introduces the idea that the usefulness of data for a particular purpose may be affected by its source, that is, the person who recorded the information. For example, a respondent who records her answers to a survey may selectively present only information that conveys a desired image, thus editing out potentially useful information for the researcher. A researcher can bias a data set by deciding what information to record and what to ignore.

Awareness of Data Collection and Purpose

The second property of the Runkel and McGrath framework addresses the issue of whether the person, whose behavior is the basis for a data point, knew that the behavior was being observed and recorded. For the situation in which the respondent is the source of data, awareness is reflected in self-report techniques for data collection, such as surveys and questionnaires. Lack of awareness is reflected in trace measures, or situations in which behaviors are unobtrusively recorded (e.g., tracking site visits on the Internet).

The awareness issue is also relevant when the researcher observes and records the respondent's behavior. In the case of a focus group, for example, participants are usually aware that their conversation is being observed and recorded by a **visible observer**. If they are unaware that their behaviors are being recorded, the situation is described as **hidden observation**.

For the third data source, that of behaviors observed and recorded in the past, awareness is a bit trickier. In general, records of public behavior fall into the awareness category. For instance, taking a public stand on an issue, such as casting a vote in the Senate, constitutes awareness that a behavior is observed and recorded. More complex, however, is the situation in which a set of collected information is saved, without the respondent's awareness, and retrieved for use as data at a later point in time. Researchers must be aware of the ethical issues that may arise with different types of data.

As with the source of data property, respondent awareness may influence the usefulness of the data. When people are aware that their behaviors are being observed and recorded for use in research, they may react to the situation, potentially biasing or distorting the data. **Reactive effects** occur when respondents alter their behavior due to the characteristics of the situation in which they are being observed and recorded. To avoid reactivity effects, researchers can use **unobtrusive measures**. These measures include data that are acquired when the respondent is unaware that behaviors are being observed and recorded. Unobtrusive measures tend to be less prone to reactivity than data developed when the respondent is aware of the research process.

The two properties—data source and awareness—create a framework for classifying types of data. This framework is presented in Figure 9-8. In some situations, data may be classified in more than one category. For example, a user may be aware that a cookie has been placed in her browser, but unaware of the exact nature of the information that will be collected. The framework is useful as a general structure for evaluating the advantages and disadvantages of different types of data.

FIGURE 9-8 Two Properties Differentiate Types of Data.

Respondent Awareness

(Does subject know behavior is observed and recorded?)

Source of Data (Who observes and records?)	Respondent Aware	Respondent Unaware
Respondent	Self-reports *Online surveys, tests*	Traces *Individual's Web sites, IP addresses, Shopping carts, Information requests*
Researcher	Visible observer *Internet: Online focus groups, interviews*	Hidden observer *Data profiling, chat rooms, Cookies, infomediaries (e.g., DoubleClick), clickstream*
Recorder	Records of public behavior *Newsgroup postings, Mailing list correspondence*	Archival records (secondary records) *Email correspondence*

In the following sections, we will look at the characteristics and concerns associated with characteristic types of data that can be obtained from the Internet.

Bits & Bytes 9-4
Online surveys save time. Research indicates that a survey that takes 19.4 minutes to complete by phone takes only 12.5 minutes on the Web.
(*Source:* Burke Interactive, 2002.)

Internet-based Sources of Data About Customers

Technological advances and their widespread adoption by many people make the Internet an important source of insights into buyer behavior. To simplify discussion, we can look at the data sources as a function of awareness.

The Respondent as a Data Source
Respondent Aware: Online Surveys
Surveys provide businesses with information about customers' awareness, perceptions, attitudes, intentions, and behaviors regarding companies and their offerings. The Internet enables marketers to develop and fine-tune survey questions and formats so that pertinent information can be obtained, often at a lower cost and with

a better response rate than traditional mail or phone surveys. Surveys can be conducted through e-mail or through the Web. An e-mail survey is comparable to a mail survey; both tend to have fixed, text-based question formats. Web-based surveys provide a wider range of survey design possibilities than standard text formats (Figure 9-9). As e-mail format capabilities become more varied, and more widely adopted, however, additional rich media opportunities can be integrated into e-mail-based surveys.

The multimedia, interactive nature of the Internet creates the potential for Web-based survey methods that are interesting and involving. In addition, technical capabilities of the Internet mean that surveys can use flexible formats that tailor the questions in a survey, thus reducing the probability of obtaining irrelevant information, or of tiring a respondent. For instance, a survey on a Web site can be designed so that information that clarifies a question can be acquired by clicking on a button or link in the question. This capability is helpful for respondents who need the information, without annoying respondents who do not.

Several cautions guide online survey research. Marketers who use the Internet to collect survey data must consider how issues associated with the online medium might

FIGURE 9-9 **Procter & Gamble™ Uses an Online Survey to Collect Information That Can Be Used to Enhance Product Benefits.**

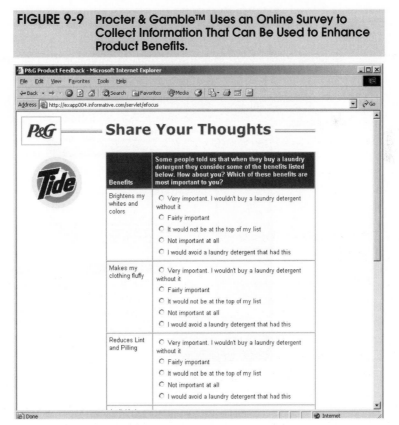

Source: Reproduced with permission of The Procter & Gamble Co. Copyright 2003. All rights reserved.

influence the quality of the data. Three such issues are sampling, equipment, and respondent characteristics.

Sampling refers to the process by which respondents are obtained from a larger population pool. With an e-mail survey, a sample of respondents is identified and contacted. For a Web-based survey, initial contact can also be made via e-mail. Many surveys, however, rely on the user to find the site and complete the survey, an approach known as **self-selection**. This approach may lead to a **selection bias** in the data. The researcher needs to know whether the sample of survey respondents is representative of the larger population to which research conclusions will be generalized. Control over survey respondents can be implemented by requiring a respondent to use a password to access the questionnaire. In addition, researchers can obtain information about each respondent that can be used to determine the representativeness of the sample.

Several methods can be used to minimize potential biases. To address concerns about selection bias, researchers can use pop-up surveys. Pop-up surveys are used in place of surveys contained in banner ads. A **pop-up survey** is programmed to "pop up" on a screen for every n^{th} customer, soliciting input, perhaps in exchange for a coupon or sweepstakes entry (Figure 9-10). The idea is that while a banner ad is always on the screen, and may be ignored—much like comment cards that sit on tables in fast food restaurants—pop-up surveys create a sense that the visitor's

FIGURE 9-10 Pop-up Software Attracts Attention and Guides Visitors to the Survey.

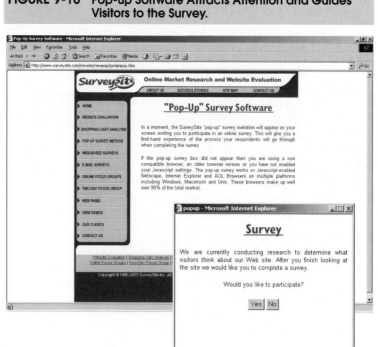

input is valued, and that not all visitors have the opportunity to contribute. (Remember from Chapter 2 that exclusivity creates status, exchanged, in this case, for information.)

To boost the response rate for a survey, and to manage access to a survey instrument, researchers use e-mail invitations to participate in surveys. The e-mail may contain an embedded link that, when clicked, takes the user right to the survey. To insure that only the intended respondent takes the survey, a computer-generated password code can be sent with the e-mail. Entering the code allows the respondent to get one-time access to the survey, thus keeping out uninvited sources of data.

Equipment characteristics can also influence the quality of Internet-based survey data. Surveys can be designed that use the full range of technical possibilities to provide a tailored, engaging research experience for the user. However, not all users may be able to take advantage of the experience. Capacity issues may limit a user's ability to download graphics-rich pages, or to play video and audio files. In addition, different types of computers (e.g., Macintosh and IBM) and different browsers (e.g., Netscape and Microsoft Explorer) may lead to different displays of survey pages.

Respondent characteristics, such as a user's level of familiarity with the Internet, may influence the quality of data obtained through an online survey. Business researchers often assess respondents' knowledge of the product or service that is the focus of a survey, to better understand the implications of the data. Because the Internet is a fairly new medium for data collection, however, researchers must also consider the possibility that the interaction between the user and the computer-mediated environment may influence the type of responses provided by the user. To reduce the likelihood of experience-based biases, researchers can directly assess respondents' levels of expertise. In addition, online surveys should be designed to minimize effects that may occur due to miscomprehension or confusion about how to move through the survey or record responses.

Bits & Bytes 9-5

Getting site visitors to provide feedback can be tough. On average, fewer than .002 percent, or 1 of every 500 visitors, clicks through a feedback banner. (*Source:* SurveySite.com, 2003.)

Respondent Unaware

Business researchers can collect information provided by site visitors even when they are unaware that they are providing data. For instance, requests for information about a product, or complaints to a customer service center can be useful for understanding what customers want, or for diagnosing problems with an existing product (Figure 9-11). In addition, analyzing the contents of shopping carts can provide insight into links between products that can be used to guide strategies for bundling products in promotions. Carts that are abandoned before the transaction can also be examined to see whether particular products or search sequences appear to trigger the decision to leave a site.

FIGURE 9-11 What Types of Data Might Be Collected from this Site?

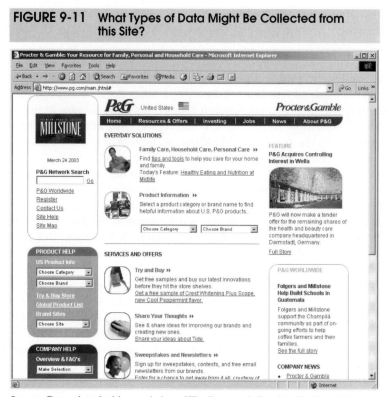

Another source of data in which the respondent is not aware of the data collection comes from individuals' Web sites. The information that people post about themselves, and their interests, activities, and experiences, can be a useful source of data. Because the respondent's Web site is not created for the purpose of serving as data for research, and because the respondent may not even be aware that her site is interpreted as data, individual sites are categorized as respondent-generated data, but without awareness. The researcher opportunistically obtains data from whatever sites are available through targeted searches.

The Researcher as a Data Source

Respondent Aware: Online Focus Groups

A traditional focus group consists of several people who are physically present in a room. A moderator may guide the discussion. The data from a focus group is the information that the researcher determines is relevant in the group interaction, and that the researcher records for further examination.

Focus groups conducted online enable a researcher to observe and record focal behaviors that occur during the interaction of geographically dispersed respondents. The interaction may still be face-to-face, through the use of cameras.

Online focus groups can be conducted using software that enables a researcher to form a discussion group (e.g., NetMeeting). Respondents type responses into a text box, and then send the comments to a group board. The board provides an ongoing record of the conversation that each respondent can review by scrolling backward and forward (Figure 9-12).

A primary advantage of the online focus group is the ability to integrate the beliefs, experiences, and opinions of respondents who are not in the same location. This ability may enable a researcher to gauge reactions to a product or concept in greater depth and with more generalizability than with a traditional focus group. In addition, the online technique is often more economical than a traditional focus group.

A primary disadvantage of online focus groups is the loss of some contextual richness that is available through physical presence. For instance, tone of voice and body language convey information that influences people's interactions. As a result, the text-based communication that serves as the record of the group interaction may provide the researcher with impoverished information in two ways. First, nonverbal information may be less able to be tracked and interpreted. Second, the absence of nonverbal information as cues for participant interaction may affect what people say and how they say it, thus introducing a possible bias into the data.

Respondent Unaware: Cookies, Clickstreams, and Data Profiling

A researcher can create data from several different Internet sources. One source of data is obtained through cookies. A **cookie** is a text file that contains a unique user identifier. When the user visits a Web site, the site's server may place a cookie in the

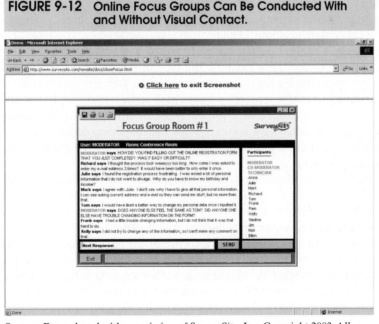

FIGURE 9-12   Online Focus Groups Can Be Conducted With and Without Visual Contact.

Source: Reproduced with permission of SurveySite, Inc. Copyright 2003. All rights reserved.

user's browser. As the user goes from page to page in the site, the identifying information in the cookie can be sent back to the server. In this way, the server can track the movement of the user through the Web site.

More interesting, however, is the situation in which a company can acquire information about a user's across-site behavior. For instance, a company that operates as an ad server, like DoubleClick, has subscribers who pay to have the company serve their advertising. When the user visits a site with an agreement to display ads from the ad server's subscribers, the ad server places a cookie in the user's browser. When the user moves to another banner or site that also subscribes to the ad server, the ad server is able to review the cookie information and update its database about the user's preferences. This information can be used to target advertising to the user. Even when the advertising is targeted, the user remains anonymous to the company who uses the Doubleclick service.

Clickstreams provide information about navigation within and across Web sites. They are a trace of a person's sequence of clicks through content files. Although techniques for analyzing clickstream data are still in the early stages of development, academic researchers have used clickstream data to develop descriptive and predictive models of site navigation and product choice. This type of quantitative research is gaining popularity in businesses as part of the broader area of **Web analytics**, the effort to understand how site use affects visitor behavior. **Web analytics software** combines individual-level clickstream data with aggregate-level site use to provide a researcher with comprehensive information about how users travel through a path, and which forms of navigation tend to result in sales, or other desired behaviors.

The value of cookie and clickstream information to a business increases when the information about site visits can be combined with information that identifies the user to the company. The combination of this demographic information with behavior information is called **data profiling**. Data profiling is possible when databases of user information can be linked to the Internet search habits of a specific user. These types of databases exist in several forms. For example, the type of information needed to identify a user is available when the user makes a purchase from a Web site, or when the user completes a registration form. All a researcher has to have is the identifying information, and a way to match up that information to the database of Internet search activity, stored by the unique user identifiers on cookies. With the match-up completed, the researcher has detailed information about the user and about his or her preferences, based on past Internet behavior.

The ability to identify users by name, and to combine identities with behaviors has ethical implications for digital business. Consumer groups have argued that data profiling violates consumers' privacy, and that adequate notification of consumers about the profiling activities is necessary, but not widely practiced.

One issue in the use of cookie data is that the cookie is associated with a browser—not with an individual user. As a result, the tracked information comes from anyone who used that browser. A related issue with trace data is that even when the cookie is mapped to a single user, the user's behavior may not reflect personal preferences. For instance, suppose that you search a site for vitamin supplements for the geriatric set as a favor to your grandmother. The person who interprets the information from the related cookie may target ads to you for a variety of products for the elderly.

The Recorder (in the Past) as a Data Source

Respondent Aware: Online Newsgroups and Mailing Lists

Businesses can use newsgroup postings and mailing lists to ascertain users' reactions to companies and to brands and products. Because the content of the newsgroup is public, and because users are aware that their communications will be made public, this potential source of information falls under the respondent aware heading. Because the records of behavior (i.e., the postings) can be interpreted as data for a particular research purpose other than the original reason for the recorded correspondence, newsgroups and mailing lists fall into the recorder category of data sources.

Newsgroups Newsgroups are collections of people with Internet access who wish to exchange information about various topics. Each newsgroup has a specific topical focus, and the postings of messages to the newsgroup tend to revolve around the central subject matter. The user networks newsgroups are often shortened into the contraction, "Usenet newsgroups." Newsgroups are organized in hierarchies, which serve as a way to organize and transmit related information between different news servers. The nine primary hierarchies and their content focus are given in Figure 9-13.

Newsgroups may often be a form of online word-of-mouth, in which communications between users about products and services provide the users with the benefits that characterize off-line word-of-mouth. These benefits include two-way communication, increased credibility of the information source, and vicarious experience. The interactive nature of the Internet is particularly conducive to the exchange of information. It is important to note that while off-line word-of-mouth may often take a sequential form, in which Person A speaks to Person B, who then speaks with Person C, the Internet may expose several people to the exchange of information simultaneously. As a result, the transmission of information between individuals about a product or service, regardless of its accuracy, may occur more rapidly online than off-line.

FIGURE 9-13 The Primary Usenet Newsgroup Classifications Are a Source of Information About Consumer Interests and Opinions.

Hierarchy	Content
alt	discussions about a wide range of issues and topics not typically contained in the remaining hierarchies
comp	discussions of computers, and technology-related issues
humanities	topics pertaining to the arts and humanities
misc	topics that do not clearly belong in any other hierarchy
news	discussion of issues regarding newsgroups
rec	discussion of recreational opportunities and activities, including hobbies
sci	issues related to the study of science
soc	discussion of cultural and social issues
talk	anything and everything that does not clearly fit in one of the preceding groups

In some cases, the information from a newsgroup discussion may be used instead of running and analyzing a focus group discussion. Newsgroup participants, with their demonstrated interest in a particular product, may represent viable target markets. The likes and dislikes reflected in message postings can be used by businesses to design effective communications for the target, while the newsgroup itself presents a forum in which the commercial communication can be made available to interested participants.

Internet Mailing Lists Online mailing lists are classified by the same reasoning as newsgroups—behaviors recorded with the user's awareness, but not for a specified purpose of research. A **listserv** is a collection of online users who have chosen to belong to an e-mail-based information exchange. Listservs can be announcement or broadcast lists, in which subscribers merely receive mail, but do not send e-mail to the list, or they can be discussion lists. Discussion lists enable subscribers to engage in communications with other list subscribers. Discussion lists may be moderated, in which case one person receives all messages for the list and determines whether they should be sent on to all subscribers, or unmoderated, where all messages are transmitted to all subscribers.

Listservs differ from newsgroups in at least two ways that influence the nature of their usefulness for business research. First, a user must sign up to participate in a mailing list, but not for a newsgroup. For the researcher, a user's willingness to sign up may indicate a stronger commitment to the topic addressed in the list than to a similar topic in a news group.

Second, mailing lists are automatically delivered to subscribers' e-mail addresses, while users must actively seek out newsgroup discussion content. For the researcher, this requirement may indicate greater interest in the topic on the part of users who frequently access the newsgroup, compared with users who access it infrequently. Passive receipt of mailing list information may mean that the user is more likely to be exposed to the message content than if it had to be actively sought, but it may also mean that the message content is simply ignored.

Getting information from discussion groups and mailing lists can be effortful, given the size of the Internet and the speed with which content can change. Software, like IntelliSeek's BrandPulse™ helps business researchers keep track of what people are saying online about their products (Figure 9-14). These types of software sift through online discussions, and track and report brand-related activity. The format of the report created by the software can be customized to meet research needs and objectives.

Respondent Unaware: E-mail and Databases

E-mail As noted in Chapter 6, regulation to protect the privacy of Internet-based communications in the private sector is sparse. For instance, employers can monitor the e-mail correspondence of employees. In addition to the absence of regulatory policy on the privacy of e-mail, technology also creates situations in which information recorded at one point in time may turn up as data at another point. As e-mail travels over the networks of the Internet, it may pass through many servers—visible to anyone who is willing and able to take a look at the content. As with data profiling, e-mail as a data source has ethical implications due to the user's lack of

FIGURE 9-14 Online Software Makes It Easy to Keep Tabs on Consumer Opinion.

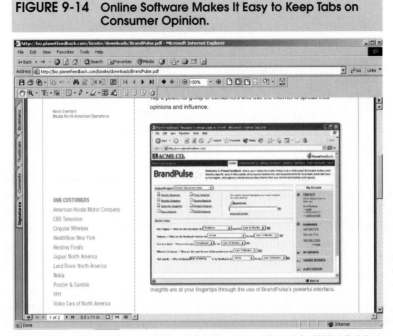

Source: Reproduced with permission of Intelliseek, Inc. Copyright 2003. All rights reserved.

awareness of the unintended use of information, combined with the expectation that the information is confidential.

Archival Records: Databases on the Internet Databases on the Internet are an important source of data for research that can be conducted with information recorded in the past. A **database** is a collection of information related to a particular purpose, and that can typically be organized for efficient search. The collection of databases contained on the Internet can be loosely classified into three categories: government, not-for-profit, and commercial.

Government-provided databases contain information gathered and structured by federal agencies. For example, census data—useful for understanding general societal trends, such as age, occupation, and income—is made available on the Internet by the Census Bureau of the U.S. Department of Commerce. In addition, the Central Intelligence Agency and the Environmental Protection Agency provide online access to compiled data. These types of sources can be used to explore trends and conditions that may affect business strategy.

Not-for-profit organizations also provide access to online databases. These databases offer many different forms of information, including statistics, archives of research papers, descriptions of organizational objectives and agendas, and personnel. Many organizations are international in scope, such as the World Health Organization. Their information can be used to develop insights into economic, technological, and societal characteristics that may facilitate the formulation of comparative market performance projections for domestic and international strategy.

'Net Knowledge

SITE-CENTRIC SENSE

We've considered several different types of data collection, as well as different sources of data. Now it's time to put them to work. Suppose that you have a Web site, and you want to know whether it's working for you, and, if not, what changes you should make. Descriptive and diagnostic measures of within-site behavior can help you predict what changes are most needed—and likely to work.

Tracking the effectiveness of your site can be done by combining log file information with self-reports of site perceptions. Descriptive measures of site use include measures of visitors, measures of what the visitors do in the site, and measures of where your visitors came from (i.e., the referring sites). For instance, you can examine the numbers of *unique users* (total number of visitors per day), *repeat users*, and *new users* to understand how well your site draws traffic, and whether first-time visitors return. In addition, you can look at what people do in your site, in order to determine what content they looked at, when, and for how long. To this end, metrics of *page views, pages per user*, and *average session length* provide aggregate-level insights into the value of your site and its content.

These passively collected measures describe visitor behaviors, but they don't tell you what the visitors thought and felt about your site. To tap the psychological dimension, you can use online, pop-up surveys and open-ended response boxes. Self-reports of what visitors liked or disliked, or what they would like to see on your site can be used to diagnose problems, and to gauge the success of possible changes to the site.

With the basic descriptive metrics in place, you can examine how well your company has performed in moving visitors from awareness of your product, to purchase and repeat purchase of the product. For instance, *customer acquisition cost* can be calculated to determine whether the resources allocated to promotional activities generated a reasonable amount of traffic. In addition, the *conversion cost* metric can be used to determine whether you are spending too much or too little money to generate each transaction.

Commercial databases are a source of potential insight about competitors' actions. We consider commercial databases and other data sources for competitor research in the next section.

Developing Competitive Intelligence

The sources of data in the framework can also be applied to organize information from the Internet for competitor analysis. Competitive intelligence seeks to answer "Who is the competition?," "What are their strengths and weaknesses?" and "How well are they competing?" In general, given the nature of competition and the importance of protecting proprietary information, efforts to find answers to these questions are undertaken without the awareness of the competing company.

Applying the data framework provides three sources of data: (1) the company, who is the respondent; (2) the researcher, who is the party conducting the research; and (3) the secondary data sources, such as databases or other publicly available information recorded at an earlier time.

The Company as a Respondent Data Source

Two forms of information can be obtained from the company as the respondent. Data can be derived from information posted by a company in its Web sites, such as company objectives, product initiatives, and customer outreach activities. In addition, information can be acquired about a particular product or service. For instance, e-mail can be used to request product information. In the case of Web sites, the information can provide a general overview of the company, while for requested information, the returned data may be more specific to a product. In both cases, however, the respondent is the source of the data, because the company conducts, observes, and records the behavior that will comprise the data. As with consumer-side analysis of self-reported behaviors, the researcher must recognize that the information being recorded and transmitted may be subject to distortions, whether intended or not, by the company that provides the information.

The Business Researcher as Data Source

When a business researcher collects information about competitors' action and records it for analysis, the researcher is the data source. Benchmarking studies and link analysis of competitors' sites are examples of situations in which the researcher is the data source.

In a **benchmarking** study, the researcher identifies a set of characteristics or goals that the business would like to achieve. The definition of the set may be based on what competitors are presently doing, and how well they are doing it. Alternatively, the set may be based on a behavior that would be new to the industry segment, but observable in other companies' activities. In either case, the researcher tracks and records the actions of the other companies on the focal behavior, as well as the actions of her company. The data from the benchmarking process is used to guide the company's effort and direction in achieving its goals.

Benchmarking may take the form of establishing standards that must be reached, hurdles that must be surpassed, or pitfalls that must be avoided. The information used to define the company performance objectives may be obtained from a content analysis of the Web sites and Internet-based communications (e.g., newsgroup postings, press information) of the companies who serve as the focus of the benchmarking study. Because the information to be used for benchmarking is determined and recorded by the researcher, the researcher is the data source.

Reverse linking can provide information about the performance of a competitor. **Reverse linking** is the process used to develop a data set about the nature of the Web links between a competing company and other companies. A researcher can use Internet search engines (e.g., Google) to generate a list of links to a specified URL, or Internet address. Analysis of the types of organizations uncovered by this search can be used to develop insights about a competitor's target markets, as well as the nature of partnership arrangements.

Previously Recorded Information as a Data Source

Competitive analysis can be conducted using data from sources of observed and recorded information in the past. Two such sources include databases and press-related information on the Internet.

Databases

Several different types of databases can be used to research the competition. These types include databases compiled through public sector initiatives, and databases compiled through private sector initiatives. For instance, patents filed by competitors can be examined using the Community of Science patents database, while information about a competitor's industry rating can be obtained from the Dow Jones online database of company profiles.

While databases provided by government and not-for-profit organizations tend to be available at no cost, the same is not always true for databases with a commercial focus. Some of the largest online databases are created by companies that conduct detailed research on businesses within a range of industries (e.g., Dun & Bradstreet, Hoover's) (Figure 9-15). These research firms provide the results of their research to interested buyers.

In contrast, other databases reflect a focus within a particular industry. Many such databases are available at no cost (e.g., Trade Show Central). For example, a database might contain information provided by a group of companies that specialize in a single product type. The purpose of the database is twofold. First, the database enables peo-

FIGURE 9-15 Commercial Databases Provide a Comprehensive Look at the Competition.

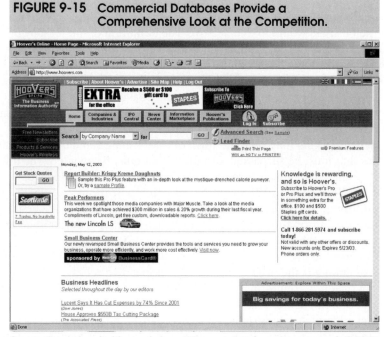

Source: Reproduced with permission of Hoover's Inc. (www.hoovers.com). © 2003. All rights reserved.

ple with a need for the product to search for and find vendors. Second, the database can be used as a way to generate revenue through advertising on the database site. This advertising opportunity may be particularly desirable because anyone who uses the database has already implicitly provided the information that he has an interest in the database focus—a good opportunity to gain brand awareness for a company that markets an item related to the database focus.

Press-Related Information

Several sites on the Internet provide services that search for and deliver news items about companies and their products. For example, eWatch provides companies with a clipping service—for a fee—that scans the Internet looking for specified search terms. The software collects the relevant content, and delivers a report to a subscriber of the service.

Cautions for Internet-based Research

The Internet can provide business intelligence, but ultimately the judgment of whether the information has value for decision making is up to the human decision makers in the process. The nature of the Internet raises several issues that influence the use of its information in business research. These issues include the relevance of information and the role of time constraints.

Information Relevance in Business Research

In an online environment, the manager has access to the information resources that comprise the Internet. The ready availability of information may enable a researcher to search for and acquire information needed for decision making more efficiently online than in a traditional off-line context. The information that may be obtained through standard search facilities on the Internet (e.g., search engines) may, paradoxically, provide the manager with too much information and not enough information at the same time. Search tools may return results of search matches in the thousands, but there is no guarantee that the results will be useful (i.e., high quality, relevant information) for the researcher's purpose.

Concerns with information quality are also raised by the freedom with which information can be published on the Internet. The Internet is largely unregulated in terms of the content that can be published. In addition, publishing software has decreased in cost and complexity to a point where it is readily available and usable. These characteristics combine to create an information environment that varies widely in terms of quality, credibility, and depth.

One way to manage concerns associated with online information is to combine online and off-line aspects of business research. Insights obtained from environmental scanning that leverages the array of information on the Internet can be used to guide the acquisition and interpretation of additional, detailed data from off-line expert sources.

Time Constraints on Information Use

The online environment may also introduce time constraints into decision making that are not experienced in the traditional, off-line decision processes. One time

---

InSite

E-EXPERIMENTS: WWW.ELAB.VANDERBILT.EDU

eLab is a virtual laboratory for studying the impact of the Internet on business activity—and commercial success. Founded in 1994 by two academic researchers at Vanderbilt University, Donna Hoffman and Tom Novak, the initiative has grown to encompass a wide range of research objectives and capabilities. For instance, eLab manages a panel of online consumers who provide information about a variety of e-commerce topics. Between 10,000 and 20,000 people make up the panel. In addition, eLab warehouses clickstream data for analyz-ing site navigation behavior, and it main-tains the server capability to run large-scale surveys and experiments online.

So what do they do with all the data? While some research results are made available only to the corporate sponsors who provide financial support for the lab, other information is avail-able on the eLab site, including acade-mic papers and data sets that provide e-commerce insight.

Any questions? Visit the eLab site and talk with Paige, your digital verbot guide!

---

constraint reflects an increase in productivity expectations. As the availability of information and communications resources spreads, demands on performance may escalate. These demands can result in heightened expectations of the business researcher.

Another type of time constraint is introduced when the rate of information with which information is published on the Internet increases the rate at which information becomes obsolete. The ease with which information can be posted and transmitted in online environments effectively shortens the life cycle of many types of information. Time constraints on information use can be managed by decreasing the cost needed to acquire the information. Internet support tools, such as search engines, can efficiently examine many information sources and return lists of sites that match the search key-words.

Trends in Online Research

The growth and development of the Internet, both technologically and commercially, has implications for business research. Several trends influence the nature and quality of online intelligence that can be gathered to guide business activity.

Trend 1: Decreasing Difference

When the makers of the Jaguar automobile line wanted to revamp the brand's Web site, one advantage the company had was that the demographics of its target market fit well with the profile of a large number of Internet users in the late 1990s—especially for income. For many companies, however, online research raised concerns about the extent to which information gathered from the online population could be applied to off-line customers, given differences in demographics and psychographics. As the

Internet has penetrated popular culture, the differences between online and off-line consumers have decreased. As a result, online research is appropriate for an increasingly broad range of products and services.

Trend 2: Increasing Richness

A second trend that affects business research is the development of rich media technologies and the spread of access capabilities, such as broadband, that enable people to experience a variety of sensory-rich experiences. Business researchers can use the Internet to create survey and interview situations that enable research respondents to interact with the product, and information that describes the product, without being in the same place as the product, or the researcher. Rich, interactive, virtual communications can reduce research costs and time, and provide businesses with insights from a broad customer base, across geographic boundaries.

Trend 3: Increasing Automation

Another trend for business research afforded by the Internet is the ability to track, record, and update visitor behaviors rapidly and automatically. In contrast to off-line business research that operates on an as-needed basis, and can be time-consuming to set up, implement, and analyze, online research can be conducted with software that records behaviors of interest to the researcher, provides ongoing analyses and updates of key metrics, and enables rapid responses to systematic behaviors in the target population.

These trends underscore the need for business research to keep pace with the changes in the online population, using online technologies as tools for identifying and understanding opportunities in the Internet environment.

CHAPTER SUMMARY

In this chapter, we examined the role of the Internet as a resource for developing business intelligence. The Internet can be used to acquire, store, and communicate the results of research on customers, competitors, and market conditions. The results of internal and external information acquisition can be integrated using Internet technologies to provide input for business strategy and implementation.

We considered the impact of the Internet on the marketing research process. The marketing research process consists of five stages: defining the problem, developing the research plan, collecting the data, analyzing the data, and presenting the results. We saw that each stage in the process may be influenced by Internet characteristics that facilitate or inhibit progress through the stage.

As a tool for conducting research, the Internet makes available a variety of data sources. A framework was used to describe the types of data sources, and to indicate the advantages and disadvantages of each type. Two properties were used to classify data types: (1) the source of the data, and (2) respondent awareness of the research. Sources of data are defined in terms of the person who observes and records the behavior of research interest—the respondent, the researcher, or a recorder in the past.

The framework was applied to research that uses the Internet to develop business intelligence about customer and market behavior, and about competitor behavior. Forms of data collection for each objective were discussed.

CONTENT MANAGEMENT
USEFUL TERMS

- acquisition cost
- benchmarking
- clickstream data
- conversion cost
- cookies
- data mining
- data profiling
- database
- datum
- descriptive
- diagnostic
- first purchase momentum

- hidden observation
- hits
- listserv
- log files
- marketing information system
- pop-up surveys
- predictive
- primary data
- qualitative research
- quantitative research
- reactive effects

- retention rate
- reverse linking
- sampling
- secondary data
- selection bias
- self-selection
- unobtrusive measures
- visible observer
- Web analytics
- Web analytics software

REVIEW QUESTIONS

1. What are three benefits of using the Internet for developing business intelligence?
2. How can business researchers assess the reliability of information gathered on the Internet?
3. Briefly describe the elements that comprise a marketing information system.
4. What is the overall purpose of the research process?
5. Distinguish between primary and secondary data.
6. Distinguish between qualitative and quantitative research.
7. How can a business researcher reduce the risk of being misled by data?
8. According to the Runkel and McGrath framework, what four events occur in the development of data?
9. Why is it important to know the exact source of data?
10. Explain the problem of selection bias.
11. What is an advantage of data profiling? What is a disadvantage?
12. What are the benefits of using newsgroup content as a source of market intelligence?
13. How can the data framework be applied to describe a strategy for developing competitive intelligence?
14. What Internet-related trends affect online business research?

WEB APPLICATION

Getting Answers: Building and Using an Online Survey

As General Mills learned, the Internet can streamline research, and cut the costs of collecting the data, too. You don't have to be a large corporation, however, to pull off an online research project. Many tools are available to help you get started. In this exercise, you'll build an online survey, collect data, and analyze the results. Although this example refers to the use of a specific survey site, many other free survey sites are available, and the fundamental processes for building the survey, distributing it, and collecting and analyzing results are similar.

1. Go to: free-online-surveys.co.uk/
2. Complete the brief registration to establish your survey account.
3. Enter your account to build your first survey.

4. Provide a title, "Favorite Fast Food."
5. Create questions. For instance, "At which of the following restaurants have you eaten in the past 6 months?" Note that you have several formats for responses, including "select one response," "tick all that apply," and ratings scales.
6. Develop a list of 10 people who will take your survey. Create an e-mail to request their participation. E-mail the survey as an embedded link in request.
7. When your respondents have completed the survey, it's time to examine your results. Use your survey account to access your results. How many people responded? Which restaurants were preferred?

CONCEPTS IN BRIEF

1. The Internet creates new opportunities for conducting business research, providing benefits in terms of collecting, storing, and using information.
2. Developing an effective online research strategy begins with asking the right question, whether descriptive, predictive, or diagnostic.
3. Online research can be used to guide many aspects of business strategy, both online and off-line.
4. Online research can be conducted in-house, or be outsourced. Primary and secondary sources of data can be obtained with the Internet.
5. Different types of data and tools for gathering data are available online, including qualitative focus groups and interviews, and quantitative log files and clickstream data.
6. When we develop primary data from respondents, we can characterize the data by its source, and the awareness of the respondent of the research. These distinctions are useful for understanding potential biases and limitations of the data.
7. Some issues to consider when collecting online data include sampling and self-selection biases.
8. The Internet can be used to develop competitive intelligence, through benchmarking research and from publicly available corporate information databases.
9. The relevance of online research for many businesses is increasing, as the number and variety of customers online increases.
10. Given the vast array and amounts of data sources, technology developments that automate aspects of business research and intelligence management are growing in number and popularity.

THINKING POINTS

1. The Internet is often described as an information-rich environment. Does the amount of information that can be obtained from the Internet increase or decrease the importance of business research that is designed to provide actionable intelligence to businesses? In other words, is the Internet likely to affect the value of business research?
2. How does the open nature of the Internet affect the type of information available to businesses? What complications or issues are raised by the use of the Internet as a source of market intelligence?
3. One goal of some practitioners is to facilitate the sharing of information collected from online shoppers. What impact might such widespread access to common data have on the need to conduct business research, and the methods for developing market intelligence?
4. What are the advantages and disadvantages of (a) the Internet as a tool for conducting research, and (b) the Internet as a source of information for research?
5. Issues of sampling and subject/respondent consent are common in many forms of research. What aspects of business research using the Internet make these concerns particularly salient? How might a researcher address these concerns?

6. What is the value of differentiating between different types of data using the properties of the Runkel and McGrath framework (i.e., data source and respondent awareness)?
7. What Internet-based data collection situations can be accommodated by the framework that would not exist in traditional environments for gathering data?

ENDNOTES

1. Sources include www.generalmills.com, www.businessweek.com, and www.bandt.com.
2. As noted in *BusinessWeek Online*, October 2001.
3. wsj.com, 1998.
4. Uniform Resource Locator.

SUGGESTED READINGS

"Online Experiments: Ethically Fair or Foul?" by Beth Azar. *APA Monitor on Psychology* 31 (April 2000), pages 50–65.

"Internet and Interactive Voice Response Surveys," in *Mail and Internet Surveys: The Tailored Design Method*, 2nd edition, by Don A. Dillman (John Wiley & Sons, Inc.: New York, 2000, pages 352–412).

"Planning to Gather Evidence: Techniques for Observing and Recording Behavior," in *Research on Human Behavior: A Systematic Guide to Method*, by Philip Runkel and Joseph E. McGrath (Holt, Rinehart & Winston: 1972, pages 173–193).

"Interactive Marketing: Exploiting the Age of Addressability," by Robert C. Blattberg and John Deighton. *Sloan Management Review* (Fall 1991), pages 5–14.

"Information Technology, Marketing Practice, and Consumer Privacy: Ethical Issues," by Ellen R. Foxman and Paula Kilcoyne. *Journal of Public Policy & Marketing, 12* 1 (Spring 1993), pages 106–119.

LEARNING LINKS

Sources of Data and Research News

cyberatlas.internet.com
www.idc.com
www.statmarket.com

Research Tips and Assistance

www.mra-net.org   (Marketing Research Association)
www.emarketer.com

Sponsored Academic Research

elab.vanderbilt.edu

Data Outsources: Consumer Insight

www.surveysite.com
www.forrester.com/home/0,6092,1–0,FF.html
web.informative.com/home.jsp
www.intelliseek.com

Data Outsources: Competitor Insight

www.ewatch.com
www3.gartner.com/Init

Digital Content and Business Activity

Focus and Objectives

In this chapter, we focus on the role of the Internet as a content resource for achieving business objectives. Topics include the sources of content for use by businesses, as well as the different types of content that are made available through the technology and business relationship. Different purposes for online content with respect to elements of business activity are discussed. Content-related issues are considered for each of the perspectives in the exchange framework.

Your objectives in studying this chapter include the following:

- Recognize the role of content as a resource for businesses.
- Know the different sources of online content and their pros and cons.
- Understand the differences between different forms of content that are enabled by technology.
- Understand ways in which online content affects business activity decisions.
- Develop familiarity with issues for each perspective that are raised by online content.

The Case of the Raging Cow

When the Dr. Pepper/Seven-Up company was ready to introduce its new, flavored dairy drink, Raging Cow, company executives decided to try an innovative way to create buzz among the target market. Prelaunch research indicated that zippy milk drinks would be in highest demand by young people, who, coincidentally, are also among the most technologically savvy Internet users. The plan was to leverage viral marketing via the Internet to spur interest in a drink designed to appeal to people who don't want to "run with the herd."

The company created a Web site, RagingCow.com, to chronicle the adventures of a bovine heroine who has purportedly escaped from a dairy in search of milk excitement. To herd new and repeat visitors to the site, marketing execs recruited six leading lights of the Web logging phenomenon to use their sites to spread the word.

Not familiar with Web logs? A **Web log** is like a diary. It's a frequently updated set of entries by a "blogger," about a theme or topic of interest to its creator. Typically, entries are arranged in reverse chronological order, so it's easy to track the origin and development of an idea. Blogging software has developed to enable even the not-so-savvy Internet user to develop and maintain a blog. All that's needed is the desire to provide frequent updates to the site. The ever-changing content of a blog keeps interested visitors coming back.

In the case of the raging cow, Dr. Pepper/Seven-Up wanted to build brand awareness and image by using a blog-like Raging Cow site to emphasize the similarities between the brand image—different, bold, independent—and the targeted consumers. In addition, the marketing promotion, in which the cow toured metropolitan areas to pique interest as the product was introduced, fit well with the chronological nature of a Web log.

Did the cattle drive succeed? The jury is still out. Veteran bloggers are upset by what they viewed as the misuse of blogging for marketing. They organized a boycott, providing links to a site that explained their opposition to the pseudo-blogging approach. Others, including company spokespeople and marketing experts, argue that blogging is a novel and viable way to create word-of-mouth. The only drawback, of course, is that the company can't control whether the buzz is positive or negative. In any event, the promotion has had the desired effect of creating attention, both for the brand and the marketing technique. The idea of using a Web log to develop a relationship between a product and its market is new, but it has many potential applications for business activity.

In this chapter, we will look at the different sources of Web content, including Web logs, and consider when they might be most effective for achieving different business objectives. In addition, the types of content, including the technologies that make them possible, will be discussed. To better understand the issues that might arise in the development and use of Web content, we will examine the implications of Web content for business activity. Content can be a product, as well as a way to develop a product and to promote a product. In addition, content can be used to create a virtual place, or a context for business activity. Finally, content may affect pricing, as when price comparisons are readily available to customers.

Defining the Purpose of Website Content

Businesses use Web sites to accomplish a range of strategic objectives. For instance, The Walt Disney Company uses its Disney.com site to build the Disney brand, by helping children "play, learn, and explore." In contrast, Re/Max, the nationally known real estate firm, uses its site to create relationships between site visitors and local realtors, and to provide information about buying and selling homes.

With more than 3 billion pages of content on the Internet, it's not surprising that Web content exists for many different reasons. For a company, however, it's important to understand the relationship between site content and business objectives. Look at the different types of Web content displayed in Figure 10-1. What appears to be an

FIGURE 10-1 Site Content Is Used to Achieve Different Objectives.

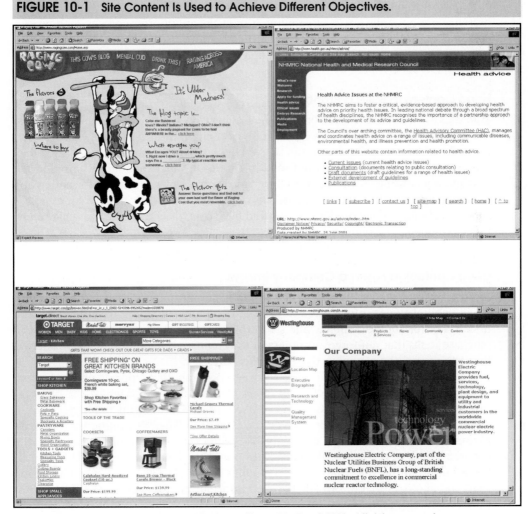

important goal of the site for the company in each case? How does the site content and its presentation work toward achieving that goal?

For commercial purposes, Web sites can be categorized into four main types, depending on the focus of the site's content: (1) enabling transactions; (2) building brands; (3) building a corporate image; and (4) managing customer relationships.

Using Content to Enable Transactions

Web sites that provide consumers with the opportunity to buy goods and services via the Internet are transaction-based sites. Sites with digital content products, like e-books, newsletters, and music, enable the entire process of purchasing—from searching to paying to consuming—to occur online. Other transaction sites allow shoppers to research and compare products, and pay for products through online services like PayPal and C2It, but they require off-line delivery of the physical product.

As we saw in Chapter 4, companies with an entirely digital inventory and company presence are pure-players. A large number of clicks-and-mortar companies, however, combine an online sales capability with off-line storefronts. We will consider aspects of managing a multichannel structure in Chapter 11.

Using Content to Build a Brand

Web sites are also used to build brands. The Raging Cow site was developed to promote the Dr. Pepper/7-Up Company's new milk product, building brand awareness and image by creating ongoing interest in the Web log. Although you can't buy the product through the site, you can obtain information about product rollouts and promotions. This site is an example of content used to build a brand, by providing information and entertainment as value-adding components of the site. Other examples of sites that use content to build a brand are Disney.com and Nick.com, the site created for children by the Nickelodeon television channel.

Using Content to Foster a Company Image

A company can use the Internet to create and foster a company image. General Mills' home page provides information about the company, including its businesses and brands, a history of the company, and a wealth of information for investors. Visitors can purchase items that reinforce awareness of the company's main brands, like Cheerios, but sales are not the core objective of the Web site.

Westinghouse also maintains a Web site to promote its corporate image. Known to many consumers for its electric products, like light bulbs and lamps, the corporation shifted from an early focus on household and industrial appliances to an emphasis on nuclear fuel and power technologies. The Westinghouse Web site chronicles the history of the company, providing customers and investors with a coherent, bird's-eye view of the corporation and its many businesses. This type of site is important for the company, as it enables Westinghouse to describe its mission to its stakeholders, and to provide detailed information about changes to the corporation's strategic focus.

Using Content to Manage Customer Relationships

This class of Web site encompasses a wide variety of types of content. Companies can use the Web to provide different forms of customer support, from FAQs to online manuals, to live support. Regardless of the form used, the objective is to increase customer satisfaction, and encourage repeat purchase and positive word-of-mouth. Sites that work as brokers between companies and consumers also use content to manage customer relationships. For instance, travel aggregators, like Travelocity and Orbitz, store customer preferences to create a streamlined, personal experience for returning consumers.

Sites that provide information to help consumers make informed consumption decisions are another means of managing relationships. For example, a site that provides reliable information about healthcare products can develop a loyal following. Such a site can also influence the relationship between a customer and the manufacturer/vendor of the reviewed product.

While many sites can be classified into one of these four categories by their primary focus, companies often combine several objectives in a single Web site. For instance, Coca-Cola uses its site to build company image, to provide information about its products worldwide, and to build brand with online games, screensavers, e-cards, and promotions.

Bits & Bytes 10.1

People are increasingly willing to pay for online content. U.S. consumers spent $675 million for content in 2001, up 92 percent from 2000. In the first quarter of 2002, more than $300 million was spent—just in the United States.

(*Source:* Online Publishers Association Report, 8/1/02.)

What Guides Content Development?

Once the focus of the Web site has been determined, it's time to decide what the nature of site content should be. This decision is based on careful assessment of several factors (Figure 10-2). Developing an online presence that effectively communicates the objectives of the company requires businesses to understand what sources of content are available, and whether or not they are appropriate for the site purpose. In addition, businesses must take into account the nature of the targeted market. What information will be valued by potential customers? What are the typical computing capabilities of the target? Content decisions require the company to understand how Internet technologies can be best implemented to create a Web site that balances the goals and needs of the company and its intended customers.

The sources of content for commercial use are often similar to the information sources encountered in traditional, off-line commercial environments. For instance, in each environment, customer-to-customer communications can provide information as word-of-mouth, and businesses can develop informational presentations about

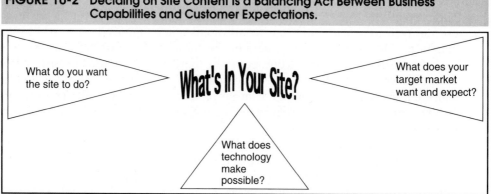

FIGURE 10-2 Deciding on Site Content Is a Balancing Act Between Business Capabilities and Customer Expectations.

themselves and their products. Two main differences exist between the environments, however. First, the Internet differs from a traditional business environment in the speed with which content can be amassed and distributed, and in the scope of sources from which content can be gathered.

A second difference between online and off-line environments for presenting information is the ways in which content from different sources can be made available with Internet technologies. Technology is an important factor for determining what content should go into a site, and how it should be presented. In the next two sections, we'll look first at the sources of Web site content, and then at the different ways that content can be presented in a Web site.

Where Does Content Come From?

Content can come from sources internal to a company, or from sources external to a company (Figure 10-3). Examples of internal, company-generated content include product information and promotional material. External sources of content may be customers, competitors, or publicity. A company may decide to use only one type of source, or a combination of sources, depending on the objectives for the content.

FIGURE 10-3 Web Site Content Can Be Obtained from Different Sources.

COMPANY	CUSTOMER	COMPETITOR	OTHER
- Product information - Promotional information - Databases - Articles - Employee posts - Weblogs	- Testimonials - Articles - Product reviews - Content submission (e.g., photos, stories) - Chat rooms - Bulletin boards - Weblogs	- Site links for comparisons - Product information	- Press (e.g., reviews, articles) - Links to databases - Link lists (e.g., partners, related sites) - Syndicated, purchased content

Internal Sources of Content

Internal sources of content can address several purposes. For instance, a company may develop content in order to make product information accessible online. Web sites that provide product specifications, or that describe applications for a product, reflect a product information focus. Company-created content may also be used to promote a product. Web sites can be used to create a brand image, and to provide incentive to purchase (e.g., with online coupons and rebates). In addition, a company can create content that will be displayed on an external Web site, as through an ad server who places the company's banner ad on a set of subscriber sites.

Another reason for a company to create content is to enhance the benefits of a product experience for its customers. For example, companies can provide answers to common questions about product usage and performance. These sets of frequently asked questions, or **FAQs**, can decrease demand on human customer service resources. Content can also consist of product manuals and online descriptions of product installation and troubleshooting processes.

When interactive customer service is necessary, content can be developed to serve as the interface between the customer and the company's customer service representatives. For instance, a company can use software designed to assess the general nature of a question or problem, and to direct the user to the most appropriate source of help. This form of filtering creates efficiencies for the customer and for the company.

External Sources of Content

A company can integrate information from external sources with content developed within the company, to meet business objectives. External sources take a variety of forms. Each form offers unique opportunities and challenges for business activity. In the following sections, we will look at several external sources of content in depth.

Customer-created Content   Content can be developed with input from customers. Solicited input, as in the form of testimonials or product reviews, has advantages for businesses. These advantages include the ability to provide additional content to site visitors, as well as the potential to use the customer input as a form of word-of-mouth. Customer recommendations of a product may tend to decrease skepticism about stated product benefits, because they come from a source with less vested interest in the sale and adoption of a product than a salesperson.

Customer submissions are another form of customer-created content available to companies with a digitally transmitted product. For example, online magazines and other digital forms of information can, as products, make use of customer submissions. One such Web site exists as a forum for displaying tattoos as art. Magazine readers provide the photographs that are organized into galleries of tattoo types (e.g., symbols, concepts). To keep visitors returning to the site, photo submissions are organized as contests. Pictures of tattoos that are deemed superior on specific criteria are the winners, and they are displayed on the home page of the magazine. These forms of solicited input enable the marketer to exercise control over which material will be presented as content.

To promote its brand in conjunction with NASCAR racing, the Coca-Cola Company invited visitors to submit racing stories to be posted on the community pages of the company site. This tactic was part of a multipronged strategy to keep visitors returning to the site and to encourage word-of-mouth.

Forms of customer-created content differ in the extent to which a business can control the content. For example, online bulletin boards and chat rooms serve as forums in which customers can discuss product experiences and make suggestions to other participants. These features serve to draw visitors to the site, and they encourage repeat visits, which provide opportunities for a company to provide new products and new information about existing products. In addition, they operate as a more traditional form of word-of-mouth, in which communication is two-way, between customers.

A potential downside to online word-of-mouth as an established source of site content is its unpredictability. Long dry spells in which postings to the forum diminish may devalue the content and decrease site traffic. More problematic, however, is the potential for negative information about the company's product or service being published as customer-created content. Because the marketer only controls the availability of the forum, and not the content, constant oversight is needed to insure timely remediation of concerns or complaints that are voiced in the online context.

Competitor-created Content   The Internet facilitates comparisons of products and services across sites. Businesses with a competitive advantage on a product can create

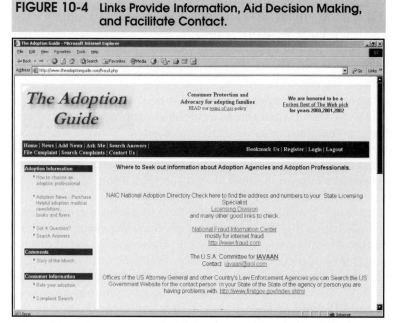

FIGURE 10-4   Links Provide Information, Aid Decision Making, and Facilitate Contact.

Source: Reproduced with permission of *The Adoption Guide.* Copyright 2003. All rights reserved.

links to competitors' sites to make salient a product advantage. In addition, product information provided on competitors' sites can be used to develop internal content that draws comparisons between competing products.

The effects of Web-provided information are substantial. Research conducted by Yankelovich Partners (2000) indicates that 93 percent of online shoppers researched a product online. Eighty-eight percent felt that it was important to have all the necessary information in one place, thus underscoring the importance of content completeness.

Links as Content   Publicly available information can be used as an external source of content. Links to related sites provide content that can augment the central focus of a company's site. These links may provide background about a product, or they may facilitate desirable comparisons between a company's product and competitors' products. The Web site in Figure 10-4 illustrates the use of links to provide prospective adoptive parents with information about the international adoption process.

Links can also serve as product benefits when the set of links enhances the value of a product or brand to the customer. For instance, a company that sells camping equipment may provide links to other companies that sell related, noncompeting products, to travel companies and tour guides, and to sites of national parks and campgrounds.

Companies use lists of links to indicate partnership agreements. These lists not only serve as information resources for visitors, but they may also influence visitors' perceptions of the company or product. A visitor's attitude toward a brand may be improved when the product is evaluated against a backdrop of well-known, reputable companies with whom the selling company has partnership agreements. When such a **halo effect** occurs, the positive affect and attitude associated with another company or its product is transferred to the evaluation of the present product.

These opportunities for using links can enhance the value proposition of a business model through the 3 I's initially discussed in Chapter 8: image, improvement, and incentive (Figure 10-5). For instance, links can promote image through association with other companies or organizations with a desired reputation. Comparisons with competing brands through links to their sites can demonstrate price and other attribute advantages, thus creating incentives for consumers. Links to sites with related products and information that enhances the value of the company's product can serve an improvement objective.

Choosing the right links is important not only for developing the site, company, and brand image, but also for boosting a site's position in search engine listings. Search engines often incorporate link popularity as a factor in determining how high to place a site in a list of search results. **Link popularity** is defined as the number and quality of sites that link to a particular site, relative to other sites with a similar focus. Search engines, such as Google, assess link popularity by counting the number of **backlinks** to a site. A backlink is a link that points to a particular page. Backlinks are different from **backward links**, although the terms are often used interchangeably. Most links on sites are **forward links**; click on the hypertext and you are directed to

FIGURE 10-5 Links Can Enhance the Value Proposition.

Model	Sample Link Type	Desired Effect
Image	Prestigious partners	Halo effect; recategorization of product as higher level or quality
Incentive	Competitors who are inferior on a key feature	Highlight product dominance on one or more features
	Public sites/databases (e.g., health-related)	Underscore product function or need
Improvement	Sites with related products	Position product as central; simplify acquisition of other, complementary products
	Sites with product use-related information (e.g., camping sites)	Stimulate product involvement; increase perceived benefits

another site—a unidirectional process. In contrast, a backward link is a link back to the site that contains the original forward link. In short, the backward link completes the loop of information.

Businesses can use a **reciprocal linking strategy** to increase the link popularity of a site. A **reciprocal link** is related to a backlink, in that a link to an external site is accompanied by a request for a link from that site back to the requesting site. An effective reciprocal linking strategy involves choosing sites with high quality content relevant to the content of your site, requesting the reciprocal link, and maintaining the value of your site as a link destination. Because managing a linking effort can be time-consuming, some companies outsource the process to businesses, like Links4Trade, who manage the process (Figure 10-6).

Syndicated Content To maintain quality content that is fresh, and updated on a regular basis, companies often turn to sources of syndicated content. **Syndicated content** is material that has been developed for distribution across a variety of outlets, for a price. For instance, the Associated Press (AP) writes approximately 400 news stories each day, and sorts them into topic categories for its online market. Subscribers to the AP service can sort through the categories and publish selected stories on their sites. AP subscribers include Yahoo! and MSNBC.com. Web sites often use syndicated content to augment site information, enhancing the value of the site to visitors. Content can be purchased on a wide array of topics, and content providers can customize content packages to meet a variety of needs and budgets.

FIGURE 10-6   Link Management Software Provides an Efficient Solution for Companies with Many Reciprocal Links.

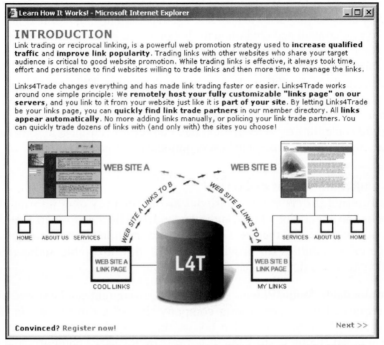

Source: Reproduced with permission from Links4Trade, Inc. Copyright 2003. All rights reserved.

Bits & Bytes 10.2

The rich get richer. Although there were an estimated 1,700 sites charging for content by mid-2002, U.S. consumers spent 85 percent of the total money to buy online content at only the top 50 sites.

(*Source:* Online Publishers Association Report, 8/1/02.)

How Is Content Published on the Internet?

We have seen that content can be obtained from many different sources. Deciding what and how to present the content is the next step in developing an effective Web presence. In this section, we will consider the different forms in which content from various sources can be published on the Internet.

Defining Types of Content

Advances in technology have made new types of content available to businesses. To illustrate the impact of technology, consider the importance of telepresence, introduced in

Chapter 5, which is defined as the user's perception of being present in the computer-mediated environment. In theoretical terms, telepresence is due to vividness and interactivity. In actual practice, telepresence is created by using different types of media, such as audio and video formats that provide sensory richness. In addition, interactivity is created by using technologies that enable the user to change the form, or representation, of the computer-mediated environment. Telepresence is the result of the carefully balancing of technical capabilities with consumer characteristics.

Different levels of multimedia capability and interactivity characterize the types of content that are possible in the Internet environment. The desired level of complexity in content type is a function of the business' objectives for the content, as well as the technical capabilities of the business or the content creator, and the anticipated behaviors and computing capacity of the target market. The business must decide which combinations of content types will best communicate its goals.

Multimedia Types of Content

The Internet differs from traditional media for providing information because it enables the integration of text, audio, and video in flexible formats that can be, to some extent, controlled by the user. Three types of multimedia technologies illustrate the range of possibilities for providing content: downloadable audio/video, streaming audio/video, and three-dimensional animation.

Downloadable Audio/Video   Audio and video content can be stored as files that can be requested by a user from a company site. In a **downloadable file**, content is transferred from the server that houses the site's files to the user's computer. Once downloaded, the file is stored in its entirety on the user's computer and is available to be played. Examples of downloadable files include a television commercial that is available on a Web site, or clips from an audio recording or a televised speech. Downloadable files can be used to provide product exposure (e.g., with a movie or music), or to create links between the different media used in a promotional campaign. The ability to provide audio and video content can be used to enhance the vividness of a site's content. Another benefit of the downloadable format is that it can be retrieved and replayed by the user whenever revisiting the experience is desired: once downloaded, the file exists until the user deletes it from the computer's memory.

The disadvantages of a downloadable file are the time needed to download the file, and the space that files can require for storage on the user's computer. For instance, with a 28.8 kbps modem, it can take nearly 2 hours to download a 60-second commercial in a format that is not compressed for the downloading process. The amount of information that must be digitized in order to create the file—and that makes the long downloading time inevitable—means that the file will require a lot of room for storage. In a world where Internet time is a fact of life, it is reasonable to assume that not many people will be willing to invest large amounts of time and computer memory to download an advertising message!

Streaming Audio/Video   An alternative to a downloadable file is a **streaming file**. As the name suggests, a "streaming" file provides the user with the file content at the time that the file is being accessed. Streaming content offers real-time playback; no content is downloaded and stored, so there is no wait to receive the file and no demand

FIGURE 10-7   RealPlayer Enables Users to Receive Streaming Audio and Video.

Source: Reproduced with permission of RealNetworks, Inc. Copyright 2003. All rights reserved.

on computer storage capacity. Examples of streaming content include Internet radio and live broadcasts of concert footage. In order to play a streaming file, a user must often download a plug-in. A **plug-in** is a piece of software that interprets the information in a streaming file and communicates it in a recognizable form to the user's computer. Plug-ins with basic playback capabilities are often available free of charge to users (e.g., RealPlayer as shown in Figure 10-7).

Three-Dimensional Animation   Much like Saturday morning cartoons, 3-D animation on the Internet provides visual interest and vividness to otherwise static content. Software packages (e.g., Shockwave and Flash) provide marketers with the tools to create content with action. Similar to streaming files, animated files may require an appropriate plug-in to enable execution of the file.

Animated images are related to the concept of virtual reality. A goal of virtual reality is to create a computer-based environment that provides the user with the sense of being in the computer-created environment, or telepresence. Programs to create virtual reality environments, such as VRML (Virtual Reality Mark-up Language), operate by translating geometric elements of objects into a series of mathematical equations that can be represented digitally.

Virtual reality environments are a hybrid of multimedia and interactive capabilities. These environments are often created with **virtual reality photography.** This technology creates an environment by connecting several photographs of an object (e.g., a car) or a scene (e.g., a store) to produce a panoramic image. The user can use a mouse to examine different parts of the image as if he were moving around in the actual environment. Because the user can navigate a virtual reality scenario, and because the context changes as the user exerts control over the environment, the situation exhibits interactivity. This type of rich media publishing is becoming increasingly prevalent among marketing organizations, as consumers acquire high-speed, broadband Internet access.

Bits & Bytes 10.3

Nearly 25 percent of the advertising done by Ford Motor Company in mid-2002 used rich media technologies to appeal to consumers.

(*Source:* Nielsen NetRatings, August 2002.)

Types of Interactive Content

In addition to the user actions that affect content with virtual reality applications, businesses can incorporate interactive content into a Web site with contests, games, and customer service. The role of interactivity differs across applications in the extent to which the behaviors of a site visitor affect the business activities of the company. For instance, interactivity can be used to accumulate information about customer needs and preferences, as with an online survey that uses a respondent's answers to structure subsequent parts of the questionnaire. This application reflects the role of interactivity as a way to develop and refine business action. In contrast, interactivity in the form of a game may promote user involvement with the site, brand, or company, but the visitor's actions are not tracked and used as data for business decision making. A continuum of the role of interactivity is presented in Figure 10-8.

Online Games

Online games can be used to increase visitor involvement with a Web site. Companies can use games as interactive content to keep visitors in a site longer, thus potentially

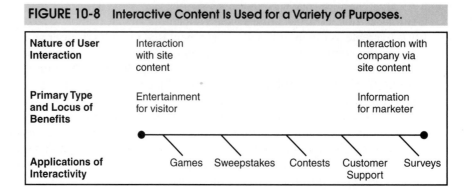

FIGURE 10-8 Interactive Content Is Used for a Variety of Purposes.

Nature of User Interaction	Interaction with site content				Interaction with company via site content
Primary Type and Locus of Benefits	Entertainment for visitor				Information for marketer
Applications of Interactivity	Games	Sweepstakes	Contests	Customer Support	Surveys

increasing exposure to the company's brands, or exposure to advertising and promotional material offered on the site. In addition, companies can use games to encourage to visitors to return to a Web site, as by changing the nature of the game (e.g., playing options, difficulty level). To participate in an online game, a visitor may be required to provide registration information. This information can provide the business with simple data about site visitors.

Online Sweepstakes

A sweepstake is often used to lure visitors to a site, or to encourage visitors to become registered members of a site. Sweepstakes operate by providing participants with a chance at winning a prize, without any investment on the part of the player. No skill is necessary, and winners are randomly determined. Online sweepstakes are attractive to marketers because the random selection of winners enables the sweepstake process to be largely automated, and to manage large numbers of participants.

Online Contests

Businesses can use online contests not only as sources of customer leads, but also as a source of content. The key difference between a sweepstake and a contest is that in a contest, the element of chance is replaced with skill, and the demonstration of superior skill determines the winner. As with online games and sweepstakes, participation in a contest may require the participant to provide registration information. (It is hard to acknowledge a winner if you cannot identify the contestant.) In addition to serving as a source of user information, contests can be developed that require the user to provide information that can be placed on the site as content. For example, an online publisher of a camera magazine might run a digital photography contest in which winners' photographs are displayed.

Because contest entries must each be evaluated to determine the winner, contests are more effort-intensive than sweepstakes. This cost is often offset, however, by the benefits of the contest in engaging participants in activities that encourage them to think about the brand, or company. As a result, contests are frequently used to build brand image and customer loyalty. They can also be used as a resource for developing promotional campaigns, based on the insights obtained from content submissions. For example, an essay contest on the topic of "Why I Like Brand X Soda" might provide the company with product perceptions about their product and the competition, as well as information about product consumption, including frequency and occasions.

Online Customer Support

Online games are served to the user as interactive content, and online contests can result in the interactive creation of content. Even farther along the continuum of interactive purposes is customer support. Interactive applications to create content to facilitate communication between company and customer include moderated discussion groups and mailing lists, as well as more private forms of communication, such as real-time live help.

InSite

WWW.EPINIONS.COM: A WEB OF WORD-OF-MOUTH

Suppose you've just learned that you're going to be the parent of triplets—yes, three of them. It's time to start shopping, but where do you go, and who do you trust? At Epinions.com, you can find information about more than 2 million products, from buying guides and product definitions to product reviews. The site also sorts information about price and product availability, so that you can find a merchant to sell you that triple stroller you know you're going to need.

What sets Epinions.com apart from other buying guides is its wealth of reviews written by real, live customers. Products are rated by customers, who also have the opportunity to submit reviews with their ratings. To help site visitors gauge the credibility of a review, contributors are themselves rated by other site visitors. For instance, suppose you read a review of the Terrible Trio Transporter. You may choose to rate the review. The rating is combined with other visitors' ratings, and the average rating is posted on the site for subsequent shoppers.

So what's in it for the reviewer? Why invest time and effort to write helpful, informative reviews that steer customers away from bad products and toward good ones? If the warm glow you feel from helping fellow shoppers make good choices isn't enough, money is also part of the operation. Reviewers receive Eroyalties, based on a calculation that takes into account the quality and quantity of reviews each person submits. Eroyalties can be cashed in monthly, for cold, hard cash. In effect, customers receive cash for creating content, while providing a free information resource for other customers. In addition, the site sells advertising space, trading on traffic to build exposure for advertising.

Online Research

Web site content can provide companies with information for developing and implementing aspects of business strategy. Insights can be obtained from customer support activities, such as online discussion groups and bulletin boards, as well as from interaction with individual users. Online contests can also provide information. For example, Budweiser uses its Web site to foster brand image. In the past, site visitors could take a quiz to assess whether they were "beer meisters." The quiz was scored instantly, and the results were displayed to the visitor. In addition to providing entertainment and information to the user, the results of this type of quiz, if tracked and analyzed, constitute a set of data about visitors' knowledge of the product and the product category.

Interactive surveys in which users are aware of the data collection serve as content that provides the company with user feedback. This feedback can be directed toward a business, a product, or even the Web site. Data collection as content may have an additional benefit; unhappy customers who are able to complain directly to a company may be less likely to complain to other customers.

Putting Content to Work: Implications for Business Activity

Businesses can use content to carry out aspects of business management related to each element of moving a product from production to sales, including the four P's: *product, price, place*, and *promotion*. As a result, online content is often developed for widely varying purposes. In this section, we will consider the way that the Internet as a content resource can influence each of the four P's, and we will look at several issues that may stem from this influence.

Content and Product

As a content resource, the Internet influences decisions about product strategy. For example, the Internet can influence a company's product strategy by creating an opportunity for new types of products and services. Consider the role of Internet Service Providers (ISPs), such as Compuserve and America OnLine. An important benefit of these services is to make Internet content accessible to users. Without an Internet, who needs an ISP? In addition, content can be used to provide information about a product, and even as a tool for developing a product.

Using Internet Content as a Product

The Internet can influence product strategy by changing the nature of the need for a product. This situation occurs when the technologies pioneered through the Internet make existing products that fulfill a similar need less desirable. For example, audiophiles can have music on demand by purchasing a compact disc, a cassette, a record, or even an eight-track tape. With the advent of Internet technologies such as MPEG3, a format that enables people to download a huge variety of recorded music, the benefits of previous formats pale dramatically.

Obviously, not all products are suitable for a digital medium. In addition, even when a product is a viable candidate for digitization, businesses must decide whether the Internet environment presents advantages for developing and selling products in a digital form. The digital form may complement or replace existing product forms.

Decisions about whether a digital product form is desirable should consider customers and competitors as factors in developing a product strategy. For instance, books are a product that can be readily digitized. Suppose that a bookseller determines that production costs will be substantially reduced if books are sold in a downloadable form from the Internet. Eliminating the hard copy production component of the business makes sense only if the bookseller correctly understands the nature of the target market. Do customers in the target market have Internet access? Are these customers likely to adapt their buying behaviors to adopt the online form of the product?

If the market is identifiable, accessible, and sufficient, the decision to switch product forms may be guided by competitors' actions. For example, EMI International, a recording company that produces and markets records and compact discs, recognized that the availability of music over the Internet created a challenge for EMI's ability to be successful selling recorded music in traditional formats. In this case, the challenge came not from competitors in the traditional marketplace (e.g., other recording companies), but from competitors in the digital business environment. The company was faced with the need to work proactively to create a product strategy capable of providing long-term opportunities for surviving and thriving, given the increasing popularity of online sources of music. As a result, EMI partnered with LiquidAudio, a provider of software and services for digital music formats, to explore opportunities for developing an online product presence. More recently, Warner Music has worked with Apple Computer to develop the iTunes product that enables consumers to download music tracks for 99 cents apiece.

Using Content to Provide Product Information

From the early days of brochureware, the use of the Internet as a way to provide information about products and services has changed dramatically. Businesses can use the technological characteristics of the Internet to provide information in ways that augment forms of communication available in traditional media. For example, a catalog that arrives in your mailbox contains a specific set of product descriptions. All, some, or none of them may be of interest to you. With the Internet, however, a business can maintain a database of product information, but provide to customers only those descriptions that match stated needs or interests. As a result, the content can be customized to provide a better match between the customer's needs and the company's offerings.

The ability to tailor information displays to customer preferences reflects the dynamic nature of online content. Early commercial Web sites tended to provide largely static displays of product information, such as brochures and catalog pages. Today, however, Web users are exposed to dynamic content. **Dynamic content** refers to the changeable nature of a display, whether triggered by a customer action, such as clicking on a link or image, or as the result of a programmed response to a user behavior. For instance, a news site might provide extra links to technology news for a user, based on automated collection and analysis of the user's clickstream.

Businesses can use the Internet as a content resource to provide product descriptions, to suggest product applications, and to facilitate product use. As an illustration of the latter benefit of the Internet, a business might create a Web site that contains technical manuals that can be downloaded on demand for different products. In addition, the site could contain step-by-step installation instructions, and even tips for troubleshooting. By storing a user profile—complete with purchase history—for each registered visitor, the site can provide dynamic content by filtering for display only the manuals for the products purchased by the visitor. As a result, dynamic content enhances site ease-of-use and functionality.

Developing an effective Web presence is important for sites that are not transaction-enabled, as content from the Internet affects off-line shopping. A study by Jupiter Communications (2000) describes **Web-impacted spending** that combines the revenue from online purchases with off-line purchases influenced by Internet-based information to provide a quantitative estimate of the Internet's influence. In 2000, Web-impacted spending was estimated at $235 billion, with projected growth to $831 billion in 2005.

Using Content to Create a Product

Internet content can be used as a tool for product development. Using the Internet as a content resource may influence the activities related to each phase of a three-stage framework for product development: planning, design, and implementation.

In the planning stage, multiple information sources are used to determine desired product characteristics. These sources might include the anticipated market and its needs, as well as input from the production and marketing personnel in the organization. As a content resource, the Internet can be used to conduct business research about customers' needs, and to investigate competitors' products and actions.

In the design stage, the inputs from the planning stage are used to guide the development of a product, from a set of desired characteristics to a coherent product concept. Digital content can be used to develop product plans and to create product simulations that can be shared and revised despite geographical differences. Digital design packages such as CATIA (Computer Aided Three-dimensional Interactive Application), through IBM, enable teams of engineers and planners to work simultaneously to develop product prototypes. This development serves as a map for the implementation stage, in which the product moves from a concept to reality.

To implement a concept, Internet content in the form of product component databases and relationship histories between suppliers and producers expedites the process of manufacturing a product.

Bits & Bytes 10.4

Looks matter. Of 2,684 consumers asked to evaluate the credibility of 100 Web sites, nearly half took site appearance into account in judging the credibility of the content.

(*Source:* Internet Advertising Report, October 2002.)

Content and Price

The ready availability of information on the Internet makes it easier for shoppers to acquire price information about products and services. This **price transparency** has advantages and disadvantages for businesses. For instance, when a business has a competitive price, it is advantageous to have that information easily accessible to customers. Suppose, however, that the price is substantially higher than that of the competition. Even if there are product characteristics, such as extra features or performance capabilities that cause or merit the higher price, customers shopping on the Internet may tend to focus on the price.

The focus on price may result from consumers' ability to use shopping agents on the Internet to gather and create spontaneously generated content about sets of products. A **shopping agent** is an application that can be provided with specific information that serves as the basis for a search through Internet content. For instance, a user could look for digital cameras made by a particular company, and within a set price range (e.g., Kodak cameras between $500 and $1,000).

FIGURE 10-9   A Sample Merchant-based Brand/Attribute Display.

Kodak DC215 Zoom Millenium Edition				
Merchant	Price	State	Shipping	In Stock
Buy.com	$273.95	CA	5.95	No
eCost.com	$274.99	CA	FREE	No
Camera Sound	$275.00	PA	see site	call
Egghead.com	$288.99	WA	FREE	Limited
BuyDig.com	$293.00	NJ	19.95+	Yes

Shopping agents often create brand/attribute matrices that display available specifications for a designated set of products. A brand/attribute matrix may contain information about a set of different brands with comparable features, or a display of the different locations and purchase characteristics associated with a single brand. In the latter instance, the location, or storefront, becomes the brand. An example of this type of display is shown in Figure 10-9. Typically, price information is listed from cheapest to most expensive, in a set. As noted, a company with a low price can benefit from the exposure provided by shopping agents.

For a business, one difficulty with shopping agents is that they result in a presentation of content that the business does not control. Of course, situations like this exist in traditional media, too. For instance, product reviews and ratings in *Consumer Reports* provide the shopper with an across-brand comparison benefit similar to the shopping agent function. With the Internet, however, the ease with which informational content can be posted and altered increases the importance of frequently monitoring competitors' price-related actions. In addition, the flexible nature of the brand/attribute displays means that a business must consider the likely specifications for a user-initiated search, and how the results of different searches might depict the product, relative to the competition.

Content and Place

Two ways in which the Internet as a content resource affects decisions about the place component of business activity are (1) by serving as a source of information about consumption locations, and (2) by creating contexts for consumption, or virtual places.

Whether the product is digital or physical, a business can use Internet content to guide customers to purchase opportunities. For instance, e-mail marketing is content created to directly market to a delimited set of targets. Alternatively, a Web site might contain a list of locations from which a product is available, perhaps divided into geographic regions.

The Internet can also act as a place. One goal for developers of virtual reality is to create contexts that provide realistic simulations of physical environments. This technology can be used to create shopping malls and stores. A customer can navigate through a store, looking at items on racks and shelves. Some programs enable the user to use a computer mouse and cursor to "pick up" an item from a shelf, turning it around and over to examine the product from different angles. Real estate companies have used the Internet to guide prospective buyers through homes, and museums use the virtual modeling technology to provide tours to distant visitors. These examples illustrate situations in which the role of the Internet as a content resource is closely related to its role as a channel resource. We will consider this interaction in detail in Chapter 11.

To create a more vivid perception of experience, some programs that create virtual places allow the user to enter the environment with a virtual persona. These images, called **avatars**, act as the digital representation of a person in the virtual environment. For instance, suppose that you wanted to go shopping in an online store that welcomed avatars. You could send your virtual representative to the store to meet with the store's sales representative, perhaps another avatar. In spite of the science fiction nature of the scenario, the technology can help businesses create a more involving and realistic experience for their customers.

On a simpler level, the format and appearance of a Web site can create a context that influences user perceptions and behavior. Researchers have demonstrated that the choice of a background for product information can alter the importance that a visitor places on a particular product attribute. For example, vague images of coins on a description of a car result in increased weight placed on price by shoppers who examine the description. Pictures of clouds on a background of sofa profiles increase the importance of comfort as a product attribute. The effects of these subtle changes to context illustrate the potential importance of content elements as factors that resemble more traditional effects of place as a context for product evaluation (e.g., atmospherics).

Content and Promotion

The Internet has received attention as a means for promoting goods and services. It is a channel of communication that has the potential for reaching a global audience. In addition, the technologies that comprise the Internet make it possible for companies to create promotional content in forms capable of addressing very different promotional objectives. We will look at the use of content for the three objectives of image, improvement, and incentive. The vehicles used to deliver the content to users, such as banners, buttons, and mailing lists, receive additional attention in Chapter 12.

Using Content to Enhance Image

Image-based business models use content to influence customers' perceptions of a brand or a company. With this approach, the business' goal is to provide content that adds value for the customer without functionally changing the experience of product use. For instance, companies have developed Web site content designed to create exposure to a brand or a company, even when the site does not enable product purchase. For example, Procter & Gamble's Crest site contains an interactive brushing demonstration that is applicable for any brand of toothpaste. The interest and involvement experienced by a user who visits the site and tries out the demonstration, however, may increase the favorability of an attitude toward the Crest product.

Using Content to Create Incentive

Incentive to purchase a particular product can be created with promotional content that demonstrates the advantages, as in time efficiency or cost reduction, of the company's product over other, competing products. For instance, content can facilitate product trial, making it easier for a shopper to determine whether a product is appropriate for her or his needs. Examples of companies who use content for product trial are research firms, such as Nua Online and Dun & Bradstreet. These companies make available sample reports, and they routinely provide free research results that indicate the focus and scope of their for-a-fee services. Free online trials create time efficiency by reducing search and evaluation costs, as well as financial risk.

Internet content can be used to reduce the costs associated with product production, and with creating and maintaining the relationship formed by the product transaction between company and customer. These savings can be passed on to customers in the form of lower prices, without narrowing the producer's profit margin. An important benefit of the Internet is the ability to provide shoppers with customer support, any time. For businesses, providing self-help content that a customer can search through and use on demand may not only enhance company–customer interactions, but it may also be less costly to manage the relationship through the Internet than through phone, mail, or in-person customer service interactions.

Incentives that reduce risk and lower price offer indirect savings to the customer. Many businesses have used the Internet to take a more direct approach, as by simply giving customers money to reward them for making purchases through their Web sites. For example, Barnes and Noble sought to increase holiday traffic through its Web site in 1999 by giving first-time buyers $20. Other merchants have provided rebates, free shipping and returns, and gift certificates to induce purchases and repeat purchases.

Some online retailers use electronic coupons to spur purchasing. E-coupon Web sites such as Coolsavings.com and Valupage.com provide shoppers with collections of vendors' coupons that can be printed and redeemed. The results of a June 2000 study by the NPD Group, Inc. indicate that e-coupons for products typically associated with online sales, such as toys (87 percent) and books (83 percent), were redeemed online more frequently than e-coupons for products in other categories. E-coupon redemption in off-line stores was highest for fast foods (96 percent) and groceries (94 percent).

As the screen in Figure 10-10 illustrates, businesses can use coupons as content to create purchase incentives.

Using Content for Product Improvement

Promotional content that provides the user with extra product-related benefits accomplishes an improvement objective. Using promotional content to augment product benefits often blurs the distinction between product and promotion. For example, Procter & Gamble has used its Crest site to enable visitors to sign up for free dental check-up reminders. The reminder was delivered via e-mail to the user, and provided an opportunity for the company to remind the user about Crest. Even though the reminder does not affect the performance of the toothpaste, it may become stored in memory as one of a set of associations between the brand name and product benefits.

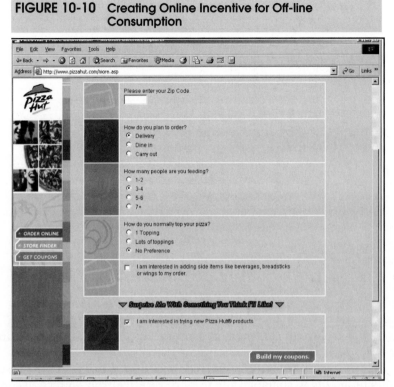

FIGURE 10-10   Creating Online Incentive for Off-line Consumption

Source: The Pizza Hut name, logos and related marks are trademarks of Pizza Hut, Inc., and are used with permission.

What Works in a Web Site? Putting It All Together

We've seen that businesses have different sources of content, and different forms in which content can be presented. In addition, we know that decisions about the relative importance of different goals for the Web site should guide the design and function of its content. A key factor in the success of a Web site, however, is the reaction of visitors to the site. Does the site meet or exceed their expectations? Companies need to know whether their sites are accomplishing strategic objectives and meeting customer needs.

While business research designed to elicit customer perceptions could be conducted for a particular site, research has shown that across companies, products, and target markets, some aspects of Web site design and function are more important than others. For instance, shoppers want Web sites to be easy to navigate, with good content that is updated frequently and regularly. In addition, research results underscore the importance of using file formats that can be downloaded quickly, without stretching the limits of patience. The graph in Figure 10-11 shows the results of a survey of 990 Internet users, conducted in 2001. The survey assessed the importance of site characteristics on the decision to make a repeat visit to a Web site. Respondents rated the importance of each characteristic out of 100 points. The average ratings are

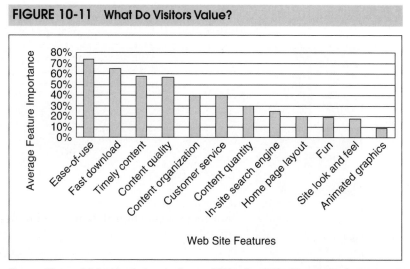

FIGURE 10-11 What Do Visitors Value?

Source: Data published by Arthur Andersen, LLP, collected by Knowledge Systems and Research, Inc.

described as percentages, and a higher percentage indicates greater importance of the characteristic.

As you can see from the graph, the visual appeal of the site is outweighed by the ability of the site to communicate its purpose effectively with good content that can be readily accessed. Of course, different purposes for Web sites change the importance of the site characteristics. A site that provides subscription-based financial reports for investors might emphasize content quality and timeliness, while a children's entertainment site might focus on visual appearance and entertainment capabilities.

Cautions for Content

The extent to which the Internet as a content resource can be used effectively in different aspects of business activity depends on the interaction of people and technology. People create content and interpret content, and technology enables the representation of that content. The interaction between people and technology can raise issues about the nature of content, and how it affects the behaviors of people. In using the Internet as a content resource, companies must be aware of the possible issues that may impede the effectiveness of business activity. We can look at these issues from the different perspectives that influence digital business.

Consumer Issues

Commercial inputs as digital content differ from commercial inputs in traditional consumption environments. Some of the characteristics that differentiate the content environments include the amount of readily available content, the cost to search the content, and who controls the format of the content (i.e., company or customer).

Each of these three differences may affect the ways that customers use Internet content, and the extent to which their behaviors differ from what might occur in traditional commercial contexts (e.g., television, radio). For example, the sheer amount of information from the Internet as a single source often exceeds the amount that can be acquired from traditional, off-line sources, in the same amount of time.

In addition, the costs of searching for information with the Internet may be lower than the costs associated with information acquisition in other venues. Consider the costs, in terms of time, that are incurred by typing a request for car specifications on a car site, compared with those incurred by driving to an equal number of car dealerships. The ease with which information can be obtained may lead people to gather more information than they would in other environments.

The third difference in content focuses on control. Many traditional sources of content are pushed to customers (e.g., television ads), who are passive recipients of the information and its format. With Internet content, however, users can actively search for and construct displays of desired commercial content.

Research on information processing provides a basis for understanding and predicting how people might use content as the basis for making product-related decisions. This knowledge provides a basis for helping businesses develop effective presentations of content. For example, we know that people tend to trade off effort to process information against anticipated decision accuracy, or quality. This result can be extended to include information search and evaluation. That is, more effort to search for information may lead to less effort invested in understanding the information to make product judgments. In addition, given the user's ability to actively structure some types of Internet content (remember interactivity?), more effort to structure content may be followed by less effort to process information to make a decision. Businesses should provide content in a form and amount that does not overload or confuse customers.

Other insights from information processing and decision making research suggest that people often use heuristics to process information. For example, if all of the brands but one in a comparison format provide information about a feature, users will tend to eliminate the incomplete brand from consideration. An alternative behavior is to infer a value for the brand that tends to be lower than the values for other brands. Either outcome works to the brand's disadvantage. These findings suggest that marketers must be aware not only of how the content they provide will appear to customers, but also how the type of information in a site compares with that of the competition, in terms of completeness.

Bits & Bytes 10.5

Although online shoppers say they judge sites on substance—not appearance—42 percent of consumers who judged health sites used site design to assess the credibility of site content. Only 7.6 percent of the health experts who judged the same sites did likewise.

(*Source:* Internet Advertising Report and Stanford University, October 2002.)

Business Issues

What Is the Content? Goods or Services

Consider the traditional manner of defining a product. In the business literature, products are often described as bundles of benefits that satisfy particular needs of a consuming populace, whether individuals or organizations, for which the populace is willing to give up something of value in exchange. Both goods and services are products.

The Internet influences the range of possibilities for bundles of benefits, by making new goods possible, and by enabling changes to existing benefit bundles. Of course, services can also provide bundles of benefits to customers. Because selling services can require the development of a strategy that is markedly different from a strategy for selling goods, it is important to understand what is actually being conveyed, and whether the benefits of the offering are perceived as characteristic of a good or of a service.

The Internet may affect our ability to differentiate goods from services using accepted characterizations of their differences. For instance, goods are sometimes differentiated from services by tangibility: goods are generally tangible, services are intangible. The Internet is an environment characterized by intangible, digitized information. Given the nature of the medium, goods that can be conveyed by the technologies that enable the medium are definitionally intangible, thus blurring one possible way of discriminating goods from services.

Services have also been differentiated from products by the nature of their consumption. Goods and their benefits, whether tangible, like an ice cream cone, or intangible, like software code, can be purchased and consumed at another place or time. (Although, with ice cream, it is generally best to consume sooner, rather than later.) In traditional venues, services are consumed at the time of production, like a maid service, a car wash, or a hair cut. Another way of characterizing the difference is that the benefits of any product offering are not obtained until consumption for either a product or a service. However, for a service, the benefits are not even available until the offering is consumed. Under this approach, goods have some created, existing, untapped potential for need satisfaction that services do not possess. Services have the benefit potential only when the service is enacted, or performed.

With the Internet, concepts of time and place differ from traditional exchange environments. Internet services create value in the form of digitized results of actions that are designed to provide desired benefits. The ability to digitize the end result of the service means that the result can be stored, and the benefits of its existence can be consumed at a later time. This capability means that the outcome of actions can be viewed as a good. In short, the difference between Internet-based goods and Internet-based services is blurred by the technological capability to digitize and store the results of the activities that create the offering.

To determine whether an offering should be promoted as a good or a service, it is necessary for the business to recognize how visible the benefits of a technology are to the end user. For instance, the Internet has created many opportunities for products that enable users to perform Internet-related activities, such as sending and receiving e-mail, and searching online databases. In many cases, however, the consumers of the informational benefits of these activities may be unaware of the underlying hardware or software products that make receiving the benefits of the activities possible. Instead, they may simply focus on the entity that makes available the benefits. Depending on the company's goals, making salient either the benefits or the underlying technology product may shift the user's perception, evaluation, and adoption of an offering from one vendor to another.

In general, the nature of the Internet as an environment of intangible, digitized information may suggest an increasing importance and emphasis on the role of service marketing issues and tactics in the development of business strategy. In addition, traditional approaches to product strategy, in which goods are often described and promoted on the basis of tangible features, may be largely replaced by marketing efforts that emphasize the relatively more tangible *benefits* of Internet-related products, rather than the intangible products themselves.

The Internet and Product Innovation

A frequently encountered term with respect to the Internet is "innovation." The Internet has itself been described as an innovation with respect to communication. In addition, the Internet has been characterized as a set of technologies that has resulted in the development of innovative products that capitalize on the technological capabilities of the Internet. In many instances, these products are digital content. Developing effective business strategy for a digital product may depend on the extent to which the product will be perceived as innovative. It is necessary to separate the Internet as an innovative environment for business from Internet content as products that may (or may not) be innovative.

Defining Innovation   Several different definitions of *innovation* have been proposed and defended by researchers, including firm-oriented, product-oriented, and market-oriented perspectives. A firm-oriented perspective describes as innovative a product that is new to the producing organization. A product-oriented perspective characterizes a product's newness in terms of the extent to which it differs from existing products. Note that neither of these two perspectives takes into account the impact of the product on the people who will use it. In contrast, a market-oriented perspective focuses directly on the impact of the product on the target market. That is, will the product change the way that the market carries out activities related to the purpose of the product? If so, how dramatic a change will be observed?

Because we have defined products as a function of the effect they have on the market—that is, the benefits that can be obtained through consumption—it makes sense to employ a parallel definition of innovation. For our purposes, then, **innovation** is determined and defined by the impact of a product on the user's behavior. Products that exert a greater influence on patterns of behavior are more innovative than products that exert less influence on patterns of behavior.

The impact of an innovation can be further classified by the nature of the product's impact on behavior. If the consumption of a product affects whether or not a behavior is carried out, the product is described as a **discontinuous innovation**. In other words, the product creates a break in the behavior pattern, hence the discontinuity. If, however, the product still enables the user to carry out the same behavior, but affects the way that the behavior occurs, the product is classified as a **continuous innovation**. An ISP is an example of a discontinuous innovation, because it requires a fundamental change to the way people communicate and obtain information. In contrast, MPEG3 is an example of a continuous innovation; people don't need to dramatically change their music listening patterns to enjoy the product.

An important point to remember is that it is possible for a product to be new, but not to be particularly innovative. This distinction is important because it may affect the way people adopt the product, as a function of its similarity in appearance, usage, performance, or benefits to existing products. In addition, it is possible for a product to be similar in application to an existing product (e.g., online newspapers), but to completely change the manner in which the application-related behavior is carried out (e.g., online newspapers from around the world, focused with push technology to provide specific, topical information). Recognition of these differences should guide the development of marketing strategy.

Policy Issues

Two issues illustrate the role of the policy perspective in content provision. One issue is the source of online content, an issue that introduces concerns of copyright. Another issue is the nature of online content; that is, what content is allowable?

Copyright Concerns: The Source of Content

The rapid growth of information on the Internet, and particularly on the World Wide Web, raises concerns about how to protect intellectual property. The importance of protecting intellectual property has increased with the development of technologies that make it easier to copy and distribute protected works.

The importance of protecting people's creative efforts has a history in the United States almost as long as the history of the country. In the United States Constitution, Congress was given the power to secure ". . . for limited times to authors and inventors the exclusive rights to their respective writings and discoveries" (Article 1, Section 8). Congress passed the first copyright law in 1790.

The advent of computer technologies led to the need to refine and expand the classification of works that would be considered protected by law. The National Information Infrastructure (NII) Copyright Protection Act of 1995 updated existing copyright laws to encompass the digital transmission of a work. This simply means that the creator of a copyrighted work has the right to authorize or forbid the distribution of a piece of work, even through the Internet.

A key concern with copyright protection on the Internet is how to enforce the legislation that protects the creator of a work. The ease with which information can be adapted, or even copied, into a Web site, coupled with the ease of altering the site should the violation be detected, provides a challenge for policy makers.

From a business perspective, however, understanding the restrictions of copyright protection, as well as the intent behind the legislation, can reduce the potential for inadvertent violations of the law. In general, content that is created with original, creative material from someone else, and which is to be used within a commercial context, can only be reproduced and made available to an audience with the consent of the original author.

In the case of Web sites that provide computer software as part of their content, explicit contracts with the software developer may transfer the copyright, or provide a license to use or sell the material. In addition, software for which distribution is not restricted, such as **freeware** or **shareware**, should be clearly noted as such to potential users.

The Nature of Content

As a means of disseminating information, the Internet has an unparalleled reach. Of concern to policy makers is the type of information that can be transmitted. In creating or reusing content from another source, businesses must be careful not to violate legislation that exists to protect two sets of people: (1) Internet users who should not be exposed to certain types of material (e.g., children and pornography, or anyone and child pornography); and (2) people who might be unjustly harmed by negative material provided as Internet content.

The policy focus that protects both sets of people is freedom of expression. In the United States, policy makers attempt to strike a balance between protecting people's ability to express themselves, and protecting those who might be placed at risk by unfettered expression. Laws that place limits on freedom of expression have been developed prior to the advent of the Internet, and this legislation extends to Internet content.

Three areas of content restriction are addressed by specific legislation. One is the restriction on content designed to provoke or incite unlawful behaviors. For instance, a Web site that provided plans for building a bomb, and information about how to distract authoritarian attention at a high school in order to facilitate bomb placement would likely be deemed in violation of the law.

A second limit to freedom of expression that restricts Internet content is defamation. Defamatory content consists of remarks that might harm the reputation of another person. For instance, a person who posts on a Web site the comment that a competitor's hamburgers are "chock full of *E. coli*" might risk a defamation lawsuit. Given the large numbers of people with access to the Internet, the potential for harming someone's reputation is great, and cases are decided on the likelihood of harm, rather than on the actual harm done. It is important to remember, however, that remarks that are true are not considered defamatory.

A third type of content restricted by existing legislation is material that is indecent or obscene. The determination of what constitutes obscenity is made on a state-by-state basis, and the local community has served as the standard for applying the law. Because a company will be governed by the law of the state in which the material is received, purveyors of obscene or indecent material must be aware of the laws that guide legal action in each state to which the content might be transmitted.

Technology Issues

A major technology issue for businesses in using the Internet as a content resource is bandwidth. Limits to bandwidth and demands on bandwidth affect the speed with which content can be transmitted and received. In general, backbone providers

'Net Knowledge

CREATING EASY-TO-USE WEB SITES

As a new marketplace for consumers, the Internet is characterized by a large range of ways in which opportunities to consume can be provided. Similarly, technological developments have also created novel ways to present content to consumers. Banners blink and wiggle, buttons glow, and animated images dance across the page to attract attention.

As the ability to develop online content becomes available to a wider range of businesses, basic rules for how to create and present persuasive information displays can get lost in the scramble to develop a Web presence. The result can be a Web site that confuses rather than enthuses, and frustrates rather than facilitates.

To leverage the power of the Internet as a content resource, businesses can develop sites that make it easy for customers to find what they need by taking advantage of widely accepted conventions

for information display, both online and off-line. For instance, U.S. consumers read from left to right, and from top to bottom. A road map, or navigation bar, for the site should appear at the top or to the left of a page to guide the visitor through the site. In addition, a search feature that can take the visitor to a specified item or location is helpful.

Online, we have become used to seeing links to other information provided in blue. A clicked-through link is typically magenta. By using these color conventions in your site, you can streamline travel by your visitors; they can readily see where more detailed information could be accessed, as well as where they have already been. In addition, sticking to tradition in naming buttons—such as Home, Help, FAQs, and Contact—can also make life easier for visitors.

attempt to make available sufficient bandwidth to meet demand, but supply is limited. This constraint applies to all who wish to use the Internet to transfer content.

A more specific bandwidth concern is what is often called the last-mile problem. The **last-mile problem** is a capacity issue that refers to the line constraints that transfer digital information from a service provider into the user's computer. Both the general and the specific bandwidth constraints suggest that businesses should exercise caution when deciding what forms of content to use.

Efforts to reduce the demand on bandwidth can create additional issues for businesses that attempt to make their content widely available on a frequently changing basis. The reasons for the additional issues are **proxy servers** and **caching functions**. A proxy server works as an intermediary between a user and the Internet. The proxy server takes the request for Web content (e.g., a particular page or file) from the user. To the user, the proxy server is invisible. The proxy server simply transfers the requested content from the Internet to the user's computer.

In the interest of reducing demand on bandwidth, however, some organizations coordinate the actions of a proxy server with a cache server. For instance, if a Web page is in high demand by the users within an organization, the page may be stored after an earlier retrieval into a cache—sort of like an electronic filing system. Then, when the user requests the Web file, the proxy server gets it from the cache, without contacting the Internet. Suppose you are a business with a policy of updating your Web site prices daily, in order to match your competition. If your file has been stored in a cache, users who request the file may only receive an outdated version.

Caching also creates problems for promotional content in the forms of banners and buttons. Companies that operate as ad servers may be less able to distribute advertising content to interested users, and less able to track the number of impressions for a banner. A banner that is cached with a heavily demanded file may receive high exposure among users associated with the proxy server, but the ad server will not be able to track exposure. In contrast, a banner on a site that is not being requested by a proxy server because a cached version is available will receive less exposure than it should.

Several programming options can help overcome the issues associated with proxy servers and caching. Businesses must be aware of the potential for a problem, and knowledgeable about the appropriate means for handling the different types of file concerns.

CHAPTER SUMMARY

The Internet serves as a content resource for businesses. The rapidly increasing rate of content production on the Internet underscores the importance of understanding the role of content as a resource. In this chapter we looked at the decisions that businesses make in order to create an effective Web presence. First, we examined the relationship between site objectives and site content. Then we considered the different sources of content that can be used for digital business activities. The sources were classified as internal sources and external sources. Internal sources reflect content developed by the company, while external sources include content provided by customers, press, and publicly available information.

Technology makes it possible to represent information as Internet content. We reviewed different types of content that reflect the integration of the two dimensions of telepresence: vividness and interactivity. The ability to integrate different forms of media, such as print, audio, and video with Internet technologies enables businesses to create multimedia presentations of content. In addition to multimedia characteristics, some types of content also enable the user to interact with the digital environment. Different types of interactive content serve different purposes for marketers, ranging from increasing the entertainment value of a Web site to providing businesses with data to use in marketing decision making.

As a content resource, the Internet has the potential to affect strategy regarding many aspects of business activity. For instance, the ability to create digital products may influence product strategy. In addition, the availability of product information as content and content-creating tools, such as shopping agents, can affect pricing strategy by making price comparisons between competing brands transparent. Content can also be used to create a context, or a virtual representation of place, that can affect product and brand evaluations. For promotion, content can be used to create brand image, to provide an incentive for a customer to carry out a desired product-related behavior, and to provide the customer with added value in the form of benefits related to product consumption.

In addition to its benefits as a content resource, the Internet raises several issues for businesses. These issues reflect an interaction of people and technology, and can be organized by each of the four main perspectives on digital business. Companies must recognize limits to consumers' information processing capabilities and be able to respond to the heuristics and biases that different forms of content may engender. In addition, businesses must understand the implications of the Internet as a content resource for defining offerings as products or services, and as innovative or not. These determinations may affect the appropriateness of a selected business strategy.

Policy and technology also come into play in terms of content-related issues. Policy makers determine the level and nature of regulation about the protection of the sources of content, in the form of copyright. They must also deal with issues related to the nature of content, such as whether the content violates legislation that limits freedom of expression. Technology works to overcome constraints on the form and reception of content dictated by capacity limits. In some cases, however, the technological solutions, such as proxy servers and caches, create additional problems for marketers. Business must look across issues and perspectives to create, implement, and manage effective business strategy.

CONTENT MANAGEMENT
USEFUL TERMS

- avatars
- backlinks
- backward links
- caching function
- continuous innovation
- discontinuous innovation
- downloadable file
- dynamic content
- FAQs

- forward links
- freeware
- halo effect
- innovation
- last-mile problem
- link popularity
- plug-in
- price transparency
- proxy servers

- reciprocal link
- reciprocal linking strategy
- shareware
- shopping agent
- streaming file
- syndicated content
- virtual reality photography
- Web-impacted spending
- Web log

REVIEW QUESTIONS

1. Name three people-based sources of Internet content.
2. Describe how technology-enabled interactivity changes commercial content.
3. What benefits do links provide, in terms of satisfying strategic objectives?
4. How can content facilitate telepresence?
5. What is the difference between a downloadable file and a streaming file?
6. How can online games or contests benefit businesses?
7. What are the possible advantages and disadvantages of price transparency to a business?
8. How might the Internet affect a company's product strategy? Pricing strategy? Place strategy? Promotion strategy?
9. Is the Internet itself a continuous or discontinuous innovation? Why?

10. What challenges face public policy makers with respect to Internet content?
11. What problems do proxy servers and caching functions create for businesses? What benefits do they provide?

WEB APPLICATION

Getting Found on the Internet: Link Popularity

Your company, Uncle Martha's Unique Knitwear, is online, but so are hundreds—perhaps thousands—of your competitors. How can you improve the odds that potential customers will find your site? When they type in a search engine query for "argyle socks," how can you help your site, woolystuff.com, appear early in the list of results?

Search engine ranking technologies have become increasingly more sophisticated in the way that they evaluate site content and index it for relevance and quality. As a result, simply relying on keywords in your site content to get your site found may not be sufficient to get the placement you want.

Many companies use linking strategies to enhance their search engine placement. Very simply, some search engines, like Google, evaluate sites in their indexing process as a function of how many sites contain a link to your site. The logic is that each link is a "vote" for your site. More votes for you, relative to your competitors, earns you a higher rank in the results listing. In addition, some links are more important than others. Links from sites that are also heavily linked to carry greater weight in determining placement.

So how can you implement a link popularity strategy?

1. First, you need to know who's linking to you.

To see what you can learn about a site's link popularity, go to Google.com. In the search box, type link: landsend.com. What do the results tell you? Who is linking to the Lands End site? Are some links more important than others?

2. The next step is to find out who is linking to your competitors.

Again, you can use Google to conduct a sample search, by typing link: eddiebauer.com. Analyze the results. Do any of the links look familiar? Are there some important sites that do not link to Lands End? Who has more links?

Now, you're ready to get some good links for your site. Remember, links on your site can be valuable content for your visitors, when they provide access to relevant content on another site. By the same token, linking to your site can add value to a related site.

3. Develop a list of sites that (a) add value as content on your site, and (b) would benefit by adding a link to your site on their sites.

4. Persuade the sites in your list to link to you.

At this point, what you say in your site about the site to which you are linking is important. If you provide some details about the value of the linked-to site, you increase the value of your content, to your visitors, as well as the linked site. As a result, the site may be more inclined to provide a reverse link to you. Develop the content for the desired links before you contact the sites.

5. Contact the set of sites from whom you are requesting a link.

It's important to find the right person to send your request. Look carefully at the contact information on a site, or contact the company to request the appropriate e-mail address. Next, draft the e-mail. Include your company name and URL, as well as the brief description you would like them to include. It's also helpful to provide an embedded link in the e-mail to the page on your site that contains their link and description, so that they can assess the merits of your request. You should also include any additional information that indicates the benefits of a link from you, such as exposure (number of unique site visitors, per day, week, or month).

6. Follow-up.

Check to see who is linking to your site. If companies have not added a link, a polite e-mail reminder can be helpful.

CONCEPTS IN BRIEF

1. Online content can be an important tool for achieving business objectives, such as completing transactions, building a brand image, or fostering relationships with customers.
2. Developing effective content requires businesses to balance what can be done using technology with what customers expect and can handle.
3. Web content can be developed from several different sources, including company material, popular press, and customers. Content selection depends on goals for the site.
4. Content from sources external to the company, such as syndicated content, is often an expensive and satisfactory way to keep content up-to-date and comprehensive.
5. How content is presented to visitors can be described by the ways in which technology is used (multimedia capabilities), and the nature of interactivity between the site and the visitor.
6. Online content can influence how businesses are able to develop and manage each element of business activity.
7. Content can be used to describe a product, create a product, or even *be* the product.
8. Content can also be used to enhance price transparency, by enabling price comparisons.
9. Web site content is a virtual context for shopping, and many aspects of physical world atmospheres and situations can be represented, and altered, with Web content.
10. Because it blurs the boundaries between business activity components, such as place and promotion, and product and place, the Internet makes it important for businesses to anticipate and understand the impact of Web content on the outcomes of business activity.

THINKING POINTS

1. Content can take on different roles: as a product, to develop a product, and to promote a product. How does the flexibility of content as an Internet resource suggest how we think about digital business?
2. What are the costs and benefits that a business might encounter when using content from internal sources (i.e., company), compared with external sources (e.g., customers)?
3. What characteristics of the Internet environment affect business' ability to create content to encourage telepresence in ways that differ from traditional media?
4. Businesses place great value on creating sites that can attract and hold consumers' attention. How is telepresence related to this objective?
5. Is telepresence always beneficial? Consider situations in which complete immersion in the computer-mediated environment by consumers may have undesirable results for businesses and for customers.
6. What are some implications for market competition of being able to use the Internet to develop products?
7. Is the Internet an innovation? If so, why is it? What type of innovation is it? Does its classification as an innovation depend on its intended use?

SUGGESTED READINGS

1. "The Ascent of Content," by Edward D. Horowitz. In *The Future of the Electronic Marketplace* (The MIT Press: Cambridge, MA, 1998), pages 91–114.
2. "In Virtual Fashion," by Stephen Gray. *IEEE Spectrum* (February 1998), pages 18–25.
3. "Less Than Zero Margins," by Brian E. Taptich. *Red Herring, 64* (March 1999), pages 46–53.
4. "Made to Odor," by Jeffrey Davis. *Business 2.0* (December 1999), pages 216–228.
5. "Giveaways—They Pay Off on the Web," by Richard Shim. *ZDNet News*, June 12, 2000.

LEARNING LINKS

Content Sources

www.inc.com/articles/biz_online/manage_si
te/traffic_increase/18491.html
www.isp-planet.com/equipment/2001/
vircom_3d.html (customer-created)

Content Management Systems

www.microsoft.com/cmserver/default.aspx
www.vignette.com

Content-Related Issues

www.hisoftware.com/uaen/WebHelp/case_
study_i_-_common_issues_with_dynamic_
content_as_seen_in_a_major_e-commerce_
site.htm
gewis.win.tue.nl/~koen/www9dd/slide9.htm
www.traffick.com/article.asp?aID=106

Evaluating Content Credibility

www.library.cornell.edu/okuref/webcrit.html
www2.vuw.ac.nz/staff/alastair_smith/evaln/
evaln.htm

Measuring Link Popularity

marketleap.com/publinkpop/default.htm

CHAPTER

Digital Channels and Business Activity

Focus and Objectives

This chapter addresses the role of the Internet as a channel resource for businesses. Differences in channel structure, function, and management are considered for online and off-line distribution approaches, using a relationship perspective. The impact of the Internet is considered on the dyadic interactions between channel members, and characteristics of Internet middlemen, or intermediaries, are discussed. Implications of the Internet as a channel resource for business activity are considered.

Your objectives in studying this chapter include the following:

■ Know the basic forms of channel structures.

■ Recognize the relationship aspects of channel structure and performance.

■ Understand the possible influences of the Internet on channel structure and performance.

■ Understand the ways in which the Internet as a channel resource can affect business activity decisions.

■ Be familiar with the issues raised by the Internet as a channel resource for each of the four perspectives on the Internet environment.

Stapling It All Together

From paper clips to built-to-order computer systems, and even staples—18 different kinds of them—the Staples, Inc. line of office supply superstores has it all. When the company opened its first store in Brighton, Massachusetts, in 1986, it also pioneered the office superstore industry, offering a large array of supplies and services to small businesses, with price discounts usually reserved for large companies.

People liked the one-stop convenience of the superstores, strolling through the 20,000 square foot stores to shop from an array of over 7,500 business-related items. To make it even easier to buy office supplies, Staples provided a catalog service to provide information and accept orders. The company grew rapidly, expanding to more than 700 locations and $7 billion dollars in annual sales worldwide by 1998.

On their mission to provide convenience and an ever-larger product assortment, Staples recognized the opportunity of the Internet as a channel for meeting their goals. Staples.com opened for business in 1999, enabling the company to overcome physical shelf space limitations and quadruple the number of products they offered. Now customers could get Staples' products any time, any place.

The increasing assortment of channels for buying office staples posed challenges for the company. Would consumers buy through the Internet channel? Would Staples.com hurt the sales of the off-line stores? How should inventory be managed to balance the online and off-line demand? Would Staples' product suppliers be willing to change their distribution processes to make the online channel work efficiently?

The challenges that Staples faced are not uncommon for businesses that integrate the Internet into their distribution strategies. Even companies who begin as pure-players must persuade visitors to become buyers, and they still have to grapple with issues of order fulfillment between the online and off-line worlds. Cross-channel integration of the physical stores and catalog sales with an online outlet required Staples to incorporate new technologies and marketing tactics to integrate existing processes and systems with the Internet outlet, and to provide a satisfactory shopping experience.

What did Staples do? The company brought in outside help, including consultants from Sapient and Molecular, to design and implement the channel strategy (Figure 11-1). To make the shopping experience easy to navigate, in-store kiosks were set up to provide information to customers and employees about products available in the store, through the catalog, and through the Web site. Distribution arrangements with suppliers were revamped, so that an item listed as "in stock" on the Web site could be shipped to the customer straight from the manufacturer. A data warehouse was developed to capture and store information about products and customers from many product managers in a single location. The database streamlined inventory management and provided market intelligence for strategic decision making.

Did the channel integration work? The success of Staples' channel strategy can be measured in several ways. The online product assortment grew from 6,000 stock-keeping units (SKUs) to 130,000 SKUs in 2 years. Customers appeared to like the variety, spending nearly $17 million on the site in the first year, without decreasing spending in traditional channels. Better data tracking enabled managers to more precisely target sales and marketing to repeat customers, thus reducing costs and increasing customer satisfaction. In 2003, Staples reported nearly $12 billion in revenue, leading the competition in office supply sales.[1]

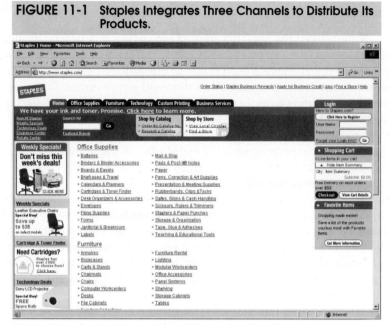

FIGURE 11-1 Staples Integrates Three Channels to Distribute Its Products.

As the Staples experience illustrates, the Internet has the potential to affect all aspects of distribution. For example, the Internet can be used as a channel itself, directly linking the manufacturer to the end customer. In this situation, many activities that are conducted by channel members in traditional channels can be eliminated. For example, a magazine that can be delivered digitally eliminates the need for distributors to stock the newsstands and magazine racks.

A second use of the Internet as a channel resource is as one component of a channel, rather than as the entire channel. Like Staples, Amazon.com uses the Internet as a retail outlet. The company relies on off-line channel members, such as wholesalers, to carry out traditional functions. The physical products—originally just books, but now a wide variety of product categories—are still stored in warehouses until shipped to consumers. The Internet eliminates the need for a bricks-and-mortar retail location.

The Internet can also influence distribution strategy by serving as a tool for channel planning and implementation. In addition to using the Internet as a channel for distributing its product to consumers, Dell Computer leverages information technologies of the Internet to move information and customer orders from its Internet site to the appropriate suppliers. Dell uses the Internet to let customers design the configuration of their computers. The company communicates with its suppliers, often using Internet capabilities, to put together the computer system. This approach enables the company to achieve cost savings on warehouse needs and to manage inventory efficiently. Dell's actions illustrate one way to use the Internet to simplify and streamline channel structure and function. Retail outlets are not necessary for Dell, and customers get customized computers, quickly.

These examples illustrate opportunities to use the Internet as a component of channel strategy. As with most opportunities, however, the Internet also presents unique challenges that must be managed in order to obtain the desired benefits for distribution strategy. For instance, channel members may have concerns about their importance in distribution processes that use the Internet, potentially resulting in power struggles between channel members. In addition, a shift from selling products to customers through a traditional retailer to making them directly available through the Internet may lead to customer confusion. These issues, among others, suggest that successful integration of the Internet into distribution strategy can be best accomplished by considering not only the benefits of doing so, but also the possible pitfalls.

In this chapter, we will examine the impact of the Internet on channel strategy. We begin by looking at the different roles played by channel members, and how the Internet affects the relationships between channel members. Next, we build on these topics to understand the Internet's role in developing and managing distribution channels, and we apply the implications of the Internet as a channel component to business activity. We also consider several issues that channel applications of the Internet raise for the different perspectives on the Internet environment—buyer, seller, policy maker, and technology developer.

> **Bits & Bytes 11-1**
> The Internet creates upheaval in the distribution channels of knowledge, too. Of 34,000 professors surveyed by UCLA researchers, 67 percent said that keeping up with information technology is stressful. Computer-related stress outranked teaching (62 percent) and publishing (50 percent).
> (*Source:* Nua Online, citing Associated Press, August 31, 1999.)

Building Channels with the Internet

A channel of distribution is defined by the set of organizations involved in the processes for transferring ownership from a producer to customers. Distribution channels exist to match customers with products. Most manufacturers produce a small range of products that they need to distribute to a wide range of customers. In contrast, most customers would like to obtain small quantities of many different products. Middlemen facilitate the spread of the product, thus matching up manufacturers and buyers.

The organization of a distribution channel, in terms of the specific types of channel members, is based on the idea that different channel members have different competencies that facilitate product distribution. For example, channel members enable a channel manager to exploit efficiencies and develop economies of scale. Each member provides a skill or skills that are necessary. As a result, the channel members depend on each other to create an efficient distribution system from manufacturer to consumer.

Who Distributes? Types of Channel Members

A **channel member** is an organization that is involved in the **negotiatory functions** associated with moving a product from producer to end user. Negotiatory functions include the actions of buying, selling, and transferring title to goods and services. For the majority of product categories, there are four main channel members: the manufacturer, who produces the product; the wholesaler, who buys goods for resale; the retailer, who buys goods to sell to the end user; and the consumer, who buys goods for personal or household use. The different combinations of these members reflect different **channel structures**. Figure 11-2 illustrates several types of channel structures.

Of course, distribution strategy is also necessary in the business-to-business market. These channels of distribution often differ from the members and the structure of channels in the business-to-consumer market. We will examine the implications of the Internet as a channel resource for the business-to-business market in Chapter 13.

Channel members who perform negotiatory functions are active exchange agents in the distribution process, taking ownership of the product and selling it to another channel participant. Other organizations conduct activities that facilitate the exchange process, but they do not become involved in the negotiation and transaction activities that affect product ownership (e.g., transportation companies and advertising agencies). Still other organizations may function to facilitate the transfer of ownership, as by brokering transactions and representing the interests of the active exchange agents. These types of organizations comprise the **ancillary structure** of a channel. Despite the different functions that they service, all of the organizations share a common goal: to facilitate the exchanges that result in the transfer of ownership from the producer to the consumer (Figure 11-3).

What Do Channel Members Do? Functions and Flows

At a very basic level, channels exist to distribute goods and services. Getting the job done requires businesses to carry out three sets of **channel functions**. **Exchange functions** consist of activities related to the transaction, including buying, selling, and pricing. **Logistic functions** involve the activities by which products are available to channel members at the appropriate times. The process of moving

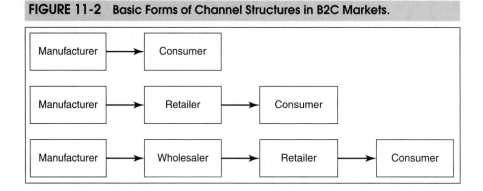

FIGURE 11-2 Basic Forms of Channel Structures in B2C Markets.

FIGURE 11-3   Channels Use Ancillary Participants to Aid Distribution Processes.

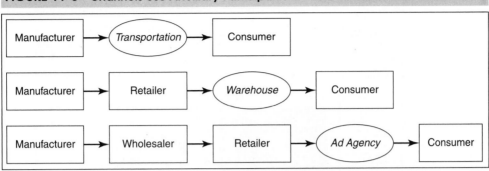

products through the channel, including transport and storage, is known as **logistics management**. The third objective of business activity in distributing is a facilitating function, consisting of activities that support exchange and logistics. Activities within the facilitating function include managing credit and financing, assuming and managing risk, and developing communications for channel members and end consumers.

Carrying out channel functions results in **marketing flows**. These flows are the actions taken by channel members to complete channel functions. The primary flows are of information, money, negotiation, and promotion. These flows, in conjunction with **product flow**, comprise **channel strategy**. Manufacturers rely on information about customer needs and competitor actions to determine the optimal form and amount of a product. This information often comes from channel members who have closer contact with sources of demand than the manufacturer. For instance, a wholesaler in frequent and ongoing contact with retailers has access to information about the quantity of product requested. Retailers in contact with the end customers often have information about the liked and disliked features of products. As a result, **information flow** is central to product distribution strategies.

Negotiation is a mutual exchange between channel members that determines the conditions of product ownership at different points in the distribution channel. For instance, a manufacturer and a wholesaler negotiate to reach an agreement about how much money the manufacturer will receive in order to transfer the title of ownership for an amount of product to the wholesaler. The **money flow** reflects the agreement reached in the **negotiation flow** about the terms of payment for ownership: how much money will be paid, and when. The **promotion flow** creates awareness of the product and incentive to take ownership of the product by different members in the channel.

The Internet can affect channel structure by changing the ability of channel members to carry out flow activities. Some flows can be carried out more readily with the Internet than others. For instance, negotiations about product inventory, delivery, and promotion can be facilitated by the Internet. In addition, the Internet can provide a channel for completing money transactions for products that will be delivered offline. In short, the Internet can be a new, specialized channel for single flow, or it can be used to integrate combinations of flows. As the screenshot in Figure 11-4 illustrates, some traditional retailers of goods and services can integrate the Internet into their

---

FIGURE 11-4 A Web Site Can Serve Multiple Functions as a Channel Component to Distribute a Service.

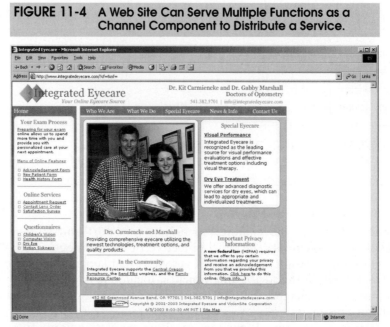

processes for distribution. For instance, an optometrist can use a Web site to provide information about the service, to facilitate communication with the consumer, and to transact contact lens sales online.

Internet Effects on Channel Structure

Because it can change the ability of channel members to transfer flows, the Internet affects the complexity of channel structures. If the Internet facilitates the ability of a channel member to do the work of another channel member, then the opportunity exists to eliminate the newly redundant member. In contrast, the decision to shift some portion of distribution activity to the Internet may create the need for a channel member who manages functions that are conducted online. The first situation reflects disintermediation, while the second situation reflects reintermediation.

Disintermediation: Fewer Middlemen in the Middle

The ability to use the Internet to perform aspects of all of the channel functions—barring transfer of a physical product—creates the possibility that fewer channel participants will be needed to effect distribution strategy. The process of reducing distribution reliance on middlemen is known as **disintermediation.** This potential for disintermediation is significant because it suggests that the services of some types of wholesalers and retailers will no longer be necessary. For instance, if a manufacturer can use the Internet to provide information about its products and their direct acquisition to a large enough number of consumers, middlemen are not needed.

Bits & Bytes 11-2
Twenty-somethings prefer online news sources to print newspapers. They are 75 percent more likely to see the Internet as the preferred source for news, classifieds, and other information than older newshounds.
(*Source: Media Life Magazine*, 2/12/02, from Forrester Research data.)

Reintermediation: More Middlemen in the Middle

While the potential for disintermediation does exist, it is not equally likely for all channels. In fact, for many businesses, managing distribution using the Internet has resulted in increasing the number of channel participants. This phenomenon has been labeled **reintermediation.** For physical products, the Internet may often lead to the inclusion of an additional channel participant to handle the virtual representation of the product. In the case of Amazon, the inclusion of book wholesalers is an example of reintermediation.

Infomediaries: New Middlemen in the Middle

As more companies integrate the Internet into their channel strategies, it is increasingly clear that some industries are more likely to disintermediate traditional channel participants than others. For instance, people have quickly adapted to finding and buying airline tickets online, without the services of a travel agent. Consumers have also shown a growing tendency to get their news from Internet sources, rather than television and newspapers.

Although traditional channel participants are disintermediated in the online channel for tickets and for news, new types of channel participants are added. For travel purchases, vendors rely on companies that aggregate travel opportunities, including plane seats, hotel rooms, and cruises. For news, portals such as AOL, Excite, and Yahoo! combine news with other types of information, serving as the go-between for news agencies and end customers. The increasing integration of the Internet into distribution strategy has prompted an increase in the participation of Internet-based organizations that operate as **cybermediaries**, or **infomediaries**. These organizations may develop solely for the purpose of operating as online channel members, designed to effectively meet channel needs in the digital business environment.

The development of infomediaries as participants in channel activities underscores two ways in which the Internet changes the way we think about channel strategy. First, the infomediaries often do not take ownership of the product being distributed. Strictly speaking, they are not channel members, but part of the ancillary structure. They do, however, exert an influence on channel complexity. This means that the term *disintermediation* should be used with caution. A change in channel structure may eliminate traditional channel members, thus exhibiting disintermediation. At the same time, however, the change may lead to the inclusion of infomediaries through reintermediation.

The nature of the activities performed by the Internet-based middlemen reflects the second change to the way we think about channel strategy. In traditional views of distribution strategy, the primary function of channel members is to move the product—by taking ownership—from the manufacturer to the customer. Infomediaries can facilitate product movement, but they do not tend to have contact with the actual product, unless the product is digital in nature. Instead, they provide a service. The increasing prevalence of Internet infomediaries suggests that the service functions of Internet-based intermediaries will occupy a central position in the formulation of channel strategy. In business-to-consumer markets, these services tend to emphasize one of three channel-related flows: (1) communicating information, (2) enabling monetary transactions by connecting buyers to sellers, or (3) aggregating product/service purchase opportunities for buyers.

Information Brokers   The role of an **information broker** is to provide buyers with information about the price and availability of products. Information brokers do not enable shoppers to complete transactions through their Web sites. Instead, shoppers must go to vendors' sites to consummate exchanges. An example of an Internet information broker is CNET. The company provides product descriptions and reviews for a wide range of technology products, as well as links to vendor sites, but it does not provide any products of its own. Another example of an information broker is Epinions.com, a company we met in Chapter 10. Epinions publishes consumer reviews of goods and services, along with links to sources of many of the reviewed products.

Transaction Brokers   In contrast to information brokers, the primary focus of **transaction brokers** is to facilitate buying and selling. Transaction brokers create links between buyers and sellers, thus serving a function similar to traditional retailers, but without incurring the risks of product ownership. Sites such as eBay.com and AutobyTel.com are examples of transaction brokers on the Internet. In each case, the Internet is used to match a buyer to a seller, thus creating the potential for a direct relationship between the buyer and the seller (Figure 11-5).

Marketplace Concentrators   **Marketplace concentrators** are Internet intermediaries that aggregate products available from a variety of vendors in one location. Customers

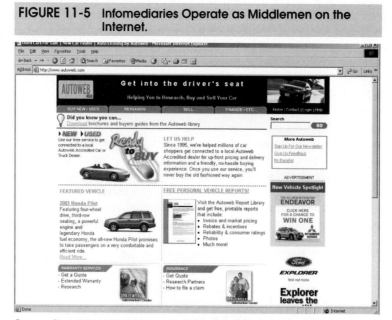

FIGURE 11-5   Infomediaries Operate as Middlemen on the Internet.

can make purchases through the site by paying the site host, who then pays the vendor. For example, Travelocity.com enables customers to search for airfares and complete ticket purchases online. The service includes a range of different airlines. Customers reserve flights and make payment to Travelocity, who then delivers the ticket, either digitally or by traditional mail. Other examples of marketplace concentrators are online shopping malls, and services such as online ticket sales for events and online stock trading. In general, marketplace concentrators do not result in the formation of a direct relationship between the buyer and seller.

Online marketplace aggregators differ in the amount of risk they assume. While some online aggregators do take ownership of the products they sell, many do not. For instance, Orbitz.com provides reservations and processes payments for a range of hotels in a single location. However, Orbitz does not buy all of the rooms. They obtain a list of available rooms from a hotel, mark up the price, and sell the rooms, taking payment from the traveler to make the reservation. Orbitz keeps the payment. When the stay at a hotel is completed, the hotel bills Orbitz, who pays the initial, unmarked up cost of the room to the hotel. In contrast, Hotels.com buys up blocks of rooms, assuming the risk of not selling the product. The company buys blocks of rooms from hotels at discount rates, and then sells the rooms to travelers, at rates often lower than those offered by the hotel itself. The ability to spread the risk over a large number of hotels, locations, and dates enables the company to balance fluctuations in demand for rooms.

Channel Management: Internet Effects on Channel Member Relationships

The transfer of a product from a producer to the customer is often a complex process that may involve several middlemen who serve different functions in the distribution process. The nature of the relationships that exist between each pair of agents in the distribution process can differ greatly, depending on the product type, and on the distribution objectives. The Internet can influence the relationships that exist between members of the distribution channel.

The Internet can facilitate the formation of new relationships, as between a manufacturer and a customer or a retailer and a customer. In addition, the Internet can alter the nature of an existing relationship. For example, FedEx uses the Internet to provide customers with a way to track the delivery progress of shipped packages. Although the distribution of the product—in this case, a service—occurs through standard, off-line means, the Internet affects customer and company activities, as well as perceptions of the interaction. For instance, a customer can check the status of a package at any time. From the company's perspective, automated, online tracking reduces demand on customer service personnel. In this use of the Internet as a channel resource for relationship management, the Internet's communications capabilities affect the relationship between the service provider and its customers.

The interactions between channel members can be viewed as dyadic relationships. A **dyadic relationship** refers to the communications and activities that take place between a pair of entities, such as channel members. Some examples of dyadic relationships in a channel include manufacturer–retailer dyads, wholesaler–retailer dyads, and manufacturer–customer dyads.

Power in Relationships

The concept of dyadic relationships is important for channel strategy because characteristics of each member in a dyad influence the ability of the dyad to meet its responsibilities. For example, dyad members can differ in terms of the amount of power, or influence, that each member exerts in the relationship, and the nature of the power. Power can be exercised—if possessed—by any channel member.

Five main sources of power characterize relationships between channel members: reward, coercive, legitimate, referent, and expert. Each type is relevant for understanding the relationships that may exist between channel members. A hallmark of power is that it relies heavily on perception; that is, a channel member will alter his behavior to

FIGURE 11-6   Channel Partners Exert Power in Different Forms to Influence Channel Behavior.

Type of Power	Description	Situational Example
Reward	One channel member acts in a way that conforms to the desires of the other member, in order to obtain some set of benefits, or reward.	In channel relationships, the reward tends to take the form of financial gains. A manufacturer who has a reputation for market success will be better able to use reward power to influence channel member behavior than a manufacturer with weak market performance.
Coercive	Flip side of reward power. Coercive power reflects the perception that the other member of the relationship can impose some cost for behavioral nonconformity.	A retailer can refuse to sell a wholesaler's products.
Legitimated	The perception that one party has the authority to direct the behavior of the other party in the relationship. This type of power is seen in contractual relationships, in which one channel member has formally agreed to complete certain activities in a predetermined manner.	In a franchise operation, the franchisor has legitimate power over the franchisee. The contractual agreement typically specifies how the franchisor will exercise power if contractually agreed conditions are not met.
Expert	One party in a relationship perceives that the other party has skills or knowledge that make conforming to influence attempts more likely to result in benefits for both parties.	Retailers who accept the advice and assistance of manufacturers in displaying and promoting products tend to do so when they perceive that the knowledge possessed by manufacturers has provided beneficial results for conforming behaviors in the past, or for other retailers.
Referent	Occurs when one party serves as a referent, or a point of comparison, that influences another's behavior.	Most instantiations of referent power in channels reflect influence attempts based on perceived, desirable similarity in goals.

the extent that he perceives that the other party in the relationship has power. The table in Figure 11-6 summarizes the different types of power.

Relationship Development and Influence Tactics: Applying Power

An important goal of channel strategy is to develop, grow, and maintain the relationships that facilitate distribution (Figure 11-7). Different tactics and processes for influencing relationships may be needed at each of these different stages. For instance, the benefits of exercising different power bases may vary by relationship stage. In addition, different stages and power bases in relationships may indicate different uses of negotiation. For example, it may be desirable to give up a benefit (i.e., foregoing a reward) early in a channel relationship to get it established. In contrast, increasing the salience of shared goals may be more effective to maintain an established relationship (i.e., referent power).

We have seen that the Internet makes it possible for businesses to develop new types of channel structures. One factor that guides the determination of which structure to use is the nature of the relationships within the structure. The overall success of a channel is related to the way in which each relationship contributes to channel efficiency. The Internet may influence the nature of more than one channel member's participation in a channel at a time. In addition, the relationship between any pair of channel members who take and transfer ownership of the product can be viewed as a unique central exchange environment; the channel members make use of technology to facilitate exchange. These characteristics mean that businesses must be aware of the interplay between each dyad in the channel, and the effects of that interplay on overall channel performance.

Power and Channel Structure with the Internet

A business that opts to use the Internet as a component of a channel strategy will be more successful in altering the channel organization if it is in a position to influence the behavior of other channel members. For example, a manufacturer with reward or coercive power based on market success can induce its retailer partners to develop an online presence more effectively than a weak manufacturer can.

In contrast, a powerful retailer can influence the ability of its manufacturers to set up direct distribution channels online. This influence may occur due to expert power, when the retailer is able to demonstrate potential pitfalls with the online plan. Alternatively, other forms of power can be employed to influence channel member behaviors. For instance, in 1999, Home Depot, a large retailer of do-it-yourself home products, sent a letter to its suppliers. The letter was an attempt to exert coercive power

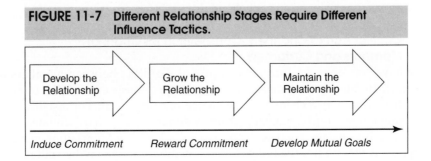

FIGURE 11-7 **Different Relationship Stages Require Different Influence Tactics.**

Develop the Relationship → Grow the Relationship → Maintain the Relationship

Induce Commitment   *Reward Commitment*   *Develop Mutual Goals*

to dissuade the suppliers from using the Internet as a direct channel for marketing their wares to consumers. Suppliers were warned that Home Depot would view any online marketing efforts as competition, and that Home Depot would be disinclined to carry the products of competitors in their stores.[2]

Conflict within Channels: Changing Roles

A concern with the use of the Internet as a channel resource is the potential for creating channel conflict. **Channel conflict** occurs when a channel member's perceptions of roles, responsibilities, and accomplishments are not consistent with the perceptions of these facets of behavior by other channel members. For instance, the Internet introduces the potential for conflict when it enables a channel member to carry out tasks that were previously the responsibility of another channel member. For example, a manufacturer who sets up an Internet site to sell products may antagonize members of its existing channel, such as wholesalers and retailers. The online site may be perceived as a threat to the financial well-being of the traditional middlemen.

Such a situation occurred when Levi Strauss attempted to control all of its online sales of made-to-fit jeans, excluding long-time retail partners, such as J. C. Penney's, from the effort. The online site was not successful. A primary reason for the failure was the inability to appeal to the targeted teen market, due, in part, to Web site characteristics that required more bandwidth than possessed by the targeted market. Levi's concluded that the tasks of product fulfillment and customer support were better left to those with more experience. In the meantime, however, retailers in the channel shifted their marketing focus to private-label brands, thus creating additional sales losses for Levi's. After a year of attempting to make the online operation a success, Levi Strauss gave up. The company handed the online operations to their retailers.

Concerns about potential channel conflict have kept several large manufacturers from using the Internet to sell directly to consumers, among them Rubbermaid, Maytag, and Black and Decker. The Gartner Group, a research and analysis firm, estimates that in 2000, 90 percent of manufacturers avoided direct sales through the Internet due to concerns about channel conflict with their traditional distributors. More recently, some companies have opted to use the Internet for direct sales, managing potential conflict with strategies such as limiting the numbers or types of products offered online, and targeting the online store toward a particular subset of the potential market that isn't the focus of other channel partners. For example, Harley-Davidson uses its Web site to provide information about its popular motorcycles, and to sell related, branded merchandise, including clothing and motorcycle accessories (Figure 11-8). To avoid conflict with its dealers, however, the company does not sell its core product online. Instead, the Web site provides a dealer locator function for visitors.

Conflict Across Channels: Competition for Channel Members and Customers

We have seen that the Internet can provoke conflict between members of a single channel, by altering the balance of power that previously existed. The Internet can also create conflict across channels, in the name of competition. For instance, suppose that a manufacturer courts channel partners with technology that facilitates channel functions, such as using an extranet to distribute leads and marketing materials. If this support is viewed positively by channel members, they may be willing to enter into exclusive distribution arrangements with the vendor, forgoing participation in other

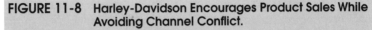

FIGURE 11-8   Harley-Davidson Encourages Product Sales While
Avoiding Channel Conflict.

Source: Reproduced with permission of Harley-Davidson Motor Company.
Copyright 2004. All rights reserved.

channels. Ricoh Silicon Valley, a data storage company, found that using channel management software to provide a personalized interaction between channel partners and the company resulted in increased partner loyalty, and enhanced channel performance.

The issue of how to reduce the potential for across-channel conflict is often centered on the concern with how to manage disintermediation within an industry. One strategy is for channel members to develop alternative capabilities or characteristics that provide value to the channel. Leveraged cooperation is an example of one approach for managing potential conflict and disintermediation.

Leveraged cooperation occurs when members of competing channels create partnerships to provide a new, online source of value to channel members. For example, one online information broker for the airline industry, SABRE, encouraged travel agents to develop content sites that described their individual offerings. The resulting network of agent-developed content provides benefits for all channel members: richer content for the broker, additional visibility for the airlines, exposure for the travel agents, and greater selection for customers. This situation illustrates the importance of understanding how the Internet changes not only the functions of traditional channel members, but also the importance of developing new competencies to manage the changing patterns and habits of buying goods and services.

The Internet's Impact on Channel Strategy

As a channel resource, the Internet can influence the effectiveness of channel strategy, often described as channel efficiency. **Channel efficiency** is achieved when the combination of efforts undertaken to distribute a product optimizes possible output.

Businesses must understand the nature of the Internet's influence on different aspects of channel strategy in order to maximize channel efficiency. Each of the basic concepts of channel strategy—functions, flows, and relationships—can be influenced by the Internet as a channel resource.

Establishing Distribution Objectives for the Internet

The role of the Internet as a channel resource should be guided by the determination of the role of the distribution strategy, in general, for achieving strategic business objectives. For instance, how important is distribution relative to other business activities? How much emphasis will distribution receive, in terms of company resources? Will the Internet change the relative importance of distribution? A key factor in establishing the weight to be placed on distribution is the extent to which it can be used to create competitive advantage.

Next, the business must evaluate the costs and benefits of integrating the Internet into distribution strategy. At this point, the questions focus on the impact of the Internet as a way to increase channel efficiency. For instance, the Internet can be used as a tool for managing existing channels to increase flows of information and negotiation. An alternative role for the Internet is as a channel for distribution, or as one part of a channel of distribution.

One issue in determining the role of the Internet as a channel resource is the nature of the product. This issue is related to product flow. Internet technologies have made rapid and remarkable advances in the past few years, but they are still not capable of digitizing and transmitting a soft drink. Products that can be conveyed in a digital format, such as books, software, and music are all viable candidates for an entirely Internet-based distribution channel. Other products, with some amount of physical attributes, can still benefit from the Internet, but the channel members complete functions that are ancillary to the actual conveyance of the product between channel members.

Although the Internet's inability to transfer a physical product may be a limitation, the ability to facilitate many other functions, including all aspects of completing a transaction that do not entail physical exchange of product, make the Internet a viable channel for many goods and services. The issue is to be able to determine how and to what extent the Internet can be leveraged in such a way that the benefits outweigh the implementation costs.

Possible uses of the Internet cover a wide range: from managing a traditional strategy with Internet capabilities, all the way to dropping the traditional distribution channel in favor of a direct, online channel. The benefits and costs of using the Internet as a channel resource at any level may depend on the nature of channel members, and the relationships between these members, in the actual and potential channels.

Bits & Bytes 11.3

Nearly 70 percent of information technology products are distributed through indirect channels. Using Internet-based channel management software can shave nearly 25 percent off the time from lead generation to order acceptance.
(*Source:* InforWorld.com, 10/4/01, and Meta Group.)

Which One, What Kind, and How Many? The Internet and Channel Partner Decisions

Once the marketer has decided that the Internet should be integrated into channel strategy, the next set of decisions revolves around the appropriate channel structure (Figure 11-9). In situations for which the Internet will facilitate performance of off-line channel activities, the channel structure may not need to change. For instance, the Internet can be used to complete negotiations, automate order processing, and coordinate product transfer—all for the existing set of channel members. In this situation, one effect of the Internet may be to improve the relationships that exist between channel members.

If channel objectives cannot be met with existing members, then a business must consider changing the channel structure. Two situations illustrate the reasons for which change may be necessary. First, suppose that a manufacturer has decided that Internet capabilities for information transfer can be leveraged to increase channel efficiency. The only way to achieve the desired channel performance is for all members to adopt and effectively use a new, Internet-based tracking system. If one or more members is either unwilling or unable to make the shift, however, the system falls apart. A new structure is necessary.

A second situation that indicates a need for channel restructuring occurs when the Internet makes it possible for a channel member to carry out activities that were previously carried out by another channel member, or when a set of activities that were once necessary are no longer needed. The former situation occurs when a manufacturer decides to create an online channel to market directly to consumers. The latter situation occurs when the Internet can be used to coordinate customer orders with supplier inventory, to ship directly from the supplier. In the first situation, the traditional retailer becomes obsolete. In the second situation, the traditional distributor arrangements lose their value.

In the following sections we will consider four channel strategies that involve differential emphasis on the Internet as a channel resource: direct channel strategy, indirect channel strategy, hybrid channel strategy, and multichannel strategy.

The Internet as a Direct Channel

One possible online channel structure is a **direct channel**, in which the manufacturer sells directly to customers. No middlemen are used. This type of structure is used in the

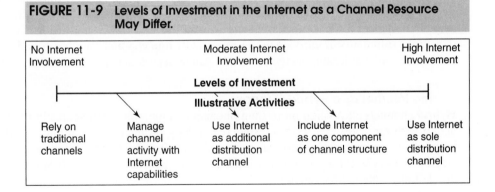

FIGURE 11-9   Levels of Investment in the Internet as a Channel Resource May Differ.

No Internet Involvement	Moderate Internet Involvement			High Internet Involvement
	Levels of Investment			
	Illustrative Activities			
Rely on traditional channels	Manage channel activity with Internet capabilities	Use Internet as additional distribution channel	Include Internet as one component of channel structure	Use Internet as sole distribution channel

off-line world by companies such as L.L. Bean and Avon. In the online world, examples of direct channels include sales of computers by Dell, and software by Egghead.com.

In each case, the company has decided that the benefits of marketing directly to the end customer outweigh the benefits that could be provided by middlemen. Shifting from a traditional retail setting to an online setting may reduce costs associated with the need to maintain a physical location (e.g., rent and utilities), as well as costs associated with the need to maintain a physical inventory (e.g., warehouses and personnel). Inventory advantages can be obtained by maintaining a **virtual inventory** that spans several suppliers and distributors. Product manufacturing and shipping can be coordinated electronically, without the need to maintain a central warehouse. On the retail side, the Internet enables online retailers to virtually aggregate a large assortment of products in a way that might not be possible in a physical location. This **virtual aggregation** can provide customers with the ability to pick and choose products that best meet their needs.

> **Bits & Bytes 11-4**
> Direct channel sales of recorded music online have faded in volume. Since the beginning of 2002, dollar sales have dropped more than half, from an all-time high of $278 million in late 2001. Meanwhile, traffic to file-sharing sites continues to increase.
> (*Source:* ComScore Networks, 11/4/2002.)

The Internet as an Indirect Channel Component

An **indirect channel** includes middlemen. Many traditional channel structures take an indirect form, by including wholesalers or retailers. Online examples of indirect channels consist of companies who rely on other, online channel members to create assortments of goods from a number of manufacturers, and to manage interactions with customers. Indirect channels that are entirely online are a rare animal, because unless the product can be moved, aggregated, sorted, and shipped digitally, some functions will necessarily be conducted by off-line members.

Amazon.com is an example of a company with an indirect distribution channel. The books that you buy online through Amazon originate with one of several book publishers. Wholesalers buy books from the publishers. Amazon collects orders from customers with its Internet retail site, and then sends the collected orders for books owned by a particular wholesaler to be processed. The wholesaler fills the order and ships it to Amazon's warehouse. At the warehouse, the wholesale order is broken down into shipments to individual consumers. Off-line channel members conduct the publishing and wholesaling activities, while Amazon conducts the retail effort online.

The Internet as a Hybrid Channel

Hybrid channels exist when more than one channel member participates in the transaction with the consumer. For example, technology products that combine hardware with software, produced by separate companies, to provide an integrated product in a single transaction for a consumer are the result of hybrid channels. Hybrid channels are definitionally indirect channels.

InSite

SAY "CHEESE!": WWW.OFOTO.COM

In 1888, George Eastman introduced the first user-friendly camera to the mass market. During the next 100 years, the company pioneered developments in photography that made taking pictures easier, and which produced prints of better and better quality. By the late 20th century, however, the company found itself mired in an "old-economy" morass of camera film, fighting competition that had moved rapidly into the "new-economy," with digital imaging. The company saw the negatives of its position, and it recognized the need to refocus, but it had invested heavily in the development, distribution, and processing capabilities for its core product, silver-halide film. Shifting to digital imaging would mean doing away with traditional processes and channels, in order to develop a new image and competency in the digital world.

Could nothing be salvaged? Digital photography offered many new benefits to amateur photographers: no film, more picture storage capacity, and instant "development." Fortunately for Kodak, however, digital photos printed on laser and inkjet printers just didn't look very good. People still wanted the crisp, clear quality of traditional prints.

In 2001, Kodak bought Ofoto.com, an online company that specialized in producing silver-halide prints from digital and film-based cameras. Photographers send their pictures to the site with OfotoNow, proprietary software that lets people edit and upload digital images to the Internet. Within days, customers receive the trusted, traditional, Kodak-quality prints by regular mail. Ofoto also stores digital images in password-protected scrapbooks, for free. Ofoto customers can send links to the scrapbooks to friends and relatives, thus virtually marketing the business for Kodak.

By using a hybrid channel that combines the benefits of digital equipment and technologies with traditional prints, Kodak was able to make the shift from the old economy to the new economy, leveraging its core investments to provide revenue for research and development in new, digital technologies.

Many information technology goods and services use hybrid channels. The hybrid channels are necessary to integrate the application that will be used by the end customer with the infrastructure, such as computing capability, needed to make the application work. Because hybrid channels require the coordinated activity of multiple channel members in the transaction phase with the consumer, they are often more complex and difficult to manage than direct or indirect channel structures.

Hybrid channels for goods and services that leverage the Internet are often managed through strategic alliances. For example, AOL's alliance with Target means that AOL subscribers will be able to purchase Target products through the AOL Web site. In this situation, the "product" is really the capability, or service, that the partners provide—being able to purchase target products through AOL. To make this hybrid channel operate effectively, both AOL and Target must coordinate their activities to bring consumers to the transaction stage.

The Internet and Multichannel Strategy

With a **multichannel strategy**, more than one type of distribution channel is used to achieve distribution objectives. For instance, a manufacturer may sell directly to customers through a catalog, through a set of off-line retailers, and through a Web site maintained by a different organization. Multichannel strategies are common in traditional marketplaces. Sears & Roebuck Company used catalogs and storefronts for many years, to increase product availability and convenience for shoppers. Companies such as The Gap, J. Crew, and L.L. Bean exemplify multichannel strategies in which two direct strategies are used, combining the benefits of different types of infrastructure for developing relationships with customers.

Each type of channel structure may provide businesses with unique sets of advantages and disadvantages. For example, for a company with a physical product, a traditional channel member who can use the Internet to complete sorting tasks, and also take physical possession of the product to create product assortments, may be more efficient than a channel member with only an online presence. The online channel member must introduce an additional organization to complete the sorting function. Companies with off-line retail experience and facilities are also often better equipped to manage product returns. Online retailers must develop the back-end applications and infrastructure that are needed to manage the reversed channel flow of returns.

The introduction of online channel members to a channel structure may alter the length and complexity of the structure. Changes to structure are important because they affect the performance of the channel; that is, they influence the level of channel efficiency that can be obtained. This effect may occur due to the reduction or addition of channel participants, and because of the motivation of channel members. As a result, marketers have to be aware of the effect that structural changes to a channel might have on psychological and sociological factors that affect channel member performance. We will look at the issues raised for marketers by channel structure changes in the following section.

The increasing role of the Internet in channel strategy reflects the growth of clicks-and-mortar companies, relative to pure-players. In the early stages of online commercial development, many companies began as pure-players, attempting to establish direct channels with consumers. The failure of many of these companies during the dot-com collapse in 2000 was due to many factors, but an important factor was the concern of targeted market segments with the reputability of newly formed, Internet-only, endeavors. Would the companies deliver through the online channel? Was transaction information secure and protected from dissemination?

Off-line companies who already had strong reputations were well-positioned to move into the void created by the disappearance of many dot-coms from the Internet landscape. Using the Internet as a channel resource has enabled many companies to balance and streamline marketing flows. For instance, a company can provide product information and take orders through a Web site, thus facilitating information and money flows, while using physical delivery services to complete the exchange. The SmoothFitness company (Figure 11-10) sells fitness equipment through its 10 Web sites and four retail stores. Although the company was started as an off-line venture, in the early 1980s, management saw the value of the Internet as a channel resource. On its SmoothFitness.com site, the company offers treadmills for sale at large discounts, compared with equipment sold in retail outlets. The company takes the order online, and has the treadmill **drop-shipped**—shipped directly to the buyer from the manufacturer.

FIGURE 11-10   Levels of Investment in the Internet as a Channel Resource May Differ.

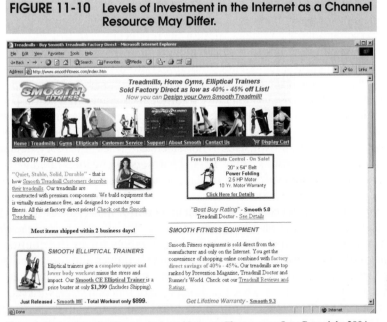

Source: Reproduced with permission of InternetFitness.com, Inc. Copyright 2004. All rights reserved.

This delivery method cuts costs by eliminating the middleman mark-up for warehousing, distribution, and retailing.

Channel Management and Performance: Is the Channel Strategy Working?

The outcomes of a channel structure can be described in terms of channel performance. Deciding whether a channel has performed as effectively as expected is based on the match between the objectives established for a particular distribution strategy and the results of measures developed to reflect the extent to which the desired outcomes were achieved.

Different channel strategy objectives necessitate different measures of outcomes. An objective of increasing distribution coverage suggests the use of different measures of channel performance than would be suitable for an objective of reducing the time to move a product from producer to consumer. This may seem quite obvious. (After all, not many people would suggest using a ruler to determine the temperature outdoors.)

More complicated, but equally important, however, is the determination of how the Internet influences channel performance, and how to measure the performance. For example, the relationship between a technology agent and a wholesaler may include rapid transmission of information about the types and amounts of products that need to be transferred to retailers. The technology agent may provide a means by which the wholesaler can accumulate information about product distribution needs from a number of producers. These products can then be combined into product assortments that are desired in different forms and quantities by various retailers. The use of the Internet to transmit the product information provides channel benefits by speeding the flow of information, and potentially reducing the logistical difficulties of product inventory storage. In addition, the

Internet increases the wholesaler's ability to create product assortments, thus enabling him to supply a wider number and variety of retailers. This benefit increases both distribution coverage and the product sales for the producer.

The effect of the Internet on channel performance can be gauged with several measures. These measures include the amount of timesavings, product sales, and distribution reach. At a general level, the types of measures used to assess channel performance may be very similar to those used in more traditional channels. At a more specific level, however, the way that the information is obtained may be different. For instance, much of the information can be obtained through the Internet. Online retailers can track site traffic and compare it with sales. Wholesalers can track inventory, demand, and rate of product flow. Input from several channel partners can be integrated with Internet-based channel management software and made available, as appropriate, through the Internet to selected channel members.

In addition to direct measures of channel performance, measures of channel partner satisfaction and loyalty can also be used to gauge the effectiveness of the channel strategy. Depending on the type of product and the strategy for its distribution, a vendor can improve its competitive position by providing incentives and tools that facilitate partner satisfaction and performance. For example, Harley-Davidson uses its Web site to stimulate buyer demand and loyalty, while the dealer locator function steers the cycle buff to pages in the site that provide contact information, maps, and driving directions to the nearest dealers. The company recognizes that its dealers are the primary connection between Harley-Davidson and its customers, and it uses the online presence to enhance dealer capabilities.

Mix Implications of the Internet as Channel Resource

What does having the Internet as a channel resource mean for business activity? In this section we will consider ways in which the Internet can influence strategic decisions about product, price, place, and promotion.

Effects on Product Strategy

As a channel resource, the Internet affects decisions about the type of product to produce, given distribution capabilities. Changes to the way that a product can be delivered to an end user create opportunities to change the form of an existing product, and even create opportunities for entirely new products. As described in Chapter 10, EMI, a recording company, was concerned that with the increasing popularity of digitally formatted music, its traditional profit base of compact disc and cassette sales was at risk. EMI concluded that the popularity of digitally formatted music, as evidenced through consumer demand, necessitated a change in product strategy for the company. EMI teamed up with Liquid Audio, a company that specializes in delivering digital music, to develop new product options. In 2002, EMI introduced a subscription-based download service, BurnITFIRST, that allows consumers to download music, burn a CD with the music, and then transfer the music to portable devices of their choice.

EMI's decision to consider alternative product forms illustrates the effect that the Internet can exert as a channel. EMI's actions also make evident the role of power in channel relationships. Demand for digital music by customers, a position often supported by the artists (e.g., singers and songwriters), resulted in diminished

FIGURE 11-11   Kazaa's Digital Channel Fills the Napster Void.

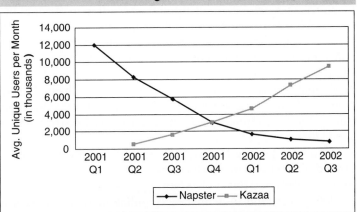

Source: comScore Networks, 11/4/02.

sales of recorded music by traditional retailers, and reduced benefits for all channel members, except the customers. The role of the Internet in shifting the balance of power from the recording industry to the customer is also indicated by the growth in traffic to sites that provide or enable access to MP3 files, even after Napster's demise (Figure 11-11).

The Internet creates product opportunities even for companies whose core business is not threatened. For example, major newspapers and magazines have developed online content as product, an action only made possible by the existence of the Internet as a channel resource. The publishers use the Internet in conjunction with off-line publishing activities, increasing brand exposure and recognition, and familiarity with the editorial style of the publication.

For retailers who use the Internet as a storefront, the Internet may affect product strategy by increasing the assortment of products that can be displayed. As Staples' experience illustrates, virtual aggregation enables a retailer to relax constraints on inventory that are imposed in a physical space. Staples was able to quadruple the size of its average SKU inventory in its physical stores when it opened its virtual store in 1999.

The Internet can also affect product strategy decisions about product line depth and product mix width. **Product line depth** is the number of items in a particular product line. **Product mix width** refers to the number of product lines offered by a company. Companies attempt to maximize sales by matching the depth of a product line to target segments of viable size and accessibility. Expanding product mix width can reduce company risk by increasing sales and profits.

With the Internet as a distribution channel, companies can tailor line and mix width decisions to capitalize on Internet channel capabilities. For instance, the global reach of the Internet may create opportunities for new products in a line, if new market segments can be identified and served with the Internet. In addition, the ease with which storefronts can be constructed and altered on the Internet, compared with their bricks-and-mortar counterparts, suggests that very different lines in a product mix can be marketed in specially designed Web showcases. The ability to separate the display of product lines enables businesses to tailor presentations to different target segments, and it reduces the potential for confusing customers.

Effects on Price Strategy

Internet effects on price can occur through two different avenues of the Internet as a channel resource. One avenue is through channel performance. In general, if the use of Internet increases channel efficiency, then a company will realize cost savings. In a competitive market, the increased cost savings may be passed on to customers in the form of price reductions. Several companies with a strong Internet presence credit their substantial cost savings to use of the Internet as a channel resource. For instance Cisco Systems, the manufacturer of network components that make the Internet a reality, estimates that the ability to use the Internet as a distribution channel saves the company $130,000,000 per year.

A second way that the Internet affects prices as a channel resource reflects the nature of the channel, and of who has power within the channel relationships. Consider the notion of supply and demand. When supply is high, prices tend to be lower. When supply is low, prices tend to be higher. In online markets, these principles apply. For instance, in an online auction for a one-of-a-kind item, increased demand results in an increased price. In this situation, the balance of power is tilted in favor of the seller. Because the Internet serves as a channel of potentially global reach, one effect of online auctions as a channel for goods may be that prices tend to be higher than they would be if the audience, or source of demand, were more restricted.

An alternative effect of an Internet channel on price is evident with companies who use the Internet to coordinate product volume and price. For example, several Web sites, such as Letsbuyit.com, enable customers to use group buying power to drive down the cost of a product. As the number of people in a particular purchase situation who commit to buy an item increases, the price decreases. In this situation, the buyers, collectively, exercise power.

Effects on Place Strategy

As more and more products become available through online channels, shoppers have the opportunity to examine and compare products, and the price and promotional material associated with the products. This situation approximates what economists describe as a state of **pure information**. The problem with pure information is that it makes it difficult for businesses to create perceptions of differences between product offerings to develop a competitive advantage.

One potential benefit of the Internet as a channel resource is as a way for businesses to differentiate a product offering from that of the competition. For online channels, companies can use the Web site, and the manner of distribution through the Internet, to leverage customers' perceptions of the site as place. As a virtual location for product distribution, Web sites can be structured to create shopping experiences that are perceived as benefits that are not attainable through competitors' distribution practices. For this purpose, the uses of the Internet as a content resource and as a channel resource are closely related. The content provided via the online channel can be used to develop a company's image and reputation, much as the store atmosphere does off-line. When products and services are sold through online intermediaries, the quality of the online experience offered by the intermediary can influence customers' perceptions of the product or the company offering the product through the intermediary channel partner.

Effects on Promotion Strategy

As a channel resource, the Internet may affect promotion strategy at different points in the channel structure. For example, marketers may alter the emphasis on the promotion element to persuade channel members to adopt Internet-related channel activities. In this situation, promotion is a means to obtain a desired channel strategy structure. It is important to note that promotion strategy must be developed for each dyad in the channel structure, and that the nature of the promotion strategy should be tailored to reflect the type of relationship (e.g., who has power, and what type). Promotion strategy should also be based on the stage of relationship development. For instance, a manufacturer might provide promotional deals to wholesalers and retailers early in a relationship, in order to motivate channel member performance.

> **Bits & Bytes 11-5**
> Through its online, retail outlet and telephone channels, Ticketmaster sold more than 95 million tickets in 2002. Online sales accounted for nearly 40 percent of the total, which was valued at $4 billion.
> (*Source:* www.Ticketmaster.com, 2003.)

Cautions for Using the Internet as a Channel Resource

The Internet creates opportunities for businesses to redesign channel structures, and to develop new avenues for distributing products to customers. At the same time, the Internet also serves as a source of challenges for each of the key perspectives in the exchange environment. Businesses must anticipate and understand the source and effect of these challenges on channel strategy.

Business Issues

For any company that plans to use the Internet as a channel for selling to customers, an important issue is that of how to initiate contacts with potential customers, and how to develop those contacts into ongoing relationships. A key function of a middleman in a channel is to link sellers, such as manufacturers, with buyers, such as retailers and consumers. The advantage to companies of an intermediary, in terms of reducing contacts, is shown in Figure 11-12.

Without the intermediary, the total number of different contacts between companies (e.g., manufacturers) and customers is equal to the number of companies times the number of customers. In this example, the total number is 12. With an intermediary to manage the manufacturer–customer contacts, only 8 contacts are needed: 2 from the manufacturers to the intermediary, and 6 from the intermediary to the customers. From the perspective of each company, the benefits are even greater. Instead of managing 6 contacts, the companies only manage 1 contact — with the intermediary.

FIGURE 11-12 Middlemen Reduce the Number of Contacts for Sellers.

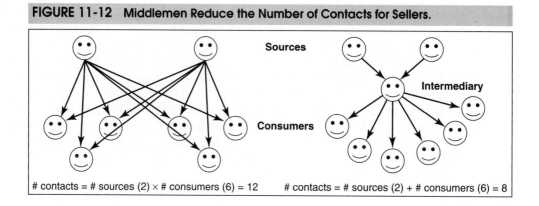

contacts = # sources (2) × # consumers (6) = 12   # contacts = # sources (2) + # consumers (6) = 8

Suppose that a company decides to shift from a channel structure in which middlemen, such as retailers, undertook the responsibility for customer contact to a direct, online channel. Because the retailer has been the source of contact for consumers with the product, the retailer may have information about customer preferences pertaining to product form and use. The manufacturer must develop this knowledge base. In addition, the original intermediary, such as wholesaler, may have a database of existing customers and qualified prospects. If the manufacturer disintermediates the wholesaler, then the manufacturer must work to construct a targeted set of customers.

The costs of acquiring customers are not insignificant. The Boston Consulting Group surveyed 100 e-commerce companies and found that they spent, on average, 40 percent of revenues on marketing costs. This amount is substantially higher than the 14.2 percent typically spent by department stores, and the 7.2 percent averaged by specialty stores. The chart in Figure 11-13 shows estimated customer acquisition costs for a range of companies that market through an online channel. We can see that some types of online services have much higher acquisition costs than others.

It's important to note that the variation in acquisition costs often reflects the fact that value of a customer can differ widely by industry or type of company. A consumer of online brokerage services may complete many transactions with a single company, while a consumer of online mortgage services may need only one loan from the company. As a result, companies use metrics such as **average revenue per user (ARPU)** and **return on investment (ROI)** to evaluate customer acquisition strategies.

Using the Internet as a channel component creates other challenges for businesses. For instance, for physical products sold via the Internet, the company must still manage the logistics of distribution. In traditional channels, some distribution functions can be carried out economically by combining sets of products or amassing substantial orders for a single product, and then shipping them at one time, as to a retailer. With a direct Internet channel, order fulfillment may be necessary in a more piecemeal fashion, which may increase shipping and handling costs to the company. In addition, the absence of expertise early in the process of developing relationships with customers may lead to frustration—on both sides—and a decline in brand loyalty.

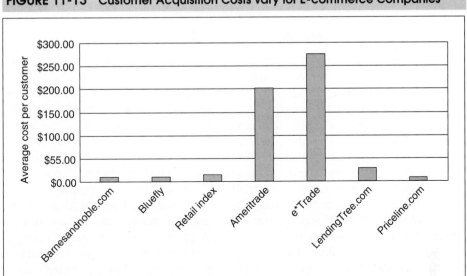

FIGURE 11-13   Customer Acquisition Costs Vary for E-commerce Companies

Source: www.emetrics.org, July 2002.

Customer Issues

A major issue for shoppers who purchase through the Internet is that of trust. Trust takes different forms. For instance, creating a storefront on the Internet is fairly simple, compared with creating a bricks-and-mortar counterpart. As a result, many small businesses have developed, often touting exotic, unique wares. For a shopper who finds one of these "stores," however, it may be difficult to evaluate the quality of the company, and of its product. In traditional marketplaces, customers use heuristics such as company reputation, store location, and atmospherics to determine whether a company's claims about its products should be trusted. With new, online businesses, these heuristics are less useful.

Even when the company is well known, with a long and reputable history off-line prior to developing an online channel, the issue of trust is still central for customers. Many people are concerned with the security of providing personal information or financial information through the Internet. Companies must use policies and procedures that not only ensure the security of information, but that can also be clearly communicated to customers.

Policy Issues

The Internet can serve as a channel for distributing many different types of goods and services. Some of them may be illegal. Policy makers are concerned with consumers' ability to obtain products that have the potential to do harm. For instance, the Internet can be used to convey information about where and how to negotiate a transaction of weapons and services for violent intent.

Even when product distribution is not intended to result in harm, the potential for the misuse of products obtained through Internet channels does exist. For example, online drugstores enable consumers to effectively write their own prescriptions. On some sites, diagnosis of a medical condition can be made using an interactive

'Net Knowledge

MANAGING CHANNEL CONFLICT

Many companies realize the potential benefits of the Internet for their distribution strategies. For some companies, the Internet represents an opportunity to completely do away with old channels, moving to a single, direct, online channel. Although the change in channel structure may be dramatic, it may also be easier than attempting to alter existing indirect channels, in which the continued participation of the partner—though perhaps in a different form—is still necessary.

Getting channel partners to accept change can be difficult, especially if the change is going to affect their revenues. Even when you have the power to force or encourage a change, it does not mean that your partners will adjust their practices readily, or happily. Managing conflict during the shift to a channel strategy that incorporates the Internet is important for the long-term success of the channel structure and its performance.

Two basic strategies are possible: avoidance and management.[1] First, you can simply avoid the conflict induced by the Internet. For instance, limit what you will do on your Web site. For example, you can simply provide product information. Alternatively, you can answer product inquiries and provide your dealers with any sales leads. If you decide to actually sell products on your site, limit the range of products you sell, to avoid stepping on the toes of your other sales outlets. Another approach is to target a certain subset of customers, typically underserved by your other partners.

If conflict is unavoidable, you have to manage it. The first step is to determine the nature and amount of conflict. A channel partner's hurt feelings may evaporate over time without any action on your part, but a partner's threat to defect to the competitor may require substantial attention and effort. To remediate conflict between channel partners, create territories, defining which products will be sold where, and how, and to whom. Establish rules for setting prices, so that all partners who sell to the end consumer are competitive within their markets. If an Internet channel threatens traditional sales, as when a manufacturer can undercut the prices offered by channel partners, share the wealth, letting the increased sales volume from site sales subsidize incentives to channel partners.

---

[1]These strategies and accompanying tactics follow guidelines presented in Jakki Mohr's book, *Marketing of High-Technology Products and Innovations*, Prentice-Hall: Upper Saddle River, NJ, 2001, page 241.

questionnaire. On other sites, doctors answer questions and make suggestions. In some cases, consumers can order medication directly from the site. Of concern to policy makers is the potential for misuse or abuse of drugs that are not prescribed for a particular person by a qualified doctor or nurse.

Technology Issues

The ability to use the Internet as a channel resource underscores the importance of technology. As more companies develop an Internet channel presence, or use the

Internet as a means for managing channels, the need for enhanced technologies will continue to grow.

Early forms of electronically aided coordination between channel members used electronic data interchange (EDI) technologies. The present-day version of EDI leverages the network infrastructure of the Internet to form extranets that can enable information, negotiation, and money flows. Many extranets are developed as public networks. A **public network** consists of two or more company intranets, or internal networks, that are connected by the Internet. One concern with public networks is that information is only protected when it is within the companies' intranets, and not when it moves across the Internet. A company can form a virtual private network that relies on passing information over the Internet through **encrypted tunnels** to keep data secure.

Despite the advances in technology, extranets still present disadvantages to businesses. First, the price of security is computing power. Keeping data safe means a need for powerful computers, at each part of the network. A related issue is that substantial effort and financial investment is required to develop the extranet. Thus, companies must be confident that the channel structure and the relationships within the structure are worth the investment.

Chapter Summary

In this chapter, we examined the role of the Internet as a channel resource. We began by examining the nature and function of channels, both with and without an online component. Differences between channel members and ancillary members were described, and the implications of the Internet for the development of new types of channel partners were discussed.

Because the Internet may alter the ways that channel members carry out market functions in distribution channels, it also has the potential to alter marketing flows. Information, negotiation, product, and monetary flows were described in terms of the Internet's impact on channel activities and flow structures.

We also examined the implications of the Internet on relationships between channel partners, including changes to power and the rise of channel conflict. The Internet may influence the types of relationships that exist between dyads, or pairs of channel members. We considered the effects of different types of power bases in relationships, and the likely effect of different relationships on the willingness to accept Internet-related channel structures. The effect of the Internet on relationships was also considered in terms of reducing channel length through disintermediation, and extending channel length, through reintermediation.

Reintermediation is often characterized by the introduction of new middlemen to an Internet-based distribution channel, often known as infomediaries. We examined several types of infomediaries, and their effect on channel relationships. One possible effect of change to channel structure is channel conflict. Attempts to avoid or reduce channel conflict may take the form of creating new roles and responsibilities for channel members.

Subsequent sections of the chapter addressed the impact of the Internet as a channel resource on characteristics of channel strategy, including issues of channel design and management. The Internet can influence channel strategy with varying degrees of invasiveness. For instance, the Internet may be used as a tool for managing an existing channel structure. Alternatively, it might serve as a medium for an online channel member, in conjunction with other, off-line members. In its most extreme form of impact, the

Internet might be used as the sole alternative to a traditional, off-line structure. Given the newness of the Internet as a channel resource, and the costs associated with developing efficient channel structures, it is likely that many companies will adopt a multichannel strategy, in which the Internet is merely one aspect of an overall channel strategy.

As a channel resource, the Internet affects business activity decisions. For example, the Internet may increase the desirability of new forms of products, or new products. The nature of the Internet as a channel for distributing goods and services may increase companies' ability to successfully lengthen product lines and widen product mixes. Different types of channels for product purchase may influence pricing strategy. The difference in the Internet's influence on price may reflect different amounts of power between buyers and sellers. This power, in turn, may stem from increased access to products on the Internet.

Reduced ability to create a competitive advantage with product, price, and promotion may increase the importance of place. Promotion strategy is affected by the need to tailor promotion to the different relationships in the channel structure, and by the need to build relationships in new channel structures that involve the Internet.

Each of the four key perspectives in the Internet environment is affected by the role of the Internet as a channel resource. Businesses must deal with issues of contact management, customers with issues of security, policy makers must manage the distribution of harmful products, and technology developers 1work to provide hardware and software solutions that can keep up with the demands of an increasingly sophisticated channel strategy.

CONTENT MANAGEMENT

USEFUL TERMS

- ancillary structure
- average revenue per user (ARPU)
- channel conflict
- channel efficiency
- channel functions
- channel member
- channel strategy
- channel structures
- cybermediaries
- direct channel
- disintermediation
- drop-ship
- dyadic relationships
- encrypted tunnel
- exchange functions
- hybrid channel
- indirect channel
- infomediaries
- information broker
- information flow
- leveraged cooperation
- logistic functions
- logistics management
- marketing flows
- marketplace concentrators
- money flow
- multichannel strategy
- negotiation flow
- negotiatory functions
- product flow
- product line depth
- product mix width
- promotion flow
- public network
- pure information
- reintermediation
- return on investment (ROI)
- transaction brokers
- virtual aggregation
- virtual inventory

REVIEW QUESTIONS

1. Name two ways in which the Internet may be used as a channel resource.
2. What is the main goal of a channel of distribution?
3. What is the role of ancillary channel structure?
4. What types of flows exist in a distribution channel?
5. Explain the concept of a dyadic relationship.

6. Why is power an important consideration in channel relationships?
7. How does the Internet influence channel efficiency?
8. How can marketers determine the appropriate channel structures for their businesses?
9. What different types of channel strategies can be implemented by organizations?
10. Describe how disintermediation and reintermediation are inextricably linked.
11. How may channel conflict arise when using the Internet as a channel resource?
12. What are the effects of using the Internet as a channel resource on product strategy? Price strategy? Place strategy? Promotion strategy?
13. What issues do buyers and sellers face when using the Internet as a channel resource?

WEB APPLICATION

Balance of Power: Managing Channel Conflict

The Internet has made it possible for some manufacturers to shorten the distribution channel that transfers their products to customers. In some cases, companies have been able to eliminate the need for traditional middlemen functions, and sell directly to the consumer. In other cases, however, companies have developed multichannel strategies that provide customers with different ways to buy the product. In this exercise, we'll look at an example of each approach, to consider the pros and cons of the online channel.

Dell Computer is a well-known example of direct selling with the Internet. The company was founded in 1984 by Michael Dell, with a goal of selling custom-built computers directly to consumers. Hewlett-Packard (HP) is one of Dell's leading competitors. Hewlett-Packard was started in the 1930s, and produced its first computer in 1966. With its wide array of products and its long history with different channels and partners, HP adopted a multichannel approach to compete with other computer manufacturers.

1. Visit the Web sites for Dell Computer (www.dell.com) and for Hewlett-Packard's computer sales (www.hp.com). Select a computer at each site, choosing comparable features. Customize the selected product. Who has the better price? The faster ship date?
2. On the HP site, visit the page entitled, "How to Buy." What channels does HP make available to consumers?
3. With the availability of online shopping, similar to that offered by Dell, why might consumers select other channels? For what situations might a customer opt for a preconfigured computer through an online retailer, rather than a customized computer ordered directly from HP?
4. What benefits does the multichannel approach provide for HP's online and off-line retailers?
5. How does HP's retailer locator system address the potential cause for concern among retailers that one retailer is more prominently featured in a list of nearby stores?
6. Now visit Apple Computer's site, at www.apple.com. What channels does Apple use? How does the company's strategy for managing channel information provided to customers compare with that of Hewlett-Packard?
7. Both HP and Apple sell their products through resellers, like Best Buy. What types of power might be used by the manufacturers to persuade a retailer to carry its product? Conversely, what types of power might be used by the retailer to persuade multiple manufacturers to let it sell their products?

CONCEPTS IN BRIEF

1. The Internet facilitates channel function in three ways: 1) it can serve as a channel; 2) it can serve as a channel member; and 3) it can enable channel management.

2. The Internet's introduction into channel strategy can be a disruptive force, resulting in conflict and changes to existing channel structures.
3. Two primary changes to channel structure are disintermediation and reintermediation.
4. Traditional channel members assume ownership of a product, or assume risks related to ownership under contract.
5. Internet intermediaries, or infomediaries, often do not assume ownership of products.
6. Three main types of informediaries are information brokers, transaction brokers, and marketplace concentrators.
7. Relationships between channel members are often described as dyadic, or pair-based, relationships.
8. Each dyad in a channel may exhibit a different type and balance of power from other channel dyads.
9. Different uses of power within a channel structure may be appropriate at different times in the relationship between dyad members.
10. Channel conflict may occur between channels, as channels compete for desirable channel members.

THINKING POINTS

1. Channel participants operate in dyadic relationships, and different forms of power are used to influence partners. In the Internet environment, are any types of power likely to be disproportionately influential? Which ones, when, and why?
2. Different influence tactics may be more or less effective at different stages of relationships. How might Internet time be expected to affect the selection and efficacy of influence tactics?
3. What issues might a business encounter in deciding
   a. to move from a traditional to a virtual channel
   b. to create a hybrid channel
   c. to use the Internet as an additional channel?
4. How might the level of investment in the Internet as a channel resource be influenced by the nature of the product? The company? The industry?
5. Are infomediaries middlemen? Why, or why not?
6. Relate the concepts of disintermediation and reintermediation to the concepts of power and conflict in channels.
7. What tradeoffs does a company make that opts to use a middleman to reduce the number of contacts with customers? How does the Internet potentially influence the desirability of the tradeoffs?

ENDNOTES

1. This example is based on material from Staples.com, Sapient.com, and Molecular.com.

2. Reported in Forbes.com, April 17, 2000.

SUGGESTED READINGS

"Coping with Internet Channel Conflict," in *Now or Never*, by Mary Modahl (New York: HarperCollins Publishers, Inc., 2000, pages 169–186).

"Electronic Marketing: the Dell Computer Experience," by Kenneth Hill. In *Electronic Marketing and the Consumer*, edited by

Robert A. Peterson (Thousand Oaks, CA: Sage Publications, Inc., 1997, pages 89–100).

"501 Blues," by Cindy Waxter. *Business 2.0* (January 2000).

"Intermediaries and Cybermediaries: A Continuing Role for Mediating Players in the Electronic Marketplace," by Mitra Barun

Sarkar, Brian Butler, and Charles Steinfield. *Journal of Computer-mediated Communication, 1,* 3 (1995).

"Disabling the System," by Karl Taro Greenfeld. *Time Digital* (September 6, 1999), pages 26–31.

LEARNING LINKS

Online Channel Management

www.saleslobby.com/OnlineMagazine/0900/channelmanagement_mmetzner.asp
www.saleslobby.com/OnlineMagazine/0900/channelmanagement_jkrist.asp

Channel Conflict

www.janal.com/channel.html
digitalenterprise.org/channels/channel.html
faculty.darden.virginia.edu/bodilys/eStrat/topic3_2002/Managing%20channels%20of%20distribution.pdf

Channel Strategy

Multichannel Approaches

www-1.ibm.com/services/strategy/files/IBM_Consulting_Integrated_multi_channel_retailing_IMCR_A_roadmap_to_the_future.pdf

Channel Management Solutions

www.corp.origin.channelintelligence.com
www.responsys.com/landingpads/irbuyersguide.asp

CHAPTER

Digital Communications and Business Activity

Focus and Objectives

Chapters 10 and 11 focused on the dual roles of the Internet as a source of information and as a channel for delivering content. This chapter is focused on the role of the Internet as a vehicle for communicating content, through the channel infrastructure of the network. We consider the nature of communication, and the impact of the Internet on the interactions between buyers, sellers, and content that is the basis for communication. Different forms of communication enabled by the Internet are discussed, as are the impacts of these forms on aspects of business activity. Issues raised by the role of the Internet as a communications resource are considered for each of the four perspectives.

Your objectives in studying this chapter include the following:

- Know the basic components of a model for communication.
- Understand the different forms of interactivity in the computer-mediated environment of the Internet.
- Recognize the implications of interactivity for communication, including personalized content.
- Know the difference between personalization and customization.
- Understand the implications of the Internet as a communication resource for business activity decisions.

Creating a Cyber Community

Sherwood Forest, in Nottingham, England, was home to Robin Hood and his band of outlaws, including Friar Tuck, Little John, and Maid Marian. The outlaws waged their unique version of guerilla warfare against the excesses of King John and his courtiers, robbing from the rich to give to the poor.

Some 900 years later, Nottingham is once again the scene of unique forms of warfare. This time, the combatants often number in the hundreds, and are rarely more than 2 inches tall. They are, however, very fierce. The highly detailed plastic and metal warriors are produced by Games Workshop, PLC, as the mainstay of a war-gaming hobby that began in England, but which now has a global presence. Enthusiasts build armies to do battle in one of two main forums. Warhammer Fantasy lures gamers into a dark, medieval world, with battles between dark elves, orcs and goblins, and lizardmen, among others. Warhammer 40,000 is a gothic, futuristic scenario, in which armies such as Necrons and Space Marines square off.

Preparing for battle isn't easy. The human commander of each army must master a complex set of rules and capabilities for his forces. In addition, the little guys have to be meticulously painted, with at least three colors per fighter. Clearly, the hobby requires a lot of time, attention, and dedication, to defeat the enemy.

How does the company market its unique product? The focused, intense, nature of the hobby means that it appeals to an equally focused and intense target market. Tom Kirby, the CEO and chairman of Games Workshop, notes that the niche market appeal of the hobby doesn't lend itself to mass marketing tactics. Instead, the company banks on word-of-mouth to build its loyal following. In the 15 years since the company entered the U.S. market, hobbyists have been exposed to the games through traditional channels of company stores and independent retailers, known as rogue traders. To generate enthusiasm for the hobby, the retail outlets not only sell the miniatures, they also sell the paints and other materials needed to build realistic battle scenarios. In addition, the stores often provide space to paint, and gaming tables for doing battle with other patrons. These tactics foster a loyal community and encourage novice gamers to build their armies and participate in battles and tournaments. The company also publishes a monthly magazine, *White Dwarf*, to keep hobbyists abreast of what players in other communities are doing, as well as developments in the Games Workshop product line.

The Internet plays a big role in the company's quest for world domination. The company site, games-workshop.com, serves as a new channel for direct sales, augmenting the existing mail order and telephone avenues. Perhaps more importantly, the Web site provides a means of communication between the company and its stakeholders, including hobbyists and investors. Most importantly, the site's community features enable players to interact with each other, through archived message boards and moderated online chat sessions. Players exchange insights and information about army characteristics and battle strategies, as well as painting tips and opportunities for gaming.

With a relatively small, niche market, it's important for the company to keep current players involved, and to provide new players with the support they need to become enthusiastic devotees. The site furthers these aims with its Warpgate Network, a list of links to independent sites that provide game-related content, and with information about Games Workshop events. Locale-specific Warhammer clubs can register in the site's club directory, Regiments of Renown, enabling individual players to find a battle in their backyard. The Hall of Heroes recognizes combatants of extraordinary skill, according them status and providing lesser players with something to strive toward.

The Warhammer world is a physical world, based on hand-to-hand combat between armies, whose commanders face off across a table of individually painted miniatures. Games Workshop has used the virtual world of the Internet to build community (Figure 12-1), by enabling online and off-line interactions between hobbyists that achieve the company's niche strategy of building interest and activity in its gaming hobby through word-of-mouth.

The Games Workshop approach is novel, but not unique. Companies are increasingly recognizing the value of the Internet for building brand communities. eBay, for instance, has focused heavily on encouraging the development of an eBay community. For a company based on peer-to-peer transactions, creating trust is an important element of eBay's success. To this end, community-specific chat rooms, as well as transaction feedback boards, help eBay provide its customers with a set of norms for exchange behaviors, as well as information about traders' reputations. Other

FIGURE 12-1 Games Workshop Uses Its Site to Build Brand Through Community.

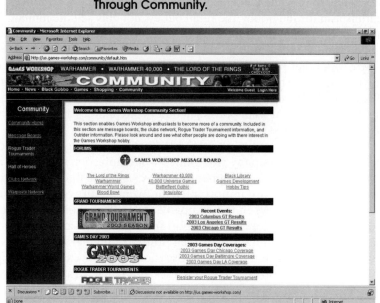

Source: Copyright Games Workshop Ltd 2000–2004. All rights reserved.

companies use community-based initiatives to meet a variety of strategic objectives, including attracting traffic, building brand image, fostering loyalty, building revenue, cutting costs of sales, improving conversion rates, and developing business intelligence. While situations for using communities may differ, a common thread ties the companies together—the use of the Internet as a resource for interactive communication.

With the Internet, businesses can communicate with many customers at once, or focus on just one person. This flexibility reflects a fundamental difference between the Internet and traditional forms for communicating promotional material to target segments. In addition, with the Internet, shoppers can exercise flexibility in the use of commercial information. They can pick and choose the format of information they would like, such as text-only or text plus graphics, and they can determine how much information they would like to acquire about a particular topic. A third key difference stems from the interactivity enabled by the Internet technology: Buyers and sellers have available to them a variety of ways in which they can communicate—from the in-your-face tactics of banner ads to virtual, real-time exchanges of information.

These differences affect the way that digital business activity is conducted. A popular view of the role of business activity is that product, price, and place issues must be addressed to create an opportunity to buy a product. In contrast, promotion is needed primarily to communicate the existence and desirability of the opportunity. With the integration of the Internet into business activity, the role of promotion, as a form of communication, becomes a central one. In fact, some researchers have argued that with the Internet, "the medium is the message!"

This shift in the relative emphasis placed on components of business activity underscores the importance of the Internet as an information-rich commercial environment. The Internet blurs the borders of elements that have tended to be treated as separate components. For instance, the ability to offer products that can be digitized and transmitted via electronic channels, such as music, videos, software, and books, means that strategic issues related to product, place, and promotion can be combined to achieve business objectives. The central role of information in this process means that businesses will need to understand and use the Internet to develop effective communications campaigns.

In this chapter, we will examine the role of the Internet for commercial communication. We begin with a discussion of the characteristics, such as interactivity, that differentiate the Internet from other forms of commercial communication. With a general description of the communications environment in place, we then look at the implications of interactivity for commercial communication. Next, we consider the effect of the Internet as a resource for communication on elements of business activity. We also consider several of the issues that Internet-based communications raise for each of our four perspectives: buyers, sellers, policy makers, and technology developers.

Bits and Bytes 12-1

e-fluentials influence approximately 155 million U.S. online adults. What influences them? In a 2001 survey, 85 percent of a set of surveyed e-fluentials said that companies' Web sites carried more clout than online magazines or opinion sites.

(*Source: CyberAtlas*, with data from Burson-Marsteller U.S.A.)

The Internet as a Resource for Communication

The Internet provides businesses with a context that can be used to deliver content in a variety of ways to customers. This capability underscores the distinction between the information in the commercial communication, and the vehicle used to deliver the information; that is, content differs from communication. In addition, the context in which information is communicated on the Internet can be described independently of the infrastructure that transmits the information. In other words, the basic network structure and function of the Internet remains the same, whether the information is transmitted to customers as banner advertising or as e-mail.

As a communications resource, the Internet enables several types of vehicles to serve as contexts for information to be transmitted, including banner ads, e-mail, and promotions. The versatility of the Internet as a context for communications means that businesses can integrate different forms of commercial communications, such as advertising, public relations, and promotions, into a strategy that combines online and offline tactics to meet strategic promotional objectives.

Characterizing Communication

A basic model for communication consists of a source, a message, and a receiver (Figure 12-2). The **source**, such as the marketer, creates the message, determining what information it should contain, the format of that information, and the vehicle in which it will be delivered. This set of actions is a process termed **encoding**. On the other end of the communication, the **receiver**, typically the consumer, attends to, perceives, and interprets the message. This process is known as **decoding**.

The two processes are closely linked; how a message is encoded will affect how it is decoded. For instance, researchers have found that the **modality** of the message affects its decoding. Modality refers to the form of the information, and it is often related to the medium in which the information is delivered. For example, modalities include textual formats (e.g., print media), aural formats (e.g., radio), and visual or audiovisual formats (e.g., television). Different formats influence attention, comprehension, and recall. For instance, audiovisual formats tend to increase attention, presumably because of their sensory richness. In contrast, textual formats tend to increase comprehension and recall; consumers exposed to print messages exhibit more accurate knowledge of presented information, and they can retrieve more information from memory than consumers exposed to messages in other modalities.

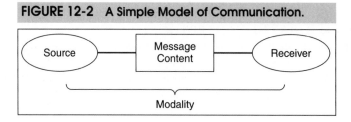

FIGURE 12-2 A Simple Model of Communication.

Commercial communications can refer to the message and its form, or to the process by which messages are passed between sources and receivers. For example, we can describe a television ad or a piece of direct mail as a commercial communication. Describing communication as a *thing* emphasizes the role of content, a topic addressed in Chapter 10. In contrast, we can think of communication as a process of sharing information between a source and a receiver. Viewed as a *process*, commercial communication emphasizes the benefits of interaction.

An important feature of the Internet is its ability to facilitate interaction between users. In the following section, we will examine how the interactivity possible with the Internet affects processes of commercial communication.

Interactivity and Commercial Communication

The Internet acts as a medium for communication, just like television, radio, newspaper ads, and other, traditional types of commercial communications. Despite the similarity in purpose, the Internet differs in two main ways from traditional media for communication. First, the Internet enables interactive communication between a source and a receiver. Second, the Internet makes it possible for customers to exercise some control over the format of the communication. These two characteristics both reflect interactivity (Figure 12-3). In the first instance, the receiver interacts with the source. This interaction reflects the role of the Internet as a channel for information exchange. In the second instance, the receiver interacts with the content. This interaction underscores the importance of the Internet's role as a source of information. In both situations, the interactions occur within the computer-mediated environment.

Source and Receiver Interactivity

From its beginning, the Internet was designed to foster communication. The technological advances that linked computers to transfer information at near real-time speeds allowed researchers to share facilities, data, and research results more rapidly and economically than they could prior to the advent of the digital network. People could interact—working collaboratively for common goals and unrestricted by geography.

Traditional forms of **broadcast communications** have several limitations. For instance, with television and radio, the message may miss its target if customers in the

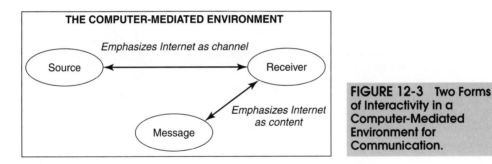

FIGURE 12-3 Two Forms of Interactivity in a Computer-Mediated Environment for Communication.

desired audience are otherwise occupied. As a result, businesses spend lots of money to place messages in programs and time slots where the likelihood of exposure is high (e.g., Super Bowl ads). The exposure problem is reduced for print media, because the window of opportunity for exposure is longer. Newspapers may sit around for a day, and magazines for a month, or more. Of course, the tradeoff between television or radio, and print media, is that the former media can be delivered to a passive audience, while print media tend to require a little more effort on the receiver's part.

With the Internet, businesses can broadcast information in forms similar to those of television and radio. For example, Victoria's Secret, a lingerie company, previewed its line in an Internet fashion show. Although demand for access to the online preview overwhelmed the company's server—a problem that does not exist for television technology—the presentation of the message was similar to televised fashion events.

The Internet and Narrowcast Communication   In addition to broadcast communications, the Internet enables narrowcast communications, and even pointcast communications. **Narrowcast communication** refers to messages that can be selectively provided to a targeted audience that is typically smaller than a target audience for a broadcast message. For instance, qualified prospects can be invited to visit a site to preview a product. In addition to limiting awareness, businesses can also limit access by providing passwords to invited visitors. Narrowcast communication is not unique to the Internet environment. Specialized television channels, such as those available through cable and satellite services, are a form of narrowcasting. What is different about narrowcasting with the Internet is that the business must take a more active role to initiate the communication process than in television narrowcast situations, because exposure to the narrowcast opportunity is less likely to occur through Web surfing than through channel surfing. As a result, the Internet may have higher targeting costs than traditional media. Companies who aggregate categories of product or interest sites, such as Narrowcast Media, provide a way to reduce targeting costs by identifying sites with relevant content for the business, effectively creating a focused target for the narrowcast campaign.

FIGURE 12-4   Traditional Media Emphasize One-to-Many Communications.

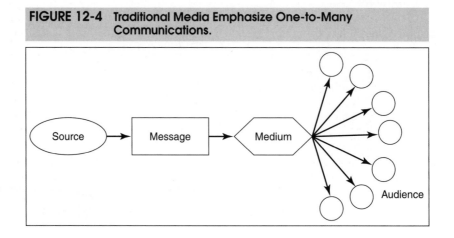

Academic researchers have used experiments to determine when narrowcasting should be used.[1] Preliminary results indicate that an important factor in the success of a narrowcasting strategy is the buyer's search cost. That is, when product awareness is low, as for a specialty product, and the effort to seek out and learn about the product is high, narrowcasting is more effective than broadcasting for generating profits. In short, the costs of targeting customers with narrowcast advertising are outweighed by the benefits of reducing the buyers' search costs with desired product information.

The Internet and Pointcast Communication   Pointcast communications are a form of one-to-one interaction. In contrast to broadcast, pointcast communication is the provision of a unique message to a single receiver. This capability can overcome limits to communication effectiveness that may occur in a more impersonal medium, such as radio or television.

Pointcast communications take many forms. The one-to-one nature of the communication may be as simple as sending a largely standardized message to a set of receivers, changing only the name of the receiver in the message. This approach to pointcast communication is reflected in some types of direct mail. In contrast, one-to-one communication may take the form of highly individualized messages, tailored to meet the receiver's needs, habits, and preferences, and personalized to emphasize the uniqueness of the comunication and the individual.

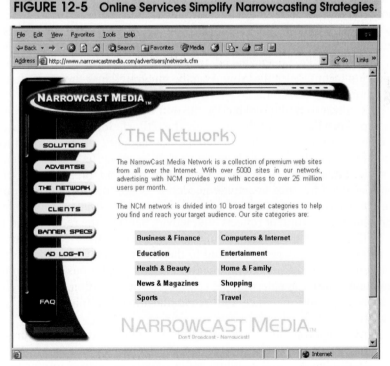

FIGURE 12-5   Online Services Simplify Narrowcasting Strategies.

Source: Reproduced with permission of Narrowcast Media, Inc., Copyright 2003. All rights reserved.

A business' ability to provide individualized messages is often a result of interaction with a customer. A customer can provide information about his needs to guide the commercial communication. Alternatively, information obtained simply as a result of the customer's interaction with the business via the Internet can provide information that can be used to structure a commercial message. For example, a domain name can provide occupational information, and information stored in cookies can provide insights into product interests. Sites that let consumers design custom displays of information and news, such as Yahoo!'s My Yahoo! feature, also provide the business with information about what is important to the customer, thus enabling the business to target future communications to the customer's interests.

Receiver and Content Interactivity

In the last section, we considered communication as interaction between a receiver and a source. Now, we shift to the interaction between the receiver and the content. With the Internet, businesses can combine print, audio, and video modalities. For instance, a message can be created in which persuasive elements are presented with text and graphics, much like a magazine ad. In addition, moving images can be presented using animation technologies, and sound can be integrated into the presentation of the message, similar to television.

In contrast to traditional media, the user can influence the combination of modalities, and hence the form of the message. The ultimate form of the message may be influenced by user preferences for content and for modality, and by constraints on the user's computing capacity. The user is an active participant in the construction of the communication, rather than a passive recipient of a preset presentation of information. Consider the difference in activity needed to obtain product information from a Web site, compared with watching an ad on television. The receiver's ability to influence the representation of content reflects interactivity between the receiver and the content.

Differences in the extent to which the receiver controls exposure to a message and the form of the message are related to the idea of push versus pull forms of information delivery. Broadcast communications are typically push communications. **Push communications** originate with the commercial organization, and they are delivered to a relatively passive audience. **Pull communications** are initiated by the receiver, and hence require higher levels of activity.

For Internet communications, all forms of communication—from broadcast to pointcast—may be pushed to the receiver. Unlike traditional broadcast media, however, the Internet also enables pull communications. When a receiver interacts with content to structure the form of the information, the selectivity that creates the message reflects a pull approach, rather than a push approach, to communication. Information acquired from a Web page by a receiver reflects pull, while information obtained from an e-mail sent to a receiver reflects push. Other pointcast forms of pushed information are also provided by software that tailors content, based on specifications provided by the receiver or by the source (e.g., customized content of an online news service).

Implications of Interactive Communications for Content

We have seen that interaction between the user, or receiver, with the source and with the content can be used to change the nature of the content that is communicated. Businesses can use the Internet to provide content that matches the individual needs of customers. That is, the nature of the product in the exchange relationship is different for each customer. The process of using the Internet to create an individualized offering, such as a site presentation or a product, is called **personalization**.

The idea that underlies personalization is that of uniqueness; the outcome of personalization is an entity in a form that has higher value to the user than it would to anyone else. Personalization exists outside the Internet. Monograms on towels and shirts, and names on plaques and certificates illustrate the concept of personalization. Who else would place as high a value on a Mickey Mouse cap, replete with ears, as the child who's name is embroidered across the front?!

The difference between push and pull forms of communication is related to personalization. Receiver specifications about the form of content to be delivered reflect pull in the set-up stage as in creating a personal support site at Dell.com (Figure 12-5), but when the preferences are recorded, up-to-date information about a

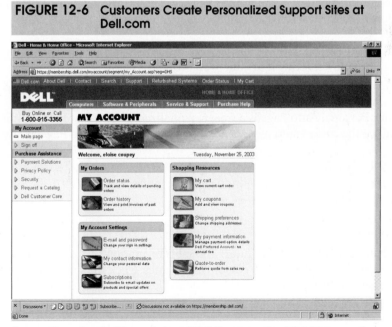

FIGURE 12-6 Customers Create Personalized Support Sites at Dell.com

desired topic can be pushed to the consumer, as with online news services. In contrast, a communications source can use information about user preferences, as from cookies or from registration information, to develop personalized communications for individual users. This approach is a push form of communication. Recognizing the difference in pull and push forms, even when the end goal of personalization is the same, is important for businesses. In general, pulled information may be a closer match to the receiver's needs and expectations than pushed information that has been developed based on inferences about user preferences. The relevance of information sent to a user based on pulled preferences can also vary depending on the amount of time that has elapsed since the consumer specified information preferences. The push communication in Figure 12-7 was received in 2000 for a vehicle that was sold in 1999.

FIGURE 12-7   Decreasing in Value: The Relevance of a Pushed Communication Can Diminish Over Time.

Subject: Oil Change Reminder: Chevrolet S10 Blazer
Date: Tue, 18 Apr 2000 16:55:55 -0700
From: Carpoint Notifier notifier@microsoft.com
To: ecoupey@vt.edu
Tuesday, April 18, 2000
Dear ecoupey@vt.edu,

According to your Personal Auto Page on MSN CarPoint, your 1994 Chevrolet S10 Blazer is due for its 63,000 - mile oil change very soon.

Visit your Personal Auto Page now for money-saving details by clicking the following link or by entering it in your Web browser's address line.
http://ownership.carpoint.msn.com/ownership/home.asp?veh=1105787&m=4#o

Your Personal Auto Page is a free, personalized service that helps you manage and reduce the cost of auto ownership. Visit your Personal Auto Page at any time to see:

```
YOUR CAR'S CURRENT BLUE BOOK VALUE
YOUR NEXT SCHEDULED SERVICE OF $100 OR MORE
YOUR CAR'S RECALL HISTORY
SEASONAL ADVICE ARTICLES
```

Advertisement: Jiffy Lube International is the nation's largest fast lube service franchise, with more than 2,000 centers in 49 states. Click the link below for special offers from Jiffy Lube.
http://ownership.carpoint.msn.com/ownership/qlube.asp

Source: Personal correspondence with MSN CarPoint.

Online Communications and Business Activity

Communication is central to the existence of an exchange relationship. There must, of course, be resources for which exchange is desirable, and a means of carrying out the exchange, such as a channel. Communication is necessary, however, to determine the availability of an item for exchange, and the extent to which it meets needs. As a means for communication between agents in exchange relationships, the Internet may influence all aspects of business activity.

Communication and Product Development

By the beginning of the 20th century, the development of technologies that spurred the Industrial Revolution had resulted in the mass production of goods for consumption. Cottage industries and one-of-a-kind production gave way to the efficiency and quality consistency of assembly line production in large factories. Advances in communications technology, and the diffusion of radio, telephone, and television, created mass markets for standardized products.

By the end of the 20th century, technological advances had once again changed the face of production and influenced the nature of consumer demand. Leveraging the communications capabilities of the Internet, businesses can meet the demand of mass markets through mass customization. **Mass customization** is the ability to provide a product that is differentiated from other forms of the same product that are produced by the same company. The Internet enables businesses to assess customers' needs for particular features of a product, and to develop product forms that reflect these needs.

Mass customization with the Internet is aided by two factors: (1) receiver-content interactivity, and (2) product modularization. Receiver-content interactivity enables a business to develop online menus of product features from which a customer can specify a product configuration. This capability automates the product design process. Product modularization is necessary to create menus of product features. **Modularization** is the ability to separate a product into sets of features that can be flexibly rearranged to create different product forms.

Customization and Personalization

Customization is not the same as personalization. A customized offering may be developed for an individual customer, but the demand for the customized form of the product is not necessarily unique to that customer. For instance, a custom built Rolls-Royce may be produced for a customer, but it *is* possible that there could be other people who might have a similar level of interest in owning the identical vehicle. Another distinguishing characteristic of customization is the nature of the process used to create the customized product. In many instances, a customized product is the result of a customer's selection of desired product features and their configuration from a bounded set. This set of possibilities is made available to other possible customers, and it is expected that multiple, identical versions of the product will be produced.

Source: (left panel) Copyright ChildImageDolls.com, 2004. All rights reserved. (right panel) Copyright The Lifelike Company, Inc., 2003. All rights reserved.

Customization and personalization can be described as relative locations on a continuum of uniqueness. As is illustrated in Figure 12-9, mass production anchors one end of the continuum: a single product form is produced for everyone in the market. Personalization is at the other end of the continuum; in its extreme instantiation, a personalized product is matched to a single customer. For instance, a Barbie doll is an example of a mass-produced product, while a My Twinn doll reflects the other end of the continuum. A doll produced by putting selected levels of different modules together reflects customization.

FIGURE 12-9 Products Occupy a Continuum of Feature-to-User Uniqueness.

Mass production	**Customization**	**Personalization**
One product form, n users		n customers, n product forms
	Charateristic Interactivity	
Low source-receiver interactivity	⟶	High source-receiver interactivity
	Characteristic Process	
Develop feature profile for target market, Optimize feature set interactivity	⟶ Develop sets of features and feature levels	Develop features and levels based on individually measured preferences

How the Product Is Built: Interactivity and Processes of Customization

At a fundamental level, customizing a product depends on communication; businesses have to know what customers want. The exchange of information via the Internet facilitates customization. This exchange can differ in terms of the nature of the interaction between the seller and the buyer; that is, whether the interaction is a direct communication between source and receiver, or an indirect one, between the receiver and the site content. For instance, customization may result from a direct interaction with a consumer about the desired form of a product. Visitors to the Dell Computer site are active participants in the process of designing the configuration of their computers (Figure 12-10). This situation reflects source-receiver interactivity used for **collaborative customization**, because the source, Dell, participates in the creation of the final product.

In contrast, a product can be customized based on the customer's interaction with Web site content without active participation by the source at any point in the creation of the end-product. This interaction can take two forms. In one form, the customer selects content options to specify the customization. For example, users can select subsets of preferred radio channels from the set of 3,200+ options provided by RealPlayer, an online audio media player, to meet individual interests. This is a pull form of indirect communication that results in **adaptive customization**. In a second form of interaction, customization is based on information provided by the customer, as through a cookie, but without any direct communication between seller and buyer—and without awareness on the part of the buyer. The result of this process is

FIGURE 12-10 Customers Create Customized Computing Products at Dell's Web Site.

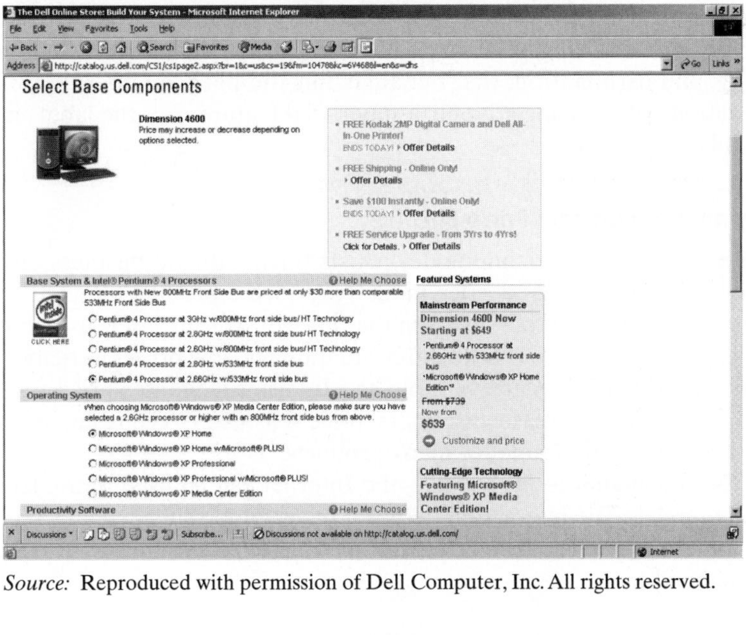

Source: Reproduced with permission of Dell Computer, Inc. All rights reserved.

called **transparent customization**. For example, an online news service might track a user's previous site behavior to selectively push information that matches categories or topics previously viewed.

How Customized Is Customized? Interactivity and Forms of Customization

Interactivity can result in different forms of customization. These forms are described with two dimensions: (1) the extent of product change, and (2) customer awareness of the change.

For the first dimension, product customization can be as simple as a cosmetic change to the way a product is represented. For instance, a business can collect user information by asking site visitors to register. Communication back to the user can then be customized by including the user's name on an otherwise standard offering. After registering with Travelocity's online reservation service, users are greeted with a personal welcome, even though the basic form of the product, as online content, is undifferentiated. This process reflects cosmetic customization. Alternatively, customization can be as complex as a change to the nature and function of attributes that constitute the product, as by building a custom computer.

The second dimension that characterizes customization is the extent to which the shopper is aware of the customization. For example, ad servers target ads to users based on information gathered from the users' past site behaviors. This is a form of passive communication that results from receiver-content interactivity. Active collaboration based on source-receiver interactivity can result in a dramatic reconfiguration of the base, or standard, product. When the nature and configuration of product features is developed solely on the basis of a customer's preferences, and is not limited by the set of features and possible levels, the product is personalized.

It can be difficult to categorize some products as forms of customization. Jones Soda, for instance, lets customers create their own labels, including pictures and copy, for bottles of soda (Figure 12-11). The actual product features, including sweetness, flavoring, and carbonation, don't change, but the package does. Is this cosmetic customization, with a change to only a superficial feature, or is the label an integral part of the soda experience?

Communication and Price Strategy

A range of possible pricing models exists for the digital business environment. One option is to follow a fixed-price model, in which a product targeted to a specific segment has one price for all buyers in that market. This model is useful for products and services for which there is little differentiation and low price elasticity. For product categories in which prices are variable, the Internet facilitates price transparency. Price transparency may increase customers' price sensitivity. As a result, a fixed-price model may become less desirable for many products.

As a communication resource, the Internet can be used to implement alternative pricing models. The interaction between buyers and sellers creates an opportunity for real-time, or dynamic pricing. **Dynamic pricing** reflects variations in prices due to supply and demand.

FIGURE 12-11   Web-enabled Customization Can Enhance the Consumption Experience.

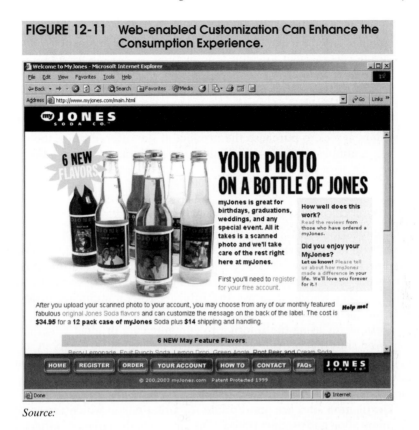

Source:

Dynamic pricing models are often implemented online with infomediaries. For example, online auctions are a form of dynamic pricing that reflects forces of supply and demand. Online auctions rely on Internet-based communication between buyers and sellers to set prices. In general, auctions tend to be effective for products that depreciate rapidly, or that have a finite expiration date. These are products for which there is a limited window of sales opportunity; companies have to get rid of them, and customers have to want them. Otherwise, customers could simply wait for a bargain. Auctions also tend to be more effective for unique items than for readily acquired commodities, and in fragmented markets. A **fragmented market** is a market in which product availability and characteristics are difficult to compare across a range of options.

Another form of dynamic pricing is practiced by intermediary companies that establish price. For example, Priceline collects customer requests and schedule constraints for airline reservations (Figure 12-13). Then they attempt to buy the ticket from an airline, for a set amount less (e.g., $10) than the amount stated by the consumer. If an airline accepts Priceline's offer, Priceline buys the ticket and resells it to the consumer. By communicating schedule and price preferences to Priceline, customers often get tickets at lower prices than through traditional channels. For the airline, the benefits include the ability to sell more tickets, while maintaining their usual retail pricing structures. Because Priceline acts as the intermediary and negotiates directly with a set of airlines whose anonymity is protected, the airlines avoid alienating customers who purchase tickets directly from the airline at higher prices than ticket holders who purchase cheaper tickets through Priceline. The method for pricing used by Priceline is called **buyer-driven commerce**.

A British-based company, LetsBuyIt.com employs a different form of buyer-driven commerce. The company uses group buying to obtain manufacturer discounts. A product is offered for a limited time, at a starting price. When a specified number of customers agrees to purchase the product at the offered price, the price drops. The process continues until the time limit expires. All buyers receive the product for the most recent, lowest price.

Communication and Distribution Strategy

Communication enabled by the interactive nature of the Internet provides businesses with new options for deciding where to market their products. As we saw in Chapter 11, the Internet can be used as a point of distribution. Whether a virtual store is the best strategy for a company may depend on the company's understanding of its product, and how to use the Internet to communicate product benefits to potential customers.

Options for using the Internet to communicate product benefits run the gamut from Web sites that provide comprehensive communications about all aspects of the product and its consumption to simple banner advertising. Three approaches illustrate the decisions a business must make: destination sites, microsites, and Internet promotion strategy.

Destination sites are appropriate for situations in which aspects of commercial communication and product transaction can be conducted more efficiently online than off-line. Creating an effective destination site entails the use of Internet-based communications to provide an engaging and entertaining experience that guides the user through all aspects of the buying decision, including postpurchase and repeat visits. Dell.com is an example of a destination site; it provides product information to visitors, guides them through the product design process, allows them to complete the transaction, arrange and track product delivery, and receive customer support. In essence, all aspects of the transaction are available on a single site, hosted by the company.

Microsites are collections of information about a company's brands that are hosted by content sites or networks. In essence, a microsite is a small virtual store that depends on traffic to its host site for product exposure. Microsites enable the business to communicate detailed, focused information to customers, without the expense of maintaining a destination site. In addition, microsites can capitalize on the visibility of the host site. Microsites tend to be effective for products characterized by higher degrees of consideration and lower efficiency of online channels (e.g., home appliances, furniture). Examples of microsites include eBay Stores, used by eBay sellers to list their auction and fixed-price items under a unique URL. This practice helps the seller by using the eBay brand name to attract store visitors, and it benefits eBay by making it desirable for sellers to list large number of items for sale on its site.

If neither a destination site nor a microsite is appropriate, a third option is to use the communications capabilities of the Internet to implement cost-effective aspects of a promotion strategy. For instance, a company can choose to use interactive banners to build brand awareness, sponsor product-related content to enhance brand image, or build a corporate site to foster public relations. We will consider these possibilities in greater detail as aspects of promotion.

Communication and Promotion Strategy

Many of the forms of commercial communications for the Internet that tend to come quickly to mind are those that mirror promotion activities in traditional media, like advertising on television and in magazines. These forms have tended to appear on the Web, given the existence of graphics support and communications standards. It is important to remember, however, that other forms of communication, such as direct mailing to targeted lists of Internet users, can also be very effective methods of promoting a product or service online. In this section we will consider applications of the Internet as a communications resource for promotion strategy that include advertising, sales promotions, publicity, and personal selling.

Advertising as Commercial Communication

The Internet makes possible two main types of advertising: e-mail-based and Web-based. While text-based, e-mail advertising can be conducted throughout the Internet, multimedia advertising is found primarily on the Web, which facilitates transmission of graphics and other media forms (e.g., animation, streaming audio and video). With the development of new, rich media technologies, however, e-mail is becoming an increasingly important, and engaging, form of promotion.

The Internet and E-mail Advertising   Text-based forms of advertising are often used by businesses with an advertising goal of eliciting a direct response. **Direct response** refers to the goal of getting a customer to carry out a behavior that is related to an end goal of product purchase. For example, requesting further information after receiving an e-mail notification of a product, or actually purchasing the product are forms of direct responses. E-mail advertising can be conducted by buying or renting distribution lists of e-mail addresses. As with traditional forms of direct mail, lists vary in expense and quality.

E-mail works. A Bizrate (2000) survey found that television ads accounted for only 6 percent of online purchases, while commercial e-mail accounted for 13 percent. In another study, NFO Interactive (2000) surveyed 1,000 users and found that 89 percent believe that e-mail is a good way to get product information. E-mail can also be an effective form of viral marketing, from consumer to consumer (Figure 12.12). To avoid unsolicited, commercial e-mail overload, customers prefer to receive permission-based e-mail. **Permission-based**, or **opt-in e-mail**, allows shoppers to decide whether or not they wish to receive additional e-mail from a particular company.

Permission-based e-mail is not only preferred by consumers, but it's also effective for influencing purchase intent. Market research conducted in 2002 by DoubleClick, an online advertising broker, found that 78 percent of the 1,000 online customers they surveyed had made a purchase after opening a permission-based solicitation. E-mail promotions, such as coupons and promotion codes are also effective for stimulating purchases.

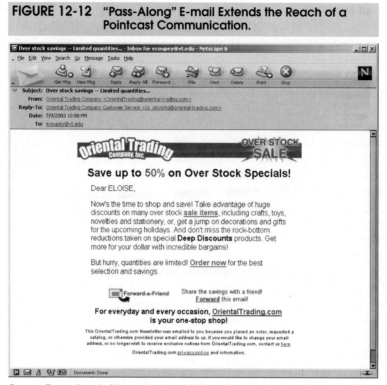

FIGURE 12-12 "Pass-Along" E-mail Extends the Reach of a Pointcast Communication.

Two cautions should be noted about e-mail advertising. Both suggest that estimates of e-mail's influence on purchase behavior may tend to be pessimistically low. First, shoppers may become aware of purchase opportunities through e-mail, but make the purchase at an off-line channel. Therefore, it is important to develop cross-channel tracking, in order to adequately assess the impact of an e-mail promotion. Second, e-mail is easily forwarded to others, potentially reaching a larger number of potential customers than the original target market. Being able to track the viral marketing spread of e-mail can identify new sales leads and new markets.

Given the potential influence of permission-based e-mail on aspects of buyer behavior, it's not surprising that more and more businesses are turning to e-mail as a key component in sales and marketing campaigns. In a 2002 study conducted by e-Dialog, Inc., researchers found increased spending for e-mail promotions from 2001 to 2002. The chart in (Figure 12-13) shows the increasing prominence of e-mail in business activity.

The Web and Multimedia Advertising: Banners, Buttons, and Beyond The World Wide Web has facilitated the development of several forms of multimedia advertising. Most popular among these forms are banner ads and buttons. Other forms of advertising are increasing in frequency, including daughter windows and interstitials, or online commercials. As with traditional media, the success of banner advertising depends heavily on the extent to which the environment in which the ad

FIGURE 12-13   Changes in Promotional Spending from 2001 to 2002.

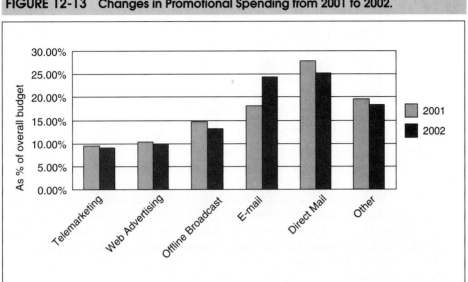

Source: e-Dialog, Inc., April 2002, as reported by eMarketer.

is placed will be viewed, as well as on the ad content. Reflecting this reality, many advertisers have tended to place their banner ads on a relatively small number of Web sites.

Early banner ads were simple in design and performance, intended to increase brand awareness and to get users to click through to the vendor's site. Newer generations of banner ads incorporate animation to capture attention. Many banners also make use of interactive technology to provide pull-down menus within a banner. Some banners allow the user to complete a transaction solely within the banner. These banners reduce frustration caused when a user clicks through a banner and then cannot return to the site that hosted the banner.

Daughter ads and interstitials are newer versions of online advertising. **Daughter windows** are small windows that appear in the corner of a screen view. Their existence depends on the presence of the larger, parent window. The main window spawns the daughter window. For instance, when opening a browser, a daughter window may appear to inform the user about a new version of the browser software that is available. Daughter windows are also known as **pop-ups** and **pop-unders**, depending on whether the new, smaller window opens over the current browser page, or behind it.

Interstitials are virtual clones of television ads. They can be programmed to appear in the time that elapses while a file is loading. Interstitials have benefits and drawbacks. Because of their full-screen size and sophisticated multimedia presentation, they are attention-getting. These same characteristics, of course, may irritate users for whom computing capacity limits the speed needed to execute the high bandwidth advertising. In addition, interstitials cannot be ignored in favor of other parts of the screen view, because they *are* the view. As a result, they may be perceived as an unwelcome intrusion into a medium over which the user typically exercises viewing control.

Animation can be used to attract and hold attention in banners, daughter windows, and interstitials. Another use of animation is to create figures that can move around a screen view. These ads, called **Shoshkeles**, are produced by United Virtualities, a company that provides the animated advertisers with the ability to speak, thus making them very attention-getting. In addition, Shoshkeles do not disappear as a screen is scrolled, as do banner ads. Shoskeles have an added advantage in that they do not slow the perceived page download time for the viewer.

Understanding Online Advertising Costs   Online advertising costs vary with the size and position of the banner or button, and with the quality of the site. Sites that can provide greater exposure, and sites that can provide highly targeted audiences tend to command high prices, as with traditional media. Pricing models for online advertising also vary. The models reflect assumptions about the effectiveness of the form of advertising (Figure 12-14). Some of the more common models include pricing by **cost-per-thousand exposures (CPM)**, **cost per click-through**, and **flat-fee pricing**.

A CPM model is based on assumptions about the ability of a banner to achieve brand awareness and brand building through exposure. This approach resembles ad pricing in traditional media. In a click-through model, the publisher is responsible for viewer response. Because revenue is based on behavior (i.e., clicking through to the vendor's site), click-through models may reflect higher levels of viewer involvement. The click-through model differs from traditional ad models that separate the ad content responsibility from the ad availability responsibility. Of course, the ultimate measure of click-through activity is the transaction.

Flat fee models are typically used in two very different situations. They are popular for sites where there is no history of visitor activity on which to base pricing: often for new sites or content. The other situation in which flat fees are popular is for highly desirable sites, such as search engines with high traffic, although there are still no visitor traffic guarantees.

Expectations about advertising performance often lead businesses to develop hybrid strategies that integrate two or more forms of online advertising. As you can

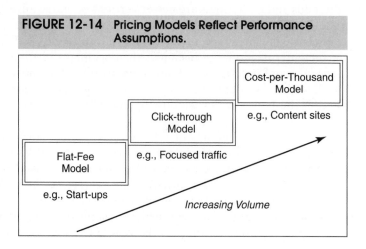

FIGURE 12-14   Pricing Models Reflect Performance Assumptions.

Cost-per-Thousand Model

e.g., Content sites

Click-through Model

e.g., Focused traffic

Flat-Fee Model

e.g., Start-ups

Increasing Volume

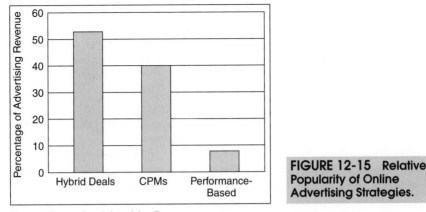

FIGURE 12-15 Relative Popularity of Online Advertising Strategies.

Source: Interactive Advertising Bureau.

see from the percentages in Figure 12-15, performance-based advertising, such as click-through ads, accounts for a relatively low portion of advertising revenue. Two related concerns with click-through advertising are (1) its low impact on brand enhancement, and (2) difficulty in assessing the value of a click-through. In the earlier-cited study commissioned by the Internet Advertising Bureau (IAB), banner exposure accounted for 96 percent of brand enhancement, compared with only 4 percent enhancement attributed to click-through. Click-through was originally envisioned as an online analog to the direct mail response of opening a letter. Companies, however, are less interested in the behavior of opening an envelope or clicking on a banner than they are with whether the behavior results in a sale. Click-through rates, therefore, tend to be an incomplete measure of advertising effectiveness.

One way to assess the value of an online advertising strategy is to calculate the expected return on advertising investment. When compared with the actual return, the resulting difference provides information about whether advertising goals were met. A formula for calculating return on investment is

Number of impressions purchased × average click-through rate × average customer turnover (visitors to customers) × average net profit/sale = expected return

For example, suppose that you purchase 100,000 impressions, and you make an average profit on your digital widget of $2.00. With statistical averages of 4% for click-through and 5% customer turnover, your formula is now

$$100,000 \times .04 \times 05 \times \$2 = \$400$$

This means that the online advertising is responsible for $400 in new sales. To evaluate the merits of your approach, you would need to compare the cost of the campaign with the $400 result. For example, if you paid $30 for each 1,000 impressions, your cost was $3,000. Unless you have reason to believe that turnover or click-through rates will improve over time, this seems like an unwise investment! If you can get one of every two visitors to purchase, the return increases to $4,000.

> **Bits and Bytes 12-3**
> Internet advertising is big business. In its annual advertising revenue report for 2002, the Interactive Advertising Bureau (IAB) reported that revenues for online ads topped $5.95 billion dollars.
> (*Source:* www.iab.net.)

Online Sales Promotions   Sales promotions are short-term incentives to induce purchase. Sales promotions on the Internet share similarities with sales promotions in traditional commercial media, both in the types of promotions that can be implemented, and in the manner in which they can be implemented. For example, coupons and rebates, as well as games and sweepstakes, are used by online merchants for the same purposes as they are used by off-line merchants: to create interest and enthusiasm for a product, and to promote product trial. The promotion serves as an incentive to carry out a specific activity related to the company's objective in offering the promotion. For example, a customer who completes an online survey about her perceptions and attitude toward a brand is entered in a sweepstake where the winning player receives the brand—free. The business receives information about the customer's evaluation of product features and creates product trial through the sweepstakes prize giveaway. All aspects of the promotion, including prize delivery of the prize, can be digitized and be administered through the Internet.

The short-run effects of promotion activity can be interpreted in terms of their effect on behavior. That is, people participate in promotions to receive the relatively immediate benefits of the participation, such as the coupon, the excitement of competing in a contest, or the chance of winning the prize in a sweepstake. Businesses can use online promotion tactics to influence the early stages of a relationship. That is, a promotion, such as an online contest or a coupon, can create interaction between a buyer and a seller.

The challenge for an Internet-based promotion resembles that for a traditional promotion—to make the customer aware of the link between the promotion and the product, in order to create long-term effects of the promotion. One tactic for online businesses is to combine different forms of commercial communications to increase brand exposure and to build brand recognition. For example, businesses can encourage viewer interaction by drawing users to ads with incentives, thus combining sales promotions and advertising. This combined approach has a dual goal of capturing attention and generating interaction (e.g., content traded for viewing ads, money for surveys, and so on).

Public Relations and Publicity   One goal of promotion is to create positive public relations. **Public relations** reflect corporate image, or the way a company represents its objectives and characteristics to internal and external stakeholders. Public relations are important for organizations with a primary online presence, due to market concerns with the intangibility and viability of digital products and their benefits.

Publicity is a form of promotion used to influence public relations. Publicity refers to information about the products or services produced by the organization, but that does not typically come directly from the organization. Good public relations are linked to publicity; a company with a favorable corporate image is more likely to garner positive publicity than a company with poor public relations.

The Internet can be used to carry out traditional approaches to publicity, such as sending product release information to editors, writers, and publishers via the Internet. Businesses can use the Internet to facilitate the processes for publicity. For instance, the Internet can be used to create a database of publicity targets, and to distribute information through discussion groups and mailing lists. In addition to a push approach to publicity, the Internet provides a means to provide publicity-related information on demand. This form of pull communication can result from the direct interaction of inquiring media with the company, or from the indirect interaction with a company's Web site content. Promotional events can also generate publicity (e.g., online concerts and charity auctions).

The opportunity for content-receiver interactivity with the Internet reflects a technology-enabled form of public relations that is unique to the medium. The ability to provide searchable content for publicity purposes may enable businesses to bypass traditional public relations intermediaries. Content can be frequently updated, and organized to address different public relations interests. For example, a site might include pages for community relations, new product releases, and previous publicity. This type of content structure can shift the emphasis on promotional activity for public relations from an active approach to a passive approach on the part of the company.

Personal Selling   Advertising, promotion, and publicity can all be effectively implemented in electronic environments. Personal selling is more difficult. The essence of a personal selling interaction is the personal contact, typically embodied in the set of cues exchanged in a face-to-face communication. Although the Internet enables real-time interactivity between active agents in the exchange, it does so through the computer-mediated environment. The presence of the electronic mediator that makes the exchange environment possible is also what makes the personal exchange encounter not possible. At a fundamental level, computer mediation means that the exchange environment is definitionally impersonal.

Definitionally impersonal does not, however, completely preclude the possibility of using the Internet for selling efforts that emulate face-to-face encounters. Technological capabilities make it possible for customers to interact with digital representations of salespeople. That is, you can see them, hear them, and talk with them, just as if they were in the same room. Of course, other sensory experiences are limited by the digital medium, including touch, taste, and smell. These limitations seem less a drawback for sales encounters, however, than for product encounters. Smelling and tasting salespeople would seem to account for an infinitesimally small percentage of face-to-face sales encounter activity.

While the Internet does not enable full implementation of personal selling online, it does, however, serve as a useful tool for facilitating personal selling off-line. For example, a salesperson can use the Internet to amass a database of contact information in order to generate lists of prospects that are characterized by desired qualifications (e.g., past histories of purchase characteristics). In addition, decision support tools that operate via the Internet can be used for personal selling by scripting sequences of activities that, if carried out in a proscribed manner, increase the likelihood of a sale. To augment information provided in a face-to-face encounter, content-laden Web sites can be used to present product descriptions or usage information. These and other uses of the Internet's communication capabilities can augment the credibility of a salesperson in a personal sales exchange.

Bits and Bytes 12.4

To boost the personality quotient of their Web sites, some companies have turned to **bots**, brand-related characters who carry on pre-scripted conversations with site visitors. For instance, an Austin Powers bot was used to promote the movie, *Goldmember,* online. Said the International Bot of Mystery, "I was built by the Ministry of Defense to serve, protect, and put the grrr in swinger, baby! Yeah!" (*Source:* Forbes.com, 7/26/02, and www.austinpowers.com.)

Issues for Digital Business Communications

The ideas of communications and interactivity are tightly linked. With the Internet, the way in which interactivity enables communications can create unique challenges for each of the four key perspectives. To make effective use of the Internet as a communications resource, businesses must be able to recognize and understand the situations in which these issues may arise.

Businesses and Commercial Communication

Communications may influence what people think and feel, as well as what they do. Businesses must develop ways to track and evaluate these different influences of online communications. For instance, a banner ad may increase brand awareness, even though people who see the ad do not click through to the vendor's site. In contrast, a button that provides downloadable software, such as the plug-in necessary to view a file, may result in a behavior (i.e., download the product), but without an effect on brand awareness (e.g., improve attitude toward the brand).

These examples illustrate the need for performance measures for online communications that reflect the different objectives and outcomes of the communication effort. Measures of online activity can be obtained from information that is automatically tracked and recorded by software programs. This information can be customer-centric, such as data obtained from a cookie file, or server-centric, as with log files of site activity. To assess psychological dimensions of communication effects, however, businesses may need to design and implement primary research programs that require active, aware communication between the company and the customer.

Customers and Commercial Communication

With the Internet, and more specifically, the World Wide Web, businesses can combine the modalities of television, print, and radio into a single presentation of video, text, and sound. This combination of modalities may influence shoppers' information search, choice, and memory. For example, if shoppers are typically exposed

InSite

SETTING THE STANDARD: WWW.IAB.NET

A key difficulty for many businesses that want to know whether their online ad budgets were well spent is trying to determine what to measure, and, once measured, what the results mean. Many of the terms used to describe advertising effectiveness are defined differently by the businesses and the advertisers who use them. In addition, the lack of standards for different forms of online ads, such as banners, can create confusion for businesses that attempt to develop a single type of rich media advertisement for display by several different advertising sites.

The Interactive Advertising Bureau (IAB) wants to help. The organization has worked toward the development of standards across several areas of online advertising, including terminology, measurement and reporting practices, and rich media advertising formats.

In April 2003, the IAB announced its interactive Universal Ad Package (UAP). The UAP was developed as the result of survey research on the ad size practices and preferences of advertising agencies, Web content publishers, and online advertisers. The goal of the UAP is to provide guidelines for the development of rich media ad content that make it easier for advertisers to design creative content, and to find publishers who will present the content in the desired format. By adhering to the UAP guidelines, Web publishers can assure online advertisers that the UAP-compliant ads they place on the publishers' sites will reach a majority of the sites' audiences.

The UAP consists of four standard units: a banner of 728×90 pixels, a skyscraper of 160×600 pixels, a medium-sized block of 300×250 pixels, and a small block of 180×150 pixels. The IAB guidelines also include recommendations for the size of the files used to create the ad, a measure that can reduce lengthy download times for viewers, and a 15-second time limit for animation used in the ad units.

to advertisements in a print media (e.g., some prescription drugs), then use of an interactive medium that combines video and print components may cause retroactive interference for cognitive processes that involve memory. **Retroactive interference** occurs when newly presented information reduces a person's ability to retrieve previously stored information. The potential for interference increases when the new information is similar on some dimensions (e.g., the brand information), but is dissimilar on others (e.g., the modality). Interference may reduce the quality of consumers' decisions about—and memory for—the information contained in the advertisement.

On the Internet, customers can exercise greater amounts of control over the variety and amount of commercial communications that they view. The "pull" nature of the environment also means that customers can determine, in varying degrees, the form and content of the communication. For instance, shoppers can specify desired characteristics of a product as the basis for information that will be included in the constructed display (e.g., products under a cut-off price). In addition, shoppers can acquire information about products and services from multiple sources and restructure the information to facilitate decision making. Each of these differences may affect how much and what type of information customers acquire, the strategies with which they integrate the information to make a choice, and the amount and structure of information they can store in memory for subsequent purchases.

With many sources of information available on the Internet, it is possible for shoppers to be exposed to brand or product-level information from sources with a perspective on the brand or product that conflicts with the company's message. Such situations include dissatisfied customers who post to message boards, or customers or product reviewers who miscomprehend or miscommunicate the benefits of a product. Because these sources of information and communication can result in the formation of negative attitudes toward a brand or company, the Internet increases the importance for businesses of monitoring and managing negative sources of information.

Policy Makers and Commercial Communication

Two characteristics of the Internet as a communications resource raise issues for policy makers. One characteristic is the ease with which consumers can become targets of commercial communications. Another is the global reach of the Internet as a communications medium.

User Control and Spam

As we have seen, commercial communications on the Internet are characterized by greater amounts of user control than are communications on traditional media. One outgrowth of this characteristic is a resistance to unwanted information that is "pushed" to the customer. A key offender in this area is **spam**, or unsolicited commercial e-mail (Figure 12-16). The practice of sending large amounts of unsolicited e-mails

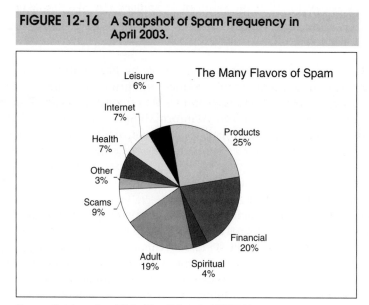

FIGURE 12-16   A Snapshot of Spam Frequency in April 2003.

The Many Flavors of Spam

Leisure 6%
Internet 7%
Health 7%
Other 3%
Scams 9%
Adult 19%
Spiritual 4%
Financial 20%
Products 25%

Source: Brightmail, published by *Cyberatlas,* 5/5/2003.

is known as **spamming**. Spam is a common occurrence. Similar to the complaints of fax-based junk mail recipients, spam recipients claim that spam uses up computer processing capacity and wastes human time. The annoyance expressed by spam recipients is often due to the low relevance of the unsolicited e-mail to the user, and to the spread of computer viruses and unwanted pornographic material that may be opened by the unwary recipient.

Lack of relevance reflects an additional concern: that of how the e-mail addresses are collected. **E-mail harvesting** is the process by which e-mail addresses are gathered from newsgroups and bulletin boards by programs designed to scavenge the Internet and record e-mail addresses. These automated scavengers sift through sites and return e-mail information, often with few restrictions on source content. As a result, the correlation between user needs and interests and spam based on the use of mailing lists created with harvested addresses is unsurprisingly low. Businesses should evaluate the ability of a mailing list to provide qualified, relevant leads. They should also be aware of the negative effects on brand image that may result from a spam-based introduction.

Policy makers determine what types of commercial communications are permissible on the Internet. To illustrate the challenges faced by policy makers, consider the question of whether e-mail should be subject to the regulations that govern regular mail, or to those that govern fax machine communications? It is illegal to send unsolicited commercial communications to fax machines, under the Telephone Consumer Protection Act of 1991. The legislation was enacted because the recipient incurs a cost to receive a fax (i.e., paper, ink, and fax machine time). Unsolicited marketing mailings are not illegal via the postal service, however. Junk mail is a nuisance—not a crime.

Federal regulation[2] states that computer-based communications equipment is similar to a telephone fax machine, making it illegal to send unsolicited advertising to an Internet address. Each violation is punishable thorough action to recover the actual amount of money lost, or $500, whichever is larger.

Bits and Bytes 12.5

In mid-2003, experts estimated that nearly one-half of all e-mail is spam. This figure represents a 43% growth from 2001.

(*Source:* Enrique Salem, of Brightmail, as quoted in CNN.com, 5/22/03.)

Local Legislation and Global Reach

A variety of techniques can be used to persuade shoppers to buy a product. These commercial offers can be communicated via the Internet to a global set of targeted users. The potential for global reach of online promotional offers is a concern for policy makers, particularly when national restrictions on the form of commercial offers differ. For instance, contests are often used to provoke customer interest in a product. In the United States, legislation prohibits contests that take the form of a lottery. In other countries, however, legislation is less restrictive.

One issue for policy makers is that of how to protect consumers from exposure to the potentially negative effects of a commercial offer that is communicated from a source in a less restricted location. A second issue is that of how to prevent advertisers from shifting bases for developing offers and promotion attempts from a more restrictive locale to a less restrictive locale.

Technology Developers and Commercial Communication

The desirability of products often depends on their ability to be meaningfully differentiated from other, related products. Personalization is one way to effect meaningful differentiation on an individual level. Effective approaches to personalization can be very effort-intensive. For instance, personalization requires an often detailed and complex understanding of a customer's preferences and values. The nature and scope of knowledge that must be elicited, stored, and incorporated into personalized product design and production presents a challenge for technology developers.

Technological approaches exist to facilitate some forms of product customization. For example, **rule-based systems** are used to track user behavior and present products and information that best match inferences based on behavior patterns. Another approach to online customization is to involve the customer more directly in the customization process by allowing the customer to specify preferred features, a process of **customer-assisted customization**.

Each of these methods has drawbacks. Because they operate on relatively rudimentary bases of information, rule-based systems may result in incorrect inferences about preferences for product form. Customer-assisted approaches may fall short of effective differentiation when the set of customization options does not reflect the range or specificity of customer preferences. Moving from customization to true personalization will require technology to advance to a point at which processes for assessing individual customer needs and preferences can be measured, interpreted, implemented, and stored for efficient product development and delivery.

CHAPTER SUMMARY

In Chapters 10 and 11, we considered the Internet as a content resource and as a channel resource. In this chapter, we looked at ways that businesses can piggyback on content and channel capabilities, building on different types of interactivity to facilitate commercial communication.

To set the stage for an examination of Internet interactivity as communication, we reviewed a basic model of communication. This model included a source who encodes a message and embeds it within a modality (e.g., textual, graphical) and a vehicle (e.g., ad, press release), and transmits it via a medium (e.g., television, Internet) to a receiver, who decodes the message.

Using this basic communication model, we considered characteristics of the Internet that differentiate it from traditional media for delivering content, including many-to-many communications, real-time interactivity, and user control over the content and form (e.g., modality and organization) of the message. These characteristics underscore the need for businesses to recognize the importance of the interactions that may occur between the processes used to encode a communication, and the processes used to decode a communication.

'Net Knowledge

TWEENSPEAK—TECHNOLOGY INFLUENCES COMMUNICATION

The Internet not only influences our ability to communicate, but also the way in which we communicate. Of course, we're all familiar with the Internet's ability to facilitate near real-time, digital conversations, even across vast geographic distances. For some digital consumers, however, the Internet has altered even the basic elements of communications, including the symbols and the syntax that guide our ability to understand one another.

This phenomenon is most prevalent among the younger set of online consumers, consisting of children from 8 to 12 years old, who have grown up in a digital world. This group, called Tweens, are comfortable with instant messaging (IM) services on the Internet, and with **short messaging services (SMSs)** that send text through cell phones. The constraints of tweens' typing ability and limited patience, combined with characteristics of the messaging technologies, have resulted in abbreviations, terms, and communication conventions that have been widely accepted among the peer group. Consider the following IM exchange between Jill and Joan—in different locations, cobrowsing for clothes on a Web site. Looking at a pair of jeans, Jill asks, "IS IT ME?" Joan responds, "2 QT 4 U! 4 ME '-)" Is Jill offended? No, she knows that the winking emoticon means that Joan is just kidding.

Why do tweens and their communications matter? Very simply, because they have a lot of influence on what others buy. Research conducted by Millward Brown,[1] a research institute, found that 90 percent of tweens' brand choices are influenced by other tweens, and that 67 percent of their parents' automobile decisions take tween preferences into account. Businesses need to understand how to talk to the target segment in a way that it will understand, and to which it will respond favorably.

[1]As reported by Martin Lindstrom on www.clickz.com, on 3/25/03 and 4/1/03.

Within the computer-mediated environment, we considered two different processes of interactivity. First, we looked at the interaction between the source and the receiver. Types of source-receiver interactivity were characterized on a dimension that reflects the size of the target audience: from broadcast to pointcast. Second, we examined the influence of receiver-content interactivity on push and pulls forms of communication.

The Internet's ability to facilitate interactive communications enables businesses to tailor product forms to meet customers' needs. We considered the role of interactivity for product personalization and customization. Personalization results from the unique match of customer needs to feature configuration. In contrast, customization matches needs to feature configuration, but the configuration is based on a constrained set of options, and assumptions about uniqueness are relaxed.

Interactive communications influence business activity. Opportunities for customization and personalization affect product strategy. Dynamic pricing strategies result from the widespread interaction between buyers and sellers. Decisions about the Internet as a distribution channel are affected by the nature of anticipated information exchanges. Finally, the Internet's communication capabilities influence the costs and benefits associated with different forms of promotional strategy. For instance, banner ads, the most popular form of online advertising, exert a stronger influence on brand-related perceptions than on purchase-related behaviors. Online sales promotions and public relations can be used to establish a customer–product relationship.

Challenges for integrating the Internet into business activity as a communications resource were considered for each of the four main perspectives on digital business. For companies, these challenges include measuring communication effectiveness, and integrating online and off-line forms of commercial communications. Customers must manage issues associated with the effects of the online medium for communication on decoding processes. Global reach and the ready availability of an audience who can be reached with unsolicited commercial communications create headaches for policy makers. As the group largely responsible for creating the environment that facilitates interactive communications, technology developers must grapple with the ever-present need to develop technology that advances present capabilities. A key concern is the desire for applications capable of remembering users' previously expressed preferences for customization, and predicting future preferences.

CONTENT MANAGEMENT

USEFUL TERMS

- adaptive customization
- bots
- broadcast communication
- buyer-driven commerce
- collaborative customization
- cost per click-through
- cost-per-thousand exposures (CPM)
- customer-assisted customization
- daughter windows
- decoding
- destination sites
- direct response
- dynamic pricing
- e-mail harvesting
- encoding
- flat-fee pricing
- fragmented market
- interstitials
- mass customization
- microsites
- modality
- modularization
- narrowcast communication
- opt-in e-mail
- permission-based e-mail
- personalization
- pointcast communication
- pop-unders
- pop-ups
- public relations
- publicity
- pull communications
- push communications
- receiver
- retroactive interference
- rule-based systems
- short-messaging services (SMS)
- Shoshkeles
- source
- spam
- spamming
- transparent customization

REVIEW QUESTIONS

1. In what two main ways does the Internet differ from traditional media for commercial communication?
2. What benefits are provided by narrowcasting?
3. Distinguish between customization and personalization.
4. How is the Internet characterized by both "push" and "pull" communications?
5. What types of pricing strategies address supply and demand issues in the digital business environment?

6. What is the key focus for the IAB (Internet Advertising Bureau)?
7. What performance assumptions are implicit in each of the advertising pricing models discussed in this chapter?
8. Discuss the merits and demerits of click-through advertising.
9. If you purchase 50,000 impressions, assume 6 percent customer turnover, carefully estimate click-through at 3 percent, and make an average profit of $4.00 per sale, what is your expected return on investment (i.e., calculate)?
10. What form of promotion is used to influence public relations?
11. Why is retroactive interference a big concern for businesses that use the Internet as the context within which to transmit commercial communications?
12. What are two technological opportunities available to assist businesses with product customization?

WEB APPLICATION

At the Auction

Online auctions are a popular way to buy and sell many different items. There are different types of auctions sites, as well as different auction formats. In this exercise, you'll visit several auction sites to analyze the characteristics of an effective auction site. As you examine the sites, keep in mind that what makes an auction site appropriate for one type of product may not work equally well for other products.

1. Visit the following URL's. It may be helpful to pull up several browser windows, in order to compare site characteristics readily.
   eBay.com
   uBid.com
   OnSale.com
   Amazon.com(on the home page, scroll down to the heading, "Bargains," and select "Auctions" from the menu of options)
2. On each site, examine the set of items that are the result of a search for "lunchbox." How many items are available on each site? Next, scan through the sets of auctions. Which sites are more active? That is, which sites have bidders, as well as sellers?
3. To explain the differing numbers on each site, get an overview of the types and sizes of product categories auctioned in each site. Select the "Browse Categories" option, where available. Which sites appear to have a larger selection of products?
4. Auctions can be classified as person-to-person auctions or as commercial auctions. Person-to-person auctions generally mean that a seller is auctioning off a single item. Commercial auctions enable a seller, such as a retailer, to list large number of products from an inventory. Based on the browse category results, which of these sites appears to have a commercial focus?
5. To test your conclusion in 4, examine several listings in a product category that you think reflects a commercial auction (*hint:* "Computers" is generally a safe bet). Are there multiples of the same product?
6. Person-to-person and commercial auctions often offer different bidding processes. Most person-to-person auctions operate with a standard English auction format, in which bidders compete against each other, raising the price of the item until a winner is established, generally within a set time

frame. In commercial auctions, however, auction sites may support what is commonly called a Dutch auction process. In a Dutch auction, bidders state the number of items they want to buy, and the price they are willing to pay. Each successive bidder increases the total value of the bid, until the auction ends. Because there are multiple items for sale, there may be multiple winners. The winning bidders all pay the same amount, however, regardless of what they bid. The winning amount is the price of the lowest successful bid. If there are more winners than items, the winners who bid the higher amounts are more likely to receive the number they requested. Which of the auction sites supports a multiple item bidding process?

7. Developing trust online can be difficult, but it may also be critical to successfully selling products on an auction site. Look through the services of each auction site. How do the sites enable buyers and sellers to determine whether either side is trustworthy? How do the sites ensure that the information is credible?

8. As an online intermediary, some auction sites facilitate the financial transaction. What payment methods are supported by each site? What safeguards are provided?

Concepts in Brief

1. Changes to the ways companies communicate with customers, using the Internet, has changed the relative importance of business activities.
2. The Internet enables interactivity between the company and a customer, and also between the customer and a company's Web site content.
3. Source–receiver interactivity can take the traditional broadcast and narrowcast forms, but it can also increase the opportunities for one-to-one interactions between a company and its customers.
4. Receiver–content interactivity can be either push or pull in nature.
5. This type of interactivity provides a way for businesses to present personalized content to customers.
6. By using the Internet as a communications resource, businesses can implement mass customization processes that leverage the receiver–content interaction.
7. Source–receiver interactivity is typically needed to produce a product that exhibits personalization, in terms of a unique, one-of-a-kind product.
8. In addition to changing the flexibility of the product in the mix, the Internet allows buyers and sellers to use dynamic pricing schemes, as with auctions and bid-ask brokers.
9. Online promotions use traditional communications tactics, such as direct mail via opt-in e-mail or spam. They also take new forms, such as banners, pop-ups, and Shoshkeles.
10. As shoppers accept and adapt to new forms of online commercial communications, their willingness to be influenced by the communications may change. Businesses should be aware of the implications of attitudinal change toward online communications for their business strategies.

Thinking Points

1. What characteristics of the Internet as a communications resource differentiate it from traditional means of communication?
2. A simple communications model includes a source, a message, and a receiver. In general, how a message is encoded affects how it is decoded, and characteristics of the source and the receiver affect the encoding and decoding processes. How might the Internet affect the importance of the interaction that may exist between the source and the receiver?

3. What benefits do the two different types of interactivity with a computer-mediated environment provide businesses?
4. The Internet can facilitate personalization for promotions, such as targeted ads, and for products. Relate the types of personalization (i.e., promotion or product) to push versus pull forms of delivery.
5. Personalization can be accomplished in a variety of ways. What types of personalization are most likely to be associated with higher perceived value by customers?
6. Why is the concept of modularization critical to the ability to mass customize products?
7. It has been argued that the Internet has increased buyer power, relative to seller power. How is the Internet as a communications resource related to this power shift?

ENDNOTES

1. Rajiv Dewan, Bing Jing, and Abraham Seidmann, "Narrowcasting and Buyers' Search for Specialty Goods on the Internet," working paper, University of Rochester.

2. US Code Title 47, Section 227 (a) (2) (B) and Section 227 (b)(2)(C), to be specific.

SUGGESTED READINGS

1. "Conversations with Practitioners," edited by David W. Schumann. In *Advertising and the World Wide Web,* edited by David W. Schumann (Lawrence Erlbaum Associates, Publishers: Mahwah, NJ, 1999, pages 287–300).
2. "Offering Custom Products on the Internet," in *Understanding Electronic Commerce,* by David Kosiur. (Microsoft Press: Redmond, WA, 1997, pages 117–132).
3. "The Impact of Interactive Communication on Advertising and Marketing," by Edward Forrest, Lance Kinney, and Michael Chamberlain. In *Cybermarketing: Your Interactive Marketing Consultant*, edited by Regina Brady, Edward Forrest, and Richard Mizerki. (NTC Business Books: Chicago, 1997, pages 79–92).
4. "Whither the Banner," interview by Kim Cross. *Business 2.0* (December 1999), pages 137–144.
5. "eBay vs. Amazon.com," by Robert D. Hof and Linda Himelstein. *BusinessWeek* (May 31, 1999), pages 128–140.

LEARNING LINKS

Mass Customization Concepts and Solutions

www.mass-customization.de
www.core77.com/reactor/mass_customizati on.html
www.build-to-order-consulting.com/mc.htm

Managing Spam

everythingemail.net/email_unsolicited.html
www.drak.net/support/m_spam.html
surveyhost.com/email.html

Dynamic Pricing

digitalenterprise.org/auctions/auctions.html
www.crmproject.com/documents.asp?d_ID = 733

Rich Media Advertising

www.clickz.com/rich/rich_media/article.php /839851
www.unitedvirtualities.com/shoshkeles.htm
www.macromedia.com/resources/richmedia

Extending the Framework Over Time

Exchange Relationships in Digital Business

The impact of the Internet environment on exchange relationships has been emphasized throughout this book. Different types of relationships exist in the business environment, and the Internet affects many of them. In this final section, we focus on relationships in greater detail. In Chapter 13, we examine the Internet's influence on business-to-business (B2B) exchange. Of particular interest is the way in which the Internet creates opportunities for new markets that facilitate exchanges of goods and services.

Relationships change over time, and as a function of many factors. While earlier chapters in this book address issues related to starting business relationships, businesses must understand how to develop and maintain relationships. In Chapter 14, we look at issues that affect ongoing relational exchanges, such as satisfaction, trust, and commitment. We consider factors that foster or inhibit relationship development in the business-to-consumer (B2C) and B2B markets.

CHAPTER

Digital Business-
to-Business

Focus and Objectives

This chapter is focused on business-to-business (B2B) exchange. B2B exchanges entail the formation of relationships that differ in predictable ways from the relationships that describe business-to-consumer (B2C) exchanges. These differences are discussed with respect to the influence of the Internet as a resource for content, channel, and communication. The impact of the Internet on strategies for B2B exchanges, and on the structure of the processes for B2B exchanges is examined. Electronic hubs are described as a new form of intermediary in the exchange process.

Your objectives in studying this chapter include the following:

- Identify the key differences between B2B and B2C exchange processes.
- Know the main types of customers for B2B exchange, and the characteristics usually associated with B2B exchange processes.
- Understand the influence of the Internet as different forms of resources on different stages of B2B exchange processes.
- Develop familiarity with the role and types of online market-makers as intermediaries for B2B exchange.

Cooperating to Compete: The Battle of the B2B Networks

In 1999, Ford Motor Company took a long look at its supply chain and decided that things could be better. Costs could be lower, purchasing could be easier, and channel partners could get along better. To make these goals a reality, Ford decided to use the Internet to create a network between its suppliers and the company. Auto-xChange was born.

Of course, it wasn't that simple in practice. Many of Ford's suppliers also provided the necessary ingredients for auto manufacture to other companies, including Ford's key competitors, General Motors (GM) and DaimlerChrysler. Some suppliers didn't like the idea of Auto-xChange, as it added one more proprietary system that had to be installed and mastered.

At the same time that Ford was developing Auto-xChange, GM was also working to develop an online market for suppliers and the manufacturer. Realizing that they could streamline the process by working together, the two companies agreed to develop an industry-based exchange that connected suppliers with manufacturers around the globe. With DaimlerChrysler signed on, the three auto companies were ready to roll.

The result was Covisint, short for Collaboration, Vision, and Integration.

The enterprise grew rapidly, due in part to Ford and GM's wide-ranging contacts with other automobile manufacturers. Recognizing that companies each do business differently, and so have different needs for the online exchange, Covisint developed a range of capabilities to meet the needs of its members. To help manufacturers in the procurement process, Covisint offers catalog and auction tools, as well as a system for managing quotes from suppliers. Suppliers can easily publish inventory and manage transactions through the exchange. Covisint also serves as a portal, providing news and content management capabilities for suppliers and manufacturers.[1]

If an industry-wide exchange is so beneficial, why don't they exist in every industry? In addition, why aren't all automotive suppliers members of Covisint?

These questions illustrate the complex issues that underlie online B2B. In each case, an important factor is power. For Covisint, Ford, GM, and DaimlerChrysler are leaders in the industry, with access to hundreds of thousands of suppliers around the globe. As a result, collaboration between only three companies was enough to streamline large portions of supply chain activity, lowering vehicle costs to consumers and raising the hurdle on effective competition for nonmembers. As a result, there are clear advantages to joining the network. Many other industries are characterized by a broader distribution of company influence; power is held by the many, rather than by the few. In these cases, developing more localized online solutions may be preferable.

As for why all auto suppliers and manufacturers haven't joined Covisint, power and control are important reasons. Just as not all manufacturers are created equal, neither are suppliers. Tier 1 suppliers work directly with manufacturers, selling parts and preassembled equipment built from materials procured from Tier 2 suppliers. In the automotive industry, Tier 1 suppliers are often concerned that information flows that previously went from the lower to the higher tier have the potential to communicate directly with the manufacturer, possibly disintermediating the Tier 1 suppliers, or at least reducing their control over marketing flows. The development of Internet-based networks reduces the costs of developing and deploying software to manage

---

[1]Sources of information include www.softwaremag.com, business.cisco.com, and www.darwinmag.com.

supply chain interactions. Therefore, Tier 2 suppliers who once did not have the resources to invest in private EDI (electronic data interchange) networks can now use the Internet to access standardized exchange processes. Concern that they could lose their power over lower-level suppliers has caused many major Tier 1 suppliers to develop their own, private, online exchanges, focusing on customized solutions as the differentiating benefit not offered by Covisint.

Manufacturers share the concerns about power and control. The ability to use Covisint to work collaboratively with suppliers on design issues is nice, and cost-effective. But how do you protect the privacy of intellectual property? How secure is the network? Will suppliers be able to protect your proprietary activities from other suppliers and manufacturers? Concerns like these have led many suppliers and manufacturers to develop their own, private networks.

The issues faced by Covisint are not limited to the automotive industry. The need to streamline B2B purchases and manage related supply chain activities has led many companies and industries to explore the potential of the Internet as a vital force in buying and selling. In addition, the factors that enable a company to successfully implement an Internet initiative are similar across industries—power and security concerns, coupled with company characteristics that may help or hinder the adoption of online B2B processes.

What does the future hold for Covisint, and for online exchanges in other industries? What characteristics of B2B exchange are affected by the Internet, and how? What do the possible changes mean for managing the supply chain? What types of online B2B activities will be successful, and for which types of companies?

Bits & Bytes 13.1
In its first 6 months up and running, Covisint managed transactions worth more than $33 billion. Not a lot, compared with the $240 billion of parts and supplies that the Big Three purchase annually, but still an impressive opening.
(*Source:* Knowledge@Wharton, Managing Technology series.)

The Internet can be used to carry out a range of B2B activities. Many of the influences of the Internet on exchange relationships that we have considered in earlier chapters are relevant for exchanges in the B2B environment. For instance, the activities that reflect a B2B relationship involve the bidirectional exchange of resources. In the B2B marketplace, these exchanges may include transfers of information, money, services, and goods. In addition, the role of the Internet as a set of resources that can facilitate exchange is applicable to the B2B environment. For example, as a content resource, the Internet enables businesses to provide information about the goods and services that they provide. As a channel resource, the Internet can be used to transfer purchased goods and services. As a communications resource, the Internet facilitates negotiations between businesses that may affect the price, quantity, and form of the products that are purchased.

Because the nature of B2B exchanges is substantially different, in many cases, from B2C exchanges, the influence of the Internet on B2B exchange relationships is also different. In this chapter, we will consider the nature of the Internet's influence on B2B activities. We begin with a description of key characteristics of B2B exchanges, including a discussion of contrasts with B2C exchanges. Then we will look at the impact of the Internet on three aspects of B2B exchanges: (1) why businesses engage in buying and selling, (2) how they conduct their exchanges, and (3) who they work with to buy and sell.

Online Business-to-Business Is Big Business

The Internet has received a lot of attention as a marketplace for consumer goods. Behind the scenes, however, B2B markets have developed that have quickly outpaced the amount of revenue associated with B2C activity on the Internet. We can describe online B2B activity with demographics, and by the types of activities that are facilitated by characteristics of the Internet environment.

Online Business-to-Business Demographics

Although estimates of B2B revenues vary, they consistently reflect the belief that online B2B revenues have increased disproportionately, relative to B2C revenues, in recent years. The table in Figure 13-1 reflects growth in each area in the United States, and Figure 13-2 shows the comparative growth of B2B in the United States versus worldwide.

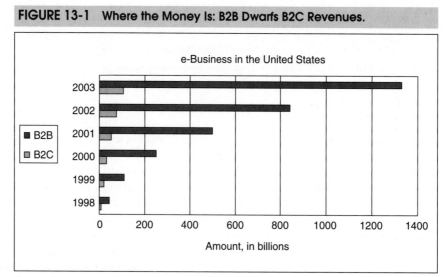

FIGURE 13-1   Where the Money Is: B2B Dwarfs B2C Revenues.

e-Business in the United States

Source: Forrester Research.

FIGURE 13-2   Worldwide B2B Growth Leaps Ahead.

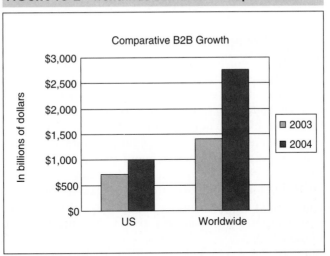

Source: eMarketer April, 2003.

The sheer size and relative weights of these numbers indicate the importance of the Internet for B2B activity. In the next section, we will look at how B2B exchanges differ from B2C exchanges as a first step to identifying the implications of the Internet for conducting B2B activities.

How Is Business-to-Business Different?

Although the goal of completing a transaction is common to B2B exchanges and to B2C exchanges, many other aspects of exchange activity are different. These differences include the type of customer, the nature of product demand, and the processes associated with B2B exchanges.

Difference in the Targeted Customer

A focal distinction between B2B and B2C exchanges is the purpose for product purchase. In B2C exchanges, customers typically buy products for personal or household consumption. For companies, these exchanges emphasize the importance of customers' perceptions of personal consumption. In contrast, B2B exchanges involve product consumption that is needed for the production of good and services, or for the sale of goods and services.

The difference in *why* the exchange occurs is related to the difference in *who* is involved in the exchange. For example, B2B exchanges occur when manufacturers sell products to distributors, who in turn sell the products to retailers. In addition, B2B exchanges occur when parts suppliers sell product components to product manufacturers. Another B2B exchange is characterized by sales of products and services that do not become part of the product sold to end customers, but that are necessary for the company to be able to do its part to create the product. For example, a company may purchase computers to manage its internal functions to efficiently produce a product. These examples illustrate different types of B2B transactions.

Difference in the Nature of Demand

Many B2B exchanges are conducted to facilitate the manufacture and distribution of products to customers. The demand for industrial products is termed **derived demand**, because it only occurs as the result of the demand for the consumer product. Derived demand tends to be characterized by sharper increases and decreases in demand than consumer demand, given the difficulties in developing accurate forecasts of consumer demand. As a result, manufacturers tend to overestimate inventory needs when consumer demand increases, and they tend to overestimate the need to reduce the inventory when consumer demand decreases. The difficulty in estimating demand is often attributed to the imprecision of inventory tracking and sales reports. The Internet has the potential to automate speed tracking, recording, and reporting procedures, thus tightening forecasting of demand for industrial products.

The nature of demand for industrial products also differs from consumer products in the number of buyers who will be interested in a product. Because industrial products are often asset-specific and may be built to meet a narrow set of needs, the market for any given industrial product tends to be smaller than for many consumer products. B2B exchanges also differ from B2C exchanges in the variability of purchase volume. B2C purchases are for personal consumption, so many purchases occur in volumes of one. After all, how many rubber gasket seals for a clothes dryer door does a single consumer need? In contrast, the gasket manufacturer may supply tens of thousands of gaskets to an appliance manufacturer, and additional thousands to several different appliance repair companies.

Differences in Exchange-related Processes

B2B exchanges also differ from B2C exchanges in terms of the processes that the buyers and sellers use to complete the transaction. The greater cost and complexity of many business purchases means that procurement processes are often conducted with formalized buying procedures and may be conducted by **purchasing agents** or **purchasing managers** who have professional expertise in making buying decisions. These agents may conduct negotiations with the sellers that are more extensive and complex than buyer-seller negotiations in B2C markets. In addition, the need for asset-specific industrial products means that B2B exchanges are often characterized by more direct interaction between the seller and the buyer, which may be conducted to obtain higher levels of product customization. Figure 13-3 summarizes the differences that are typically present between B2B and B2C exchanges.

Another characteristic difference between the B2B and the B2C markets is the volume of sales. Sales volume in the B2B market is higher than in the B2C market, even though the total number of customers is lower. The volume difference makes sense, however, if you consider that several industrial purchases may be necessary to create the product that results in a single sale to a consumer. The volume difference is also observed in the digital business environment. In the next section, we will examine the demographics of online B2B exchanges.

FIGURE 13-3   B2B and B2C Exchanges Differ in Who They Sell To, Why, and How.

Business-to-Consumer Exchanges	Business-to-Business Exchanges

Target customer
  ♦ Consumer
    - Personal use
    - Household use
	Target customer
	  ♦ Business consumer
	    - Reseller
	    - Industrial market

Nature of demand
  ♦ Consumer-driven
	Nature of demand
	  ♦ Derived, based on
	     consumer demand

Exchange processes
  ♦ Informal
    - Fewer constraints on
     purchases
    - Fewer decision makers
  ♦ Indirect producer-consumer
    link
  ♦ Simple negotiation
	Exchange processes
	  ♦ Formal
	    - More constraints on
	     purchases
	    - More decision makers
	  ♦ More direct producer-
	    consumer contact
	  ♦ Complex negotiation

Bits & Bytes 13.2
Online B2B trade in the European Union is expected to grow to 22 percent of total B2B business—from 77 billion euros in 2001 to 2.2 trillion euros in 2006.
(*Source: CyberAtlas,* August 2002, reporting Forrester Group data.)

The Internet and Online Business-to-Business Exchange

In this section, we examine the Internet's influence on three aspects of B2B activity: the "why," "how," and "who" of B2B. More formally, these are: (1) purposes of exchange, (2) processes for exchange, and (3) participants in the exchange.

Purposes of Business-to-Business Exchanges: Why Do Businesses Buy?

We can divide the B2B marketplace into three main categories. These categories are defined by the motivation of the buyers and the sellers for conducting the exchange. The categories include the following customers:

1. Buyers who serve as middlemen to resell products to consumers (buying to sell).
2. Buyers who incorporate a product into the manufacture of their own product (buying to build).
3. Buyers who use a product to facilitate business operations (buying to function).

Who Are Business-to-Business Customers?

First, a B2B exchange may involve selling to an organization that then sells the product to the end consumer. In this market, wholesalers and retailers act as **resellers** who add value to the product through business activity. As we saw in Chapter 11, the Internet affects the nature of exchange relationships within the reseller segment with its ability to serve as a channel resource. For example, Wal-Mart operates as the reseller for one or two major, national brands in each of the product categories it stocks.

Second, an exchange may involve selling to an organization that uses the product to manufacture its own product. For example, an **original equipment manufacturer (OEM)** may purchase product components from a supplier to assemble another product. This exchange is motivated by the purpose of adding value through manufacturing. In addition, a company may procure products that are needed to enable manufacturing, but that do not become part of the end product (e.g., machine parts of an assembly line). Automotive manufacturers are OEMs; they buy parts for vehicles from suppliers, and they buy parts needed to engineer the production processes used to assemble the vehicles.

Third, an exchange may involve selling to an organization that uses the product to operate. For instance, purchases of computer equipment and office supplies, and janitorial services are often needed to facilitate the normal operations of a business. These types of sales are often referred to as **MROs**, for *m*aintenance, *r*epair, and *o*perating. Staples, Inc. was founded to provide large organizations and companies with office supplies, in bulk and on a regular basis, prior to developing its superstore interaction with end customers.

The OEM and MRO categories that emphasize manufacturing and operations are often classified under the label of industrial marketing. The types of processes that may be carried out under this general label, however, are also found in markets for which the government and institutions are the target customers.

The division of business customers into the second and third categories of manufacturing and operations can be described as two different forms of markets: vertical and horizontal. A **vertical market** is a market that emphasizes products and services necessary to the manufacturing and sales of products in a specific industry. Vertical markets tend to be narrow in focus. For example, a vertical market in the lumber industry might include B2B marketing of products for logging and sawmill functions. In contrast, **horizontal markets** are focused on providing products and services that fulfill functional needs that may exist across a variety of industries. For example, a horizontal market for transportation services might include trucking services capable of moving loads of lumber from sawmills to lumberyards, as well as steel from mills to factories, and bolts of cloth from factories to stores.

The markets exist off-line and online. With the Internet, the ability to digitally connect companies to buy or sell parts and services needed to build products has resulted in the development of vertical, industry-specific markets, like PlasticsNet, and in across-industry, horizontal markets like Employease, a service for filling short-term employee needs.

Bits & Bytes 13.3

B2B companies are turning to the Internet to attract customers. Overcoming concerns about their ability to adequately target a business market with Web advertising, B2B companies are predicted to make up 22 percent of online ad spending in 2005.

(*Source: CyberAtlas,* July 2002, reporting GartnerG2 study results.)

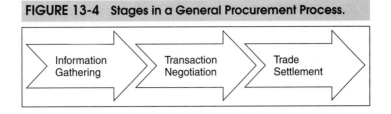

FIGURE 13-4   Stages in a General Procurement Process.

Business-to-Business Exchange Processes

B2B exchanges, just like B2C exchanges, involve buyers and sellers. As we saw earlier, however, the nature of the exchanges between buyers and sellers is different. These differences, including higher costs and greater product complexity and asset-specificity, increase the importance of choosing the right seller. In B2B exchanges that are likely to occur repeatedly, establishing an efficient, trusted, and effective buyer–seller relationship is an important goal of the buying process. Within B2B exchanges, regardless of whether the purchase is by an OEM, or for an MRO, the formal processes for carrying out the purchase tend to be similar. This process of selecting and completing a B2B purchase with a vendor is called **procurement**.

Stages in the Procurement Process

The exchange process for procurement consists of three main stages: information gathering, transaction negotiation, and settlement (Figure 13-4). In the **information gathering stage**, the buyer decides what type of product is needed and develops information about possible sources for the product. In the **transaction negotiation stage**, communication with potential sellers establishes terms for the exchange, including product configuration, price, quantity, and delivery. In the **settlement stage**, the transfer of the product is completed.

Types of Business-to-Business Exchanges and Procurement Stages

Depending on the newness of the procurement situation, different emphasis may be placed on each of the three stages. Three types of B2B exchanges often illustrate the history of the relationship between a seller and buyer: **new buy**, **modified rebuy**, and **straight rebuy**. These situations range from an entirely new purchase situation, in which no relationship exists, to a routinized purchase decision, based on a long-term relationship with a seller. In a new buy situation, information gathering is disproportionately important. In a modified rebuy, attention is often directed to negotiation that alters some aspect of the previous arrangement. In a straight rebuy, a preexisting agreement to effect an exchange is enacted with no changes to terms of the transaction. The table in Figure 13-5 reflects the amounts of activity that are typically conducted in each stage of the procurement process, as a function of the type of exchange relationship. The shaded boxes reflect heightened activity.

Internet Effects on Business-to-Business Exchange Stages

The Internet affects what companies can do to conduct B2B exchanges, depending on the type of exchange relationship to be conducted. Businesses can leverage the

FIGURE 13-5 Stage-related Activity Changes as Relationships Develop.

	Type of Relational Exchange		
Procurement Process Stage	**New Buy**	**Modified Rebuy**	**Straight Rebuy**
Information Gathering			
Transaction Negotiation			
Trade Settlement			

Internet's ability to serve as a resource for content, channel, and communication to effect B2B exchange activity as a function of the stage of the procurement process. More simply put, different capabilities of the Internet are emphasized at different stages of the buying process (Figure 13-6).

The Internet and New Buys   A new buy situation is often characterized by the absence of an ongoing seller–buyer relationship. In the new buy situation, the buyer must complete all stages of the procurement process. Information must be sought about possible vendors, and negotiations must be effectively concluded before the product is transferred to the buyer.

FIGURE 13-6 Internet Resources Provide Different Benefits for B2B Exchanges.

	The Internet as a B2B Resourse		
Type of Relational Exchange	**Content**	**Communication**	**Channel**
New Buy	Buyer: Internet facilitates acquisition of product information Seller: Internet facilitates lead generation		
Modified Rebuy		Buyer: Internet facilitates negotiation Seller: Internet facilitates pricing	
Straight Rebuy			Buyer: Internet facilitates automated ordering Seller: Internet facilitates scheduling and delivery

Getting information that is accurate and timely can be difficult in situations where the market is fragmented. A **fragmented market** exists, for example, when a buyer cannot get ready access to comprehensive information about the products and terms of sellers, and vice versa. One or both sides may exhibit a high degree of separation. In this situation, the Internet can be used as a source of information for sellers and buyers, enabling buyers to accomplish information gathering tasks. In the information gathering stage, the Internet exerts its strongest effect as a content resource. Business buyers can request information from sellers through e-mail. In addition, information can also be acquired from sellers' Web sites. Banners with links to sellers' sites also provide information.

The Internet and Modified Rebuys   In a modified rebuy exchange, the Internet is primarily effective as a communication resource. It facilitates negotiations that enable buyers and sellers to alter various aspects of an existing exchange agreement. For instance, two-way interactivity provides buyers and sellers with the ability to conduct a near real-time negotiation to change the form of an ordered product part, as well as its amount, and the timing and destination of its delivery. In this role, the Internet enables the buyer and the seller to customize a product order, and to personalize aspects of the exchange process.

An important aspect of the interaction capabilities of the Internet for modified rebuys, however, is the need for the seller to understand the expectations of the buyer, and to incorporate recognition of them into the processes for reaching customized product agreements. A modified rebuy represents a middle-ground position in relationship development. Business customers may tend to expect that sellers will incorporate previous experience with them into present and future attempts to solidify business relationships. When used effectively, technological characteristics of the Internet can enable sellers to record and track buyer information, as through server-based data (e.g., log files) and through user-based data (e.g., cookies). This ability to retain information about buyer preferences and past behaviors can reduce the transaction costs associated with the new buy situation. It can also increase switching costs when the effort to provide the seller with company-specific requirements is not negligible.

The interactive, immediate nature of the Internet-enabled relationship places a new requirement on sellers to not only recognize the import of previous interactions on a current interaction, but to be able to integrate and develop the implications of the interaction rapidly. In this respect, Internet-based exchanges resemble personal selling in the business marketplace.

In addition to the communications that are conducted between the buyer and the seller, communications that affect the specifications for the exchange can take place via the Internet within the company. For instance, private internal networks, or **intranets**, can be used to obtain information about needed product characteristics, as well as cost constraints and purchase approval.

The Internet and Straight Rebuys   For an exchange that is a straight rebuy, the Internet functions as a channel resource. Because the exchange does not need to be negotiated, and because all necessary information is already available to both parties, the primary benefit of the Internet is as a conduit for transmission. This transmission may take the form of the request to complete an automated exchange, or to manage the logistics of the product's delivery, or both.

Prior to the Internet, companies often used privately established networks for electronic data interchange (EDI). EDI makes it possible for organizations to efficiently conduct standardized business exchanges, such as straight rebuys. EDI does, however, have several significant drawbacks. These networks are often expensive to establish, and their complexity requires trained users. In addition, EDI networks tend to limit users to the transfer of a small number of properly formatted documents.

The Internet enables business buyers and sellers to overcome several obstacles associated with the use of EDI to process business exchanges. Because the Internet is an open network, companies can use its infrastructure to develop private intranets and extranets that allow users to transfer documents in a wide variety of formats. Because a selling organization can receive exchange-related documents in a variety of formats, buying organizations can transmit purchase orders that fit their organizational requirements, thus facilitating movement toward repetitive, straight rebuy situations by decreasing implementation costs.

The Internet and Supply Chain Management

As we just learned, the Internet can influence all phases of the procurement process. Procurement, however, is just one part of the set of activities needed to move a product from design to distribution. **Supply chain management (SCM)** is the set of processes by which a company interacts with suppliers to locate necessary parts and services (sourcing), to arrange for their purchase and delivery (procurement), and to oversee the logistics associated with production, inventory, transportation, and warehousing. In addition, SCM involves the external interactions with chain members, including training and postsales customer support.

The number and types of supply chain activities carried out by a company can be large, and costly. In complex supply chains, it is important to coordinate the activities of supply chain members, in order to minimize costs, time, and errors, and to maximize efficiencies in internal and external logistics.

Many companies have turned to the Internet to manage their supply chains. Internet-based SCM solutions overcome the limitations of private networks for EDI by decreasing costs to participate and by increasing standardization of forms, as for orders and billing. These characteristics enable smaller companies to use SCM software and increase the ability for supply chain members to communicate and coordinate production and logistics efforts.

The effects of the Internet for SCM extend across a host of different companies, and a range of supply chain activities. For instance, Herman Miller, a manufacturer of office furniture, depends on many suppliers and distribution participants to build, store, and transport its products. Prior to using the Internet to manage its supply chain, the company's order fulfillment times were long, because orders were placed from several different sources, routed to different production locations, and subject to the availability of needed components. By centralizing its order process via the Internet, the company was able to better pinpoint what supplies were needed, and where, and when. The result was substantial. The cumbersome inventory of work-in-progress was reduced, lowering inventory costs by 30 percent, and cutting the lead time for manufacturing in half.

While Herman Miller's SCM initiative emphasized procurement, Boeing—known for building big airplanes—leveraged SCM for collaborative research and design with its suppliers. The interactive design process led to efficiencies in staffing, and in tooling up for building the aircraft; better communication of what capabilities the manufacturer had guided supplier activity, and vice versa.[1]

Herman Miller, Boeing, and Wal-Mart are all big names that have successfully incorporated the Internet into their SCM strategies. Fortunately, Internet-based SCM isn't just for large, established companies. Researchers have studied the types of companies that move most rapidly and effectively toward online SCM, and they have drawn some conclusions.[2]

Two sets of factors are important to the adoption of Web-based SCM: internal characteristics of the company, and external characteristics of supply chain relationships. The internal characteristics are the widespread acceptance of information technologies (IT) throughout the company's functional units—not just limited to a central IT department—and the presence of a formalized process for using IT, including rules and standards for conducting business activities with IT. In short, a company that is largely familiar with and committed to IT will adopt Web-based SCM faster than a company that is reluctant to use IT.

In addition, manufacturer-supplier relationships that are highly, mutually interdependent indicate that the manufacturing company is a good candidate for speedy SCM adoption. The process may be additionally speeded if some of the supply chain partners are strong champions of IT, and use them visibly.

Bits & Bytes 13.4

Online purchasing has grown steadily, especially in large companies. The Institute for Supply Management reports that 84 percent of large companies buy supplies and services over the Internet.

(*Source: eCommerce Times*, 29 January 2003).

Sourcing and Supply Chain Management

An important issue for Web-based SCM is the nature of the relationship between the manufacturer and the supplier. The type of buying need can affect the commitment to the relationship, and hence the implementation of a Web-based SCM strategy. For instance, the need for some products and services may be highly predictable, while the need for other types is more variable. For example, a car manufacturer can reliably predict that as long as production continues, tires will be needed. In contrast, the need for an employment service to handle the task of finding a replacement for a line manager who was just hired away by the competition reflects a less predictable business exchange. In general, business exchange activities that are frequently repeated—and on a predictable timetable—often result in **systematic sourcing**. Exchange-related activities due to less predictable needs are typically met with **spot sourcing**.

Systematic sourcing is often associated with straight rebuy relationships, in which product needs are clear and predictable. Spot sourcing reflects buying behavior in which need is less predictable, and which tends to result in more opportunistic purchasing behavior. A buying agent may examine several potential vendors and engage in negotiations each time the product or service need arises, thus creating situations that more closely resemble new buys than established relationships.

The Internet changes the way that companies meet their sourcing needs. We've already learned that the Internet has created new roles for distribution channel members, including a variety of intermediaries that could not exist with the digitally networked Internet. A similar situation exists in B2B marketing for sourcing and the nature of supply chain relationships.

Three types of online intermediaries largely capture the range of sourcing needs for B2B activity: aggregators, auctioneers, and exchanges. These intermediaries illustrate the role of the Internet as a set of resources for conducting sourcing activities. For instance, aggregators use the ability of the Internet to serve as a content resource. **Aggregator intermediaries** can collect information about supply sources in a fragmented market, reducing the effort to find a specific product (Figure 13-7). **Auctioneer intermediaries** are often used for spot sourcing, such as meeting an unexpected need for a generic product. **Exchange intermediaries** serve to connect buyers to sellers when fragmentation is high on both sides of the market. Aggregators leverage the Internet as a content resource. Auctioneers use the Internet primarily as a channel resource. Exchanges capitalize on the Internet's communication capabilities.

Participants in Online Business-to-Business Exchange Processes

The content, channel, and communications benefits of the Internet open up new ways for businesses to trade with other businesses. We have seen that many aspects of supply

FIGURE 13-7 As an Aggregator Intermediary, XSmaterials.com™ Combines Buying Opportunities Across a Wide Range of Industries.

Source: Reproduced with permission of XSmaterials.com, Inc. Copyright 2003. All rights reserved.

chain functions are altered due to the introduction of the Internet. In addition to changing B2B processes for exchange, the Internet may trigger changes in trading relationships. For instance, increased ease of communication may lead a company to include new partners in its trading network.

In this section, we'll consider two forms of B2B exchange, and we'll examine the processes and participants associated with each form. A **direct exchange** involves communication between the buyer and the seller, with no intermediaries. In contrast, an **indirect exchange** introduces intermediaries who facilitate the transfer of products from the seller to the buyer. Indirect exchanges are often conducted through online markets, or electronic hubs.

Direct Business-to-Business Exchange and the Internet

One challenge for participants in many types of B2B exchanges is finding exchange partners. The difficulty in identifying exchange partners exists for buyers and for sellers. From a buyer's perspective, multiple sellers may exist, but characteristics of the buyer's situation—such as budget and time constraints, and high levels of asset specificity—may narrow the range of products and vendors that are acceptable. From a seller's perspective in a B2B environment, identifying promising sales leads and developing suitable agreements can be difficult in an environment characterized by smaller target markets and greater awareness of competitors than in many B2C markets.

The Internet can be used by buyers to find sellers, and vice versa. Buyers can use Internet search engines to hunt for specific products and industries. In addition, B2B directories exist that facilitate buyer search by aggregating sellers by product or service, and by industry.

Sellers' Web sites also serve to initiate direct contact. Sellers can provide content about product offerings and customization flexibility. Sellers can also use banner ads on external sites to generate leads. Whether attached to a company's Web site or to a banner, **Web response forms (WRFs)** can be used to enable potential buyers to express interest in a particular product. A WRF is an online form used by buyers to request product information, and by sellers to qualify sales prospects. Buyers who visit a seller's Web site might leave behind information in a server's log file about in-site information acquisition, and the URLs from which they entered the site. With a WRF, however, the seller can obtain more detailed information about the motives behind the buyer's Web site visit (i.e., lead qualification), as well as a way to initiate subsequent contact with the buyer. Benefits for buyers include the ability to receive information tailored to needs and experience, as well as rapid fulfillment. A WRF can be used within a seller's Web site, or through a link placed in a banner ad on an external Web site. Many business sites use automated outbound e-mail response applications to provide quick responses to buyer inquiries initiated with WRFs.

E-mail capabilities on the Internet can be used to influence the information gathering stage of the buying process in several ways. We have noted the fulfillment capabilities of the Internet as a way to respond to inbound e-mail and WRF requests for information. In addition, business marketers can send unsolicited mailings to targeted businesses, in the hope that the pushed information is relevant. Other uses of e-mail to create direct exchanges between sellers and buyers include distribution of press releases and newsletters to potential customers. Interactive surveys can provide contact with prospects and generate interest in an existing product or in the development of a new product. Sellers can also use e-mail to manage discussion groups on industry-related issues. Buyer participation in online discussion forums can provide information for both buyers and sellers that can influence the exchange process.

Many uses of the Internet by sellers who seek to establish a direct exchange with buyers are similar to traditional forms of direct marketing. For instance, sellers can use outbound e-mail to develop pointcast messages to recipients. As with traditional mail-based lead generation approaches, the seller incurs costs associated with list acquisition. In general, however, direct marketing on the Internet reduces costs because printing and mailing expenses are eliminated. Figure 13-8 contains a sample of B2B activities that can be used by a business to incorporate the Internet into direct exchange efforts.

FIGURE 13-8   Businesses Integrate Multiple Activities to Initiate Direct Exchanges.

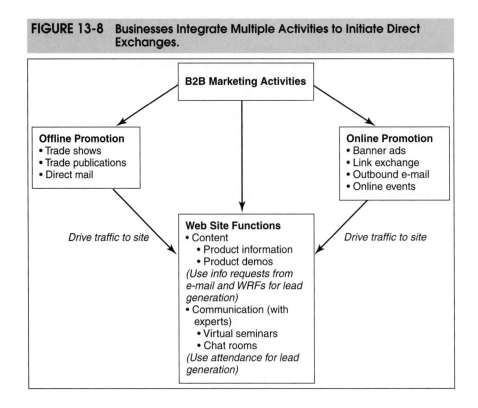

Indirect Business-to-Business Exchange and the Internet

Indirect exchanges involve the introduction of an intermediary into the buying process conducted between a buyer and a seller. In the B2B environment, these intermediaries often function to create links between buyers and sellers, thus providing an alternative means of contact to a direct exchange. The intermediaries operate by creating collections of buyers and collections of sellers through organized systems that allow information sharing between buyers and sellers. Some organized markets establish standards that affect the way that exchanges are conducted, including information gathering, transaction negotiation, and trade settlement. Firms that impose structure across the range of activities in the exchange process are called **market-making firms**.

An important benefit of organized markets is that they can reduce transaction costs associated with each stage of the exchange process. For example, a market-making firm that aggregates collections of information about the wares of different vendors in a sector of industry can drastically reduce the effort needed by a buyer to search for product information. In addition, organized markets can affect costs of negotiating. Different types of firms impose different structures and procedures for reaching agreements, as about price. These established procedures can reduce transaction costs by decreasing confusion about the types of agreements that are possible. In the settlement stage, policies that reflect norms and codes of conduct can reduce difficulties with enforcing exchange contracts.

Types of Online Markets   Three primary forms of online markets have been identified by eMarketer analysts: consortia-led exchanges, proprietary exchanges, and third-party exchanges. **Consortia-led exchanges** are collections of companies that share ownership, often in conjunction with a technology partner that creates the online exchange forum. For example, General Motors, Ford, and Chrysler joined with Covisint to create a consortia-led exchange to facilitate B2B exchanges between the companies and their suppliers. **Proprietary exchanges** are privately owned and managed by one—typically large—company (e.g., Wal-Mart's Retail Link, see the InSite feature). The goal of a proprietary exchange is to increase revenues by creating more efficient exchanges between members of the company's supply chain. In both consortia-led exchanges and proprietary markets, the owners participate in the buying and selling activities of the markets.

In contrast, **third-party exchanges** function as intermediaries that are not trading partners. In the following section, we will look at the characteristics of third party hubs as online intermediaries for B2B exchange.

Third-party Hubs as Online Intermediaries   The Internet is the host environment for several new forms of market-making intermediaries. These intermediaries are digital hubs that operate within vertical or horizontal B2B markets to mediate transactions between buyers and sellers. Some hubs are focused on particular sections of industry, while other hubs emphasize the provision of services or functions that extend across industries. For example, in a vertical hub for restaurant furniture, suppliers for products and components associated with restaurant furniture production, maintenance, and repair might offer their wares. In contrast, in a horizontal hub, a buyer might find vendors who specialize in processes that can be used in a range of industries. For instance, a company that repairs torn vinyl upholstery might sell its services in a horizontal hub to buyers in the restaurant industry, the airline industry, and the professional-waiting-room industry.

InSite

LOWERING EDLP WITH RETAIL LINK: WWW.WALMART.COM

Sam Walton, the founder of Wal-Mart Stores, Inc., had a simple philosophy. "There is only one boss—the customer. He can fire everyone in the company, from the chairman on down, simply by spending his money somewhere else." Treating the customer as king, with low prices and friendly service, works; in 1990, Wal-Mart become the country's #1 general retailer, a position it has held ever since.

What makes Wal-Mart so successful? Customer service never hurts. Wal-Mart greeters at each store entrance welcome customers with a smile. Employees are urged to stick to Sam's "10 foot rule;" an employee within 10 feet of any customer should smile, and offer assistance.

But friendliness isn't the main reason for shopping at Wal-Mart—it's the everyday low prices. Wal-Mart works to provide a tremendous variety of products, typically at lower prices than its competitors. The range of products means a host of suppliers, and a host of suppliers means that many different methods and systems are needed to keep marketing flows moving smoothly between Wal-Mart's suppliers and Wal-Mart's shelves.

Wal-Mart recognized that by streamlining the ways in which it communicated with its suppliers, it could reduce costs by reducing supply chain complexity. The company developed an EDI solution, called Retail Link that connected stores to suppliers. With Retail Link suppliers could check on store-levels' sales of their products, thus gauging demand and assessing inventory needs. Accurate and timely sales and inventory information benefited the suppliers, as Wal-Mart leaves as much as 70 percent of its store inventory under the ownership of the supplier. As a result, knowing how much product has sold enables suppliers to efficiently manage productivity, and to bill Wal-Mart for sales promptly.

The Retail Link strategy works well for the supplier and the company. Efficient flows of information allow suppliers to reduce their costs, and pass on the savings to Wal-Mart, who passes them on to customers through everyday low prices (EDLP). Wal-Mart's biggest supplier, Procter & Gamble, was one of the earliest Retail Link participants. The supplier of Pampers and other popular household brands was able to double its margins on products from 1994 through 2002. With results like these, suppliers are happy to participate in the proprietary exchange. Because the streamlined flows through Retail Link reduce the costs of goods sold (COGS), Wal-Mart is happy to have its suppliers on board the exchange.

To make it possible for more suppliers to participate in the exchange by reducing the costs associated with custom EDI solutions, Wal-Mart moved Retail Link to the Internet in October 2002. Partnering with bTrade, a technology company, Wal-Mart was able to offer its thousands of suppliers the ability to quickly and easily set up Retail Link accounts and move their transactions with Wal-Mart to the Internet. As if the benefits for suppliers weren't enough, Wal-Mart added one more—joining the private exchange network is free.

Source: Information obtained from www.walmart.com, and from Internet sources.

With its networked structure and relatively inexpensive access, the Internet is a fertile medium for third-party hubs. The ability to communicate product and price information in near real-time between buyers and sellers enables exchange participants to update inventory availability and to react to price fluctuations. This capability enables exchange participants to better manage derived demand. In addition, markets on the Internet decouple product flows from information flows; an exchange agreement can be reached without the physical presence of the product. This characteristic provides logistics benefits and increases the geographic scope of the market.

Despite the advantages they can provide, market-making intermediaries on the Internet also present disadvantages. Among the disadvantages are the increased transaction risks that arise when a buyer must rely on the computer-mediated environment to obtain an accurate understanding of the product offering. In addition, the newness of many online markets means that buyers and sellers may enter exchange agreements with little information about the performance history of either partner in satisfying terms of the agreement. These disadvantages act as barriers to adoption by B2B buyers and sellers.

First-mover Advantage for Online Intermediaries   The disadvantages associated with online intermediaries underscore the importance of a **first-mover advantage**, or benefits that can be attributed to an early presence in a market. Being early in the market for buyers and sellers increases the likelihood that an online intermediary will be able to develop a large enough base of potential buyers and sellers to create market liquidity. **Market liquidity** refers to the presence of sufficient numbers of buyers and sellers in a marketplace to enable good matches between buyers and sellers. The number of participants required to achieve market liquidity is described as **critical mass**.

The size of the participant base reduces risks for buyers and sellers in several ways. First, risks associated with the ability to locate a buyer or a seller decrease as market size increases. Second, increased numbers of transactions provide more information (e.g., via word-of-mouth) about participants. Third, increased market size is often accompanied by the development of formal standards and mechanisms for participation and performance. These requirements protect participants in the exchange process.

eBay's entry into the B2B market in 2003 illustrates the challenges faced by an online intermediary. Although the company's early presence in the online marketplace had given it the competitive advantage in terms of critical mass, the advantage was limited to the B2C market. Companies, and even entire industries, had already joined or built online exchange hubs. Many of these hubs, particularly the industry-level ones, were designed to facilitate the transaction of very specialized goods and services. As a result, eBay was faced with the need to develop a strong presence in the B2B market. They developed vertical, industry-oriented categories, including agriculture, printing, and metal working. To capture additional market, however, they also included more horizontal categories, such as computer and office equipment, and networking and telecommunications services. To attract the reseller market, a separate category of wholesale lots was developed.

Online Intermediaries as Value-adders

As we've seen, online B2B intermediaries play different roles in the exchange processes between businesses. We can describe these roles in terms of the two primary ways that the intermediaries provide value to the buyers and sellers in the exchange process: **aggregation** and **matching**. When the objective of the intermediary is aggregation, value is achieved by creating collections of buyers and sellers. When the objective is matching, value is achieved by facilitating exchanges between buyers and sellers.

In an aggregation model, value is measured in numbers—of sellers and their products, and of buyers. Intermediaries who add value through aggregation often adopt a **catalog approach**, in which the wares of a large number of vendors, in either a vertical or a horizontal market, are accumulated and made available to a collection of buyers (Figure 13-9). Aggregation models are characterized by prenegotiated prices and a large variety of specialized products (i.e., noncommodity).

A second type of value added by online B2B intermediaries is through matching; the intermediary provides a mechanism through which buyers and sellers can negotiate prices to carry out an exchange. An important aspect of matching is the need for liquidity. Because liquidity depends on an adequate number of buyers and sellers, matching models benefit from aggregation.

Matching is accomplished with auctions and bid-ask exchanges. In **auctions**, **buyer-driven pricing** occurs when buyers' bids for a product build on previous buyers' bids. This B2B model is analogous to standard bidding with eBay, an online auction in the B2C marketplace. **Seller-driven pricing** occurs when the seller sets an initial price and lowers the

FIGURE 13-9 Alibaba's B2B Marketplace Aggregates Buying Opportunities into an Online Catalog.

Source: Reproduced with permission of Alibaba, Inc. Copyright 2003. All rights reserved.

price until a buyer accepts the price. **Bid-ask exchanges** are based on real-time matching of bid and asking prices. For example, a vendor of bandwidth can "ask" a certain price for unused inventory. If the asked price matches a buyer's bid price, the exchange is transacted. Exchange models are most effective for commodity-type products that are traded in large volumes, and for which demand—and hence, price—tend to fluctuate.

Classifying Intermediary B2B Hubs   Several of the characteristics used to describe B2B exchange activity can be used to classify different types of B2B hubs as business models. Such classification is useful because it helps marketers to determine the type of hub that is most appropriate for conducting a particular business exchange.

A taxonomy of B2B hubs suggested by Sawhney and Kaplan[3] integrates *what* businesses buy (i.e., manufacturing or operating), with *how* businesses buy (i.e., systematic or spot sourcing). As a general rule, systematic sourcing is associated with aggregation models and static pricing. Spot sourcing, given the higher volatility in demand, is associated with hubs that use a matching mechanism to enable dynamic pricing. The integration of what and how businesses buy results in four different types of B2B intermediaries, each of which provides different benefits to participating buyers and sellers. The four types of hubs are (1) MRO hubs, (2) catalog hubs, (3) yield managers, and (4) exchanges.

MRO hubs focus on business processes that provide necessary functions across a variety of industries. Because the functions are needed on an ongoing basis, they reflect systematic sourcing in a horizontal market. In contrast, **yield managers** take a spot sourcing focus to provide operating inputs that have less predictable demand, such as employment services.

Online hubs that provide manufacturing products adopt a vertical focus. **Catalog hubs** aggregate products within an industry and are characterized by prenegotiated prices and systematic sourcing. **Exchanges** emphasize commodity-type products that are purchased on a spot basis. The characteristics that differentiate the online intermediary hubs are illustrated in Figure 13-10.

Kaplan and Sawhney note that online B2B hubs can be neutral or biased. A **neutral hub** does not favor buyers or sellers. Neutral hubs are most effective when there is **bilateral fragmentation**. Bilateral fragmentation refers to the presence of

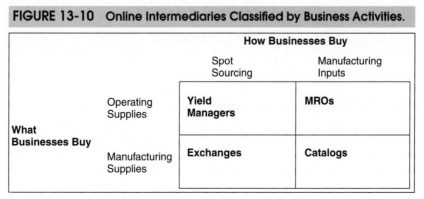

FIGURE 13-10   Online Intermediaries Classified by Business Activities.

		How Businesses Buy	
		Spot Sourcing	Manufacturing Inputs
What Businesses Buy	Operating Supplies	**Yield Managers**	**MROs**
	Manufacturing Supplies	**Exchanges**	**Catalogs**

Source: Adapted from Kaplan and Sawhney, 1999.

'Net Knowledge

CHOOSING THE RIGHT BUSINESS-TO-BUSINESS HUB

The rise in popularity of B2B exchanges, or hubs, has led to the proliferation of many new hubs, of many different types. The challenge for a B2B company is to find the one that best meets company needs. Choosing the right hub is important because the cost to integrate hub processes with company processes can be substantial, in both time and money.

There are several factors to consider in choosing a hub.[1] First, what do you want the hub to do for you? Some hubs operate like portals, aggregating content and commercial opportunities. Others work as match-makers, making the introductions between buyers and sellers. Another set of hubs goes one step further, buying goods from sellers and selling them to buyers. These hubs are market-makers. Deciding which type of hub is best requires clear knowledge of how your company wants to integrate the Internet into its B2B activities.

Another factor to consider is the amount of support the hub can provide to companies in order to get set up. Large companies often have an advantage in that they have more resources to devote to developing the infrastructure and processes required to use a particular B2B hub than smaller companies. As a result, hubs that court large companies are often not suitable exchanges for small-to-medium companies. Recognizing this constraint, some hubs target smaller businesses, providing a wide range of support services.

The size and nature of participants in the hub is also an important factor. As we saw earlier in the chapter, an exchange needs to have a critical mass of participants, and of the right sort, in order to provide value for buyers and sellers. Having too few buyers and sellers, or an extreme imbalance between the two, can reduce the value of the hub and hamper its chances of long-term survival.

The life expectancy of the hub is influenced not only by its ability to compete with other hubs, but also by its internal management team and the business model under which the hub operates. In evaluating the likely success of a hub, a company should consider whether the hub's management has a viable business plan, and whether they have the necessary resources to implement the plan. For instance, a hub with an aggressive participant growth plan should have a plan for implementing the technologies needed to manage the growth in hub activity.

---

[1]See *Software Magazine*, February/March 2001 for additional hub selection criteria.

high differentiation of participants on each side of the exchange process. Neutral hubs require participation of both buyers and sellers to provide value, whether the market uses an aggregation mechanism or a matching mechanism. With an aggregation mechanism, a neutral hub increases the value it adds by providing a wider range of opportunities to buyers and sellers. With a matching mechanism, a neutral hub increases its value by improving the quality of matches between buyers and sellers.

Biased hubs focus on providing benefits for buyers or for sellers—but not both. Biased hubs tend to be most effective when there is **unilateral fragmentation**. Unilateral fragmentation refers to situations in which only one side of the market exhibits low concentration. Biased hubs operate in favor of the fragmented side of the market. For instance, characteristics of the Internet make it possible for a hub to aggregate buyer demand from a collection of highly fragmented buyers. The aggregator can negotiate more effectively with a collection of concentrated sellers than if the buyers negotiated independently. This situation is termed **reverse aggregation**, in contrast to more traditional markets, in which an aggregator combines services offered by resellers to increase selling power, a process of **forward aggregation**.

The presence of online B2B intermediaries presents businesses with new outlets for buying and selling products. In addition, the novel characteristics of some online intermediaries, such as reverse aggregators, mean that buyers and sellers must adapt their B2B exchange processes to effectively leverage aspects of these biased markets. Shifts in the processes for conducting B2B exchanges may also affect the nature of relationships that develop between participants in the exchanges. We will consider the impact of the Internet on aspects of relationship development in detail in Chapter 14.

CHAPTER SUMMARY

The impact of the Internet on business activity is evident in the B2B environment. Businesses have relied on technologies that enable the electronic exchange of data and of dollars in B2B transactions for several decades. The impact of Internet-related computing technologies, however, has extended far beyond these early e-commerce applications to include a wide range of business marketing activities. The ability of organizations to conduct B2B activities online has resulted in projections of e-commerce revenues for B2B in excess of $1.3 trillion by 2003.

Applications for digital B2B continue to develop, often resulting in new uses of the Internet. For example, the development of industry-niched, vertical market portals on the Internet not only creates a new business opportunity for the portal developer, who provides a hub that connects buyers and sellers, but it also provides the participating vendors with a new forum for selling their products.

In this chapter, we examined the role of the Internet for aspects of B2B marketing. We began by describing the differences between B2C and B2B marketing activity. These differences included the types of customers, the nature of product demand, and the processes for conducting exchange activities. Rapid increases in the development of B2B Internet applications—as indicated by a comparison of B2C and B2B revenues—illustrated the importance of the digital environment for B2B activity.

The Internet's role in B2B activity was considered in terms of three aspects of business exchanges: exchange purposes, exchange processes, and exchange participants. The Internet exerts a strong influence on purposes for B2B exchanges. We noted that more than one-half of the B2B online revenues by 2002 are projected to stem from reseller activity. In addition, the industrial market, comprised of manufacturing and operating activities, are expected to account for approximately one-third and one-fifth of online B2B exchanges, respectively, by 2002.

We also examined the effect on the Internet in stages of the procurement process. These stages include information gathering, transaction negotiation, and trade settlement. The Internet affects the amount of buyer activity conducted in each stage, depending on whether the exchange is a new buy, a modified rebuy, or a straight rebuy. For new buys, the Internet provides benefits as a content resource for providing information in the early stage of the procurement process. For modified rebuys, the Internet exerts influence as a communications resource for facilitating negotiation and customization. In straight rebuy situations, the Internet is an effective channel for automating processes for product orders, invoices, and logistics.

The Internet affects the nature and function of participants in direct and indirect B2B processes. A key problem for buyers and for sellers in direct exchanges is the need to identify appropriate exchange partners. The Internet has introduced new intermediaries for indirect exchange that seek to address the difficulties of direct, online, B2B exchanges. These intermediaries were described as electronic hubs: organized markets that create value through aggregation and matching mechanisms. The appropriate selection of online intermediaries for B2B exchanges was considered in terms of exchange characteristics, such as the type of purchase and the predictability of product need.

CONTENT MANAGEMENT

USEFUL TERMS

- aggregation
- aggregator intermediaries
- auctioneer intermediaries
- auctions
- bid-ask exchanges
- bilateral fragmentation
- buyer-driven pricing
- catalog approach
- catalog hubs
- consortia-led exchanges
- critical mass
- derived demand
- direct exchange
- exchange intermediaries
- exchanges
- first-mover advantage
- forward aggregation

- fragmented market
- horizontal market
- indirect exchange
- information gathering stage
- intranets
- market liquidity
- market-making firms
- matching
- modified rebuy
- MRO hubs
- MROs
- neutral hub
- new buy
- original equipment manufacturers (OEM)
- procurement
- proprietary exchanges

- purchasing agents
- purchasing manager
- resellers
- reverse aggregation
- seller-driven pricing
- settlement stage
- spot sourcing
- straight rebuy
- supply chain management (SCM)
- systematic sourcing
- third-party exchanges
- transaction negotiation stage
- unilateral fragmentation
- vertical market
- Web response forms (WRFs)
- yield managers

REVIEW QUESTIONS

1. Describe three differences between B2B and B2C exchanges.
2. Explain why B2B markets account for a disproportionate amount of online revenue.
3. What three aspects of business exchanges does the Internet influence?

4. What is the difference between a vertical market and a horizontal market?
5. If a procurement officer is conducting a modified rebuy, on what stage of the procurement process is she most likely focused?
6. In a new buy situation, how may buyers take advantage of the Internet? In a modified rebuy exchange?
7. What are some of the drawbacks of EDI (electronic data interchange)? How does the Internet address some of these drawbacks?
8. How may e-mail capabilities on the Internet influence direct B2B exchange?
9. Describe some of the advantages and disadvantages associated with market-making intermediaries that may be experienced by buyers and by sellers.
10. What two ways can intermediaries provide value to buyers and sellers in the exchange process?
11. Discuss the different types of B2B hubs, in terms of what and how businesses buy.

WEB APPLICATION

Evaluating Online Exchanges: What Works, and Why?

Online markets, or exchange hubs, exhibit many differences. They can be vertical or horizontal, open or restrictive in their membership, broadly or narrowly focused, and so on. In this exercise, you'll visit exchange hubs of several types, to understand which characteristics and capabilities make an exchange hub successful. Completing the table below will help you organize your analysis.

Exchange Hub	Industry Focus	Membership	Key Benefits	Support Services
Elemica.com	Chemicals	Open	Single point of access to all members for order negotiation and processing. Streamlines supply chain management (SCM). Also has direct online selling and logistics products.	24 × 7 customer phone support. Value calculator for cost savings estimation.Data intelligence reporting capabilities.
Exostar.com				
Pantellos.com				
Food Trader.com				
Vertmarkets.com				

1. Do membership restrictions and exchange size appear to vary by industry? If so, what industry characteristics might explain the variation?
2. Which exchanges emphasize process facilitation (e.g., SCM solutions) relative to developing source or buyer contacts? Is there any apparent relationship between the emphasis and the membership? That is, do smaller, more focused exchanges seem to promote solutions more heavily than exchanges with larger numbers of buyers and sellers?
3. For which exchanges, or types of exchanges (by industry), is the range of support services largest? What characteristics of the industry indicate the need for extensive support?

CONCEPTS IN BRIEF

1. The Internet has influenced many aspects of B2B activity, in different ways from its influence on B2C activity. These differing impacts reflect fundamental differences between B2B and B2C exchange processes.

2. The influence of the Internet on B2B activity is important, as B2B revenues dwarf B2C revenues, online and off-line.

3. B2B activity differs from B2C activity in the nature of the customer, the processes used to buy and sell products, and the nature of demand.

4. The formalized processes of B2B exchange, such as the procurement process, enable us to delimit stages in which the Internet may be used for different purposes and benefits. For instance, the Internet helps companies overcome new buy obstacles in highly fragmented markets, and it helps coordinate communications in modified rebuy situations.

5. The sourcing and procurement functions that comprise supply chain management (SCM) have been streamlined by companies that use the Internet to communicate inventory and supply needs, to conduct collaborative research and design, and to manage retail delivery scheduling. The Internet is a flexible tool for SCM.

6. The Internet has influenced B2B sourcing by enabling the development of different types of sourcing intermediaries, including auctioneers, aggregators, and exchanges.

7. These intermediaries, who often function as market-makers, occupy a central position in B2B indirect channels.

8. Online intermediaries provide value for B2B exchange processes through aggregation and matching; in short, they manage fragmentation on the buy side and the sell side, making it easier for companies to find what they want to buy (aggregation), or who they want to buy from (matching).

9. Intermediaries can be classified into four types, depending on what they sell, and how they sell it. The four intermediary types are yield managers, MROs, exchanges, and catalogs.

10. The success of an online intermediary, and its value to its participants, depends on the ability of the intermediary to acquire sufficient participants to assure that there are enough buyers for sellers, and vice versa.

THINKING POINTS

1. What characteristics of the Internet might account for the disproportionate adoption of the Internet as a market for B2B exchanges, relative to B2C exchanges?

2. What characteristics of B2B exchanges may account for the disproportionate adoptions of the Internet as a market for B2B exchanges, relative to B2C exchanges?

3. How might the capabilities of the Internet serve to "smooth" the spikes in derived demand that result from overly optimistic and pessimistic forecasts of consumer consumption?

4. In which type of market, vertical or horizontal, is the formation of a personalized relationship that exists between the producer and the buyer more likely to be a central factor in the development of the relationship? Why?

5. Consider the role of the Internet as a content resource, a channel resource, and a communications resource. Are these resources likely to be differently emphasized in different types of B2B exchanges (i.e., new buy, modified rebuy, straight rebuy)?

6. What characteristics of the Internet have contributed to the rapid growth—in number and in popularity—of online markets that serve as intermediaries for B2B exchanges?

7. What are the implications of reverse aggregation for the development of market intermediaries?

ENDNOTES

1. These examples are discussed in detail, with others, in *ZDnet News*, "Why Is B-to-B Getting Such a Bad Rap?" by Stefan Heck and Jeff Arvin, 12/6/01.
2. C. Ranganathan, Jasbir Dhaliwal, and Thompson Teo, "Diffusion of Web Technologies in the Supply Chain Management Function: Examining the Role of Environmental and Organizational Factors," Diffusion Interest Group in Information Technology Workshop (DIGIT), Barcelona, 2002, 1–21.
3. "B2B E-Commerce Hubs: Towards a Taxonomy of Business Models," by Steven Kaplan and Mohanbir Sawhney. Working paper, University of Chicago, Graduate School of Business, December 1999.

SUGGESTED READINGS

1. *Business-to-Business Internet Marketing*, by Barry Silverstein (Maximum Press: Gulf Breeze, FL, 1998.)
2. "Impacts of the Electronic Marketplace on Transaction Cost and Market Structure," by Ho Geun Lee and Theodore H. Clark. *International Journal of Electronic Commerce, 1* (1), pages 127–149.
3. "Let's Get Vertical," by Mohanbir Sawhney and Steven Kaplan. *Business 2.0* (September 1999), pages 85–92.
4. "The Impact of Interorganizational Networks on Buyer-Seller Relationships," by Charles Steinfield, Robert Kraut, and Alice Plummer. *Journal of Computer-mediated Communication, 1* (3), http://www.ascusc.org/jcmc/vol1/issue3/steinfld.html.

LEARNING LINKS

Online Supply Chain Management

www.darwinmag.com/learn/curve/column.html?ArticleID = 123
www.cio.com/research/scm/

Online Sourcing

www.nwfusion.com/research/reports/IDC27219R.html
www.aberdeen.com/ab_company/hottopics/esourcing2002/default.htm

Applications of Online Sourcing

www.tiburongroup.com/html/solutions/services/sourcing.htm
www.machineshops.biz/08–52003-Internet-Sourcing-25795.html

Online Procurement

www.napm.org

Applications of Online Procurement

www.ajplus.co.uk/indeco/index/
www.eere.energy.gov/femp/procurement/online_procure.html
www.suppliersonline.com/Default.asp

Internet B2B Intermediaries

www.computerworld.com/news/2000/story/0,11280,43960,00.html
www.workz.com/cgi-bin/gt/tpl_page.html, template = 1&content = 1408&nav1 = 1&

Focus on the Future

Relationship Management for Digital Business

Focus and Objectives

This chapter addresses the role of the Internet as a force that influences businesses' ability to develop and maintain exchange relationships. The growing importance of developing ongoing relational exchanges is described, and a framework for thinking about relational exchange is discussed. We use this theoretical basis to consider ways that value is created in business-to-consumer (B2C) and business-to-business (B2B) exchanges. In B2C exchanges, we consider ways in which the Internet affects relational development by influencing satisfaction, trust, and commitment. In B2B exchanges, we examine the Internet's influence on different classes of B2B relationships.

Your objectives in studying this chapter include the following:

- Understand the difference between initiating relational exchange, and developing and maintaining the exchange.
- Recognize key shifts in business activity that illustrate the increasing importance of ongoing relational exchange.
- Understand which types of exchanges provide benefits from ongoing interaction, and how the Internet affects the creation of these benefits.
- Identify primary determinants of perceived value in a B2C relationship, and the Internet-related factors that influence them.
- Identify major classes of B2B relationships, the dimensions that define them, and the Internet characteristics that influence them.

Closing the Loop

Did you ever wonder how some businesses seem to know just the right ads to have pop up on your browser? Why does the content on your favorite Web destination seem designed just for you? The answer to these questions may be "closed-loop marketing."

Closed-loop marketing refers to the process of developing solid knowledge about customers and their likes and dislikes by tracking and using the pattern and content of communications to and from customers; in essence, simply listening to what your customers are saying with their actions. For instance, a company might run an advertising campaign that includes an e-mail campaign and a banner ad with a click-through capability to the company's site. Customers' responses to the advertising can be tracked with the Internet. Visitors at the company site who arrive through the banner ad provide the business with information about the "pull" of the banner, and about the previous location of the visitor. Each piece of the response is useful information for altering the ad campaign and for learning more about potential customers.

The e-mail campaign can provide information that can be used to build individual shopper profiles. Companies can embed links in e-mail content that, when clicked, will take the customer to detailed content about the link subject. By tracking which link customers visit, and when, and for how long, the business gains additional information about shoppers to add to their visitor profile. When it's time to correspond with the customer, the message can be customized, based on profile information, to incorporate content targeted to the shopper's needs and interests.

Macromedia, whose Flash software jazzed up the Internet with interactive, animated design capabilities, has recognized the importance of the Internet for closed-loop marketing. The company uses the Internet to take a customer-centric approach to business, building relationships with its customers that introduce them to the processes of product development. Macromedia believes that the Internet is a crucial element in leveraging the power of one-to-one relationships between a company and its customers.

How do they do it? E-mail is an important component of Macromedia's closed-loop process. Site visitors who register for product downloads or e-mail notifications of products or events are entered into a database. The responses these visitors provide to personalized e-mails are used to refine and customize future communications. In addition, sales information, and the types of customer support requested and received can be stored in a customer's profile. Macromedia also lets site visitors register to participate in product testing. Web developers and online shoppers have the opportunity to provide feedback about Macromedia's products-in-progress. Tracking responses from both sides of Web development makes sense. Macromedia has created products that can be readily used by site developers and appreciated by site visitors. These products have helped other companies use the Internet for their own closed-loop activities.

A big challenge for closed-loop marketing has been the integration of customer responses and activities across channels to create a comprehensive profile of a customer, in turn creating an appropriate Web display that uses dynamically created content tailored to the individual customer. This was the problem faced by FAO Schwartz, the well-known toy company.

How do you make your Web site suitable for new visitors—providing all the necessary information for first-time visitors and buyers—without annoying loyal, frequent visitors? In addition, how do you customize dynamic content when you don't have access to what that customer has purchased in the past, either through the site, or through a catalog or retail store?

FAO Schwartz hired an expert. Mindseye, Inc., a Web solutions developer, used Macromedia's ColdFusion software to redesign the toy store's online presence. By integrating all of the data collected from individual customers, across channels, Mindseye provided FAO Schwartz with a site that suited everyone. Customized product displays and offers are developed in real-time, based on access to customer profiles that contain comprehensive information about past FAO purchases, online and off-line. This process, known as **real-time marketing**, leverages closed-loop marketing for maximum effect.

The ability of the Internet to facilitate communications, and to track, analyze, store, and report instances and patterns of visitor actions makes closed-loop marketing an increasingly popular strategy for businesses. As Macromedia has learned, working with customers, and listening to their needs and wants, lets the company build products that maximize the benefits to its customers, whether they are buyers or sellers.

The experiences of Macromedia and FAO Schwartz illustrate several challenges faced by businesses in the digital business environment. For instance, how can businesses best use the Internet to keep customers happy and loyal? What might work for one buyer–seller relationship, or for one type of business, might not work for another. In addition, how should large amounts of customer information be managed, not only from online sources, but also across channels? In what ways can information be gathered, organized, stored, and used to improve all aspects of exchange? Each of these challenges emphasizes the central role of relationships.

The link between the Internet and relationship management is not new. Throughout this book we have seen the importance for businesses of the relationships that exist in the Internet environment. In Chapter 1, we considered the interaction between business and technology as a backdrop for the study of digital business strategy. In Chapter 2, we developed a framework based on the exchange relationships between participants in the Internet environment. The activities of these participants were discussed in Chapters 3 through 6 as relationships formed to meet the exchange needs of businesses, customers, technology developers, and policy makers.

In Chapters 7 and 8, we extended our view to examine the effect of the Internet on the nature of competition—among companies and among customers—for resources in the environment. We looked at ways in which the Internet influences strategic business, including defining objectives and leveraging resources. Using the Internet to identify relationships that meet strategic objectives was addressed in Chapter 9. In Chapters 10 through 12, we learned how businesses can leverage the content, channel, and communication resources of the Internet to initiate relational exchanges. B2B relational exchanges were the focus of Chapter 13.

The importance of relationships to business is evident when you consider the many types of relationships that can exist between a company and its customers. These relationships not only include links to the end consumer, but to all of the participants in the value chain. For instance, a company might have ongoing relationships with a set of suppliers, some value-added resellers, and a collection of retailers.

The Internet, with its ability to transmit information and to store data, can affect the ways that companies manage relationships with other participants in value chain activities. The importance of exchanges that occur—in addition to sales transactions—is evident in the influence of policy makers and technology developers on the exchanges between buyers and sellers, at many links in the value chain.

Beyond affecting the beginning of relationships, the Internet can influence the ways that businesses conduct activities that foster valued relationships and terminate ineffective relationships. In this chapter, we shift our focus to consider the Internet as a factor that affects businesses' efforts to build ongoing interactions. Earlier chapters emphasized the role of the Internet as a factor that facilitates or inhibits the beginning of exchange relationships. Now we will consider the Internet as a means for developing and maintaining relational exchange.

We begin by looking at several factors that have spurred the growing importance of relationship-oriented business. Then we take a theoretical perspective on relational exchange to describe the nature of exchanges, including the ways that relationships add value for partners, and how value is measured. We apply this theoretical base to examine the influence of the Internet on companies' ability to foster relational exchanges in B2C and in B2B markets.

Bits & Bytes 14.1

Developing relationships is important. Research results indicate that a customer must shop at an online store four times before the store profits from the customer.

(*Source:* Nua Internet Surveys, citing Mainspring, 2000.)

The Increasing Importance of Relationships

Businesses are interested in relationships for a very straightforward reason—building relationships with customers can improve profits. Researchers have estimated that the cost of making a sale to a new customer is six to nine times as expensive as making a sale to a repeat customer.

Developing an ongoing relationship not only reduces monetary costs, it also provides a business with less uncertainty about exchange-related outcomes, more time to pursue other relationships, and greater satisfaction on the part of the other partner. This latter benefit illustrates the concept that relationships provide value for both partners. Satisfaction results from the improved knowledge of preferences and needs that guides the exchange. For a company, customer satisfaction increases the likelihood of getting referrals through positive word-of-mouth.

Because it can be used to gather and store information about customer needs, and to facilitate interaction with customers, the Internet has increased the importance that businesses place on developing relationships, as well as the methods they use to do so. Strategies that are focused on developing unique, sustained relationships with individual customers are described as **1:1[1] marketing**. Because it has the capability to facilitate personalized, customized interaction between companies and consumers, the Internet is an important factor in 1:1 business activity.

As an area of academic study, relationship marketing is relatively young. Although companies have formed partnerships for mutual benefit for hundreds of years, the formal study of relationships for business activity did not receive widespread attention until the 1980s. The increased attention to the role of relationships in business practice can be attributed to changes in the way that we view business exchange.

Shifts in Perspectives on Exchange

The importance of relationships for digital business is evident in four fundamental shifts in the ways that business researchers and practitioners address business exchange. These shifts are (1) from a product focus to a person focus; (2) from a competition focus to a cooperation focus; (3) from a discrete, company-based focus to a networked focus; and (4) from a transactional focus to a relational exchange focus.

From Products to People

In both B2C and B2B markets, increasing attention is being paid to the importance of the customer, as with 1:1 marketing strategies. Many companies have shifted from a **product-centric approach**, in which a product is pushed to a target market, to a **customer-centric approach**, in which customers communicate product preferences and may even collaborate in the design and development of the product, as do Macromedia's clients.

The Internet facilitates interactions between buyers and sellers, creating an environment for relational exchange. Buyers can communicate preferences and dissatisfaction rapidly and directly, and sellers can target products and promotions to specific audiences. These two capabilities reflect accountability and addressability. **Accountability** refers to the burden placed on sellers to meet the buyers' expectations. **Addressability** refers to the ability of businesses to identify and target individual customers, as with pointcast technologies. In addition, advances in product development technologies have made it possible to modularize the construction of many products. As we saw in Chapter 12, this modularization enables mass customization, thus making it possible for companies to respond to customers' needs more effectively. One effect of the increasing ability to mass customize products is a parallel increase in buyers' expectations of seller accountability.

From Competition to Cooperation

Economists have long attempted to understand and explain marketplace behavior with models of competition. Competition means that companies treat each other as adversaries in their quests to meet their own goals. Recent efforts to describe markets, however, have been focused on cooperation. Cooperation exists when a subset of companies operates jointly, maximizing each company's core competencies for a mutual goal.

Cooperation can help companies compete. Managing competition through cooperation is reflected by the growth of strategic alliances. In Chapter 8, we learned that strategic alliances are partnerships between independent companies that might otherwise be in competition with each other. An alliance can provide each partner with needed capabilities, but without the headaches of ownership that often occur with vertical integration. A company may form multiple strategic alliances to create a network of relationships that provide the company with a competitive advantage through cooperation. Remember Covisint, the B2B automotive exchange? The exchange consists of several major manufacturers and a lot of suppliers. Rather than developing many different processes for procuring parts, the companies streamlined the buying process by connecting suppliers to manufacturers with a single, overarching process. The reduced costs, in time and money, enable the manufacturers to compete more effectively on price to end customers.

From Stand-alone to Networked

The shifts in focus we have just considered are each related to technological advances that increase the ways in which people can interact. For instance, shoppers can use the Internet to compare competing products, and to order customized products. Because the increased transparency of product offerings may affect businesses' ability to develop and sustain a competitive advantage in the product offering, companies compete for customers, often working to develop long-term relationships that add value for the customer, independent of the product offering. The interactive capabilities of the Internet provide a means by which companies can tailor business activities to develop one-to-one relationships with customers.

From Transactions to Relationships

The three shifts just discussed suggest the importance of the fourth shift from a focus on single transactions to a focus on ongoing interactions (Figure 14-1). Prior to the emergence of relationship marketing, business researchers and practitioners emphasized the importance of understanding and implementing practices that promoted a company's ability to complete transactions, such as making a sale. This orientation is often described as a functional approach to interactions between agents in the marketplace.

A relational exchange perspective provides a better description of the types of exchanges that take place daily between organizations in the business environment than does a transaction-focused approach. As we saw in the first section of this

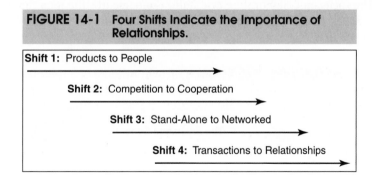

FIGURE 14-1   Four Shifts Indicate the Importance of Relationships.

Shift 1: Products to People

Shift 2: Competition to Cooperation

Shift 3: Stand-Alone to Networked

Shift 4: Transactions to Relationships

book, transactions are merely the end result of an exchange process. We also saw that exchange processes are not limited to products and money; businesses engage in exchange processes that transfer many different resources. Relational exchange takes into account the different types of resource exchange that receive little attention in transaction-focused descriptions of business activity.

Organizing Types of Relational Exchange

Relationships can differ widely. Some require little or no interaction to complete a transaction, while others reflect high levels of exchange—in ideas, negotiations, and product trial. We can organize the key differences between exchange relationships as a continuum of interaction. Relationships that take a transaction-oriented focus are at one end, while relationships that emphasize ongoing interaction between the partners are at the other extreme. This continuum is shown in Figure 14-2.

The location of a relationship on the continuum depends on the extent to which the partners adopt a collaborative orientation toward the exchange. The development of the area of relationship marketing in the 1980s led to a shift in focus from transactional approaches to relational processes for exchange. This shift underscored the idea that the true value of a customer may lie across several transactions, rather than in a single transaction. By the late 1990s, information technologies had made increasingly possible interactive communications between companies and customers that pushed relational exchange toward a collaborative orientation. A **collaborative orientation** exists when an interaction between two parties indicates cooperative actions undertaken for mutual benefit; that is, the customer becomes an active partner in creating the nature of the exchange. A collaborative orientation in a relationship suggests that both partners will be willing to make changes to accomplish relational goals, and that each party anticipates future interactions.

Procter & Gamble has taken a collaborative orientation to product development with its "Share Your Thoughts" page. Consumers provide feedback about product experiences and make suggestions about product enhancements through the company's Web site. The company estimates that online collaboration has reduced their costs to test new product concepts from $25,000 and 2 months, to $2,500 and 2 weeks.[2] The screen in Figure 14-3 illustrates the benefits of closing the loop with consumers, in the redesign of Bounty paper towels. Procter & Gamble uses the Web to collect the feedback, and to communicate the impact of the feedback to its customers.

The focus on collaborative orientation underscores the idea that the actual transaction is often not the most useful descriptor of a relationship. Many different types of

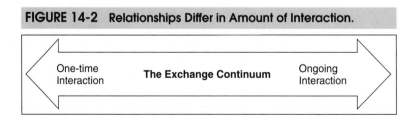

FIGURE 14-2 Relationships Differ in Amount of Interaction.

One-time Interaction   **The Exchange Continuum**   Ongoing Interaction

FIGURE 14-3 **Procter & Gamble Reaps the Bounty of Internet Collaboration.**

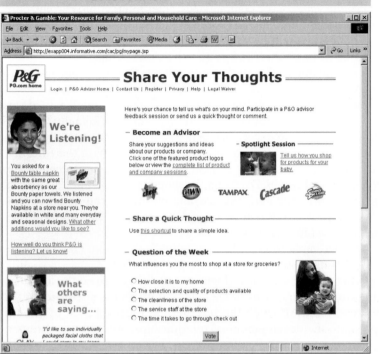

exchanges occur between the initial contact between the active agents and the final transaction of money and product. The number and nature of the exchanges may differ depending on the exchange agents and their objectives. For instance, in a B2C relationship, the exchange may involve a one-time purchase, with limited interaction and relationship development. In contrast, in a B2B setting, the exchange process may be more complex and it may be repeated.

For many types of exchanges, the process by which the transaction is reached can be critically important. For instance, in a B2B exchange, characterized by high costs and high levels of asset specificity, the give-and-take nature of the exchange between the businesses may be an important determinant of the relationship—even though transactions may be infrequent.

Applying the Continuum

Applying the exchange continuum to digital business suggests several implications for companies. As we have already noted, the continuum suggests that all forms of exchange can affect the perceived value of a relationship. As a result, opportunities for creating value are not limited to the final transaction. For both partners in an exchange, value can be created through the transfer of all forms of resources, not just products and money. For instance, the communication of product maintenance information and product updates from a company to a customer via the Internet can enhance the value of the company-customer interaction. The customer receives useful information, and the company receives the benefits of the reduced costs obtained from using the Internet to transfer the information. This implication illustrates the shift from a stand-alone to a networked perspective on exchange.

A second implication of the continuum is that the opportunities to add value to an exchange process increase as the nature of an interaction shifts from transactional to relational. An increase in the number of exchange-related activities and the extended duration of these activities provides both partners with multiple occasions and ways in which to provide and experience benefits of the interaction that are based on recognition of each other's abilities, interests, and needs. With the Internet, companies and their customers can interact in near real-time to create exchange processes that are mutually advantageous. For example, shoppers can acquire desired information about product features and performance, and businesses can obtain knowledge of shopper preferences, even in the absence of a transaction. This implication reflects the shift from a product focus to a people focus.

Another implication of the continuum is that there may be different types of relational exchanges, and that different types of exchanges may have different benefits for the partners in the exchange (Figure 14-4). We described the location of a relationship on the continuum in terms of the extent to which the interaction reflected a collaborative orientation. Although the Internet has received a lot of attention for its ability to promote the development of relationships, not all transactions require the same

FIGURE 14-4 The Internet Offers Opportunities to Enhance Exchange.

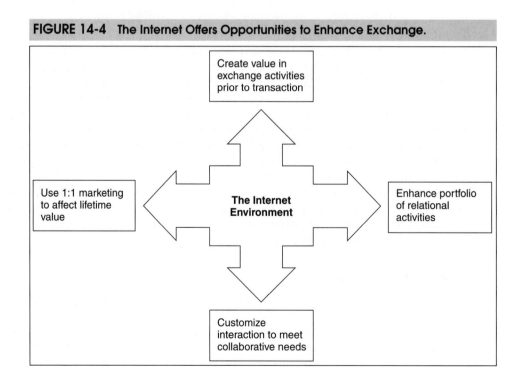

investment in the formation and maintenance of a one-to-one interaction. In addition, consumers may differ in the importance they place on developing an ongoing relationship with a marketer for a particular product. The difference in types of relational exchanges reflected by the continuum is related to the shift from competition to cooperation.

Movement along the continuum from transactions to relationships also suggests changes in the ways that businesses measure the value of exchange. An emphasis on transactions means that value is measured in market share, or how many customers in a targeted segment buy a product. With a relational, or 1:1 focus, the emphasis shifts to share-of-customer, or how loyal the consumer is to a particular company or product. This shift is assessed by considering the **lifetime value (LTV)** of a customer. Lifetime value is the total amount of profits, discounted over time, that will result from sales to a customer over the life cycle of the consumer. LTV provides a summary measure, in dollars, of relationship value. To learn how to calculate LTV, try the Web Application in the review materials at the end of the chapter.

Factors that Influence LTV and the Customer Life Cycle

Lifetime value measures a relationship in terms of dollars. Although dollars, and return on investment, or ROI, may often be the ultimate marker of business success, several factors many influence the customer life cycle. For instance, a customer who is highly satisfied with a company may be more loyal and purchase more frequently, and for a longer time, than a customer who is dissatisfied with the company. As a result, the life cycle is longer for the first customer, and more profitable for the company.

Boosting LTV involves careful management of the interactions with customers. **Customer relationship management (CRM)** is the oversight of the set of interactions between a company and its customers, from the initial contact, to sales lead, transaction, training, and customer support. The power of the Internet as a means of gathering and using customer information has increased the popularity of CRM.

Many software products and consultants provide ways to implement CRM processes. CRM software provides businesses with the means to collect and store data online about the customers' interactions with a company, a process known as **data warehousing**. By integrating and analyzing the stored data, through a process known as **data mining**, businesses can better match targeted offers to customer needs and expectations.

The benefits of these CRM activities, however, are measured with behavioral and psychological characteristics. Behavioral characteristics are the observable outcomes of interaction. In contrast, psychological characteristics are the unobservable measures that reflect the partner's perceptions of a relationship.

Behavioral Characteristics and Lifetime Value

With behavioral characteristics, we can describe a relationship in terms of the number of times that the partners have completed transactions, the frequency with which the partners interact, and the types of activities that each partner has carried out in order to facilitate the interaction. For example, in a B2C relationship, the seller might create a database to keep track of a customer's preferences. In a B2B relationship, a buyer

'Net Knowledge

THE CRM LIFE CYCLE

Life cycles are an important focus for businesses. We evaluate products in terms of their life cycle, from beginning, to growth, maturity, and decline. We also consider the life cycle of customers, in order to determine when they stop bringing profits to a company.

CRM solutions seem to have a life cycle, too. Think of all the information that a company can collect about its customers. Companies use online databases to store visitors' site activity, member registrations, referring Web sites, sales and support information, and log files of site activity. With Web analytics tools, this information can be used to fine-tune marketing efforts to better reach consumers, thus creating stronger relationships with consumers, and increasing loyalty and profits.

So why are so many online business efforts often so impersonal? Where are the 1:1 relationships? The Aberdeen Group, a business research firm, may have the answer.[1] Based on survey research designed to examine ways in which companies attempt to implement software solutions to manage customer relationships, Aberdeen detected a systematic trend. Most companies used the data they collected in a similar order of activities. First, they developed and refined the Web presence, in terms of content. Next, they tended to work on the site's functionality, by incorporating search tools. The third stage of CRM implementation was focused on customer activity on the site, including traffic patterns. The last step was to use the data to personalize communications and develop 1:1 interactions with customers.

In short, companies worked from the broadest impact of CRM tools to the narrowest. They started with the broadcast public face, the Web site. Then they moved to a focus on clusters of customers, with aggregate-level analysis of site activity and impact. It wasn't until the more general functions were implemented that companies leveraged their data to develop personalized, individual contacts with consumers.

---

[1] As described in *CRMDaily,* July 10, 2003.

---

might adjust a requested delivery schedule to accommodate the production capabilities of a valued supplier.

Psychological Characteristics of Lifetime Value

Three psychological descriptors of relationships are satisfaction, trust, and commitment. Research results suggest that these measures are related to perceptions of relationship value. **Satisfaction** is defined as the overall evaluation of the experiences related to the purchase and consumption of a product over time.[3] **Trust** is exhibited as willingness to rely on an exchange partner, based on perceptions of the partner's reliability and integrity.[4] **Commitment** is defined as a lasting desire to maintain a valued relationship.[5]

Satisfaction, trust, and commitment often affect the link between components of a customer's attitude toward a product or a company, and future intentions toward consuming a product from the company. Researchers have demonstrated that these indicators of satisfaction, trust, and commitment are influenced by the collaborative orientation of the partner in the relational exchange. In general, satisfaction is more closely related to intentions to conduct future exchanges when the collaborative orientation is weak. When the collaborative orientation is strong, trust and commitment become more influential than satisfaction.

We can use behavioral and psychological characteristics of relationships, in conjunction with the concepts from the relational exchange continuum, to consider ways that the ability to foster relational development might differ in B2C and B2B exchanges.

Differences Between B2C and B2B Relationships

Similar to B2C interactions, B2B interactions have an overarching goal of completing a transaction. As we saw in Chapter 13, however, the exchange processes exhibit several key differences. First, B2B transactions may be subject to greater time constraints than most buyer–seller transactions. Business customers may have a specific task that can be accomplished in a desired time frame only with the purchase of a particular product. In addition, they may have a clear sense of product need based on multiple past purchase experiences.

The higher incidence of repeat purchases illustrates a second difference between the two types of exchange relationships: the likelihood of developing an ongoing exchange relationship may often be greater for B2B situations than for B2C situations. As a result, B2B interactions may tend to be more relational than B2C relationships, which may tend to emphasize a transactional approach to exchange.

The process of effecting a B2B transaction may often be more complex than the process for completing a B2C transaction. More steps may be needed to obtain approval for a transaction, to assess the quality of the transaction, and to document the execution of the transaction. The increased complexity of B2B exchanges may also mean the inclusion of more people in the decision-making process. These characteristics—increased activities and participants—suggest that the impact of the Internet on the development of relational exchange is best examined using psychological indicators of value for B2C exchanges, but behavioral indicators of value for B2B exchanges.

In the next two sections, we will use the concepts of the relational exchange continuum, sources of value, and ways to assess value to consider ways that the Internet can be used to foster relational exchange in B2C and B2B interactions.

Putting CRM to Work: Building Business-to-Consumer Relationships

To illustrate the effect of the Internet on adding value to customer relationships, we will look at the decision process that initiates the exchange in three stages: prepurchase, purchase, and postpurchase. In each stage, we will take a consumer-centric approach to understanding how the Internet can be used to create value for the customer. Although there are many ways in which the Internet can help or harm value

InSite

FROM MARTINI TO WINE: WWW.VIRGINWINES.COM

For many people, choosing wines is a lot tougher than drinking them. Experience is an important factor, both in knowing what makes a wine good, and in knowing what you like to drink. After all, one person's Mad Dog 20/20 may be another's Chateau-neuf du Pape. The problem with most experts who recommend wines is that while they may know what is good, and what they like, they don't have a good idea of what you like.

Virgin Wines addresses this problem with its online wine cellar and CRM system. With over 10,000 wines available, choosing can be difficult. Working with Blue Martini Software, the company developed a Web site that efficiently and thoroughly uses the data it collects from its customers to create a personalized wine shopping experience.

The site's Wine Wizard takes customers through a three-step process, collecting information about taste preferences, and delivering a set of recommendations that can be used to create a custom-mixed case of wine—delivered to your doorstep (Figure 14-5). For repeat customers, the software incorporates information about past purchase patterns to update the preference profile used as the basis for developing recommendations. By providing descriptions of recommen-

FIGURE 14-5 The Wine Wizard Introduces Customers to Different Products.

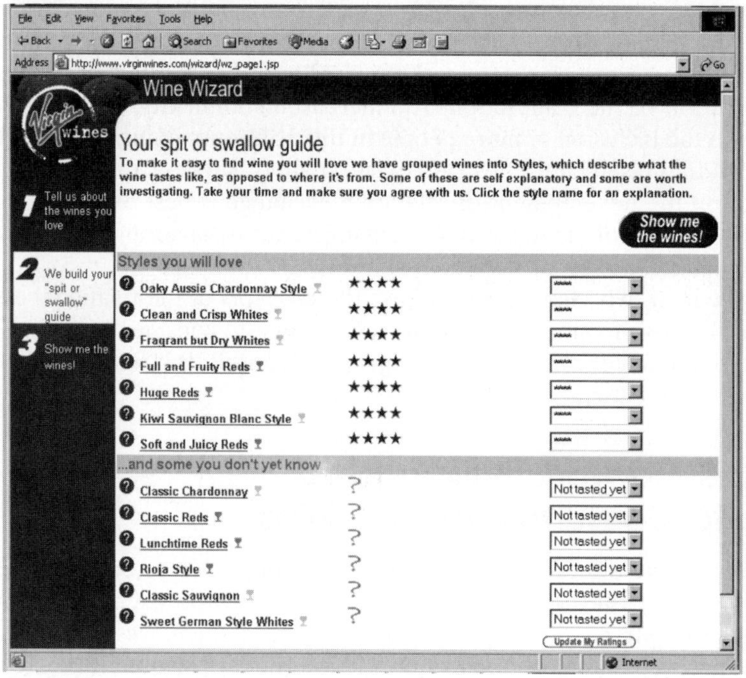

ded wines, the software enhances the company's ability to sell unfamiliar or unique wines.

With its always-on approach to personalized service, the site has been successful in developing a loyal following. By the end of its first year in business (2000), the company had already achieved a repeat customer rate of nearly 50 percent, and a 200 percent return on its development investment. To put the value of the CRM strategy into perspective, Virgin Wines is able to convert 12 percent of its visitors to buyers—nearly three times the industry average.

The only drawback? Virgin Wines only delivers in the United Kingdom.

creation, for the sake of clarity, we focus on one value source in each decision stage: satisfaction for prepurchase processes, trust for purchase processes, and commitment for postpurchase processes (Figure 14-6).

Prepurchase: Search and Satisfaction

Researchers who study consumer decision making have found that customers' confidence that they have made a good decision about a product increases their satisfaction. As we learned in Chapter 3, processes for making a decision include the ways that information is acquired, the amount of information that is obtained, and the strategy that is used to evaluate the information.

As a content and communication resource, the Internet provides shoppers with lots of information, and the opportunity to ask companies for even more. From a business' perspective, the task is to determine how to facilitate a customer's search and evaluation processes. In an online environment, search costs may be reduced by the ease with which the online environment can be used to obtain information from different vendors. A side effect of reduced search cost may be a significant increase in the numbers of sources returned by a general search; that is, more options to consider increases evaluation costs. These evaluation costs may be higher than those experienced in

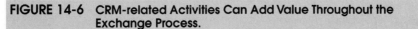

FIGURE 14-6   CRM-related Activities Can Add Value Throughout the Exchange Process.

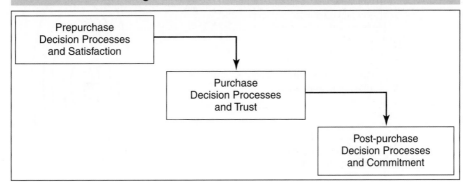

off-line situations, given the amount of information. In addition, vendors may provide information in different forms, increasing the complexity of integrating the acquired information for evaluation.

Characteristics of Software Agents for Search and Evaluation

Businesses can use Internet-based **software agents** to aid shoppers with information search and evaluation. These agents can range from very simplistic programs that execute a few keystrokes to complete a search task, all the way to very sophisticated tools that that seem to have minds of their own. Software agents can be described with three key characteristics: (1) **agency**, or the extent to which they can operate independently of the user; (2) **intelligence**, or the extent to which the agent's actions reflect an ability to build a knowledge base; and (3) **mobility**, the extent to which the agent can travel the Internet from computer to computer (Figure 14-7).

Agency means that the software tool has the ability to work autonomously, without the user's presence. Software agents can reduce search costs because they serve as a stand-in for the user, by representing the user's interests in a search task. For example, a software agent can be sent to complete a search for prices available on the Internet for a particular model of car. The customer specifies the type of car, and the price criterion, and the agent conducts the search.

Intelligence refers to the agent's ability to incorporate knowledge of the customer's preferences in its actions. In addition, intelligence is related to the amount of learning that an agent exhibits. Some simple forms of agents operate on sets of specified rules (e.g., search online dealers for a Ford Taurus; find the 10 cheapest offers). Other agents can learn a customer's preferences, and then carry out search actions that match this knowledge with knowledge of other users' preferences. These agents are called **collaborative filtering agents** or **recommender systems**. For instance, Firefly, an agent used by Amazon.com, can keep track of what a customer orders, look for other customers who purchased the same book, see what else they purchased, and then make a recommendation back to the customer.

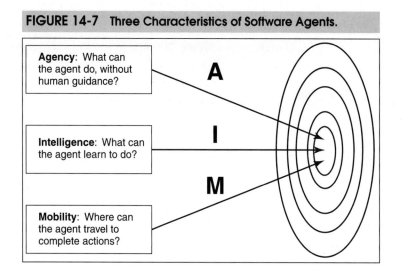

FIGURE 14-7 Three Characteristics of Software Agents.

Agency: What can the agent do, without human guidance?

A

Intelligence: What can the agent learn to do?

I

M

Mobility: Where can the agent travel to complete actions?

The ability to conduct effective searches depends on the mobility of the agent. Some software agents are designed to run on a single computer, either the customer/client or the company/server. In contrast, other agents can roam from computer to computer, gathering information and interacting with other agents. Although increased mobility has advantages in terms of a wider base for collecting information, it comes with costs due to potential security hazards.

Types of Software Agents

The effects of agents on marketing can be seen by looking at two types of software agents: search engines and intelligent agents. Search engines facilitate information acquisition, while intelligent agents can influence search and evaluation.

Search Engines   Search engines are simple software agents that operate based on opportunistic discoveries of keyword matches. Search engines, such as those available at Yahoo! or AltaVista, reduce the costs of information search. It would be impossible for a consumer to visit or find every relevant site on the Internet using a manual process.

Although they can reduce search costs, current search engines (as well as those available in the near future) also present substantial challenges to consumers. Even well-refined searches often result in an unmanageable number of hits. A large list of hits may result in information overload and create time pressure for the consumer. To help manage this complexity, most search engines order the hits in a ranking scheme. Of course, most consumers do not know and cannot control the criteria for determining the relative rankings. In addition, search engines only index a fraction of the Internet, a fact that can create uncertainty about whether all the appropriate information is available.

Intelligent Agents   An intelligent agent is a software tool that can act as a proxy for the user in the online environment. An agent can carry out tasks, such as actively gathering information based on its interpretation of the user's interests, bidding in an online auction according to the user's preferences, and completing online transactions. Search engines and intelligent agents can both provide the user with decision information. In contrast to a search engine, which only provides information from one indexing process, an intelligent agent can conduct a search with several engines, and then filter the search results to provide the user with only the hits that appear frequently. A search engine leaves the user with the task of visiting the sites, evaluating the information available, and then making a decision based on visiting all of the sites. The intelligent agent can visit many sites, extract the relevant information, compare information between sites, select the best alternative, and effect the transaction for the decision maker, all in accord with its interpretation of the user's interests.

Bits & Bytes 14.2
Satisfaction is linked to sales. A survey of 750 online shoppers revealed that 2 percent of them felt that customer service had improved from November 2001 to November 2002. They also spent more, averaging $72 during the week ending on November 15, up 28 percent from the preceding year.
(*Source: eMarketer,* 11/27/02, reporting data from Harris Interactive.)

Purchase: Transactions and Trust

In Chapter 2, we characterized the marketing process as a series of exchanges between active agents. These exchange activities can be viewed as subgoals to a larger goal of making a transaction—actually trading the good or service for money, or for some other item of acceptable value. The Internet provides buyers and sellers with new ways to complete transactions, including new forms of payment and of product delivery. Customers' perceptions of the risk involved with these methods, and their level of trust in the company's ability to deliver the good, are key factors in their decision to complete a transaction. As a result, it is necessary to know how different characteristics of a transaction situation are related to the issues that will influence the behavior of any partner in a transaction.

Transferring Payment on the Internet

Transactions can be described in terms of the expectations people have about the general characteristics of payment systems, and of the benefits of these systems for them. In addition, transactions can be described by the specific methods for exchanging a product or service for money. General characteristics of a payment system include authentication, confidentiality, and integrity.

Authentication **Authentication** simply means that each party in a transaction is able to verify that the other party is who he or she claims to be. Although this may seem like a simple concept, it can often be difficult to put into practice. Consider a face-to-face transaction, such as buying jeans in a mall store. You can verify the vendor's authenticity by dint of being in the store. The vendor can verify your authenticity by requesting some form of identification, typically your driver's license. Now consider an Internet purchase. Neither party can verify the other's authenticity in the same manner. Of course, this situation occurs in many transactions. For example, when we place orders over the phone, neither party is able to verify identity.

Advances in technology development are improving options for authentication. Some methods of authentication that are presently available include biometrics, smart cards, and digital certificates. As the name hints, **biometrics** authenticate user identity by matching a biological indicator, such as a fingerprint, a voiceprint, or even a retina scan, to a previously stored image. **Smart cards** contain computer chips that store personal, unique, identifying information. As with biometrics, authentication is based on matching; when scanned by a card reader, the information on the smart card must match stored information on the computer. Digital certificates take smart cards a step farther. A **digital certificate** is an encrypted file, protected by a password. The file contains information for user identification, much like a smart card. The encrypted file information is verified by a **certificate authority**, who creates the digital certificate.

Confidentiality The second requirement of a payment system is **confidentiality**. Purchasers expect that the financial information they provide to a marketer will be made available only to people who have an appropriate need to know the information. For instance, your credit card number may be taken from an Internet order form and transmitted to the institution that manages your card, in order to receive payment.

Integrity   The third expectation of a payment system is **integrity**. The buyer expects that the features of the transaction will be implemented as agreed; that is, the buyer will receive the product ordered, and the seller will charge the quoted or listed price, unless specific exceptions have been discussed and accepted. Suppose you place an order, using your credit card, for a pair of Tough-hide jeans, and the selling price is $26.99 with tax and shipping included. You expect to receive not only the Tough-hide jeans, but also a credit card statement that reflects a charge of $26.99, rather than a different amount.

In contrast to authentication and confidentiality, for which there are technical ways to fulfill customers' expectations, integrity is based on customers' perceptions. For off-line companies that develop an online presence, a favorable prior reputation and history may reduce customer concerns with online shopping. New companies, however, must manage the signals that their transactions' capabilities send to customers to create a basis for trust through integrity (Figure 14-8).

In an online transaction, the extent to which the buyer believes that the general expectations are met may depend on characteristics of the seller. Among these characteristics are company reputation, brand image, and company longevity. In addition, a buyer's past experiences with the company may also serve to reduce perceptions of risk about the transaction, despite a brief company history, or an unknown reputation.

Trust and Transactions

Expectations of authentication, confidentiality, and integrity underscore the importance of being able to assure online consumers of privacy and security. Being able to protect access to information during its transmission is a necessary precursor to insuring privacy. If it is possible for someone to gain access to financial or personal data, either while it is being transmitted through the Internet, or after it is stored in an online database, then privacy has been compromised by weaknesses in security.

Privacy and security are related to trust. The development of trust in the exchange environment is important to exchange partners because it may increase the likelihood of completing a transaction. In addition, trust may enhance the buyer's satisfaction with the transaction, which may influence positive relationship development in situations with a brief history of relational exchange, or for customers with low collaborative orientations.

When little is known about an online vendor, shoppers often use seals of approval as shortcuts for assessing trustworthiness. Verisign, Inc.'s service assesses Web sites to ensure that they meet established standards for protecting transactions and information. A site is submitted for review. If it passes, it receives a seal. When clicked, the seal

FIGURE 14-8   Creating Trust in Transactions: Goals for Payment Systems.

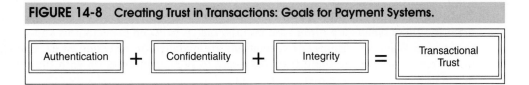

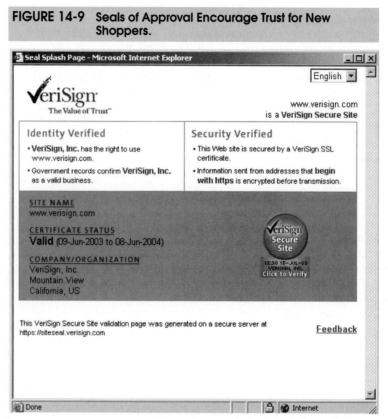

FIGURE 14-9 Seals of Approval Encourage Trust for New Shoppers.

Source: Reproduced with permission of VeriSign, Inc.[6] Copyright 2003. All rights reserved.

provides consumers with information about the company and the Verisign validation (Figure 14-9). Other organizations that provide related services include TRUSTe and BBBOnline.

Security and privacy issues must be addressed in order to create trust in the seller's ability to protect the information transmitted by the buyer. Trust, however, is not limited to the ability of the seller to meet buyers' expectations about aspects of the final transactions of money for goods. Building trust by creating interactions that demonstrate reliability and integrity can add value to a relationship at any point in the exchange process. The content, channel, and communication capabilities of the Internet provide businesses with ways to create, manage, and monitor customers' beliefs and expectations about product and company performance.

Postpurchase: Complaints and Commitment

Commitment is based on the belief that a partner's actions demonstrate reliability and integrity. These beliefs are often based on the match between expectations and actual experience. When a consumer's expectations are matched or exceeded by experience postpurchase, satisfaction and trust may lead to further interaction with the seller. When expectations are not met, future interaction may become less likely. (This notion works in the other direction, too. For instance, marketers are often reluctant to accept a personal check from a customer who has written one or more checks on an inadequate bank balance in the past.)

Internet Resources and Postpurchase Interaction

The Internet creates opportunities and challenges for managing relationships with customers after the transaction. As we have already noted, customers with high LTV to a company are an important reason for managing postpurchase processes. As a content resource, the Internet can be used to provide general product information, such as usage tips, that add value for consumers. Companies can also provide information targeted to particular customers. For instance, a recall notice on a specific model of a product can be addressed only to customers with that model, thus influencing perceived integrity and reliability by using the Internet as a channel resource. As a communication resource, the Internet serves as a **response device**, or a means for closing the marketing loop by obtaining feedback about the product experience from the consumer, as Procter & Gamble does with its "Share Your Thoughts" page. The display in Figure 14-10 illustrates another form of marketer-initiated postpurchase interaction. The automated response is personalized, based on stored customer profile information.

Postpurchase interaction is a two-way street. Businesses can follow up on sales with customers, and customers can express their views about the exchange experience. Suppose that the feedback is not positive; a customer has a complaint. Effective complaint management is important for fostering relational exchange. Researchers have shown that complaint handling is related to trust and commitment. Poor complaint management harms trust and commitment, particularly in newly developed relationships. Even a long and positive prior history with a company cannot overcome poor complaint management. A positive history of relational exchange reduces the effects of poor complaint management on commitment, but it is not enough to keep the customer's trust undiminished.

The need to manage customer dissatisfaction increases when we consider that consumers can voice their dissatisfaction to other consumers. The power of word-of-mouth means that factors that diminish satisfaction, trust, and commitment are not limited in their impact to just the dissatisfied customer. This concern is magnified in the digital business environment, in which dissatisfied consumers can create Web sites to provide forums for airing concerns and outrage. (Remember the untied.com site, created to provide a forum for complaints about United Airlines?) This possibility underscores the importance of the need to understand and manage complaints effectively, using the Internet.

Using Justice Theory and the Internet for Complaint Management

We can describe complaint management and consider the effect of the Internet as a tool for complaint management with justice theory. **Justice theory** provides a framework that integrates complaint management processes with the psychological measures of relational exchange. In a nutshell, justice is related to the appropriateness of decisions. If we think of complaint management as a process, we can see that several different decisions are made, based on the interaction between the consumer and the company. For instance, decisions are made about the processes for handling the complaint, the outcomes of the complaint process, and the nature of the interpersonal interactions. Justice theory

FIGURE 14-10 Automated Order and Delivery Confirmation Reinforce the Relationship.

Dear Eloise Jones,

Thank you for shopping with Williams-Sonoma. We have received your order, and it is currently being processed. Please see below for details.

Ship to Name & Address:

Eloise Jones

900 Highland

(For privacy reasons, the city, state and zip code have been omitted.)

Item Description	Item #	Qty	Price	Status
Mono 3-Initial Brand W/Board Personalization: DAD	63-1623164	1	$34.95	Will be shipped directly from the manufacturer

Merchandise Subtotal	$34.95
Shipping Charge	$7.75
Tax	$1.57
Total	$44.27

We will continue to email the status of your order as each item is shipped. You can always review the status of your order at *www.williams-sonoma.com/cs*. Simply enter your order confirmation number and billing zip code to access the information.

If you ordered multiple items, some items may be shipped separately with no additional shipping charges.

Thank you for your order.

Williams-Sonoma Customer Service

1.800.541.1262

Weekdays, 7:00 a.m. to 5:00 p.m., Pacific time

Saturday, 8:00 a.m. to 4:30 p.m., Pacific time

FIGURE 14-11   Dimensions of Justice Theory.

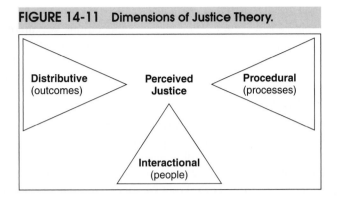

considers these decisions as the dimensions of **procedural justice**, **distributive justice**, and **interactional justice**, respectively. Customers evaluate the perceived justice associated with each type of decision to evaluate the quality of complaint handling (Figure 14-11).

Procedural Justice and the Internet   Four aspects influence customers' perceptions of procedural justice: (1) the ease with which a complaint can be made; (2) the flexibility of the complaint procedure; (3) the extent to which the customer has control over the processes that result in an outcome; and (4) the efficiency of the complaint process, measured by convenience and speed.

For companies with an established off-line presence, the Internet can provide an additional venue for placing a complaint, thus decreasing costs of traveling to a physical location, of waiting on hold by phone, or of writing and posting a letter, and increasing customers' perceptions of control. Online customer service facilities that provide immediate confirmation of a compliant, as by automated e-mail, can also increase perceptions of efficiency. An appropriate infrastructure for accepting and responding to online complaints is critical, however, given the potential of the medium for decreasing interpersonal communications. For instance, an automated e-mail response that is not followed by timely and personalized action may be more harmful to a customer's perceptions of a company and its product than the absence of the online complaint capability. This result may occur when an automated, impersonal response effectively creates unmet expectations that the problem will be addressed. In this situation, a company is now faced with a customer with two grievances: the initial complaint and a procedural complaint.

Distributive Justice and the Internet   Distributive justice is based on perceptions of outcome appropriateness. The basis for gauging whether an outcome was just may differ from situation to situation, and from consumer to consumer. For instance, for one customer, simply being able to voice a complaint may suffice, while another customer may require an apology, and yet another customer may require an apology and compensation.

The type of outcome demanded often depends on the basis for dissatisfaction, or the reason for which expectations are believed to be unmet. Three bases for assessing distributive justice are (1) **distributive needs** (Did I get what I wanted/needed?); (2) **distributive equity** (Did I get what I deserved?); and (3) **distributive equality** (Did I get what other people got?).

Managing complaints based on needs requires businesses to understand the extent to which the actual experience deviated from expectations. We can think of this deviation in terms of costs. A dissatisfied customer incurs costs not only from the consumption experience, but also from the complaint process. Building on the idea of using the Internet to increase the procedural efficiency to complain, we can see that the Internet can be used to reduce complaining costs, thus reducing the need-based sources of dissatisfaction for distributive justice.

1:1 marketing with the Internet affects the equality basis for customers' perceptions of distributive justice. Customized and personalized offerings that are delivered individually via the Internet can make it difficult for customers to assess deviation from expectation based on others' experiences. Suppose you go to a single price store in your local strip mall, where everything is $8. You pick out a shirt, and you go to the cashier. After waiting through a long line in which every one of the 16 people in front of you pays $8 plus tax for each item (remember, physical presence means sales taxes), you finally reach the counter. The cashier tells you that you owe $11, plus tax. Clearly, something is not fair; you saw what everyone else paid, and you know the store's pricing policy. If, however, you purchase the shirt from a Web site, on which prices fluctuate based on supply and demand, or on some other algorithm, the basis for comparison is more difficult.

The Internet also provides customers with a forum for airing experiences that can serve as a basis for comparison. A shopper who has just negotiated a terrific deal on a product may post that experience and the tactics on a bulletin board to other people with a similar interest. This situation creates new opportunities for comparison and perceived distributive injustice. The development of clear and defensible procedures for creating product offers can reduce the potential for postpurchase dissatisfaction, due to the outcome of the product experience and the complaint experience.

Interactional Justice and the Internet   Interactional justice is based on people's perceptions of the communication that occurred between the person complaining and the company representative. Even when a customer believes that procedures and outcomes were appropriate, a perception that the interpersonal communication was inappropriate can damage the quality of the complaint process. Bases for deciding whether the interaction was fair include politeness, effort, concern, and honesty.

With its lack of face-to-face communication, the Internet can be a difficult environment for positively influencing customers' perceptions of interactions. For instance, we may often rely on signals, such as body language and verbal intonation as nonverbal cues for politeness and concern. The Internet is better suited for communications that emphasize the content of the message, such as the description of the complaint process or possible outcomes, rather than its packaging.

For complaint situations in which an appropriate remedy is available and the processes for determining the outcome are clear-cut, interactional justice may be less important than distributive and procedural justice. When the processes and outcomes for a complaint situation are more ambiguous, however, the nature of the communication increases in importance. In these situations, a business can use the Internet to demonstrate effort and honesty. For instance, a timely response that provides a detailed, personalized understanding of the complaint connotes effort. A match between stated procedures and actions throughout the complaint management process conveys honesty.

Satisfaction, trust, and commitment are important factors for fostering B2C and B2B exchanges. As we saw earlier, however, the unique characteristics of B2B exchanges mean that we can use not only the psychological determinants of relationships, but also a set of behavioral aspects of relationships to consider ways to create value in ongoing B2B interactions.

Bits & Bytes 14.3

Weak online customer service hurts off-line sales. Jupiter Media Metrix estimates that 70 percent of online shoppers in the United States will reduce purchases at the off-line store of a merchant with poor online service.

(*Source:* RetailIndustry.about.com, March 2001.)

Using the Internet to Build Business-to-Business Relationships

The Internet can provide value to both partners in a B2B exchange. In many instances, the ability to exchange information through Internet channels can speed up the transaction process, by making necessary information available to all involved parties simultaneously. In addition, the Internet may simplify the exchange process by eliminating the need for multiple forms of documentation and of means for storing transaction-related documentation. For instance, templates for ordering, for tracking inventory and distribution, and for invoicing customers can all be stored and maintained in a single, digital, electronic database. Similarly, histories of customer interactions can be readily stored and retrieved to streamline future use. Each of these features can increase the value of interaction for the exchange partners. We will look at the behavioral characteristics that define B2B exchanges, and at the ways that the Internet can influence the development of these exchanges in the following sections.

Classifying B2B Relationships

Many different types of relationships can exist to facilitate exchange. These relationships are formed to meet organizational goals and to address environmental challenges that can create uncertainty and dependence. In this section we will use a framework[7] that integrates market characteristics and situational factors with dimensions that describe behaviors in relational exchanges to develop a classification of B2B relationships. We can use this framework to consider the implications of the Internet for fostering B2B relationships.

Environmental Effects on Relationships   Business relationships help companies manage challenges posed by aspects of the business environment. In the B2B environment, these challenges can stem from supply market characteristics or from situational characteristics. **Supply market characteristics** include the availability of alternative sources for products or product components and the **supply market dynamism**, or variability of change, in supply sources. Availability and dynamism are broad market forces. In contrast, **situational characteristics** reflect the perspective of a single buyer in the market. Situational characteristics include **supply complexity** and **supply importance**. Supply complexity is the extent to which a buyer's needs are specific and complicated. Supply importance refers to the centrality of the supply to the buyer's objectives.

Dimensions of B2B Relationships   The types of relationships that companies may form to address environmental challenges are described with relationship connectors. **Relationship connectors** are "dimensions that reflect the behaviors and expectations of behavior in a particular buyer-seller relationship."[8] Relationship connectors are operational or structural. Operational connectors affect the processes for exchange, while structural connectors affect the forms of exchange. Operational connectors are (1) information exchange, (2) cooperative norms, and (3) operational linkages. Structural connectors are (1) legal bonds, and (2) adaptation by the buyer or the seller. Brief descriptions of these connectors are provided in Figure 14-12.

Relationship connectors describe the extent to which the partners in a B2B exchange are "connected." Self-reports of connector importance in a particular relationship are used to classify the relationship as more or less connected, relative to other forms of relationships.

FIGURE 14-12   Relationship Connectors Reflect Behaviors and Expectations.

Type	Description	Example
Information exchange	Open communication of mutually useful information	Share product design specifications with suppliers
Cooperative norms	Joint efforts to achieve shared and individual goals	Develop affiliate program (e.g., Amazon.com)
Operational linkages	Merged routines and systems facilitate organizational activities of both partners	Build extranets to include suppliers and distributors
Legal bonds	Contractual agreements specify responsibilities and activities of each partner	Formalize strategic alliances (e.g., AOL and Target ally to co-brand Target products and promote them via AOL)
Seller adaptation	Alteration of process or product by seller to meet buyer needs	Change product design to meet user specifications (e.g., customizable CRM software)
Buyer adaptation	Alteration of process or requirements by buyer to meet seller needs	Change company data-entry processes to make use of CRM software

A Breakdown of B2B Relationships   Relationships can be classified into types that reflect different levels of each of the relationship connectors. Cannon and Perreault describe eight relationships with nicknames that capture the nature of the exchange. These relationships—from least connected to most connected—are (1) basic buying and selling, (2) bare bones, (3) contractual, (4) custom supply, (5) cooperative systems, (6) collaborative, (7) mutually adaptive, and (8) customer is king. The role of the relationship connectors in each type of relationship is provided in Figure 14-13.

The types of relationships are related to market and situational characteristics. For instance, when the market supply is not variable, and when supply alternatives are readily available, exchange needs can be met with basic buying and selling, bare bones, and contractual relationships. Cooperative systems, characterized by operational links, also facilitate exchange, as by adding value through customized logistics systems.

In contrast, when the market supply is dynamic, and when supply alternatives are limited, more closely connected relationships provide business buyers with ways to manage the difficulties of procurement. These relationships, such as the mutually adaptive and the customer is king interactions, emphasize operational *and* structural connectors.

Internet Implications for B2B Relational Exchange

We can use the framework developed by Cannon and Perreault to assess the effect of the Internet on B2B relationships. By extending the market and situational characteristics to encompass the Internet, we can consider ways that B2B relationships may be influenced as business partners react to the environment. In addition, we can use the classification of relationships to understand how businesses can operate proactively,

FIGURE 14-13   Relationship Profiles Are Based on Relationship Connectors.

	Information Exchange	Cooperative Norms	Operational Linkages	Legal Bonds	Seller Adaptation	Buyer Adaptation
Basic Buying and Selling	*High*	*High*	*Low*	*Low*	*Low*	*Low*
Bare Bones	*Low*	*Low*	*Moderate*	*Low*	*Moderate*	*Low*
Contractual Transaction	*Low*	*Low*	*Moderate*	*High*	*Moderate*	*Low*
Custom Supply	*Moderate*	*Moderate*	*Moderate*	*Mod*	*High*	*Moderate*
Cooperative Situations	*Moderate*	*High*	*High*	*Low*	*Moderate*	*Low*
Collaborative	*High*	*High*	*Moderate*	*Mod*	*Moderate*	*Moderate*
Mutually Adaptive	*High*	*Moderate*	*High*	*Low*	*High*	*High*
Customer is King	*High*	*High*	*High*	*High*	*High*	*Low*

leveraging the resources of the Internet to create relationships that optimize business goals for both partners.

Reactive Relational Exchange   The Internet can alter the impact of supply market and situational influences on B2B exchanges by changing the costs and benefits associated with different types of relationships. For instance, in considering supply market effects, the global communication capability of the Internet increases buyers' ability to locate alternative sources of supply. Such an effect decreases the need to foster relationships based on reducing supply uncertainty. In addition, the ability to communicate in near real-time can influence variability in supply sources. In some cases, communication can increase the unpredictability of supply, as when electronic hubs conceal the identity of participants and the amount of available supply. This outcome would indicate a need to solidify a relationship to reduce uncertainty. In other cases, increased communication can enhance buyers' ability to gauge supply availability and price, thus decreasing the need to depend on a sole supplier.

For situational characteristics, the ability to communicate needs and to interact to clarify those needs via the Internet can influence supply complexity. For instance, being able to send digital descriptions of parts, including verbal and graphic specifications, to potential suppliers may result in interactions that simplify the product. Alternatively, digital communication can facilitate the location of suppliers with qualifications that make them better able to adapt to fill the buyer's needs.

Proactive Relational Exchange   As an environment for B2B exchange, the Internet can affect the value of different relationships for their participants. As a set of resources for relational exchange, however, the Internet makes it possible for businesses to operate proactively, using the Internet to encourage forms of relationship connectors that create ongoing interactions. For example, interactivity via the Internet can foster operational connections that increase structural connections. Through increased ease of informational exchange, buyers can learn of constraints on seller abilities, and adjust planned activities to reflect those constraints (e.g., pick an alternative delivery schedule; find a different supplier). In this instance, increased information exchange increases buyer adaptation that perpetuates the relationship. Sellers can tailor products and product offers, customizing and personalizing them to better meet the needs of individual buyers, potentially increasing dependence and switching costs for the buyer.

The Internet can also be used to develop operational linkages. For instance, outside intranets and extranets provide infrastructures to facilitate B2B exchanges. In addition, the ability to share information through online databases can streamline processes and solidify interactions. For example, a supplier can create a shared database facility that monitors a buyer's inventory and makes the information available to the supplier. When the inventory is low, an automated rebuy is initiated. Benefits to the buyer include reduced costs to monitor inventory, and reduced costs to negotiate with alternative suppliers. A potential downside to the arrangement for the buyer is the lost opportunity to identify better deals.

Cautions for Business-to-Business Relational Exchange   As we have seen, the Internet creates challenges and opportunities for B2B relationships. It is important to recognize that businesses often form several relationships, that these relationships may take different forms, and that the assortment of relationships must be strategically managed so that the complete set of relationships achieves the company's objectives. As a result, the impact of the Internet on any relationship in the set can affect the entire set, in terms of relational performance.

One effect of the Internet is to create the possibility for new relationships. In Chapter 13, we learned about the growth of electronic hubs (e-hubs) as online market intermediaries. These hubs influence market supply characteristics. E-hubs can shift the partnership arrangement from between a seller and a buyer to the market maker and the buyer. In this situation, businesses must recognize the potential for decreased commitment to the producer and increased commitment to the intermediary.

Bits & Bytes 14.4

B2B customers in the high-tech industry prefer the Internet for customer service communications; 61 percent of the service-related interactions took place via e-mail on online.

(*Source:* BizReport.com, August 2002, citing data from CRM-solution provider, KANA.)

Managing B2B Relationships with CRM Strategies

Issues created by the impact of the Internet on supply market characteristics and situational characteristics increase the importance of managing business relationships effectively. While B2C CRM is focused on relationships between the company and its end customers, B2B CRM is more complex.

Supplier and Dealer Relationship Management

B2B relationships span the entire length of the value chain, including all of the participants in the supply chain, and all of the participants in the demand chain. As a result, one company may find itself managing several very different types of relationships, each of which may place a different emphasis on the reasons for the relational exchange. For instance, the central enterprise may value a relationship with one supplier because it locks in a secure source in a highly uncertain or scarce market. In contrast, the importance of the relationship between a dealer and the manufacturing enterprise may result from the ability to collaborate in product design, incorporating feedback from end customers acquired and transmitted by the dealer. Figure 14-14 illustrates the different types of relationships that can be addressed by CRM strategies, separating them into two broad classes of supplier relationships (SRM) and dealer relationships (DRM).

Understanding how the relationships differ, in terms of supply market and situational characteristics, can help businesses determine how best to implement CRM

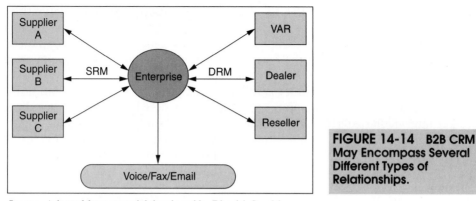

FIGURE 14-14 B2B CRM May Encompass Several Different Types of Relationships.

Source: Adapted from material developed by Bhavish Sood for "CRM in B2B," as published online at www. intelligentCRM. com

solutions. For instance, in a relationship in which operational linkages are extensive or the need for buyer adaptation is high, it may be difficult to implement a CRM strategy that requires changes to infrastructure. In addition, relationship partners may be reluctant to alter existing procedures, particularly if the primary benefits will be received by the other partner, or—in the case of a central CRM solution—by partners in other relationships.

When Does CRM Work?

Moving from a transaction orientation to a relational or collaborative orientation can be costly. The shift from a product-centric focus to a customer-centric focus can require a company to alter many of its methods for interacting with its customers. In B2B settings, the formalization of many business activities, such as procurement, can make it particularly costly to change the nature and function of business relationships. As a result, it is important for businesses to assess the costs and benefits associated with implementing a CRM strategy, or altering a present one.

In Figure 14-15, the benefits of CRM are described in terms of the likely impact of introducing a CRM solution in several types of vertical industries. Impact is determined by two dimensions: (1) dependence on partners, and (2) need for CRM. Dependence is related to the availability of supply sources, or the complexity and specificity of product needs. The need for CRM reflects the benefits or advantages of relationship management that can be obtained by the companies in an industry. For instance, some companies may have a higher need than others for characteristic outcomes of CRM solutions, such as postsales customer follow-up and support, or communications and transaction convenience.

As the figure indicates, the value of CRM varies widely. In general, however, relationship partners in industries that have the richest set of needs that are met by relationship management strategies are those that will benefit most from comprehensive CRM strategies. Internet-based solutions for knowing and growing a B2B relationship should be implemented with an eye toward balancing the costs and benefits of the strategy across the set of relationships in which the company participates.

FIGURE 14-15 Who Benefits Most from CRM?

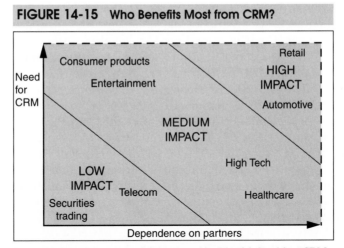

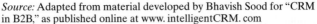

Source: Adapted from material developed by Bhavish Sood for "CRM in B2B," as published online at www. intelligentCRM. com

---

Bits & Bytes 14.5

Companies will spend big bucks to keep customers happy. Worldwide, eCRM spending is projected to increase from $13.7 billion in 2002 to $17.7 billion in 2006. (*Source*: *eCRM Guide*, July 2003, citing data from the Aberdeen Group.)

CHAPTER SUMMARY

In previous chapters, we have focused on the formation of relationships between participants in the digital business environment. In this chapter, we examined the impact of the Internet for developing and maintaining relational exchange. Relational exchange was described as an ongoing interaction between partners that provides value for each partner.

The Internet can enable the development of relationships between buyers and sellers and increase the value of relational exchange to each partner. This increased emphasis on relationship development was described as the outgrowth of four changes in the way that businesses view exchange-related behaviors. These shifts were (1) from products to people, (2) from competition to cooperation, (3) from stand-alone to networked, and (4) from transactions to relationships.

We considered the effect of these shifts on relationship development with a continuum of relational exchange, anchored by a transactional orientation at one end, and a relational orientation at the other end. This continuum suggests that the Internet can affect the value of relational exchange by (1) enabling different resource exchanges, (2) creating new opportunities for interaction in exchange processes, and (3) emphasizing the need to understand the collaborative orientation of both partners in an exchange.

Building on the idea of added value through relational exchange, we next examined the measurement of value in relationships. The concept of lifetime value was introduced, and its importance for customer relationship management (CRM) was discussed.

In addition to a simple dollar measure of customer value, we also addressed factors that affect the exchange experience and influence the length of the consumer life cycle. We looked at behavioral characteristics (e.g., number of transactions, types of interaction activities) and psychological characteristics (i.e., satisfaction, trust, commitment). Differences between B2C relationships and B2B relationships suggest that psychological dimensions better reflect value in B2C relationships, while behavioral dimensions better reflect value in B2B relationships.

Tactics for the strategic development of B2C and B2B relationships were discussed in separate sections. To illustrate how businesses can create relational value in B2C exchanges, we considered the role of the Internet at each stage of the decision process, focusing on satisfaction through information search, trust through transactional security, and commitment through effective complaint management.

For B2B exchanges, we adopted a framework that uses environmental characteristics and behavioral characteristics to create a classification of relationship types. This framework served as the basis for assessing the impact of the Internet on the types of B2B relationships that occur. We also applied the framework concept of relationship connectors, such as operational linkages and information exchange, to consider strategies for fostering B2B relationships, including applications of B2B CRM.

CONTENT MANAGEMENT
USEFUL TERMS

- 1:1 marketing
- accountability
- addressability
- agency
- authentication
- biometrics
- certificate authority
- closed-loop marketing
- collaborative filtering agent
- collaborative orientation
- commitment
- confidentiality
- customer relationship management (CRM)
- customer-centric approach

- data mining
- data warehousing
- digital certificate
- distributive equality
- distributive equity
- distributive justice
- distributive needs
- integrity
- intelligence
- interactional justice
- justice theory
- lifetime value (LTV)
- mobility
- procedural justice
- product-centric approach

- real-time marketing
- recommender system
- relationship connectors
- response device
- satisfaction
- situational characteristics
- smart cards
- software agents
- supply complexity
- supply importance
- supply market characteristics
- supply market dynamism
- trust

REVIEW QUESTIONS

1. What are the primary objectives of 1:1 marketing?
2. Describe the four fundamental shifts in perspectives on relational exchange.
3. Compare and contrast cooperation and competition.
4. Describe the continuum of exchange processes.
5. How do companies assess the value of a relational exchange? Customers?
6. Discuss the importance of satisfaction, trust, and commitment at different stages of the purchasing process.

7. Review the differences between B2C and B2B exchange relationships.
8. What three characteristics define software agents?
9. Discuss the advantages and disadvantages of different types of software agents.
10. What three characteristics are essential to a successful payment system?
11. How do payment systems in the digital business environment differ from those in a traditional marketplace? How are they similar?
12. Explain the ideas behind justice theory, and the different dimensions of justice.
13. What functions are provided by CRM software? How are these activities conducted?
14. What are operational connectors in B2B exchanges? Structural connectors?
15. What are the benefits of proactive relational exchange as opposed to reactive relational exchange?

WEB APPLICATION

What's a Customer Worth? Calculating Lifetime Value

We've seen that knowing the lifetime value (LTV) of your customers can influence how you plan your business strategy. For instance, it can affect what you are willing to pay to acquire a customer, and to retain that customer. It can also help you decide whether there are segments of your customer base that are worth more than others, and who are potential targets for up-selling and cross-selling. But how do you actually measure the LTV?

Calculating LTV requires you to know some basic facts about your business. First, what's the average lifetime of a customer, or of a segment of customers? Lifetimes can vary greatly, depending on the type of product. (For some products, the average customer may purchase regularly for a while, and then stop using the product, or switch to a competing brand. Understanding the reasons for the stopped purchasing can not only help you define the lifetime, but also assess the likelihood of winning back the customer.)

The second piece of information you need to know is the average profit per sale, after all of the costs of making a sale have been deducted (e.g., sales calls, shipping, customer support).

The third piece of information required for a basic LTV measure is the number of sales that the average customer makes during the average lifetime.

Now, simply multiply the number of sales times the average profit. Instant LTV.

Try it out. Suppose that your company sells its product, an environmentally friendly, nontoxic household cleaner, only through its Web site. The average customer buys 2 quarts a year, and stays a customer for 3 years. The cleaner sells for $25 per quart of concentrate. Of course, there are some costs to produce and sell that product. For instance, the cost to produce the product, or the cost of goods sold (COGS), is $18 per unit. (Remember this is concentrated, and it's good stuff.) Then, you have some promotion and sales management costs that average $2.80 a sale. In addition, the credit card company charges a fee per sale for effecting the card transaction (another $0.60 per sale). Next, you have to shell out an average of $3 per unit to ship the product. Fortunately, you've managed to collect a $4 per unit shipping and handling fee. Unfortunately, you discovered that not everyone is thrilled with the product, and that returns can and do happen. When they do, it's expensive. Averaged across all sales, it costs you $2.20 to complete the return—it's heavy. So, what's your net profit per unit?

Find the gross margin—the difference between the selling price and the cost of goods sold, and then subtract the additional costs, and add on the revenue from the shipping and handling fee.

Did you arrive at a profit of $2.40? If not, try the math again. Now, multiply the profit per unit by the number of sales in the average customer lifetime. The lifetime value is $14.40.

Of course, it can get much more complicated. For instance, suppose that half of your customers bring you new customers—without the costs of promotion and sales management. In addition, some of your customers may change their buying patterns over the years, perhaps underconsuming (less messy) or overconsuming (more messy), relative to the average. Finally, you don't have those future profits yet. Historically, given inflation, today's dollars will be worth less tomorrow, so to get a more accurate measure of LTV, you would have to factor in the appropriate discount rate for the time period of interest.

While there are many ways to calculate sophisticated LTVs, there are also many online tools and services that can help you. It's important to understand, however, what factors and assumptions are included in the calculations.

CONCEPTS IN BRIEF

1. Acquiring customers is costly, and keeping loyal buyers can be lucrative; hence, fostering relationships is important in B2C and in B2B markets.
2. Businesses can use the Internet to manage relationships with their customers by facilitating 1:1 marketing through personalized communications and customized content.
3. 1:1 marketing leverages the data collection, storage, and dissemination abilities of the Internet to profile customers based on their interactions with a company—the process of closed-loop marketing. This information can be used in real-time marketing to develop dynamic content that presents timely, individualized, and appropriate offers.
4. Fostering relationships from a transactional to a collaborative orientation may not be appropriate for every company. The concept of lifetime value can provide insight into the value of developing and maintaining customer relationships.
5. In B2C and in B2B markets, relationships are formed because they reduce uncertainty for the buyer. The flip side is that relationships can increase dependence of the buyer on the seller.
6. Companies want customers to be satisfied, trusting, and committed. Internet technologies can increase satisfaction (e.g., through price comparisons), engender trust (e.g., through secure online transactions), and encourage commitment (e.g., with online customer support).
7. In B2B relationships, the Internet changes the relative importance of supply market characteristics and situational characteristics for many companies, thus altering the value of old and new relationships.
8. Changes to B2B relationships are often reflected in the structural connectors (e.g., extranets and EDI infrastructure) and operational connectors (e.g., strategic alliances and legal contracts) that comprise the relationships.
9. Similar to B2C markets, B2B markets are concerned with managing customer relationships; in B2B markets, these entail supplier relationship management (SRM) and dealer relationship management (DRM).
10. In general, consolidating B2B CRM with online solutions is most effective in industries with larger sets of needs for the outcomes of CRM.

THINKING POINTS

1. Consider the types of relationships that can exist between buyers, sellers, policy makers, and technology developers. What are some implications of different stages of relationship development—of any two perspectives—for digital business activity? That is, how might an early stage relationship between, for example, consumers and policy makers in the Internet environment affect business activity differently than a more developed relationship with a longer history of interaction?
2. How does the Internet contribute to an increasing emphasis on cooperation between businesses as a way to compete? What characteristics of the Internet facilitate cooperation? What characteristics facilitate competition?
3. The concept of collaborative orientation suggests that people differ in their perceptions of the desirability of developing relationships. Different products may also affect the desirability of a

relational orientation. Does the Internet change the benefits of relational exchange for customers? For companies?

4. When difficulty to find and compare products is reduced by Internet features, customer loyalty may shift from companies/retailers to specific brands. How can businesses use the Internet to build relationships with consumers that create loyalty to the vendor, rather than to the brand?

5. Building on Q4, what does the potential shift in loyalty focus (i.e., from vendor to brand) imply for the structure of businesses on the Internet? That is, what type of business model would you recommend?

6. Why are behavioral measures of relational exchange more appropriate for a B2B exchange than psychological measures? What characteristics of the setting (i.e., B2B versus B2C) influence the measurement of satisfaction, trust, and commitment in each type of exchange?

7. In B2C relational exchange, how can the Internet be used to create satisfaction, trust, and commitment in each of the decision stages (i.e., prepurchase, purchase, and postpurchase)?

8. In B2B relational exchange, which combinations of behavioral characteristics most clearly reflect the importance of satisfaction to exchange partners? Which combinations reflect a stronger importance of trust? Of commitment?

ENDNOTES

1. Read as "one-to-one."
2. As noted in "Beyond Relationship Marketing: The Rise of Collaborative Marketing," by Mohanbir Sawhney. In *CRM Project Volume 3*, at www.crmproject.com.
3. Based on Anderson, Fornell, and Lehmann (1994). "Customer satisfaction, market share, and profitability: Findings from Sweden," *Journal of Marketing*, 58(3), 53–66.
4. Based on Moorman, Deshpande, and Zaltman (1993), "Factors affecting trust in market research relationships." *Journal of Marketing* 57(1) 81 –101, and Morgan and Hunt (1994), "The Commitment-Trust Theory of Relationship Marketing," *Journal of Marketing* 58(3), 20–38.
5. Based on Moorman, Deshpande, and Zaltman (1993), "Factors affecting trust in market research relationships." Journal of Marketing 57(1) 81 –101.
6. The Verisign seal is a graphical representation intended to indicate a Web site's compliance with the Verisign Principles and Criteria and is produced herein for illustrative purposes only.
7. Cannon, Joseph P., and William D. Perreault, Jr. "Buyer-Seller Relationships in Business Markets," *Journal of Marketing Research, 36* (1999), pages 439–460.
8. Ibid, page 442.

SUGGESTED READINGS

1. "Enhancing Customer Relationships with the Internet," In *Business-to-Business Internet Marketing*, by Barry Silverstein (Maximum Press: Gulf Breeze, FL, 1998, pages 294–324).
2. The *One To One Future: Building Relationships One Customer at a Time*, by Don Peppers and Martha Rodgers (Doubleday: New York, 1993).
3. "Paying Up: Payment Systems for Digital Commerce," by Stephen D. Crocker and Russell B. Stevenson Jr. In *The Future of the Electronic Marketplace,* edited by Derek Leebaert (The MIT Press: Cambridge, MA, 1998, pages 303 – 334).
4. "Building Consumer Trust Online," by Donna L. Hoffman, Thomas P. Novak, and Marcos Peralta. *Communications of the ACM, 42* 4 (April 1999), pages 80–85.
5. "Agents that Reduce Workload and Information Overload," by Pattie Maes. *Communications of the ACM, 37,* 7 (July 1994), pages 31–40.

LEARNING LINKS

Customer Satisfaction and Loyalty

www.theacsi.org
www.surveyvalue.com/customersat_
overview.html
bmgt2-notes.umd.edu:8080/Faculty/KM/
papers.nsf/0/1c984af952c1d89d852569dd006
ee08f?OpenDocument

Lifetime Value

www.zeromillion.com/marketing/
determining-lifetimevalue.html
www.wilsonweb.com/wmt5/customers-
value.htm

www.smallbusinessnewz.com/smallbusiness
newz-13–20010321Lifetime-Value-
Online.html

Customer Relationship Management

www.crmproject.com
www.crm-forum.com

Closed-Loop Solutions

www.closedloop.com
www.dconx.com

Bibliography

Abrams, Marc, ed., *World Wide Web: Beyond the Basics*, Upper Saddle River, NJ: Prentice-Hall, Inc., 1998.

Achrol, Ravi S., "Evolution of the Marketing Organization: New Forms for Turbulent Environments," *Journal of Marketing, 55* (October 1991), 77–93.

Alba, Joseph, John Lynch, Barton Weitz, Chris Janiszewski, Richard Lutz, Alan Sawyer, and Stacy Wood, "Interactive Home Shopping: Consumer, Retailer, and Manufacturer Incentives to Participate in Electronic Marketplaces," *Journal of Marketing, 61* (July 1997), 38–53.

Anderson, Paul F., "Marketing, Strategic Planning, and the Theory of the Firm," *Journal of Marketing, 46* (Spring 1982), 15–26.

AOL, Target in Marketing Alliance, *Yahoo News, Reuters*, June 2000.

Azar, Beth, "Online Experiments: Ethically Fair or Foul?" *Monitor on Psychology, 31*, no. 4 (April 2000), 50–52.

Bakos, J. Yannis, "A Strategic Analysis of Electronic Marketplaces," *MIS Quarterly* (September 1991), 295–310.

Benjamin, Robert and Rolf Wigand, "Electronic Markets and Virtual Value Chains on the Information Superhighway," *Sloan Management Review* (Winter 1995), 62–72.

Bettman, James R., and Pradeep Kakkar, "Effects of Information Presentation Format on Consumer Information Acquisition Strategies," *Journal of Consumer Research, 3* (March 1977), 233–239.

Bezjian-Avery, Alexa, Bobby Calder, and Dawn Iacobucci, "New Media Interactive Advertising vs. Traditional Advertising," *Journal of Advertising Research* (July–August, 1998), 23–32.

Biocca, Frank, "Communication Within Virtual Reality: Creating a Space for Research," *Journal of Communication, 42*, no. 4 (Autumn 1992), 5–22.

Blattberg, Robert, and John Deighton, "Interactive Marketing: Exploiting the Age of Addressability," *Sloan Management Review* (Fall 1991), 5–14.

Bloom, Paul N., George R. Milne, and Robert Adler, "Avoiding Misuse of New Information Technologies: Legal and Societal Considerations," *Journal of Marketing, 58* (January 1994), 98–110.

Bucklin, Randolph E., James M. Lattin, Asim Ansari, David Bell, Eloise Coupey, Sunil Gupta, John D.C. Little, Carl Mela, Alan Montgomery, and Joel Steckel, "Choice and the Internet: From Clickstream to Research Stream," *Marketing Letters 13*, no. 3 (2002), 245–258.

Canter, David, Rod Rivers, and Graham Storrs, "Characterizing User Navigation Through Complex Data Structures," *Behaviors and Information Technology, 4*, no. 2 (1985), 93–102.

Cataudella, Joe, Ben Sawyer, and Dave Greely, *Creating Stores on the Web*, Berkeley, CA: Peachpit Press, 1998.

Chase, Larry, *Essential Business Tactics for the Net*, New York, NY: John Wiley & Sons, Inc., 1998.

Cook, Don Lloyd, and Eloise Coupey, "Consumer Behavior and Unresolved Regulatory Issues in Electronic Marketing," *Journal of Business Research, 41* (1998), 231–238.

Comer, Douglas E., *Computer Networks and Internets*, Upper Saddle River, NJ: Prentice-Hall, Inc., 1997.

Coupey, Eloise, "Restructuring: Constructive Processing of Information Displays in Consumer Choice," *Journal of Consumer Research, 21* (June 1994), 83–99.

Coupey, Eloise, and Mark T. Jones, "Decision Making in the Electronic Commerce Environment: Issues and Approaches for Tool Development." *Quarterly Journal of Electronic Commerce, 1*, no. 3 (2000), 215–228.

Coupey, Eloise, David Brinberg, and Carter Mandrik, "Internet-based Consumption and Quality of Life in Rural Communities: Marketing and Policy Implications." *Quarterly Journal of Electronic Commerce, 1*, no. 1 (2000), 13–30.

Davis, Jeffrey, ed., "B2B Boom," *Business 2.0* (September 1999), 84–124.

Davis, Jeffrey, ed., "The New eCommerce Engine: How It Works," *Business 2.0* (February 2000), 112–140.

Dennis, Alan R., Susan T. Kinney, and Yu-Ting Caisy Hung, "Gender Differences in the Effects of Media Richness," *Small Group Research, 30*, no. 4 (August 1999), 405–437.

Dillman, Don A., *Mail and Internet Surveys: The Tailored Design Method*, 2nd ed., New York, NY: John Wiley & Sons, Inc., 2000.

Dillman, Don A., and Donald M. Beck, "Information Technologies and Rural Development in the 1990s," *The Journal of State Government* (1991), 29–38.

Do, Orlantha, Eric March, Jennifer Rich, and Tara Wolff, "Intelligent Agents & The Internet: Effects on Electronic Commerce and Marketing," *http://bold.coba.unr.edu/odie/paper.html*, 6 pages.

Duncan, Tom, and Sandra E. Moriarty, "A Communication-based Marketing Model for Managing Relationships," *Journal of Marketing, 62*, no. 2 (April 1998), 1–13.

EBUSINESS, "501 Blues," *Business 2.0* (January 2000), Powered by Hire.com.

Foxall, Gordon R., and John R. Fawn, "An Evolutionary Model of Technological Innovation as a Strategic Management Process," *Technovation, 12*, no. 3 (April 1992), 191–202.

Foxman, Ellen R., and Paula Kilcoyne, "Information Technology, Marketing Practice, and Consumer Privacy: Ethical Issues," *Journal of Public Policy & Marketing, 12*, no. 1 (Spring 1993), 106–119.

Garbarino, Ellen, and Mark S. Johnson, "The Different Roles of Satisfaction, Trust, and Commitment in Customer Relationships," *Journal of Marketing, 63*, no. 2 (April 1999), 70–87.

Gardner, Donald G., Richard L. Dukes, and Richard Discenza, "Computer Use, Self-Confidence, and Attitudes: A Causal Analysis," *Computers in Human Behavior, 9* (1993), 427–440.

Gebauer, Judith, and Heike Schad, "Building an Internet-based Workflow System—The Case of Lawrence Livermore National Laboratories Zephyr Project," Fisher Center Working Paper 98-WP-1030, (April 1998).

Ghose, Sanjoy, and Wenyu Dou, "Interactive Functions and Their Impacts on the Appeal of Internet Presence Sites," *Journal of Advertising Research* (March–April 1998), 29–43.

Glazer, Rashi, "Marketing in an Information-Intensive Environment: Strategic Implications of Knowledge as an Asset," *Journal of Marketing, 55* (October 1991), 1–19.

Glazer, Rashi, and Allen M. Weiss, "Marketing in Turbulent Environments: Decision Processes and the Time-Sensitivity of Information," *Journal of Marketing Research, 30* (November), 509–521.

Gray, Stephen, "In Virtual Fashion," *IEEE Spectrum* (February 1998), 18–25.

Grayson, Kent, and Tim Ambler, "The Dark Side of Long-term Relationships in Marketing Services," *Journal of Marketing Research, 36*, no. 1 (February 1999), 132–141.

Gulati, Ranjay, and Jason Garino, "Get the Right Mix of Bricks and Clicks," *Harvard Business Review, 78*, no. 3 (May/June 2000), 107–114.

Ha, Louisa, and E. Lincoln James, "Interactivity Reexamined: A Baseline Analysis of Early Business Web Sites," *Journal of Broadcasting & Electronic Media, 42*, no. 4 (Fall 1998), 457–474.

Hafner, Katie, and Matthew Lyon, *Where Wizards Stay Up Late: The Origins of the Internet*, New York, NY: Simon & Schuster, Inc., 1996.

Hahn, Robert W., and John A. Hird, "The Costs and Benefits of Regulation: Review and Synthesis," *Yale Journal on Regulation* (1991), 233–277.

Hammond, Kathy, Gil McWilliam, and Andrea Narholz Diaz, "Fun and Work on the Web: Differences in Attitudes Between Novices and Experienced Users," *Advances in Consumer Research, 25* (1998), 372–378.

Hance, Olivier, *Business and Law on the Internet*, New York, NY: McGraw-Hill, 1996.

Hannon, Neal J., *The Business of the Internet*, Cambridge, MA: International Thomson Publishing, Course Technology, 1998.

Hanson, Ward, *Principles of Internet Marketing*, Cincinnati, OH: South-Western College Publishing, 2000.

Hauser, John R., Glen L. Urban, and Bruce D. Weinberg, "How Consumers Allocate Their Time When Searching for Information," *Journal of Marketing Research*, 30, 4, (November), 452–466.

Hesse, Bradford W., Carol M. Werner, and Irwin Altman, "Temporal Aspects of Computer-Mediated Communication," *Computers in Human Behavior, 4* (1988), 147–165.

Hinde, Robert A., "A Suggested Structure for a Science of Relationships," *Personal Relationships, 2*, (March 1995), 1–15.

Hirschman, Elizabeth, "People as Products: Analysis of a Complex Marketing Exchange," *Journal of Marketing, 51* (January 1987) 98–108.

Hoffman, Donna L. and Thomas P. Novak, "Marketing in Hypermedia Computer-Mediated Environments: Conceptual Foundations," *Journal of Marketing, 60,* 3, (July 1996) 50–68.

Hoffman, Donna L., William D. Kalsbeek, and Thomas P. Novak, "Internet and Web Use in the United States: Baselines for Commercial Development," Project 2000, Vanderbilt University, Nashville. Working Paper. (Draft Date: July 10, 1996).

Hollingshead, Andrea B., Joseph E. McGrath, and Kathleen M. O'Connor, "Group Task Performance and Communication Technology: A Longitudinal Study of Computer-Mediated Versus Face-to-Face Work Groups," *Small Group Research, 24*, no. 3 (August 1993), 307–333.

Hunt, Shelby D., and Robert M. Morgan, "Relationship Marketing in the Era of Network Competition," *Marketing Management, 3*, no. 1 (1994), 18–29.

Jain, Subhash C., "The Evolution of Strategic Marketing," *Journal of Business Research, Vol. 11* (December 1983), 409–425.

Jones, Mark T., and Eloise Coupey, "A Script-based Approach for E-Commerce Applications," *Quarterly Journal of Electronic Commerce, 2*, 4 (2001), 291–304.

Kaplan, Steven, and Mohanbir Sawhney, "B2B E-Commerce Hubs: Towards a Taxonomy of Business Models," (December 1999), Working Paper. University of Chicago, Chicago.

Klein, Lisa R., "Evaluating the Potential of Interactive Media Through a New Lens: Search Versus Experience Goods," *Journal of Business Research, 41* (1998), 195–203.

Kleinmuntz, Don, and David Schkade, "Information displays and decision processes." *Psychological Science, 4* (1993), 221–227.

Kleinmuntz, Don, and David Schkade, "Information display and choice processes: Differential effects of organization, form, and sequence." *Organizational Behavior and Human Decision Processes, 57* (1994), 319–337.

Korthauer, Ralph D., and Richard J. Koubek, "An Empirical Evaluation of Knowledge, Cognitive Style, and Structure upon the Performance of a Hypertext Task," *International Journal of Human-Computer Interaction, 6*, no. 4 (1994), 373–390.

Kosiur, David, *Understanding Electronic Commerce: How Online Commerce Can Grow Your Business*, Redmond, WA: Microsoft Press, 1997.

Kraut, Robert, Sara Keisler, Tridas Mukhopadhyay, William Sherlis, and Michael Patterson, "Social Impact of the Internet: What Does It Mean?" *Communications of the ACM, 41,* no. 12 (1998), 21–22.

Lamb, Charles W., Joseph F. Hair, Jr., and Carl McDaniel, *Principles of Marketing*, Cincinnati, OH: South-Western Publishing Co., 1992.

Lambkin, Mary, and George S. Day, "Evolutionary Processes in Competitive Markets: Beyond the Product Life Cycle," *Journal of Marketing, 53* (July 1989), 4–20.

Lea, Martin, and Russell Spears, "Computer-mediated Communication, De-individuation and Group Decision-making," *International Journal Management—Machine Studies, 34* (1991), 283–301.

Lee, Ho Geun, and Theodore H. Clark, "Impacts of the Electronic Marketplace on Transaction Cost and Market Structure," *International Journal of Electronic Commerce, 1*, no. 1 (Fall 1996), 127–149.

Lee, Ho Geun, and Theodore H. Clark, "Market Process Reengineering Through Electronic Market Systems: Opportunities and Challenges," *Journal of Management Information Systems, 13*, no. 3 (Winter 1996–97), 113–136.

Leebaert, Derek, ed., *The Future of the Electronic Marketplace*, Cambridge, MA: The MIT Press, 1998.

Maes, Pattie, "Agents that Reduce Work and Information Overload," *Communications of the ACM, 37*, no. 7 (July 1994), 31–41.

Malone, Thomas W., Joanne Yates, and Robert I. Benjamin, "Electronic Markets and Electronic Hierarchies," *Communications of the ACM, 30*, no. 6 (June 1987), 484–497.

Mazis, Michael B., Richard Staelin, Howard Beales, and Steven Salop, "A Framework for Evaluating Consumer Information Regulation," *Journal of Marketing, 45* (Winter 1981), 11–21.

McKinsey & Co., "Achieving Channel Excellence: The 'Ace Up Your Sleeve' in Sales and Marketing Programs," white paper (Summer 2003), www.mckinsey.com.

Mehta, Raj, and Eugene Sivadas, "Direct Marketing on the Internet: An Empirical Assessment of Consumer Attitudes," *Journal of Direct Marketing, 9*, no. 3 (Summer 1995), 21–32.

Modahl, Mary, *Now or Never: How Companies Must Change Today to Win the Battle for Internet Consumers*, New York, NY: HarperCollins Publishers, 2000.

Molinsky, Andrew L., "Sanding Down the Edges: Paradoxical Impediments to Organizational Change," *The Journal of Applied Behavioral Science, 35*, no. 1 (March 1999), 8–24.

Morgan, Robert M., and Shelby D. Hunt, "The Commitment-Trust Theory of Relationship Marketing," *Journal of Marketing, 58* (July 1994), 20–38.

Novak, Thomas P., and Donna L. Hoffman, "Bridging the Racial Divide on the Internet," *science , 280* (April 17), 390–391.

Nowak, Glen J., and Joseph Phelps, "Direct Marketing and the Use of Individual-Level Consumer Information: Determining How and When 'Privacy' Matters," *Journal of Direct Marketing, 9*, no. 3 (Summer 1995), 46–60.

Peppers, Don, and Martha Rogers, *The One to One Future: Building Relationships One Customer at a Time*, New York, NY: Doubleday, 1993.

Pine, Joseph B., II, and James H. Gilmore, "The Four Faces of Mass Customization," *Harvard Business Review* (January–February 1997).

Pitter, Keiko, Sara Amato, John Callahan, Nigel Kerr, Eric Tilton, and Robert Minato, *Every Student's Guide to the Internet*, San Francisco, CA: The McGraw-Hill Companies, Inc., 1995.

Porter, David, ed., *Internet Culture*, New York, NY: Routledge Inc., 1997.

PriceWaterhouseCoopers, "IAB Online Ad Measurement Study," December 2001, *www.iab.net.*

Ranganathan, C., Jasbir S. Dhaliwal, and Thompson S. H. Teo, "Diffusion of Web Technologies in the Supply Chain Management Function: Examining the Role of Environmental and Organizational Factors," *DIGIT* 2002, Barcelona.

Rayport, Jeffrey, and John J. Sviokla, "Managing in the Marketspace," *Harvard Business Review* (November–December 1994), 141–150.

Resnick, Paul, and Hal R. Varian, "Recommender Systems," *Communications of the ACM, 40*, no. 3 (1997), 56–58.

Rheingold, Howard, *The Virtual Community: Homesteading on the Electronic Frontier*, Reading, MA: Addison-Wesley, 1993.

Rohner, Kurt, *Marketing in the Cyber Age: The What, The Why, and The How*, Chichester, England: John Wiley & Sons, Ltd., 1998.

Rosenblum, Bert, *Marketing Channels: A Management View*, 6th ed., Fort Worth, TX: The Dryden Press, 1999.

Runkel, Philip, and Joseph E. McGrath, "Planning to Gather Evidence: Techniques for Observing and Recording Behavior," In *Research in Human Behavior: A Systematic Guide to Method*, New York, NY: Holt, Rinehart & Winston, 1972, pp. 173–193.

Sager, Ira, Steve Hamm, Neil Gross, John Carey, and Robert D. Hof, "Cyber Crime," *BusinessWeek* (February 21, 2000), 36–42.

Sarkar, Mitra Barun, Brian Butler, and Charles Steinfield, "Intermediaries and Cybermediaries: A Continuing Role for Mediating Players in the Electronic Marketplace," *Journal of Computer-Mediated Communication, 1*, no. 3 (1995) *http://www.ascusc.org/jcmc/vol1/issue3/sarkar.html.*

Schibsted, Evantheia, "Are You Next? 20 Industries That Must Change," *Business 2.0* (March 1999), 44–52.

Schlosser, Ann E., and Alana Canfer, "Interactivity in Commercial Web Sites: Implications for Web Site Effectiveness," Working Paper, University of Illinois.

Schmidt, Jeffrey B., and Richard A. Spring, "A Proposed Model of External Consumer Information Search," *Journal of the Academy of Marketing Science*, 24, no. 3 (1996), 246–256.

Schnaars, Steven P., *Marketing Strategy: A Customer-driven Approach*, New York, NY: Macmillan, Inc., 1991.

Schumann, David W., and Esther Thorson, eds., *Advertising and the World Wide Web*, Mahwah, NJ: Lawrence Erlbaum Associates, Publishers,1999.

Scott, Judy, "Emerging Patterns from the Dynamic Capabilities of Internet Intermediaries," *Journal of Computer-mediated Communications, 5*, 3 (March 2000), *www.ascusc.org/jcmc.*

Shim, Richard, "Giveaways—They Pay Off on the Web," *Yahoo News*, from PC Data Online, June 2000.

Silverstein, Barry, *Business-to-Business Internet Marketing: Five Proven Strategies for Increasing Profits through Internet Direct Marketing*, Gulf Breeze, FL: Maximum Press, 1999.

Slivovitz, Michael, D., Chad Compton, and Lyle Flint, "The Effects of Computer Mediated Communication on an Individual's Judgment: A Study Based on the Methods of Ash's Social Influence Experiment," *Computers in Human Behavior, 4* (1988), 311–321.

Spears, Russell, and Martin Lea, "Panacea or Panopticon? The Hidden Power in Computer-Mediated Communication," *Communication Research, 21*, no. 4 (August 1994), 427–459.

Stefik Mark, ed., *Internet Dreams: Archetypes, Myths, and Metaphors*, Cambridge, MA: The MIT Press, 1997.

Steuer, Jonathan, "Defining Virtual Reality: Dimensions Determining Telepresence," *Journal of Communication, 42*, no. 4 (Autumn 1992), 73–93.

Strauss, Judy, and Raymond Frost, *Marketing on the Internet: Principles of Online Marketing*, Upper Saddle River, NJ: Prentice-Hall, Inc., 1999.

Suarez, Fernando F., and James M. Utterback, "Dominant Designs and the Survival of Firms," *Strategic Management Journal, 16*, no. 6 (September 1995), 415–431.

Tamilia, Robert D., Sylvain Senecal, Gilles Corriveau, "Conventional Channels of Distribution and Electronic Intermediaries: A Functional Analysis," Working Paper, Center de Recherche en Gestion, Document 08–2001 (2001), *www.esg.ugam.ca/esg/crg.*

Tapscott, Don, *The Digital Economy: Promise and Peril in the Age of Networked Intelligence*, New York, NY: McGraw-Hill, 1996.

Taptich, Brian E., "Less Than Zero Margins," *Red Herring* (March 1999), 46–50.

Tax, Stephen S., Stephen W. Brown, and Murali Chandrashekaran, "Customer Evaluations of Service Complaint Experiences: Implications for Relationship Marketing," *Journal of Marketing, 62*, no. 2 (April 1998), 60–76.

Tsay, Andy A., and Narenda Agrawal, "Channel Conflict and Coordination in the eCommerce Age," *Production & Operations Management Special Issue: Collaboration and Coordination in SCM and eCommerce* (in press).

Valacich, Joseph S., David Paranka, Joey F. George, and J. F. Nunamaker, Jr., "Communication Concurrency and the New Media: A New Dimension for Media Richness," *Communication Research, 20*, no. 2 (April 1993), 249–276.

Vassos, Tom, *Strategic Internet Marketing*, Indianapolis, IN: Que Corporation, 1996.

Vesely, Rebecca, "Kiddie Kash," *Business 2.0* (May 1999), 24–26.

Walther, Joseph B., Jeffrey F. Anderson, and David W. Park, "Interpersonal Effects in Computer-Mediated Interaction: A Meta-Analysis of Social and Antisocial Communication," *Communication Research, 21*, no. 4 (August 1994), 460–487.

"Web Security: A Matter of Trust," *World Wide Web Journal, 2*, no. 3, O'Reilly & Associates, Inc., Sebastopol, CA, 1997.

Widing, Robert E., II, and W. Wayne Talarzyk, "Electronic Information Systems for Consumers: An Evaluation of Computer-Assisted Formats in Multiple Decision Environments," *Journal of Marketing Research*, (May 1993), 30, 125–141.

Wilde, Louis L., "The Economics of Consumer Information Acquisition," *Journal of Business, 53*, no. 3 (1980), 143–165.

Winer, Russell S., John Deighton, Sunil Gupta, Eric J. Johnson, Barbara Mellers, Vicki G. Morwitz, Thomas O'Guinn, Arvind Rangaswamy, and Alan G. Sawyer, "Choice in Computer-Mediated Environments," *Marketing Letters, 8*, 3 (1997), 287–296.

Zeff, Robbin, and Brad Aronson, *Advertising on the Internet*, New York, NY: John Wiley & Sons, Inc., 1997.

Zimmerman, Jan, and Michael Mathiesen, *Marketing on the Internet*, Gulf Breeze, FL: Maximum Press, 1998.

Index